Zeitroman – The Novel and Society in Germany 1830–1900

Australian and New Zealand Studies in German Language and Literature

Australisch-Neuseeländische Studien
zur deutschen Sprache und Literatur

Etudes parues en Australie et Nouvelle-Zélande
en relation avec la philologie allemande

edited by
Gerhard Schulz (Melbourne)
and John A. Asher (Auckland)

Vol. 12

PETER LANG
Berne · Frankfurt am Main · New York

Roger Hillman

Zeitroman

The Novel and Society in Germany
1830–1900

PETER LANG

Berne · Frankfurt am Main · New York

Library of Congress Cataloging in Publication Data

Hillman, Roger.
  Zeitroman: the novel and society in Germany, 1830–
1900.

  (Australian and New Zealand studies in German
language and literature; v. 12)
    Bibliography: p.
    1. German fiction – 19th century – History and
criticism. 2. Social history in literature.
I. Title. II. Series.
PT763.H53 1983   833'.7'09355   83-5461
ISBN 0-8204-0010-6

Library of Congress Catalog Card Number:
83-5461
ISBN 0-8204-0010-6

Printed by Lang Druck Inc., Liebefeld/Berne (Switzerland)

INDEX

PREFACE

The novel and theories of the novel have long been favourite areas for literary studies; the interrelationship between literature and society has almost received over-exposure in recent years. Despite this, the German *Zeit-roman* of the 19th century has been largely ignored, presumably dismissed from serious discussion in the belief that the novel only made progress outside Germany in that period. Thus the present work seems to be the first in English to consider the *Zeitroman*-tradition. No large-scale rehabilitation is attempted, but the novels considered generally emerge as more than aesthetic aberrations or poor substitutes for history primers, while perspectives are opened up on the development of the German novel from the 19th into the 20th century.

With novels referred to, as well as with the frequently cited works of Hasubek and Worthmann, full bibliographical details are given in the first footnote referring to them. Thereafter the page and, if relevant, the volume number are given in the body of the text. Where the author has added emphases to quotations, a note to this effect is added in parentheses.

ACKNOWLEDGEMENTS

For supervision, encouragement and support at different stages of this work I am grateful to Professor Brian Coghlan, Professor Gerhard Schulz, Professor Hans Mayer, the late Professor Siegfried Sudhof, Dr. Dushan Stankovich and Dr. Bruce Beaton. Many thanks are also due to the University of Adelaide for enabling me through a research grant to spend three months in the German Federal Republic in 1973 and 1974. I am indebted to the Alexander von Humboldt-Stiftung for the chance to complete the book in Bamberg, and also for substantial financial assistance with publication. The Australian National University has also assisted financially, a most generous gesture towards a new member of staff. My wife Herta has earned more than the conventional thanks through her critical comments and typing the manuscript.

Work completed in Bamberg in January 1979. Through internal difficulties of the Verlag Peter Lang, and through no fault of the author, publication has been delayed till February 1983.

CHAPTER I

THE *ZEITROMAN* AS A FORM

1. Introduction

There can be few literary terms used in a more self-evident sense than *Zeitroman*. It is hard to imagine the common ground shared by Lohenstein's *Arminius* (1689-90) and Günter Grass' *Katz und Maus* (1961), yet both have been referred to recently as *Zeit-romane*. [1] At the other extreme, Hartmut Steinecke seems to be using the term in a highly specialized sense when he bypasses Immermann, Freytag, Spielhagen and many others with the following assertion about Gutzkow's *Die Ritter vom Geiste* (1850-51):

> [. . .] er ist der erste Zeitroman in Deutschland, der diesen Namen eigentlich verdient — und er blieb auf Jahrzehnte hinaus der einzige. [2]

What then is, or was, the *Zeitroman*?

In his Princeton lecture of May 1939, Thomas Mann said of *Der Zauberberg*:

> Er ist ein Zeitroman in doppeltem Sinn: einmal historisch, indem er das innere Bild einer Epoche, der europäischen Vorkriegszeit, zu entwerfen versucht, dann aber, weil die reine Zeit selbst sein Gegenstand ist, den er nicht nur als die Erfahrung seines Helden, sondern auch in und durch sich selbst behandelt. [3]

This second sense, with Time as a philosophical problem, is not what is generally understood by the literary term and can be disregarded. But with the first sense Mann is clearly referring to the term as it is commonly used. Only in this sense of an inner picture can *Der Zauberberg* be regarded as a *Zeitroman*; Davos is far removed from the trouble-spots of a Europe on the brink of war, and yet this setting is an ideal one for a cross-fertilization of intellectual currents.

> Sie [die Geschichte] arbeitet wohl mit den Mitteln des realistischen Romanes, aber sie ist kein solcher, sie geht beständig über das Realistische hinaus, indem sie es symbolisch steigert und transparent macht für das Geistige und Ideelle. (XI, 612)

Mann's novel thus represents a kind of synthesis of Classical and Realist elements. These were seen as antagonistic by Immermann, referring to Goethe and Schiller in 1829:

> Die beiden hatten es noch gut, sie konnten sich noch abschließen und auf das Reingeistige und Ideelle fixieren, während das in unsrer realistisch-politischen Zeit schon ganz und gar nicht möglich ist [. . .]. Die Wirklichkeit hat sich eine große, ungeheure Geltung erworben [. . .]. [4]

Mann sees his figures as "lauter Exponenten, Repräsentanten und Sendboten geistiger Bezirke, Prinzipien und Welten" (XI, 612), and he expresses the hope that this does not automatically make of them "Schatten und wandelnde Allegorien" (ibid.). Here he sees the dangers of this approach, dangers most acute in the Settembrini-Naphta disputations.

Mann's assessment is important inasmuch as it throws light on the difficulties involved in this kind of portrayal of an era. For it might be said, in anticipation of a more detailed investigation, that Immermann and Spielhagen did not attempt such an inner picture in their novels, but remained at the outer level of their eras. It might further be maintained that the "Poesie" Keller found lacking in *Martin Salander* [5] was akin to Mann's sense of an additional symbolic dimension. H. Mann's *Im Schlaraffenland* is concerned in its satire with an outer reality and only through distorting this makes an implied negative comment on an inner reality. Fontane alone, so much admired by T. Mann, blended the inner picture of an era with one of its exterior. Fontane never ran Mann's risk of dematerializing his figures into mere intellectual ciphers, and at the same time rarely allowed them to become so enmeshed at the outer level that they degenerated into pale types, de-individualized representatives.

To return to the problem of terminology, only Peter Hasubek [6] and Joachim Worthmann [7] have sought to establish in any depth just what constitutes a *Zeitroman*. The term has frequently figured in thesis titles with no [8] or inadequate clarification, or with only the most general of restrictions on its area of application. Thus Klemperer [9] sees politics, a concern with affairs of the State, as the domain of the *Zeitroman*. Ivo Braak, alongside the sense of "Nebenform des Gesellschaftsromans," allows the term to cover the general depiction of any age, not only that contemporary with the author. [10] Such a broad definition leads to confusion, since it embraces the backward-looking historical novel and the futuristic Utopian novel. Implicit in the Utopian novel is projection of an author's vision, which only a subsequent generation can assess against the historical reality, but the raw material of the writer of a *Zeitroman* must remain the historical reality contemporary with his work. The historical novel involves a different narrative perspective again. It implies a sovereign authorial view of the era treated rather than a vantage point from which the issues are still immediate ones. The latter still holds for Spielhagen's *Problematische Naturen* (1861-62), where the 1848 Revolution only slightly predates the novel. In this sense Gutzkow's "eagle-perspective" [11] is illusory, as a "Nebeneinander" [12] is possible with a static past, but not in any dynamic novel concerned with a present in constant flux. The absurd extreme of this direction is the kind of encyclopedic compilation of knowledge satirized in Flaubert's *Bouvard et Pécuchet* (1881).

Admittedly it is impossible to establish any clear division between the *Zeitroman* and the historical novel in terms of distance from the time of writing. Narrowing the temporal scope of the *Zeitroman* to the present and the immediate past will affect not only the perspective of the author in his lack of historical distance, but also in all likelihood the strength of his criticism. For authors tend to exaggerate the ills of their particular age, above all the uniqueness of those ills, and *Zeitkritik* is a topos. [13] Related to the issue of the historical novel is the distinction between a historian's assessment of character from external signs alone [14] and the novelist's generally more probing view (T. Mann's inner picture). The lack of psychological exploration of Immermann's characters does indeed bring their author close to being a chronicler, as he is well aware (see p. 28). With Dickens the external approach to characterization has a different effect. Unlike Immermann's pale sketches, Dickens' most characteristic figures embody overdeveloped idiosyncrasies, e.g. Mr. Micawber and Uriah Heep in *David Copperfield,* or Harold Skimpole in *Bleak House.* These parallel his skill in painting isolated scenes, but in neither case do the parts fuse to a historical panorama, to more than a highly individually coloured whole. The relationship between the novel and historical accounts was seen as complementary by Schleiermacher. In his view the novel is not bound by historical truth or figures of historical moment, "aber er muß das gewöhnliche Leben seiner Totalität nach zur Anschauung bringen." [15] Schleiermacher's conception of the novel in general could be seen as programmatic for the panoramic *Zeitroman* as developed by Immermann, Gutzkow and Spielhagen.

If we assume that any depiction of an age must be restricted, just how comprehensive must it be for the novel concerned to qualify as a *Zeitroman,* and also how primary a position should the *Zeit* have over other aspects? In attempting to answer these questions difficulties arise in demarcating the *Zeitroman* from related forms of the novel. Majut lists

Laube's *Das junge Europa* (1833-37) under the heading "Der Zeitroman," but adds that it is "wie alle Zeitromane — , ebensosehr Gesellschaftsroman, Charakterroman und Entwicklungsroman."[16] The issue seems to be one of emphasis, though not in the shadowy form of Majut's claim. A *Zeitroman* does portray society, it does include characters, though rarely with such primacy as to justify the term "Charakterroman," and it can trace the development of the latter, but it need not, as in the static approach of *Der Stechlin*. The capacity of the *Zeitroman* to integrate these and other elements without affecting the primacy of the *Zeit* is what establishes its most characteristic areas of tension and what also disqualifies it from being called a "Charakterroman" or an "Entwicklungsroman." It is far more difficult to separate the terms *Gesellschaftsroman* and *Zeitroman*. Majut sees both as describing "Formen und Sitten des gewöhnlichen Lebens seiner Periode,"[17] but then does not show where any difference might lie. The *Zeitroman* seems to encompass but at the same time go beyond the *Gesellschaftsroman*. In general its scope extends to the bases of a society in a particular age, and the span of contemporary issues and interrelationships between the social classes is wider, even when these are related back to the one class as the focus of attention — the nobility in *Der Stechlin* and the upper-bourgeoisie in *Im Schlaraffenland*.

Another related term Majut deals with is *der soziale Roman*. From the four "Kernthemen" of this category he sees in the *Wanderjahre*,[18] it seems Majut understands by it a novel tracing the economic development of society and the bearing of this progress on politics. *Der soziale Roman* is then less concerned with a rounded picture, with manners, fashions, contentious philosophical issues etc. which can do so much to conjure up the atmosphere of a given age in the *Zeitroman*. The term is the most suitable for a novel like Weerth's *Fragment eines Romans* (written in 1846-47). But such tenuous boundaries must inevitably overlap, and the issue seems largely one of emphasis, not of basically different criteria, when approaching the problem with Majut's categories.

2. Universality and ephemeral elements

In considering the *Zeitroman* one is confronted with the vexed question of universality: just how bound should a *Zeitroman* be to its own time? It almost seems required to forfeit claims to universality in its detailed concentration on a particular age. But timeless questions merely receive a certain flavouring from their particular historical setting. The attitudes of a certain age to broad issues like religion and morality will be instructive in crystallizing that age's character. This naturally presupposes that other problems are either unique to a given age or only comprehensible within its framework. Thus the relationship — crucial for the 19th century *Zeitroman* — between the nobility and the bourgeoisie changed from a clash of economic interests earlier in the century to a more united front presented to the common enemy, Social Democracy, by the end of the century.

The delineation of character will vary in accordance with the relationship between universal and historically limited concerns. Hasubek ascribes to the "Zeittypen im Zeitroman" a purely localized, non-universal significance:

Die Menschentypen in der Komödie des 18. Jahrhunderts zum Beispiel verkörperten allgemeinmenschliche Eigenschaften, Schwächen und Vorzüge des Menschen überhaupt. Gerade das kann von den Zeittypen im Zeitroman nicht behauptet werden, die als Mittel, den zeitgeschichtlichen Kosmos zu beschreiben, fest mit ihrer einmaligen historischen Situation verflochten sind und deren dargestellte Wesenszüge keine überzeitlich-allgemeinmenschliche Gültigkeit beanspruchen können. (b, 228)

But again it is surely a matter of accents, and such a clearcut distinction as is made here is misleading. Beaumarchais' figures, universal though their appeal has proved to be, still derive substantially from their age. At the other end of Hasubek's spectrum, any figure who is not the palest chiffre in a 19th century *Zeitroman* has to transcend his age in some measure to be credible in human terms, a basic level hardly reached for instance by the fevered exaggerations of Gutzkow's *Wally, die Zweiflerin* (1835). The notion of any historical situation being unique to the extent of invalidating a more general ("überzeitlich-allgemeinmenschlich") approach to its historical figures is inconceivable in practical terms. It is of course convenient to talk of "Victorian morality," "Renaissance Man," etc., but to claim a unique, epoch-bound identity for such concepts would be absurd. Scott's introduction to *Ivanhoe* elaborates on this point with regard to manners and sentiments. He indicates that these are sufficiently constant throughout the ages and across the social ranks for a writer of romances to have his materials substantially to hand in his own society.[19]

This is the basis on which realistic literature has been seen as surviving, as a work of art, the passing of the world it has portrayed.[20] In this context realism is almost an aesthetic criterion, referring to a durable quality which is precisely the element of universality. Whether through strength of characterization in a perennial mould or the quality of the world depicted, a certain exemplary nature is lent to this world in relating an eternal type to a particular age. This quality, which Tolstoy believed present in *Der Büttnerbauer,* was what caused him to enthuse about Polenz' novel:

> Such a detail, illuminating the inner life of this woman and this man, lights up for the reader the inner life of *millions of such* husbands and wives, [...].[21] (author's emphasis)

On the other hand, every work has ephemeral features, and the *Zeitroman* must by its very nature — its concern with the minutiae of life to add depth to a rounded picture of an era — be particularly prone to such dating. Although, then, a certain accessibility for subsequent generations is necessary to ensure a basic human veracity of the work, the criterion of universality is to be applied very warily when making value judgements on the *Zeitroman,* since its avowed aim is generally to be found elsewhere.

3. *The aesthetic element*

Another vital question is whether aesthetic criteria are the ultimate consideration with this novel-form. If we consider what stylistic features a good *Zeitroman* might contain, and suggest for instance vividness of depiction of a society, detachment from pamphlet-style polemics, or articulateness of social comment, it becomes clear that the aesthetic value of the *Zeitroman* leans rather more heavily than most literary forms on historical facts, and that extra-literary factors play a considerable role in the shaping of its raw material. Still, the primarily literary function remains, and historical and sociological documentation is not interchangeable with a novel by Immermann or Spielhagen, to mention the two lesser lights among those considered here. For the claim is occasionally advanced that the aesthetic quality of a novel is inversely proportional to the faithfulness of its reflection of social reality.[22] Goldmann sees this relationship as one of the weaknesses of a sociological approach to literature which seeks to establish connections between the content of literary works and the content of the collective consciousness of social groups. But there is no inherent reason why the *Trivialroman* should hold sway here, why the mere mention of the *Kreuzzeitung* or the *Café Kranzler* in a Fontane novel should not more effectively create a whole, subtly wrought atmosphere. Fontane's technique must be of interest to the sociologist too, but at the same time it contains literary overtones going well beyond the sociological level. It is easy to overlook these overtones when the narrator or a character makes an analysis of some feature of an age couched in what seems to be the form of a truism, a general assertion of historical fact. But as J. P. Stern points out:

> The truth of such generalizations is suspended, we must match them not against our historical understanding but against our understanding of the fictional whole (the 'totality') in which they occur. [23]

This is to be borne in mind particularly in the case of *Die Epigonen,* where we frequently encounter commentaries on historical events or social trends rather than seeing these actually unfolded on the epic canvas.

Hasubek claims:

> Die meisten Figuren im Zeitroman erhalten ihre Glaubwürdigkeit weniger auf Grund künstlerisch-kompositorischer Absichten des Dichters, als vielmehr aus der Tatsache ihrer zeitgeschichtlichen Relevanz. (b, 228)

Here we see an uneasy intermingling of the historical and artistic aspects of the *Zeitroman.* The credibility seems to be a historical one, whereas the contemporary relevance cannot, from a modern viewpoint, be taken as pre-established, but has to emerge from the novel's portrayal of that contemporary reality. That is, neither the figures nor the overall framework which determines whether something is of contemporary relevance can be directly transferred from a particular setting in history. They have to be artistically moulded, and the "künstlerisch-kompositorische(n) Absichten des Dichters" are always apparent. In implying the precedence of the historical over the artistic aspect, Hasubek tends to reduce the *Zeitroman* to a social document, but it remains first and foremost a work of literature.

4. *Development of the form*

a. *General survey*

Having come somewhat closer to the *Zeitroman* through formal considerations, let us seek more pointers in its historical development. In his illuminating examination of the *Novelle,* Karl Polheim [24] came to the conclusion that it was meaningless to use the one blanket term for such a wide-reaching genre, and that at best one could talk of the *Novelle* of a limited historical period with certain common features in mind. For similar formal reasons, as well as to achieve a certain unity of content, it would seem meaningful to confine discussion of the *Zeitroman* to its manifestations up to the threshold of the twentieth century. This is not to deny the further development of the form via the bridge-figures of Fontane and H. Mann in different directions in the twentieth century, with novels of T. Mann, at least *Der Zauberberg* and *Doktor Faustus,* further novels of H. Mann, Musil, Grass and others. There may be external formal similarities — e.g. between the sheer scope of Gutzkow's nine-volume *Die Ritter vom Geiste* and the uncompleted monumentality of Musil's *Der Mann ohne Eigenschaften,* which appeared in three volumes between 1930 and 1950 — in attempts from both centuries to capture a whole age. Yet the two novels are worlds apart, worlds divided not only by Freud and modern psychology, but also by the geometric progression of the pace of historical developments. Of interest in showing the transition between the two centuries is Arnold Zweig's *Der Streit um den Sergeanten Grischa* (1927). The novel forms a kind of negative answer to the hopes held out by Dubslav Stechlin for a possible restoration of the old order (see p. 97), tracing as it does the death of military glory and the honour of the last vestiges of the Friderician state. Fontane's emphasis on the individual in *Der Stechlin* is retained here with a much broader canvas as backdrop: the one issue of justice for a foreign prisoner is seen as a test case for the morality of forces waging war.

In broad formal terms, the 19th century *Zeitroman* narrowed its scope from the panoramic novels of Immermann, Spielhagen and Gutzkow, with their attempts to create a total picture of an age, to a more modest but incisive examination of a small fragment of an age in the novels of Keller, Raabe [25] and Fontane. In the novels treated in detail here, except for the Swiss conditions in *Martin Salander,* the interrelationship between a waning aristocracy and a rising bourgeoisie proved a common preoccupation, with the emergence of Social Democracy broadening this picture by the end of the century. Within the degree of uniformity in the 19th century *Zeitroman* there was also of course diversity. At the most basic level this was governed by a rapidly changing age; after decades of conservatism this diversity gathered momentum with the completely changed complexion of life wrought by the various stages of the Industrial Revolution, the *Gründerjahre* in the 1870's and a belated imperialism in the race for overseas colonies in the 1880's and 1890's, to list only some of the more spectacular developments.

From Immermann on a tradition of the *Zeitroman* did develop in the direction of more effective, because artistically more articulate, social criticism. This development is neglected in Hasubek's otherwise valuable work when he gains criteria for the *Zeitroman* largely from Gutzkow's works and at times dangerously generalizes from these (e.g. a, 92-93), implying a largely stable form. Fritz Martini sees a progression within the *Zeitroman* [26] from the tendentious form preferred by the writers of the *Junges Deutschland* to a more static one, which finds no solutions. Martini cites Gutzkow, Spielhagen and Fontane as examples. However, in *Problematische Naturen* Spielhagen does attempt, without successfully achieving, a historical progression. Worthmann places the following emphases:

Im Mittelpunkt unserer Studien steht die historische Bewegung, nicht das einzelne Werk in allen seinen vielfältigen Dimensionen und Inhaltsnuancen. (16)

The present work, though not conceived in this light, can hopefully complement this approach. While the historical background is never lost sight of, the works themselves are the focus of attention in tracing stages along the way in the development of the genre.

b. *Beginnings of the form*

The concerns of the *Zeitroman* are met for the first time in Immermann's *Die Epigonen* (1836), despite its carry-over from the past (see p. 29). It must be remembered that at the time when pioneering efforts were being made in the field of the *Zeitroman,* the novel as a whole was struggling for acceptance as a genre in Germany — continuing through to Spielhagen's apologetics much later in the century (see p. 155, n. 15) — and stood very much in the shadow of Goethe. This location of Immermann's novel at the beginning of the tradition conflicts with the wider net cast by Worthmann in his understanding of what constitutes a *Zeitroman.* A brief refutation of the earlier candidates he proposes will simultaneously clarify some of the assumptions in the present work.

Worthmann claims that Arnim's *Armut, Reichtum, Schuld und Buße der Gräfin*

Dolores (1810) was the first German *Zeitroman* of the 19th century. This view raises considerable formal problems. Firstly, the work contains a large number of poetic and dramatic insertions and even a dramatic presentation within the prose, with people speaking as if with play-roles. Secondly, much of the work is set in Italy and Sicily, whereas the *Zeitroman* requires a certain unity of place as well as time. The concluding lines of Arnim's novel, which return it to a German base, are visionary. Towards the end we follow almost exclusively the personal intrigues of the story and a generalized religious moralizing. Worthmann himself concedes: "Neben der erzählten Handlungswelt entsteht ein Überbau aus Reflexionen, der nun selber nicht mehr integriert ist" (24). Other assertions of Worthmann further make it difficult to regard this work as a *Zeitroman*, if by this term we understand a wrangling with the actual problems of an age in real, i.e. non-mythologized form. Thus he seeks to explain "warum der Dichter hier die wirklichen Probleme der Zeit verfehlte" (22) and then writes:

> Da also für Arnim die Objektivationen der "alten" Zeit in Staat und Gesellschaft ihre Legitimität aus der mythischen Urzeit herleiten können, beruhen sie letztlich auf göttlicher Setzung und müssen als solche im Kampf der Zeiten bewahrt werden. (23)

Certainly the disorder of war is present as a refrain to the work,[27] but the theme does not assume prominence. One of the interpolated tales, *Die Schule der Erfahrung*, is heralded as conveying the essence of the novel. Its religious allegory has undoubted reference to the historical events depicted, but it extracts from them a generalized, historically timeless sense which is the ultimate concern of the author. The individual age is not in itself of primary interest — surely a criterion for a *Zeitroman* — but simply reflects at this particular historical stage an eternal world-order.

Worthmann is not alone in his view of Eichendorff's *Ahnung und Gegenwart* (1815) as a *Zeitroman*. Braak[28] and Majut[29] see it as the first example of this novel-type in Germany. Certainly elements of *Zeitkritik* are present, but not as a differentiated critique of the age. The generalized, highly poetic language is more akin to mythology than the dissection of social criticism.[30] Mention of the Rhine or Danube — which might seem to be specific settings — occurs for the sake of the poetic resonance of those names.[31] Certainly the age is seen in the novel as an active agent: "[. . .] der furchtbare Gang der Zeit, der wohl keines der besseren Gemüter unberührt ließ" (193). However, the ultimate solution to the crosscurrents of the age is not to be found in any material sense, but in the higher realm of religion (335, 349). This transcends the usual domain of the *Zeitroman*, for with the notable exception of Gotthelf it is largely a secularized form, and an appeal to another dimension of reality generally goes beyond its scope. Thus Eichendorff's novel, and for that matter Goethe's *Wilhelm Meisters Wanderjahre* with the heralding of industrialism, cannot be regarded as a *Zeitroman* because of different basic concerns. Worthmann's own formulations — e.g.: "Reale Interessengegensätze sozialer Schichten spielen keine Rolle" (27) [32] — sometimes contradict his overall view of the work as a *Zeitroman*.

The same basic objection applies to Tieck's *Der junge Tischlermeister* (1836): though the work contains many elements of the age it portrays, this is not its primary concern, and thus it is not a *Zeitroman*. This can be asserted without even going into the question of genre raised by its subtitle: "Novelle in sieben Abschnitten." The second of the seven sections contains the nucleus of a work examining social conditions. However, this potential core recedes before the extended productions of plays at the residence of the Baron. These are primarily a vehicle whereby Tieck expresses ideas about the development of a German theatre, [33] a reflection of the work's direct descent from the *Lehrjahre*.

19

The novel does not range over a large number of social circles; anecdotes of a highly individual nature abound, and the personal fates of the main characters — notably in affairs of the heart — are followed with an attentiveness that makes them ill-equipped to represent an age. Worthmann notes a discrepancy between the world of the fictitious characters, constantly in the foreground, and another world they reflect upon in their conversations.[34] However, he fails to draw the implied conclusion that this is hardly a fruitful foundation for a *Zeitroman*. The tableau at the conclusion of the work ensures the preservation of the old-style guild with its patriarchal structure, but as with the ending of *Die Epigonen* this is more of a private solution, and one largely overtaken by those historical developments which are at least portrayed in *Die Epigonen*. For although both Tieck's and Immermann's works appeared in 1836, the action in Tieck's fades out some decades before.

Worthmann's perspective on "Probleme des Zeitromans" must be modified by inclusion of these three novels, which lie beyond a meaningful limitation of the term.

c. Gutzkow's "Die Ritter vom Geiste"

Perhaps the most deliberate attempt to establish the genre was Gutzkow's *Die Ritter vom Geiste*. This novel is not considered in detail here for two reasons: — firstly, because Hasubek's thesis substantially exhausts Gutzkow's contributions to the field, and secondly, because it represents something of an isolated stage in the development of the genre without immediate future thrust.[35] This is conceded by Gutzkow's apologist Arno Schmidt.[36] Gutzkow's is the most extensive attempt to capture an age through the sheer scope of a novel, though he himself acknowledges that "ein Panorama unserer Zeit" is ultimately impossible and that the most his mammoth work can encompass is "ein gutes Stück von dieser unserer alten und neuen Welt" (I, 9).

The problems raised by Gutzkow's attempt to realize his aims are legion. The ploys and trappings of the "Roman des Nacheinander" are not avoided in his own work, despite his programmatic intention. Intrigues abound, conversations are frequently interrupted when seemingly close to revealing an important fact, at the end of the first two volumes — over 800 pages, after all — some identities are still unclear and others are mistaken, the whole paraphernalia of family curses is brought into play; in short, the "Romanenwelt" (I, 7) of the older-style novel is simply transplanted to fresh soil. Quite apart from the primary sense of the term, Gutzkow's novel is a *Zeitroman* in capturing so many literary topoi of the era, contrary to its own aim. Furthermore, the "eagle's perspective" of the narrator [37] is coloured by a tendentious liberalism which works against any legitimate notion of a horizontal approach ("Nebeneinander") in a characterization like the following:

> Er war bei aller Gesinnungstüchtigkeit doch etwas Diplomat und richtete sich nach den Umständen, wie die ganze Bourgeoisie jener Stadt, die im Herzen von einer weit freiern Auffassung war, als sie seit einiger Zeit anfing, vor den Machthabern und den bedenklichen Umständen zu heucheln. (III, 173-74)

The strong editorial overtones skim over the political consciousness of a whole class, which the reader has to take on trust, for it does not emerge from the accumulation of details.

Gutzkow is not merely aware of this danger, but elsewhere seeks to exonerate himself of any such tendencies in highly self-conscious fashion.[38] A "Nebeneinander" in many speeches in the novel, expressing elevated notions in language to match, makes their effect more parliamentary than naturalistic, there being no interwoven dialogue or interruptions. The sheer number of characters in the novel means that some disappear from the stage for volumes on end. Such has been the fate of Melanie when Dankmar brings her together with Egon, Pauline, Lasally, Schlurck and Werdeck in a letter (VII, 393), but this kind of contrived entry from the wings is not adequate for the aims of this wide-ranging novel. It is more than a delayed entry when a pivotal character like Hackert is absent from halfway through vol. 6 till the beginning of vol. 8. Again the author is aware of this kind of technical problem — "Das Billet der Madame Ludmer führt uns in die lange nicht betretene Salonsphäre zurück [. . .] " (VIII, 60) — but in such an ambitious undertaking problems of this kind become insoluble.

The features discussed above should suffice to qualify Gutzkow as a base for considering the *Zeitroman.* If some of Hasubek's generalizations from the model of Gutzkow are now queried, the aim is not to cavil, but to trace the development of the genre beyond or alongside Gutzkow. Hasubek lays great stress on the " 'medialen' Charakter" of novel figures (a, 276 et passim), these being seen as undeveloped characters who simply represent a current of the age. Supposed examples of this feature observed in Fontane's works (a, 266) are either misleading or misunderstood. The figures cited from *Die Poggenpuhls* are certainly what Hasubek claims, namely representatives of certain codes, professions, etc., but this does not exhaust their being. They are also, in varying degrees of fullness, characters in their own right and not simply one-dimensional chiffres. The same would apply to *Martin Salander* and even to many of Spielhagen's creations, though additional complexity is not always a poetic virtue with his figures. Fontane's figures most certainly do not fit uniformly into this category. When they do, as in the case of Treibel's political campaigner Vogelsang or the two Berliners in *Cécile* (Hasubek's further examples), a specific effect is achieved; their very limitations or fanaticisms are ironized, and their medial nature is frequently designed to signify an incompleteness of being. It is unjust to lump a Vogelsang together with a Professor Schmidt. Hasubek does allow for a certain amount of individualization of *Zeitroman* characters to temper their medial function as types of the age. But he derives this from the practice of drawing on models from real life to imbue the fictional figures with more fullness (a, 267). Again this might do justice to Gutzkow,[39] but it certainly does not uniformly to Fontane, either in the direction his poetic practice took or in his achievements in characterization.

In the final paragraph of his thesis (a, 276-77) Hasubek lists various features which combine to make up the *Zeitroman.* This they do only in combination; the presence of some of the features is, he claims, insufficient. The absolute nature of the claim is dangerous. One feature he lists is a significant increase in the number of individual characters. There was indeed a general shift of emphasis from a main figure to a group of figures of similar weight — such titles as *Die Epigonen, Die Ritter vom Geiste* and *Die Poggenpuhls* illustrate this. Despite similar aims, these never match the achievement of Thackeray's *Vanity Fair* (1847-48), subtitled "A Novel without a Hero," where a whole section of English society about the time of Waterloo is presented, yet many more fully-drawn characters emerge than in the German novels. Working against Hasubek's claim are *Martin Salander* and *Frau Jenny Treibel,* which show that a central figure is still capable of unifying the threads of a relatively small-scale work. The title *Der Stechlin* has ramifications that are different again (cf. p. 100).

The present work seeks to avoid the pitfalls of characterizing a genre through one main author, an approach which at times becomes normative, by illustrating the development of the *Zeitroman* in the 19th century through detailed analysis and comparison of five main representative examples.

5. The "Zeitroman" and the "Bildungsroman"

The struggle of the novel as a genre is also found in the other main form of the 19th century German novel, the *Bildungsroman*. Today we regard Keller's *Der grüne Heinrich* (1854) as a cornerstone of this novel-type, and easily forget that Keller viewed this work as a major departure from his natural areas, among which he reckoned his since-forgotten dramatic attempts.[40] The diversity of different ages in the *Zeitroman* does not affect the core of the *Bildungsroman*. The form of *Bildung* of course changes, but the concept can retain a constant quality when transferred to various historical settings. Thus a tradition of a *Bildungsroman* can emerge with certain features common to all members of the genre. This is implicit in any parody of the tradition, represented for instance by Grass' *Die Blechtrommel,* for parody of a novel-type presupposes a tradition to be parodied. Could any work be said to parody the tradition of the *Zeitroman*? None is commonly regarded in this light, though Grass might again furnish the closest example with *Hundejahre.* The reason for this seems to be the historical limits to each time (*Zeit*) making such a thing impossible rather than the lack of a tradition.

The *Bildungsroman,* with its emphasis on the inner harmony of the individual and more shadowy social background, inversely reflects the aims of the *Zeitroman.* Quite apart from evaluations of the respective writers, it is possibly this division of labour which has assigned the 19th century German novel to a seemingly irretrievable obscurity compared with the contemporaneous novel literatures of England, France or Russia. For there the two strands are more frequently interrelated[41] or else separated with a specific, ironic purpose — e.g. the individual's unglorified view of the Battle of Waterloo in Stendhal's *La Chartreuse de Parme* (1839). If we agree with Keller that *Martin Salander* did not succeed, then we have to wait till Fontane for such an achievement in the German novel, and then in his wake his dual admirers Heinrich Mann, most notably in *Der Untertan,* and his brother Thomas, though bearing in mind the reservations expressed about *Der Zauberberg.*

It is interesting that Raymond Williams sees a similar split — into "the 'social' novel and the 'personal' novel"[42] — after 1900 in the realist novel, most of his examples of pre-1900 novels being English works. If this is so, it could hardly be maintained that the German novel had been ahead of its time, but rather that it largely bypassed a whole 19th century European tradition. It is hard to go past the value judgement in Williams' following assertion:

> In the highest realism, society is seen in fundamentally personal terms, and persons, through relationships, in fundamentally social terms. [43]

As mentioned above, this interpenetration is first found in the German novel in Fontane. But even if this is the "highest realism," this criterion cannot be applied absolutely to those *Zeitromane* which do not attempt an interrelationship between an individual and his age at such an intensive level. The differing emphases within this relationship will be seen to be one of the crucial issues in the *Zeitroman.*

6. Further problems

One formal problem of the *Zeitroman* is its ending. Theodor Mundt advanced in 1842 the notion that in contrast to the circular structure of the *Novelle*, the linear progression of the novel may end in an arbitrary conclusion. [...] Like the endless continuity of life which it reflects, the novel, theoretically, need not conclude at all.[44]

The problem will be particularly acute in the case of the *Zeitroman*, where because the accent is usually on a whole era rather than any individual or group of individuals, the convenient device of the death of the main character as the completion of a life-cycle cannot be employed. Fontane's technique proves to be the exception, though in *Der Stechlin* the death of Dubslav — which because of Fontane's different concerns is not a misplaced device of convenience — does not quite complete the novel. Instead there is the poetically more satisfying tapering off with the final reappearance of the title-symbol which had been ushered in on the opening page. Both *Die Epigonen* and *Martin Salander* end, as Martini says of the latter, "in der Zelle der Familie,"[45] and both conclusions are unsatisfactory. *Die Epigonen* suggests a largely personal solution to the problems of the age, while *Martin Salander* introduces an ill-prepared note of optimism for the future. The alternative is to choose a decisive turning-point in history to conclude the era represented in the novel, and this is what Spielhagen attempts in *Problematische Naturen* with the Berlin barricades of the 1848 Revolution and a brief aftermath. But his poetic realization works against this plausible design. *Im Schlaraffenland* benefits from its framework — the fairytale of the title — in being able to conclude in much the same way as it began, a testimony to the cyclical quality of the life observed. In this particular case the lack of a historical progression is not disturbing as the fairytale element is never absent despite the work's basic concern with demolishing social façades.

In her study on *Martin Salander*, Margarete Merkel-Nipperdey hints at the problem of ending the *Zeitroman* and extends it to the beginning also.[46] But the beginning does not seem to be as problematic, for the novel-writer — even the writer of a *Zeitroman* working with a panoramic depiction of society — can choose his own settings and gradually allow them to take on fictional shape. There is no need at the beginning for a historically important time-setting, because reference can always be made to past events by way of orientation, whereas at the end of a novel such sorties into the future are not possible in terms of poetic credibility. *Die Epigonen* errs on this count with the break between the bulk of the action, ending in 1829, and the letters of 1835. Nor, if the writer is concerned with a contemporary canvas, are references to the future possible in terms of historical credibility, with the resultant breach between analysis and speculation.

The whole problem of the ending of a *Zeitroman* arises because of its reliance on historical reality at the same time as it preserves its own fictional entity. The historian or literary historian can legitimately demarcate the boundaries of a period for examination, and even give pointers to what follows the limit he has chosen, it being accepted that any boundary is arbitrary in a continuous course of history. But the writer of a *Zeitroman* somehow has to mould a self-sufficient work of art, despite his raw historical material which does not come to an end, nor even generally culminates in an event like the 1848 Revolution. The fictional apparatus which requires a resolution clashes with the historical level which does not, except in the case of a work like *Problematische Naturen* where a resolution at both levels is attempted, albeit unsuccessfully, by fusing the two.

The balance between portraying the forces of an age in more abstract form and delineating figures whose primary function is to be somehow representative of that age, is one of the most delicate facing the writer of a *Zeitroman*. Hasubek sees the latter's aim as "die erzählerische Bewältigung der überpersönlichen Kräfte und Strömungen seiner Gegenwart" (b, 224). These crosscurrents of the age, though they transcend the fates of individuals, can of course only emerge through the depiction of individuals if the work is to be more than a kind of philosophical thesis. Hasubek is at pains to stress that the presentation of one-dimensional, typifying figures in the *Zeitroman* is a valid artistic possibility (b, 226-27), but one asks why, if the two levels were achieved in other national literatures, they could not be in Germany. Even if we accept the standard reasons advanced, namely Germany's disunity and lack of a capital before 1871, Fontane and to some degree Raabe are solitary beacons in the 30-odd years till the turn of the century.

7. Conclusion

These strands of investigation into the nature of the *Zeitroman* can now be summarized. The *Zeitroman* is not basically concerned with individual psychological concerns, the individual's life-cycle, indeed the primacy of the individual in any sense. It does seek to portray a society, the manners and mores of that society, its political crosscurrents, and generally, in the 19th century, the interrelationship between classes. The *Gesellschafts-roman* and *der soziale Roman* thus do not match the scope of the *Zeitroman,* and for this reason the German term has been retained in favour of the English "social novel." This would seem to be the closest rendering of all three German terms, and it could thus be misleading to use it for any one of them.

The temporal scope of the *Zeitroman* is limited to the present and the recent past. The concentration on details of the society contemporaneous with the writer risks transient accessibility. No blueprint for a *Zeitroman* can be determined within the range of its ambitious undertakings, but each example of the genre works within poles of tension. The most important of these are universal vs. ephemeral concerns, historical documentation vs. fictional restructuring of reality, and characterization of individuals vs. more abstract depiction of an age aiming at greater scope. Just as characteristics of the *Zeitroman* are a matter of emphasis rather than being clearly distinguishable from related streams of the novel, each area of tension remains a continuous spectrum, not an either-or alternative. These guidelines are lent substance by the following novel analyses.

CHAPTER II

KARL IMMERMANN: *DIE EPIGONEN*

1. Introduction

In 1835 Ludolf Wienbarg exhorted young German writers as follows:

Greift in die Zeit, haltet euch an das Leben. Ich weiß, was ihr entgegnet. Nicht wahr, es ist verdammt wenig Poesie in dieser Zeit, in diesem Leben, das wir in Deutschland führen? [. . .]
Aber gut. Haltet einmal Abrechnung mit der Zeit, entzieht einmal durch einen herzhaften Ent-
schluß dieser heutigen deutschen Literatur den Schimmer poetischer Lügen, [. . .] reißt der Zeit
den Mantel der Heuchelei, der Selbstsucht, der Feigheit vom Leibe [. . .] . [1]

Karl Immermann, whose novel *Die Epigonen* appeared in 1836, had already been working
at it for many years,[2] yet Wienbarg's remark could almost have been directed to this particular writer. That is, with the possible exception of the admonition to expose "poetische
Lügen," a point to which we shall return when discussing the novel's conclusion. Otherwise Wienbarg's theory is unquestionably realized in Immermann's practice, an achievement which lends the writer historical significance in the tradition of the German novel.

Die 'Epigonen' stellen in der deutschen Literatur den ersten bewußten Versuch dar, einen großen
Zeit- und Epochenroman zu schreiben. [3]

The work's deserts have always been seen in the light of this pioneering function, coupled
with its interest as a historical-sociological document.

In the same extract Wienbarg says: "[. . .] zeigt uns den Himmel, wie er grau und
schmuzig über uns niederhängt." This injunction is also realized in Immermann's novel,
both figuratively and, in the first chapter, almost literally. For it begins thus:

An einem deutschen Sommertage, wo Gußregen und schwüler Sonnenblick wechselten und das
Gefilde zu öfterem halb unter grauen Wolken, halb unter glühendem Lichte lag, [. . .] . [4]

Through the rather odd coupling of "deutsch" with "Sommertag," the broad setting
emerges at once, not being limited to Westphalia till the end of the second chapter. The
rest is of course only superficially a report on the weather. The atmosphere is established,
the half and half nature of the age, an image reinforced by repetition. So that what seems
to be a conventional stage-setting in fact contains the nucleus of the work in condensed
form.[5]

What is of particular interest here is the word "deutsch." The young Friedrich Engels
paid homage to this quality in his poem *Bei Immermanns Tode*:

Ich aber ging ans Tagewerk und schwur,
So stark und fest und deutsch, wie du, zu werden. [6]

Throughout the novel great emphasis is laid on the fact that the conditions portrayed are
German ones. This goes beyond a concrete historical setting to an attempt to explore
something of the mentality of a nation. The pride and confidence of later bourgeois art
have still to be established — one has only to compare the ring of the word "deutsch" in
Immermann, who in any case inclined to a more aristocratic position, with its tone in
Freytag's *Soll und Haben,* not to mention the twin historical levels of Wagner's *Meister-
singer* in its extolling of Germanic art.

When for instance one of those excluded from the Duchess' festivities suggests staging
a still more sumptuous entertainment by way of retaliation, the narrator intervenes:

"[. . .] welcher Gedanke indessen, obgleich er ein echt deutscher war" (III, 247). Excursions from German soil are few and brief. Thus the tale of the stranger returned from Siberian captivity is not told for the sake of any exotic potential. It is merely a yardstick by which to measure the misery of his present plight:

> Aber das Schlimmste sollte ich nicht in Sibirien gelitten haben; hier in der lieben deutschen Heimat mußte ich es erfahren. (III, 234) [7]

Likewise the "Philhellene" with whom Hermann is conversing when he first appears gives but a brief picture of the projected aim of his wanderings. When met with again, he is not only still in Germany but has become the embodiment of a host of philistine tendencies. The zealot's airy plans are more of a foil for Hermann's own disillusioned comments about Germany, the natural repose, he feels, for his resignation. A fleeting breath of the outside world is soon past: "Ich war in London, in Paris; ich habe sie gesehn, die sogenannten bedeutenden Charaktere der Zeit" (III, 17). The extreme counterpart to this approach, the enrichment of a still unmistakably Prussian outlook through contact with the external world, will be found in Fontane's *Der Stechlin.*

Within the bounds of his own country, however, Immermann does present a wide panorama, avoiding mere provincialism. Two areas are highlighted, the first being the social coruscations of Berlin with its many cultural crosscurrents. Together with this comes an unmasking of the emptiness and hypocrisy behind the façade of brilliance. With corresponding changes in types and tastes of the age, this is very similar to Heinrich Mann's *Im Schlaraffenland,* except that Mann goes a step further and creates his own mythical *Schlaraffenland* from the milieu he portrays. The other main sphere of Immermann's novel is the Rhineland. This proves the logical setting for his confrontation of a waning nobility with an emerging bourgeois capitalism, even though the model for Hermann's uncle, Gottlob Nathusius, had built up his enterprise near Magdeburg. For Immermann

> has only transferred the theatre of capitalist expansion from the province of Magdeburg in the West-German district to one where, in fact, the old aristocratic lordships [. . .] lay right next to industrial areas. [8]

As a novel whose action fades out in 1829 — i.e. excluding the correspondences of Book 8, dated 1835 — Immermann's is indeed forward-looking in this aspect. Despite the beginnings of large-scale undertakings in the Rhine provinces, Krupp's factory at Essen still employed only 122 men in 1846,[9] and the industrialization of Germany was even then a long way off.

Immermann's novel exemplifies the tension between literature and a kind of chronicling treatise, a tension inherent in the genre of the *Zeitroman.* [10] The issue is treated by the doctor and the editor in their correspondence in the 8th book (IV, 113, 115), while in the *Memorabilien* Immermann says of his novel:

> [. . .] daß, wenn ich einen Schritt weiter gegangen wäre, ich das Gebiet des Staatsmanns, des Philosophen oder des Predigers betreten hätte. (V, 371)

Something of a historical background is attempted at the beginning of the *Geschichte des Herzogs* (IV, 158-60). But although the doctor claims it is "ohne [. . .] Kommentar" (IV, 158), the historical details reflect a strongly personal flavour and rather less objectivity than is essayed in most historical chronicling. Laube's *Das junge Europa* inevitably moves much further in this direction with the outer books of the trilogy, "Die Poeten" and "Die

Bürger," being written in the form of correspondences. [11]

For Benno von Wiese, there is a successful integration of the characters into the historical panorama the novel unquestionably presents. Indeed, for him the two are inseparable:

> So wird das Studium der privaten Seelengeschichte für Immermann zur Voraussetzung, um dennoch Zeitgeschichte zu schreiben, da das Ich-Schicksal unmittelbar mit dem Zeitschicksal identifiziert wird. [12]

The emphases here seem wrongly placed. The ranking of "Seelengeschichte" as a presupposition for "Zeitgeschichte" does not seem tenable when one considers the thinness of individual characterization in this novel and the heavy debt of such characterization as there is to figures from Goethe's *Wilhelm Meister* novels. Certainly something of what von Wiese claims for the novel is essayed at a theoretical level when the editor writes to the doctor:

> Nie sind die Individuen bedeutender gewesen als gerade in unsern Tagen; auch der Letzte fühlt das Flußbette seines Innern von großen Einflüssen gespeist [. . .]. Jeder Mensch ist in Haus und Hof, bei Frau und Kindern, am Busen der Geliebten, hinter dem Geschäftstische und im Studierstübchen eine historische Natur geworden, deren Begebenheiten, wenn wir nur das Ahnungsvermögen dafür besitzen, uns anziehn und fesseln müssen. (IV, 116)

Yet as we shall see, the vicissitudes of the age — repeatedly lamented throughout the novel — make a mockery of the significance of individuals. And the domestic regions enumerated in the second sentence above, with the possible exception of the "Geschäftstische," are precisely those not explored in any depth in this work. Their *Biedermeier* snugness remains foreign to it up to its closing pages. The idyll of such a personal realm is ravaged by external forces, and it is to these that the writer turns his attention.

The problematic figure of Flämmchen seems too to confound attempts to view this work primarily as a "Seelengeschichte." Her role in a realistic *Zeitroman* and the intrusion of the world of fantasy embodied in her raise the question of what part allegory — she is even referred to as "die junge Furie" (III, 83) — can play in such a work. In this she does not approach the stature of Melusine, who in Fontane's *Der Stechlin* is an individual with her own integrated role in the novel, though the mythological implications of her name are never forgotten. Flämmchen is more a fantastic, exotic character who is a clear example of the inappropriateness of the framework and characterization borrowed from the *Wilhelm Meister* novels.

False resolutions like that of the "Philhellene" aside, the individual in Immermann's novel is frequently seen at loggerheads with society. As Hecker points out,[13] in the static social order of the *Wilhelm Meister* novels only the individual has any mobility, and that within the clearly circumscribed borders of the social order. With Immermann, however, all is in confusion; we see the crumbling of this order and the imprint of larger-scale historical movements. The July Revolution of 1830 has affected Immermann far more than the French Revolution did Goethe at the time of the *Lehrjahre*. But, there being no established tradition of the *Zeitroman*, Immermann employs the old props.[14] Alienated from their origins, his characters border on being clichés of the *Bildungsroman*, since the panoply of this genre no longer accords with the demands of the socially more problematic *Zeitroman*. Flämmchen's uneasy position occurs in spite of the author's elaborate attempts to justify the verisimilitude of this character and others. The doctor writes the following appraisal of the work to the editor:

> Am wahrsten sind die Figuren, welche die Menge vermutlich für Erfindungen halten wird: Die Alte, der Domherr, Flämmchen. Es ist zu loben, daß Sie diesen Blasen der von Grund aus umgerüttelten Zeit nichts hinzugefügt, noch ihnen etwas abgenommen haben. (IV, 111)

The attempt is made to justify these figures as chiffres of a disturbed age, but at this point the novel's fictional apparatus creaks audibly. [15]

The identification of "Ich-" with "Zeitschicksal" would seem to find more support in a typically sententious statement by Wilhelmi late in the novel: "Wir sehen gleichsam in einer Gruppe und abgekürzten Figur um uns her das ganze trostlose Chaos der Gegenwart" (IV, 238). Hermann's labile nature certainly does bring together several currents of the age, most notably the two great social classes. But if in one sense he combines both classes, in another he belongs to neither (IV, 265), so that he does not represent a simple fusion of the two. The conclusion of the novel shows most clearly the cleft between "Seelen-" and "Zeitgeschichte." On the first level Hermann has apparently attained happiness, but the problems of the second level have merely been recognized and by no means resolved in terms of a lasting solution. Furthermore, editorial manipulation of character accentuates the fictitiousness of Hermann. [16] In such cases any sense of "Zeitschicksal" emerges only through the intermediate stage of the author's reflections tacked on to his narrative. Thus von Wiese's appraisal seems oversimplified.

A more penetrating view of the relationship between the personal fate of the individual and the historical circumstances in which he lives is given by Manfred Windfuhr:

> Die Umwelt, die im Bildungsroman (Beispiel "Lehrjahre") dazu diente, die Entfaltung des Helden zu fördern oder zu hemmen, ihn dem Irrtum und der Bewährung auszusetzen, also trotz aller Eigenbedeutung noch auf die Hauptfigur bezogen blieb, wird in der Schlußfassung der "Epigonen" zum Selbstzweck. [17]

It is tempting to regard such a depersonalized function of the milieu as an asset for a *Zeitroman*, enabling its social import to transcend the confines imposed on it if it is just an extension of the hero's own experiences. But on closer inspection a far more satisfying, subtler possibility is realized later by Fontane when he refuses to acknowledge such a dichotomy, allowing the milieu to emerge organically from the situations involving the main characters, and in particular from their conversations.

This leads to the basic difference in characterization between Immermann and Fontane. In the *Zeitroman* of Immermann's type the age is often revealed through programmatic discussions on the part of characters. Fontane's method is to allow the nature of the age to emerge from action or, more often, detailed depictions of setting or conversation, but not conversation at such an introspective, analytical level as that employed by Immermann. For Immermann such conversations are purely the vehicles of thought, whereas in Fontane's works the mannerisms and turns of the language tend to reflect the attitudes of the characters rather than directly present ideas.

As predominantly spokesmen for ideas, Immermann's characters lose in depth of characterization. This is one of the reasons why the conclusion of the novel does not satisfy. For the resolution of Hermann's trials in his personal relationships emphasizes a side of the novel that has never been sufficiently developed to support such a weight of emphasis. Windfuhr comments on the uneasy marriage of the earlier *Leben und Schicksale eines lustigen Deutschen* with the far broader concerns of *Die Epigonen*:

> Hermann wird zur bloßen Verbindungsfigur zwischen den einzelnen Gesellschaftskreisen, die sich in der Darstellung zu verselbständigen beginnen [...]. Ist die äußere Verbindung geschehen, so

tritt Hermann in der Regel ganze Abschnitte zurück, um der Sitten- und Gesellschaftsschilderung Platz zu machen. [18]

This combination in such scenes as the concluding one is no longer consonant with Immermann's novel in its final form.

2. The nobility and the bourgeoisie

When the results are revealed of a lawyer's delvings into the family history of the Duke's ancestors (III, 101ff.) one sees the old hereditary order crumbling before the new rule of industrial wealth. This situation had arisen from the fluctuating land values and rights of possession during the Napoleonic occupation. The Stein-Hardenberg reforms (1807-11) set in motion a democratization of land ownership. A veritable leitmotif of this novel, the confusion and disorder of the times, [19] appears in the narrator's assessment: "Man weiß, wie die allgemeine Verzweiflung jener Zeit auch [. . .] den Grund und Boden, im Werte heruntergedrückt hatte" (III, 102). Hermann's uncle profits from Graf Julius' financial troubles at this time, and the latter builds up debts to the point where he agrees to cancel them by selling his estates to the uncle. The narrative comments tersely: "Die Rittergüter gingen in die Hände des Bürgerlichen über, das Geld hatte gesiegt" (ibid.). In fact, the passing of noble estates into middle-class hands

happened very often between 1820 and 1830 in the stress of the agricultural crisis which was a result of the limited possibilities of German agriculture for export. At that time eighty per cent of the aristocratic landlords lost their estates. [20]

The takeover in the novel springs from a different reason and an earlier period, but as with so many other historical phenomena treated, this instance anticipates the mainstream of historical events.

Immermann's sympathies show through at this point of the narration. The lawyer, representing the uncle's claims, succumbs to the gracious surroundings and character of his aristocratic hosts and especially of his hostess, the Duchess. Pictured as being impressionable, he falls under the spell of the Duchess' "Gartenkabinett," redolent with art that he cannot properly appreciate but whose value he instinctively realizes. As a character he forms a striking contrast to the champions of a self-assertive, overweeningly confident bourgeoisie of later in the century. He visualizes the future in the following terms:

Schon erblickte er hier, wo das Schöne gute Menschen beseligt hatte, ein ödes rechnendes Comtoir; schon sah er dort draußen, quer über die armen Blumen, über den samtnen Rasen einen Weg für Karren und Schleifen zu irgend einer trostlosen Fabrikhütte führen. (III, 110)

This vision, with its aesthetic clinging to the past and rejection of the future, is central to the work. Elsewhere these black and white shades may be more blended towards a grey on both sides, but whatever is added in favour of the uncle or his enterprise, the bleak spectre of industrialization remains and at the novel's end can only be delayed, not dispelled. Here too Immermann establishes a strain in German literature which survives much later in the century in the works of Kretzer, with construction of the "Stadtbahn" and the proliferation of factories in *Meister Timpe*, Conrad, with building speculation by the river Isar in *Was die Isar rauscht,* Raabe and others. The anti-industrialist streak is taken up in elegaic vein — again not a polemic one — in *Die Akten des Vogelsangs* (1895), as in the following example:

> Ja ja, so redet man [. . .] über die [. . .] über die Gras wächst und zu denen noch einige Zeit ihre Nächsten im Leben kommen, bis Straßenzüge, Eisenbahngeleise oder, im besten Falle, der Ackerpflug über sie weggehen [. . .] wird. [21]

In the extract from *Die Epigonen* quoted above, the lawyer is smitten by scruples as to the outcome of his investigations. From the outset the surviving inner values of the older order are counterpointed against the unpoetic, cheerless visions conjured up by the incursion of the new. The "kindische Halbwesen der Zeit" and the "ungeschickte Vermischen von Alt und Neu" (III, 105) occasion Wilhelmi's objections to the whole proceedings. This conservative view begrudges the middle-class the acquisitions which it cannot be denied, a direction pointed to by the end of the novel. On the other hand it fails to posit any revitalization of the aristocratic ranks to counter them.

The lawyer's respect is shared by Hermann, for whom it outweighs the uneasiness felt when the Duke expounds his notion of the indispensability of the nobility and the incontestability of its rights (III, 151). Hermann also finds social intercourse with the local landed nobility to be stimulating, although these were considered by their more refined peers to be "eine Sammlung völlig verbauerter Krautjunker" (III, 155). Here a distinction is made between the country nobility which had remained bound to its estates, and that which had flirted with the "Stadt- und Hofleben" (ibid.). Immermann here simply presents this distinction as an established fact without examining its implications, the "Stadt- und Hofleben" of Berlin not being related to this context. Whereas Fontane, without ever reducing his verdict to such a programmatic statement, pictures a whole spectrum of types in *Der Stechlin,* with Dubslav standing out from his more provincial peers in Immermann's first category and Barby as a most favourable instance of the second.

Elsewhere, however, Hermann is fully capable of inveighing against the nobility:

> Auch der Adel ist so eine Ruine [. . .]. Was macht den Adel? Die Abgeschlossenheit, das Kastenmäßige. Nun aber haben die Bessern sich längst mit dem gebildeten Mittelstande vermischt. (III, 158).

This intermingling of the two classes, noted by Immermann early in the century, becomes an increasingly prominent issue in the period under consideration. The strong disenchantment expressed by Hermann must make an odd impression, coming as it does close on the heels of his favourable view of the country nobility, and also in view of his general sense of wellbeing at enjoying noble patronage (e.g. III, 152). Wilhelmi sees through the contradiction in Hermann — "ein armer Bürgerlicher, der den Adel haßt und sich doch für die Hochgebornen totschlagen ließe" (III, 159). With Hermann the ambivalent attitude inclines in favour of the nobility; Oswald Stein in Spielhagen's *Problematische Naturen* veers the other way in his diatribes against the class he despises in his words but not always in his actions. Hermann sees and acknowledges the nobility's glaring weaknesses, but he at the same time stresses what he regards as its surviving strengths and defends it strongly in the face of the exaggerated protests of his uncle (III, 295-97). In the case of Spielhagen's bourgeois hero, however, the nobility emerges in far less twilight shades and is the butt of constant verbal attack.

Such duality runs a tortuous course through the novel of the 19th century into the 20th. With Hermann and Oswald the duality of attitude mirrors too the duality of their origins, since they are considered bourgeois till the revelation of their mixed births. Immermann is dealing with an era when capital in the hands of the bourgeoisie began to assert itself as a force vying with and often usurping the established order of inherited estates. Hermann and Oswald belong at least by upbringing to a bourgeoisie gaining impetus but still aggressively self-conscious. The cracks in the walls of the feudalistic order, pictured in a quite literal sense in the Schloß Schnick-Schnack-Schnurr in *Münchhausen* (I, 72-73), are already apparent in *Die Epigonen*. The uncle, in keeping with his unabashed attitude to the nobility and his pragmatic nature, has no time for the high orders he receives (IV, 28) because they bring no financial gain. He represents the extreme position of bourgeois resentment, seeking compensation for earlier snubbing through such catch-cries as "Bürgerkanaille" (III, 296). His opposition to the nobility is uncompromising, yet all his calculations are ultimately vain. A kind of noble revenge triumphs when he dies of shock at the news that Ferdinand was in fact the natural son of Graf Julius, who had resigned the *Standesherrschaft* to the uncle to ensure Ferdinand's inheritance. Thus the narrator's comment: "das Geld hatte gesiegt" (III, 102) is exposed as a provisional verdict only.

The negative side of Hermann's view of the nobility is consolidated by the Duke's exercising the "Recht des Standesherrn, eine Leibwache zu halten" (III, 163). A rumour of the imminent arrival of a general causes the workers in the garden to don their military trappings, the whole being designed to exhibit "den Glanz des Hauses" (ibid.). Such brilliance is shown as hollow by the hasty nature of its assemblage even before the ironic dénouement of the general's failure to appear. This weak point of the more flamboyant nobility was seized on by bourgeois writers throughout the century, other notable examples being Immermann's contemporary, Heinrich Laube,[22] and Spielhagen.

Behind the pantomime of the domestic guard lie other implications for the nobility. These are formulated by Wilhelmi in his following tirade:

> Aber in diesem nichtsnutzigen Kasten siehst du ein Gleichnis und Symbol von dem ganzen Tun und Treiben dieser abgelebten Klasse. Sie fühlen sich überholt von dem Sturmschritte der Zeit; Ehre, Mut, kriegerische Tapferkeit sind bürgerlich geworden [. . .]. (III, 287)

This criticism too is repeated in Laube's *Das junge Europa* (I, 111-12), and in Spielhagen's *Problematische Naturen* the wheel has turned full cycle with cases of the nobility actually seeking an injection of renewed vigour from the bourgeoisie. Wilhelmi's comment reinforces his general view of the nobility as a class out of tune with the times. It is not a jaundiced attempt at compensation, but reflects a historical situation of which Bramsted writes:

> The middle-class, hitherto repressed and politically powerless, had proved its fitness in the national armies of the Wars of Liberation, where it had shown that courage and presence of mind were not the monopoly of the aristocracy. Through the institution of the territorial army (*Landwehr*) which was led by middle-class reserve-officers, the bourgeoisie had played a great part in the victories of 1813-15 [. . .].[23]

The formation of a kind of domestic guard, with the brilliance of the noble estate being represented by workers, indicates again its brittleness. The gardeners whose charade Hermann witnesses represent a class whose presence is not strongly felt at all in this novel. The descriptions of the factory-workers make a strong impression, but the pages containing a concrete description of industrialism are few. The extensive descriptions of Coketown in Dickens' *Hard Times* (1854) mirror the gap between the respective industrial growth of England and Germany, a gap which had not been bridged in the years between the publication of Immermann's and Dickens' novels. The spread of Pietism among the factory workers is described in some detail, but in general *Die Epigonen* focusses on the nobility and the bourgeoisie. Class struggles are allegorized in the following episode. Workmen are to remove the longstanding cupboard from the archive, only to find its rotted frame collapse:

> Die Arbeiter sahen Hermann bestürzt an.
> "Ist es doch, als ob ein Feudalthron einstürzt", sagte Hermann. "Frisch, ihr Leute vom dritten Stande, die ihr gar nicht die Absicht hattet, ihn zu zertrümmern, sondern ihn nur so ein wenig beiseite bringen wolltet, tragt die Stücke hinaus!" (III, 341)

This extract embodies a characteristic frequently encountered in Wilhelmi's utterances, what Höllerer fittingly calls "das Immermannsche Pathos der Verkündigung."[24] The prophetic ring might still be convincing, but is hardly so in the case just cited. A fairly trivial event is allegorized in incredibly heavyhanded fashion, being magnified to the level of a clarion call to the new order. And whether one cares to read irony into Hermann's words or not, they are inconceivable as words actually spoken by him or any other realistic character. In short, this is a blatant breach of style, an editorial intrusion which reduces the scene to the level of the ludicrous.

The qualities of honour and courage (III, 287) are not only no longer the preserve of the nobility, they have in fact become debased within that class. This is seen most clearly in the jousting spectacle organized by the Duchess for her husband. The title of Immermann's novel is exemplified in this episode. Her reading of Sir Walter Scott is her inspiration, i.e. the idea is borrowed, not creative, and irony plus a kind of moralizing lament (III, 276) feature strongly in the account of the whole débâcle. *Epigonentum*, belonging to a generation born afterwards, is symptomatic of the dissolving of the nobility's inviolable prerogative to values of honour. Its heroism is a thing of the past according to Immermann's novel, and the symbols of grandeur it flaunts reflect no deeds, but an attempt to simulate glory by recourse to representation, as witnessed by a recent turning to heraldry (see III, 161).

Various class distinctions are crystallized in Book 4, "Das Karussell, der Adelsbrief," but their origins are not delineated in any clear, historical form:

> Auch in diesen Gegenden hatte es im Strudel der Zeiten nicht fehlen können, daß ein Teil der Bodenfläche auf Neugeadelte oder bürgerlich Verbliebne überging. (III, 246)

The Duchess intends overlooking the subtleties of class barriers in inviting these landowners too to her entertainment, but she still acts without coming to grips with the historical reality. Much fuss is made about the necessity of purely noble blood for a spectacle of this kind (III, 247-48), the highly self-conscious debate being in itself symptomatic of the crumbling of the old order. The spectacle is severely compromised. The Duchess' original conception of a tournament founders, and Hermann's suggestion for a replacement, the "Karussell," runs anything but a smooth course and is dominated by the spectacular antics of an intruder, the nephew of the disgruntled "Enterbten," a motif from Scott's *Ivanhoe*. The original notion of an exclusively noble entertainment is also compromised. Those initially excluded remain so. But the blurring of class boundaries becomes further apparent when the Duchess is obliged to extend her invitations to the "Honoratioren des Städtchens" to swell the "dünnen Reihen des Adels" (III, 292), and even then the visit of a regiment is timely to cover her embarrassment. The nobility is no longer self-sufficient and has to turn to the class from which it formerly remained distant. The old distinctions are not as sharp, but they do survive at a formal level. The nobles ride in their carriages to the arena; "die Bürgerlichen gingen zu Fuß voran" (III, 305). Inside, seats are filled democratically, but differences in standing are impressed on pages when they collect votes cast for the Queen of the Festival (III, 306-7). So that the compromise to which the Duchess has been forced by lack of numbers is an uneasy one, and while concessions are seemingly made, the original conception is basically retained.

This episode shows the folly of trying to resurrect past ages as a temporary escape from the present one. A similar phenomenon is also observed in the sphere of the church (IV, 152). Certain weaknesses of the nobility do indeed cause the class to emerge in an unfavourable light. But the ascendant bourgeoisie and its economic concomitant, the birth of the industrial era, fare no better in the novel. Here the lawyer's aesthetic rejection of the future asserts itself again. Not that this deficiency is confined to the industrial realm — "der Mangel jeglicher Poesie" (III, 409) disturbs Hermann in the Berlin circles in which he moves. Again Wienbarg's judgement comes to mind: "[. . .] es ist verdammt wenig Poesie in dieser Zeit." In one of his letters to the doctor, the editor also laments the political ugliness of the age (IV, 116).

One might compare here the attitude of the narrator in the celebrated passage from Stendhal's *Le Rouge et le noir* (1830):

> Eh, monsieur, un roman est un miroir qui se promène sur une grande route. Tantôt il reflète à vos yeux l'azur des cieux, tantôt la fange des bourbiers de la route. Et l'homme qui porte le miroir dans sa hotte sera par vous accusé d'être immoral! Son miroir montre la fange, et vous accusez le miroir! Accusez bien plutôt le grand chemin où est le bourbier, et plus encore l'inspecteur des routes qui laisse l'eau croupir et le bourbier se former. [25]

Despite the protestations of the editor, politics of course do obtrude in Immermann and also Stendhal. Stendhal in fact gives a mock apology for this:

> — La politique, reprend l'auteur, est une pierre attachée au cou de la littérature, et qui, en moins de six mois, la submerge. La politique au milieu des intérêts d'imagination, c'est un coup de pistolet au milieu d'un concert. [. . .]
> — Si vos personnages ne parlent pas politique, reprend l'éditeur, ce ne sont plus des Français de 1830, et votre livre n'est plus un miroir, comme vous en avez la prétention [. . .]. (376)

Here the aesthetic impropriety of politics impinging on literature — Stendhal's favourite image of a pistol-shot in a concert — is lightly touched upon. But in the first quotation above Stendhal very clearly differentiates the role of the novel as a mirror of society from indignation at the actual social conditions portrayed.

In Immermann's novel, Hermann's verdict is reserved above all for his uncle's factories: "Der Sinn für Schönheit fehlte hier ganz" (IV, 23). This aesthetic criterion seems to be the main criticism of the approaching industrial era. The poetic aura of the conclusion, with an autumnal backdrop to Hermann, his sister and his beloved, seems likewise an effort to provide a bastion in mood — since one in more concrete, economic terms is not presented — against the encroachments of the new age with the resultant loss of beauty. The author's presence is strongly felt in the concluding montage. This accords with the one ray of hope seen by the princely narrator of the *Mondscheinmärchen*:

> Nur *eine* Entwicklung der Schönheit sehe ich noch vor uns, nämlich die poetische; in der Dichtkunst hat, wie ich glaube, Deutschland den Gipfel noch nicht erreicht. (IV, 64) [26]

But the possibility of beauty surviving in a literature of the future is not examined in the novel, and even the prince's prophecy would seem blighted by his earlier comments on the inhibiting conditions for the plastic arts: "[...] keine Heldengruppen, [...] keine Erscheinungen, [...] kein Genre" (IV, 63).

For all this, the picture presented is not wholly dark. Even in scenes where comments on the scarring of the district by the inroads of industrialization are really scathing (IV, 14), Immermann hastens to balance the picture, acknowledging the many trades and skills to which simple peasants had turned (IV, 21) through the uncle's influence. Preceding a further bitter criticism of industrialism comes a balancing of its good and bad aspects. "Das Geld und ein diese Weltkraft bewegender verständiger Geist" (IV, 22) call forth Hermann's admiration. But this is not his overriding impression:

> Vielmehr empfand er einen tiefen Widerwillen gegen die mathematische Berechnung menschlicher Kraft und menschlichen Fleißes, gegen die Verdrängung lebendiger Mittel durch tote [...]. (ibid.)

Actually very little of the vital side of life is seen in this novel, and however vivid Immermann's pictures of mechanization are, they do not really invoke a sense of loss. For what is supposedly vanishing in their wake is posited rather than presented as a positive counterweight. The declining aristocracy is celebrated for its former glory rather than ever being seen in it, and the descriptions of Nature are so minimal as to provide no real substance for lament at its defacing. In this they differ from the accumulation of such a sense of loss in Raabe's *Die Akten des Vogelsangs*.

The accession to financial supremacy of the uncle by no means involves the extinction of those he has succeeded:

> Mit allem Gelde vermochte er daher nicht, sich vor den Reminiszenzen des Adels und der Kirche zu schützen, über deren Eigentum der Zeitgeist ihn zum Herrn gemacht hatte. (IV, 29)

He even unwittingly encourages those forces he despises: "die sitzende Lebensart" (IV, 29) required of his workers leads to an upsurge of Pietistic sentiment, presumably encouraging inwardness through curtailing physical activity. His personal antagonism to the churches does not necessarily typify his class, but this little episode does illustrate the Old surviving in spite of, and in some cases nourished by, the New. There is a constant interplay, not a steady ascent for the bourgeoisie and a descent for the nobility. Immermann attempts a balanced perspective, which if anything inclines in personal sympathies to the nobility. The resolution of this interplay will be seen in a more detailed discussion of the novel's conclusion.

3. *Contemporary history*

The central historical process presented by Immermann's novel is the class conflict between an economically waning aristocracy and an emerging bourgeoisie. But several other historical currents are also integrated into the novel's fictional framework. Historical characters appear either with name unchanged, e.g. Klopstock (IV, 245), as unnamed yet unmistakable, with direct reference being made to E. T. A. Hoffmann's works but not to Hoffmann (III, 127), or as a key-figure ("Schlüsselfigur"), with Medon being modelled on Karl Follen. The satirical part of *Münchhausen* abounds with open or veiled references to contemporary figures and institutions, while in H. Mann's *Im Schlaraffenland* this possibility of the satiric *Zeitroman* is directed instead at types intended to represent society. *Die Epigonen* has both possibilities; alongside the Klopstocks and Hoffmanns appear figures like Madame Meyer:

[. . .] dem Typus der jüdischen Salondamen nachgebildet, wie er in Henriette Herz, Dorothea Veit, Rahel Varnhagen hervortritt, ohne daß von einer bestimmten Porträtähnlichkeit zu sprechen wäre. (III, 11 — *Einleitung des Herausgebers*)

Such allusions lend much flavour to the work as a depiction of a particular time; simultaneously they can date far more quickly than the overriding historical issues.

Both Hermann and the son of the "Konrektor" are seen as chiffres of the age in accounts of their personal history preceding the action of the novel (III, 39 and 195). On successive lines we read of Hermann's participation in the Wars of Liberation and then at the Wartburg, a fiery activism present only in the past and notably absent in the era of the "Epigonen." Again, Hermann is individualized to the least possible degree, while the uncertain fate of the son of the "Konrektor" is one among many mirrors of the turbulence of the times. The "Umwälzungen der Zeit" are described as impinging on the lives of individuals such as the "Johanniter" (III, 70) and the canon (III, 254), while Hermann speaks of similar upheavals in his childhood (III, 146-47) and his uncle shifts responsibility to the "Verwicklungen der Zeit" (III, 295). Other examples, while not abstracting this general verdict on the age, reinforce the impression of its topsyturvy nature. As a survival of the novel's picaresque origins, the innkeeper suffers on the same day for "Laster und Tugend" (III, 48). The doctor arranges a love affair through conscious quackery ("Der Leutnant und das Fräulein" — III, 90-100), and the exposure of Medon is symptomatic of the age's contradictions (IV, 75). These are all comparatively small touches, but their accumulation in the lives of the fictitious characters illustrates the historical phenomenon concerning Immermann.

A more specific slice of history appears, re-formed, in Book 5, entitled "Die Demagogen." These exponents of revolution are not treated sympathetically by Immermann, but their grievances do provide more local colouring of the time. For instance the stranger who defrauds Hermann of his horse is "gehetzt von den Schergen der neununddreißig Tyrannen" (III, 351); the hopeless entanglement of the numerous states, each with its own petty interests, is still a sorely felt barrier to unification. The absurd, inflated notions and plans of a group led by one Brüggemann from Mecklenburg are catalogued, beginning with the gymnasts' slogan:

Frisch, fromm, frei, fröhlich, das ist immer die Hauptsache. Auf einen Kopf oder ein paar krummgeschloßne Knochen kommt es dabei nicht an; mehr als totmachen können sie uns nicht. (III, 360)

Empty slogans and ideas devoid of practical application typify the demagogues: before having achieved the power they envisage for themselves, they debate the issue of what should happen to the kings and princes who fall before them, and show in this issue a disunity rivalling that of the states they seek to overthrow. Their programme proclaims a non-viable alternative to the uneasy blending of old and new bewailed by Wilhelmi in the present:

Schwer Werk liegt auf teutscher Jugend: wir sollen die alte, dumm und faul gewordne Zeit wieder einrenken [. . .] . Es ruht, wie gesagt, auf der Jugend; die Alten sind nichts nutze. (III, 363)

Such revolutionary ardour betrays itself in its formulation. Furthermore, a certain despair at a revolutionary spirit in general (III, 346-47) is expressed by the editorial accompaniment in its comments on the case of the "Philhellene." The crassly philistine existence embraced by this erstwhile zealot serves to unmask the philistine at large.

Extremism is also found in education. Throughout Book 3 a comparison is made between the education systems of the "Edukationsrat" and the "Konrektor." Both systems debase initially good principles through their stubborn onesidedness. Thus they both embody and help perpetuate a malaise of the age emerging from the novel, namely an absence of roundedness, of breadth of vision. Book 3 is not as closely related to the contemporary reality as Book 5, and is concerned rather with playing off more general pedagogic principles against one another. Other issues raised, however, belong quite specifically to the day, e.g. "das Verhältnis der neu erworbnen Provinzen zu dem Haupt- und Stammlande" (III, 394), referring to the Rhineland territories which came under Prussian rule after Napoleon's defeat.

Contemporary figures enter the arena of the novel. Under the pseudonym of "der Hindu" (III, 208), A. W. Schlegel appears, as elsewhere "der Beamte" (III, 425) seems to point to E. T. A. Hoffmann. Though embodying certain characteristics of their namesakes, these figures, as frequently occurs in *Münchhausen,* are "Kunstfiguren," in no sense miniature biographical sketches. This also applies of course to Klopstock's portrayal — a further feigning of historical reality — in the letter "Graf Heinrich an Hermann, den Vater" (IV, 244-46). The appearance of Klopstock in his father's day has been motivated by Hermann's nostalgic yearning for friendship in the more ardent spirit of the era of *Empfindsamkeit.* A single generation has sufficed to distance the earlier attitude to the point where it is ridiculed (III, 415). But Hermann regrets the loss of the intense joy of close personal relationships, a closeness forfeited through striving after "weiteren und höheren Zwecken" (III, 416). Yet these prove vain, lacking the firm base of a unified nation or established public institutions, so that modern man hovers between the rejected past and the unattainable aspirations of the present. Hermann, generalizing the age's feeling when he says "unser Herz," rues "den Mangel eines Freundes, einer Geliebten, eines Hauses" (ibid.), which further contradicts the claims of the editor examined on p. 29.

A variation of the allusion-technique comes with reference to Weber's *Der Freischütz,* direct in *Münchhausen* (II, 389) but indirect here (IV, 208-9), though "Kaspar und Max" also appear (III, 276). The Kaspar-like "Kammerjäger" tells Ferdinand fragments of the opera's plot,[27] reshaping it to motivate Ferdinand's fatal attempt to snatch the leaden ring from the pump. Here it is not a matter of a historical figure appearing in fictional garb, but of a myth drawn from contemporary reality being blended with the novel's fictional 'reality.'

The method by which contemporary history is most frequently presented in this novel is that of a reflective judgement by a character. The tenor of these judgements is generally critical, a polyphonic lament on the malaise announced by the novel's title. The doctor presents a retrospective viewpoint on the age in his correspondence with the editor (e.g. IV, 112), but the most frequently heard spokesman of the period is Wilhelmi. This hypochondriac is given to violent diatribes, but these are often ironized and thus lose in impact as valid analyses.[28] His sententious but impotent utterances are seen as typical of his compatriots' expending energy on speculation rather than concrete activity (III, 131-32). But his analyses contain insights, as when he verbally demolishes the changing façades of the age:

Abwechselnd kriecht sie in den frommen Rock, in den patriotischen Rock, in den historischen Rock, in den Kunstrock und in wie viele Röcke noch sonst! (III, 55)

No deeply-rooted opinions or values, but "Röcke" to be cast off at a moment's notice and replaced by another. [29]

Wilhelmi it is, too, who is the mouthpiece for the most detailed analysis of *Epigonentum*. He exposes unsparingly the dilettantism occasioned by the inheritance of a mental and spiritual wealth, the replacement of "Überzeugung" by often completely unfounded, empty "Ansichten" (III, 136). Elsewhere he repeats the popular catchcry of an "Übergangsperiode" (III, 416), here he elaborates on the historical setting of his own age:

> Man muß noch zum Teil einer andern Periode angehört haben, um den Gegensatz der beiden Zeiten, deren jüngste die Revolution in ihrem Anfangspunkte bezeichnet, ganz empfinden zu können. (III, 135)

The concept of the *Epigone* has been treated in detail by Manfred Windfuhr.[30] It is a condition which, since Immermann reintroduced the term to more modern usage, has been spelt out under the same heading[31] or else has been described in strikingly similar terms without using the tag *Epigone*.[32]

Goethe's strong influence on Immermann inhibited rather than enhanced the latter's creations. It is thus difficult to accept Claude David's answer to the question he poses:

> Auf wen [. . .] werden wir den Begriff anwenden? [. . .] Immermann, der das Übel erkannt und angeprangert hat, zieht sich damit selbst aus dem Spiel.[33]

Certainly consciousness of the dilemma does not bring its own cure for Wilhelmi in his assaults on it, nor for the editor (see IV, 109). The essence of *Epigonentum*, an unmanageable abundance inherited from a preceding generation, is presented briefly even before the declamatory Wilhelmi appears. At the beginning of chapter two, Hermann, alone in a wood, muses on the contrast between the harmony of Nature in the ordered progression of the seasons, and his own precocious generation, transposing images from the first context to the second to show the discrepancy:

> Wir armen Menschen! Wir Frühgereiften! Wir haben keine Knospen mehr, keine Blüten; mit dem Schnee auf dem Haupte werden wir schon geboren. (III, 19)[34]

Immermann's portrayal of contemporary history in this novel thus covers a very wide field. It mentions actual historical events such as the Wartburg Festival. It incorporates figures drawn from contemporary reality as fictitious characters. Finally, it contains a verbal reckoning with the nature of the age, in which the most significant feature is the problematic state heralded by the novel's title and running through it as a leitmotif.

4. *Social manners, customs*

The age typified here inclines strongly to an observation of external politenesses and forms, to a preservation of harmony midst the divergence of opinions in all spheres, rather than coming to grips with the differences underlying these opinions. For instance Medon, idolized by the society of the Berlin salons, entered debates only once diverging opinions had been expressed:

> [. . .] so wußte er auf die glänzendste Weise zu resumieren, wo dann jeder die seinige [Meinung] in so schöner Gestalt wieder erblickte, daß dem eifrigsten Streite ein allgemeines Wohlbehagen folgte, die Sache selbst freilich unerledigt blieb. (III, 383)

The multitude of opinions finds spokesmen throughout the novel, but only rarely champions in action. The method again employed is a programmatic analysis of the issue, a conversation consisting of generalizations and abstractly presented ideas. Wilhelmi laments the fact that "Tische mit den Markenkästchen" have been replaced at social gatherings by "Musikpulte" and "Lesebrettchen" (III, 54). This change does not reflect a new level of cultural interest, but a dilettantic toleration of supposedly intellectual pursuits because they belong to good tone:

> [. . .] dieser bunte Jahrmarkt flutet zwischen Musik, Vorlesen und sogenannter geistreicher Unterhaltung hin und her, mit *erlognem* Interesse, mit *scheinbarer* Erhebung. (ibid. — author's emphasis)

What gives itself an aura of cultural refinement is in fact pretentious philistinism.

A grimmer feature of the age, the duel, appears here, though it is treated far more cursorily than for example its absurd counterpart in Turgenev's *Fathers and Sons* (1862). With Turgenev there is a lack of grandeur or tension similar to that conveyed by Immermann: "Die Sache gewann wegen des Mangels an Sekundanten ein sehr unförmliches Ansehn" (III, 82). This reflects the way in which — in both works — qualities such as heroism or old-style chivalry are shown to be no longer consonant with the age. The duel as a questionable institution also appears in *Le Rouge et le noir* (269, 327, 503), or, with the irony of a greater historical distance, in Broch's *Pasenow* (1931-32),[35] these examples showing something of a progression. Immermann's rather colourless depiction contrasts with the eloquent terseness and sense of waste in his contemporary Stendhal. Turgenev is interested in the psychology of his figures rather than in merely typifying them, while Broch turns to a historical convention of the past with retrospective irony. Immermann confines himself to locating this one duel within its historical context rather than elaborating it to be something significant in the personal fates of those concerned. Thus we hear in some detail of the differing methods of fighting employed by the opponents, and then a general observation to which this duel proves to be an unimportant exception:

> Indessen wäre dieser Handel, wie so mancher, durch die Ermüdung der Kämpfer wohl zum unblutigen Ziele gediehen [. . .]. (III, 83)

A widespread feature of the age, the secret society, is ironized by Immermann, yet another detail prefigured in Goethe's *Lehrjahre*, in the *Gesellschaft des Turms*. After expressing lofty sentiments, Wilhelmi and his neophyte Hermann give themselves over to the more worldly pleasure of immoderate eating and drinking. Flämmchen, who has caused the abrupt disappearance of the holy vessels by her intrusion, completes the deflating of the previous ceremony by drawing moustaches on the busts of Plato and Pythagoras. The masonic tradition is thus crudely satirized by Immermann as a further crumbling of traditions and ideals in the age he is portraying.

There are numerous signs of the moral decay of the times. Hermann is dazzled by the front presented by Medon and Johanna as a married couple. Later it is revealed that this is in fact a marriage purely in form. The whole basis of society seems to be this façade it presents; no longer are there any stable, unassailable values, and naïve observers like Hermann must perpetually be disappointed. The discrepancy between the fair appearance and the ugly reality is a veritable leitmotif of the age as portrayed in Immermann's *Zeitroman*.

This weakness of Hermann's must be borne in mind when appraising other judgements made by him. He finds stability and stimulation in Berlin in the society assembled at Medon's house. In this mental climate the proponents of arguments are more important than the arguments themselves,[36] not out of respect for human dignity but as a palliative to the ego. The adoration of Medon's admirers is equated with "Vasallendienste" (III, 382); Medon himself is described in terms of "Großartigkeit" rather than "Größe" (ibid.), again a reflection of the basically empty age. Hermann's feeling of wellbeing in this group thus becomes pathetic, his praise of its qualities dubious.

Immermann's editorial comments often overcome one problem of the *Zeitroman*, namely how to present a solid, more realistic picture of an age when the characters' utterances are subjective, and in Hermann's case governed by an all too palpable naïveté. The same subjectivity with regard to contemporary historical reality of course applies to these editorial comments, but they do draw together those of the individual characters and thus transcend them in general validity. As it is, Immermann achieves a vivid picture of the Berlin salons and the fickleness of their members with their successive crazes.

Immermann shows the manners and customs of his age to be a function of *Epigonentum,* a central thread which serves him well, as it unites the various strands of an age of reluctant, overburdened heirs. The past is crumbling, the future uncertain, and the present a bewildering flux of unresolved historical forces, not directed towards any climax like the 1848 Revolution. The same could be said broadly of the narrative — it is something of a hotch-potch of styles and traditions. But if it does not represent any clear break with other novel-streams, Immermann's work does broach new territory in its accentuation of the social reality as a primary concern, and through this significant step paves the way for the development of a tradition of the *Zeitroman.*

5. *The conclusion of the novel*

> Während das Werk in seinem Schlusse gerade lehrt, daß die schrecklichsten Zerstörungen die in der Zeit schlummernden Heilungskräfte nicht vernichten können, sahen viele nur die abgelebten Figuren [...]. Es war mir merkwürdig, daß gerade den frischesten und gesündesten Lesern der Atem der Hoffnung aus den "Epigonen" entgegenwehete [...]. (V, 371)

Thus Immermann in his *Memorabilien*. It must be said at the outset that poetic achievement has not matched poetic intention.

The final two chapters of the novel draw together various strands of the story. Many of these are connected with the idea of heredity, just as the novel's title implies the inheritance of a past which cannot be harmonized with the present. The age, whose upheavals have been repeatedly mentioned, does not act as an incubator, but favours abrupt and consequently stunted growth, though Wilhelmi assumes a brighter future with talk of a subsequent, more robust generation (IV, 261). We hear of Hermann's solitary walk to the "Hünenborn" and the interring of Flämmchen's bones. This action gains the approval of Wilhelmi: "Der Mensch bedarf solcher symbolischer Handlungen, um sich von einer Last gänzlich zu befreien" (IV, 261-62). In his aphoristic tone of these final pages he aspires to something of the priestly bearing of a Sarastro, a dignity ill-prepared by the earlier portrayal of a hypochondriac. A symbolic quality attaches not only to Hermann's action here, but to the whole episode of the dead child. The fact that Hermann has a child by Flämmchen shows that he, too, has been caught up in the complications leading to other births of socially mixed origins in the novel. But the child's death removes the possibility of echoing Hermann's or Ferdinand's tortuous ancestry.

The latter instance has shown the brittleness of both feuding classes. It is ironic that Graf Julius can only hope to perpetuate the noble line through the bourgeoisie, when Ferdinand accedes to the uncle's wealth. On the other side, the uncle who thrives on calculation is crossed in his reckoning and dies at the revelation of the illusion under which he has lived. The ultimate irony comes when the funeral processions for both the uncle and the Duke cross paths, and the bitter class-enemies in life are remembered simultaneously in death (IV, 222).

His child dead and his background clarified, Hermann is not subject to any further complications. But the dubious nature of his own inheritance remains. Again Wilhelmi abstracts a more general sense from the personal fates of the figures, seeing in them the "Kampf alter und neuer Zeit" (IV, 265). He berates the vain aspirations of both nobility and bourgeoisie and finds emerging from their conflict "fremdartige Kombinationen" (ibid.) whereby tensions are not resolved by any clear synthesis:

> Das Erbe des Feudalismus und der Industrie fällt endlich einem zu, der beiden Ständen angehört und keinem. (ibid.) [37]

This duality reflects onto the legal side — "diesen rechtmäßig-unrechtmäßigen Erwerb" says Hermann — and so he resolves to administer it as a "Depositar" (ibid.). Yet although he says this notion springs from Wilhelmi, the two have used it very differently. For whereas Wilhelmi envisages a positive future — "ein Depositum [. . .] für ein nachkommendes glücklicheres Geschlecht" (III, 417) — Hermann merely sets his office against the "Tag der Abtretung" (IV, 265). He consciously isolates himself from the struggle he so clearly sees and clings to an idyll which he acknowledges to be a fleeting refuge from those forces which must destroy it. The notion of being a depositary has far more positive thrust in *Die Ritter vom Geiste,* where Dankmar pursues the Wildungens' claims not in their own interest, but to re-establish in a contemporary setting the Knights Templar. He sees the inheritance issue as

> ein Symbol der Frage unsres Jahrhunderts, wie sie einmal ungelöst dasteht. Es ist unwiderleglich; um das Recht der Person, um die nachwirkende Kraft der Vergangenheit handelt sich Alles. (VI, 242)

> [. . .] mein Prozeß ist denn nun also ein Bild unsrer Zeit geworden.[. . .]. Deshalb hab' ich mich entschlossen, auch nicht persönlich zu erben. (VI, 244-45)

With Gutzkow the trusteeship is assumed with an ethical awareness of the broader claims of society. Hermann's action is much closer to the primacy of private values in Dickens' communities. [38]

Hermann then announces his policy of removing the factories and returning the land to agriculture. Within the framework of this novel, this is a gigantic step. For the factories which are anathema to Hermann have throughout been vying with noble estates, and while these presumably support farmers, the reader has repeatedly been shown the aristocratic administrators and not the rural workers. Hermann's statement: "Die Erde gehört dem Pfluge, [. . .] " (IV, 266) is nothing short of visionary, for within this novel this possibility has been neglected. The situation differs from that of *Münchhausen,* where the ethos of an industrious, virtuous *Volk* emerges organically from the novel and can justifiably be set against the nobility.

Hermann's conception is an individual's solitary defiance of the onset of mechanisation, scarcely an adequately motivated solution to the problems posed by the novel. The hybrid heir of both noble and bourgeois lines, Hermann expounds a vision at the end which is likewise hybrid, simply forestalling the inevitable. The ending of *Münchhausen* is similarly visionary:

Unsere Zeit ist ein Kolumbus. Sie sieht wie der Genueser mit den Blicken des Geistes das ferne Land hinter der Wüste des Ozeans. Desselbengleichen erlebt sie die Geschicke des Kolumbus. (II, 416)

In *Die Epigonen* "das ferne Land" is perceived by Hermann, namely a soul-destroying industrialism. Unlike the Columbus-vision, Hermann's is unbearable, and he retreats before it. In the last sentence of *Münchhausen* "der Atem der Hoffnung," to return to Immermann's verdict at the beginning of this section, does indeed waft through any delusions of the present:

Und es kann sein, daß auch die Zeit nach Ophir und nach des Tartarchanes Gebiete entsteuert zu sein wähnet und in diesem Wahne, ein erhaben phantasierender Kolumbus, abstirbt, und daß erst spätere Jahre erfahren, Amerika sei an jenem Morgen entdeckt worden. (II, 417)

No such hope for a future, more enlightened generation emerges from *Die Epigonen,* at least not as an overall impression; Wilhelmi does speak in such terms (III, 417 and IV, 261).

It is this inadequacy of motivation that makes Hermann's vision unsatisfactory on a narrative level; it seems even more problematic than the historical implications of what he proclaims. For however reactionary he might seem in acting counter to the currents of the age, he does clearly recognize those currents.[39] It is not as if Hermann's alternative society is undermined by no longer being historically viable in a matter of a few years:

Noch Ende der Siebziger Jahre war Deutschland ein Agrarstaat; die Mehrzahl der Deutschen wohnte nicht in Städten, sondern auf dem Land und fand ihre politische Repräsentation überwiegend im konservativen Altpreußentum. [40]

Thus it seems that criticism such as Hans Mayer's — "Es fehlt die Erkenntnis des geschichtlich Neuen, das Immermann zwar in einzelnen Symptomen [. . .] zu erkennen vermag [. . .]"[41] — is rendered problematic by Hermann's decision. Even if the historically new is not embraced, it is recognized and bowed to as a historical development — "wir können ihren Lauf nicht hemmen" (IV, 266) — but a stay of respite is sought as a provisional, individual solution. Mayer comments on Hermann's pronouncement: "Die Erde gehört dem Pfluge, [. . .] der einfach arbeitenden Hand" (IV, 255) as follows:

Aber dieser Rückweg ist nicht mehr möglich [. . .]. So wirkt das letzte Kapitel in der Tat wie ein Versprechen, dessen Erfüllung mehr als ungewiß bleibt. [42]

No attempt is made in the novel to regard this "Rückweg" as turning back the clock of history. The "Versprechen" Mayer speaks of is present as an individual solution against the trend of history, but not as a generalized historical verdict. By the *Memorabilien,* in support of Mayer's view, any individual solution clearly seemed untenable to Immermann: "Der Charakter des Friedens, in dem wir seit fünfundzwanzig Jahren leben, ist [. . .] der des Vermittelns, des Verschlingens des Einzelnen in ein Weltganzes" (V, 288-89).

A different kind of resolution is essayed when Hermann says:

[. . .] alle Fieber der Weltgeschichte werden endlich wenigstens in dem einzelnen Gemüte von zwei treuen Armen und Augen ausgeheilt. (IV, 267)

According to this view the turmoil of the age can be overridden by love, and the extent to which an individual will be affected by historical forces is relativized to his own personal happiness. Again, this whole side of the novel is one developed far more extensively and convincingly in *Münchhausen*. There, the editor's pronouncements in his final letter (II, 415 and 417) do serve to crystallize tendencies running through the work. In *Die Epigonen*, on the other hand, Hermann's statement above strikes virtually a new note.[43] The final tableau, which realizes his statement in his own case, is hastily assembled and then fades out almost at once. It thus neither hails a new age as in *Münchhausen*, nor — through its abruptness and the author's diffident leavetaking in the last sentence — does it give any triumphant solution to the personal vicissitudes featured throughout the novel. To return to Immermann's retrospective appraisal of his work (see p. 41), those powers brought into play ("die in der Zeit schlummernden Heilungskräfte") do not balance the dislocations of the age ("die schrecklichsten Zeitstörungen") in *Die Epigonen*. Immermann's *Zeitroman*, while crystallizing the problems of the age with clarity and variety of perspective, chooses to sidestep the historical implications which have been realized in an individual solution. The nobility, for all its weaknesses and sapped vigour, is affectionately clung to, while the bogey of industrialism, championed by the new-found wealth of the bourgeoisie, is to be averted as long as possible.

CHAPTER III

FRIEDRICH SPIELHAGEN: *PROBLEMATISCHE NATUREN*

1. Introduction

In Immermann's novel, "die Epigonen" were the successors of a particularly rich historical era. Their plight was one shared, as a result of their position in history, by all figures in the novel who were not of the older generation. *Epigonentum* was thus a collective malady, symptomatic of a whole age. In Spielhagen's novel, on the other hand, we see just three people among the novel's broad range of characters who are classed as "problematische Naturen." These are Oswald, Berger and Oldenburg, all rather extreme individuals. Their frequently divergent paths are drawn together at the end when they fight on the barricades. But the intent at least is clearly for the historical event, and above all the ideal of liberty, to take precedence over the resolution of the individuals' fates. Thus the familiar problematic relationship between the individual and his age in a *Zeitroman* is present from the outset of the novel and strained by the end to the point where it has virtually become two separate strands.

The idea behind the novel's title is first expounded by Oldenburg in discussion with Oswald. He acknowledges its origins in Goethe, referring to those people "die keiner Lage gewachsen sind, in der sie sich befinden, und denen keine genug thut." [1]

> Es ist ein grausiges Wort, denn es spricht in olympischer Ruhe das Todesurtheil über eine, besonders in unseren Tagen, weit verbreitete Gattung guter Menschen und schlechter Musikanten. (I, 344-45)

Clearly a certain general validity is essayed here ("weit verbreitet"), with special reference to the contemporary scene ("besonders in unseren Tagen"), in accordance with Spielhagen's own theoretical canon. For he says of the modern writer:

> Er muß zweitens versuchen, den Helden [. . .] zu einem für die Zeit typischen, für die aktuelle Welt repräsentativen Menschen umzubilden. [2]

Such programmed generality is reinforced in Dr. Braun's view of the same phenomenon:

> [. . .] ich habe [. . .] gefunden, daß Sie eines der vortrefflichsten Exemplare einer in unseren Tagen ziemlich weit verbreiteten Species *generis humani* sind, Nachkommen des weiland vom Teufel geholten Doctor Faustus [. . .]. (I, 422)

The idea contained in the novel's title is exaggerated beyond all proportion when Oldenburg tells of a conversation with Berger "über die schwere Noth einer Zeit [. . .] die beinahe nur noch problematische Naturen hervorbringt" (II, 453).

The poetic intention is, however, not realized — the "problematische Naturen" do not emerge as types reflecting their age. The faceless men dying beside Oswald and Berger on the barricades are presumably not governed by the same desperation or death-wish. Certainly Oswald is rebuffed by society, but these rebuffs are outweighed by his own hypersensitivity and in particular his erotic vacillations. Wilhelmi's verdict of *Epigonentum* was an attempt to formulate the essence of the existing age from observation of it. Spielhagen's central notion of *Problematische Naturen*, on the other hand, is more universal, just as the interrelationship between *Hammer und Amboß* is intended to embrace many of society's ills in Spielhagen's novel of the same title (1869). *Problematische Naturen* tries unsuccessfully to convert a formulation of Goethe into a central symbol of the time immediately preceding the March Revolution. The novel fails to transplant this notion as a general one to fresh historical soil; the type of the 'problematic nature' does not emerge sufficiently as the necessary product of this particular age. Because the choice of a representative phenomenon of the age is not a felicitous one, the work itself is rendered problematic as a *Zeitroman*.

Another difference between the two novels is the shift in perspective from Immermann's basic conservatism to Spielhagen's clamorous but inconsistent anti-nobility sentiments. The liberty visualized at the conclusion of *Problematische Naturen* is not described any more definitively in class-conscious terms, and for all its tirades against the nobility, the novel is far from being pro-bourgeois. In this it differs strongly from that bastion of awakening bourgeois self-confidence, Freytag's *Soll und Haben* (1855). The assertiveness in Freytag's novel can be quite painful in poetic terms, as when Anton, half-drowned, opens his eyes and thus shows "die Absicht, seine Stellung in der bürgerlichen Gesellschaft noch nicht aufzugeben."[3] This example shows just how firm the bourgeois core of the novel is. The inflated expression of a simple idea is wholly inappropriate to the concrete situation, but points back relentlessly to the novel's central concern. This kind of solid base is lacking in *Problematische Naturen*. The historical progress of the bourgeoisie is not sufficient to explain his case. Spielhagen's novel is set in the period before the March Revolution, i.e. predating Freytag's novel, but the "Warengeschäft" where Anton gains his grounding in the ethos of work is specifically described as belonging to a former stage in the development of commerce (39-40).

Positive values in *Soll und Haben* are lent more profile by the berating of what is opposite to or outside them. Thus the national spirit of the German bourgeoisie becomes overweeningly nationalistic in outbursts against the Poles, a people whose ills supposedly result from the lack of a strong middle-class. In *Problematische Naturen,* on the other hand, a national identity is seen as a dream belonging to the past, to the Wars of Liberation. The dream could be shattered no more rudely than in the case of Berger (II, 55ff.). There are reminders of the extant order of "deutschen Duodezfürsten" (I, 177), while Oldenburg feels all too conscious of the difference between the purposefulness of the French uprising he has just participated in, and the political naïveté of the Berlin Revolution (II, 537). *Problematische Naturen* is essentially a negative comment on the age, largely ignoring constructive alternatives except for the Brauns. This is not to say that *Soll und Haben* provided a viable alternative, either historically or poetically. The other side of Freytag's coin can be seen in the biting satire of Weerth's *Humoristische Skizzen aus dem deutschen Handelsleben* (1847-48). With Spielhagen's novel, the predominantly negative tone is not in itself a criticism of the narrative. But it does mean that the glorification of liberty at the conclusion is a greater break with what has gone before, and a greater poetic contrivance, than the problematic ending of *Die Epigonen*.

One final point in this introduction: the oft-noted discrepancy between Spielhagen's practice and his more tenacious theory is evident in this novel also. The device of "Reflexion" is anathema to Spielhagen's notion of objectivity (cf. BTT, 69). Yet it is present for instance in the extended speech of the "Geheimrat" (II, 324-26). Clearly intended to be an abstraction of the age akin to Wilhelmi's speech about *Epigonentum*, it is, in terms of the novel, little short of visionary. "Schnaubende Dampfrosse, Riesenwerke der Industrie, Triumphe der Erfindsamkeit aller Art" (II, 325) are nowhere evident. Nor is the power of the masses when they appear "in dicht geschlossener Kolonne" (ibid.), if one excludes the fighting on the barricades at the end, but even that is seen primarily in terms of a few individual characters.

The fevered individualism of an Oswald is certainly found wanting, but he finds no strength in any communal activity. Indeed, prior to the fighting on the barricades, we only see the negative counterpart to what the "Geheimrat" sees as strength in unity, namely the caste-spirit of the nobility. This is not a demonstration of constructive power through solidarity, but a cowardly acknowledgement of powerlessness without it. The whole speech of the "Geheimrat," however provocative its individual ideas, is thus not only a breach in the tone of such a private occasion, but is also poorly integrated into the work as a whole. It remains a theoretical treatise, and is not saved by the miraculously timed appearance of a male choir comprising all non-aristocratic stations of men. The text they sing and the solidarity of their ranks are intended to lend substance to the sentiment finally expressed by the "Geheimrat," that the young will continue the work begun by the old in a ceaseless march of progress. One has only to readjust the concrete setting slightly to expose it as an operatic device, and an off-stage one at that.

These structural weaknesses of the novel lead to a fuller consideration of the narrative.

2. *The narrative-structure*

The whole confrontation between Oswald and the nobility he despises hinges on his coming to the estate of Grenwitz as tutor. The motivation for his taking up this job is odd. It is offered him by Berger, who has nevertheless written "ein Buch über den Adel und gegen den Adel" (I, 15). The point of this is a gibe against the prevailing censorship; the book cannot be printed in Germany. Berger mentions as enticements the cleverness of the Baroness and the beauty of Helene, but only finally convinces Oswald with the argument that the book of life's experiences for people of their ilk takes its title from Balzac's *Illusions perdues*. His feeling of obligation towards Berger combines with this argument to sway Oswald, with his virulently anti-noble sentiments, to accept a job for four years in the bosom of a noble family. That the Baroness should accept Berger's advice so unquestioningly, without realizing he is reputed to be a democrat and an atheist (I, 260) — anathema to her Divine Right belief in royalty — is also a poor piece of motivation. But Oswald does come to work for the Baroness and her family, and the inevitable clash of personalities and ideologies is sustained for the whole of vol. I, with Oswald frequently bewildered at his own immobility but nevertheless staying on, and the Baroness' avariciousness emphasized to explain her adherence to the original contract. Further co-existence only becomes impossible after Oswald has badly wounded Helene's suitor Felix in a duel. When Oswald visits Berger at the Fichtenau asylum, the latter expresses surprise that Oswald has survived thus long and sees the whole venture in terms of a philosophy of resignation (II, 49). The pivotal point of the plot is thus inconsistently motivated.

The *Zeitroman,* like any other novel, requires a certain logic in construction. In *Problematische Naturen,* the opening situation is little more than a device for providing access to the nobility to one outside its ranks till the revelation of his birth, so as to expose noble institutions to a highly critical gaze. But this contrived conflict diminishes the tragedy inherent in those hapless individuals "die keiner Lage gewachsen sind, in der sie sich befinden, und denen keine genug thut" (I, 344). For Oswald's experience does not cover a whole range of situations in life. He is placed in a situation that is untenable from the outset, and the threads of vol. II, when he has left the Grenwitz estate, are all too closely bound up with those of vol. I for any viable alternative to present itself.

Disturbing too are the many theatrical, Romantic elements which also dogged *Die Epigonen* as a novel about contemporary reality. These are remnants of an earlier, alien literary tradition. Here one must count among other components of the plot [4] the gypsies, incredibly bound up with an earlier phase of Oldenburg's life (I, 347ff.); Mutter Clausen's tale of herself as a jilted commoner (I, 162); the riotous living of Harald and his entourage; and the motif from *Die Epigonen* of the concealed noble birth of one believed a commoner. The characters in the novel even express consciousness of these devices. When Xenobi is robbed of her child by some frivolous *Junker* and entreats Oswald to help her, Oldenburg laughs:

> Eine ungeheuer romantische Situation, Herr Doctor [. . .] Morgendämmerung, Wälderrauschen, Zigeuner, des Königs Hochstraße, — wahrhaftig: reiner Eichendorff! (I, 243)

But at the same time as Spielhagen exposes these narrative props for what they are, he does employ them, without satiric intent, as structural elements. Superimposed on a post-Eichendorff novel, they evoke literary echoes out of harmony with the realistic base of the work.

Nor is this the only instance of self-conscious usage of novelistic devices. When Berger, in trying to persuade Oswald to take up the position at Grenwitz, mentions Helene as his trump, Oswald replies he has no wish to experience for himself the stock novel-situation of a house-tutor falling in love with the daughter of the noble household (I, 17). But he does take up the job and he does fall in love with Helene. Then again, Berger describes the revelation that Schmenckel is the father of Fürst Waldernberg with grim glee:

> Der Proletarier eines Fürsten Vater, der Fürst eines Proletariers Sohn — das gäbe einen hübschen Stoff zu einem modernen Romane [. . .] . (II, 543)

Certainly, this strand of the plot is subsidiary, and Waldernberg is one of the more patently manipulated characters, reeking of the technical machinery of the novel rather than the reality it feigns to present. But the Oswald-Helene example is a more serious instance of the author utilizing a convention he simultaneously questions.

A further discordant note comes with the increasing role of chance in vol. II, as the words "Zufall" and "zufällig" recur again and again, often to explain fairly major developments in the action (see II, 124, 128, 140, 148 et passim). We have seen how, at least in one case, this same outside force appeared to great effect in *Die Epigonen* (see p. 33).[5] Chance was seen as an element proper to the novel by Hegel and Vischer, as well as in the discussion about the nature of the novel and drama in the *Lehrjahre*.[6] With Spielhagen this element is so obtrusive as to pose serious problems. Without specific reference to this novel, Löwenthal writes:

> Neben die bloße Gesinnung tritt als ein anderer bestimmender sozialer Faktor bei Spielhagen der nicht weiter abzuleitende Zufall: Tod, Ohnmacht, Abstammung, eine Gesprächssituation und dergleichen mehr vermögen bei ihm Schicksale zu formen, lassen also der Illusion, als ob in sehr weitem Maße das Leben der Menschen nicht aus ihrer gesellschaftlichen Realsituation, sondern aus individuell beiläufigen Anlässen sich bestimme, breiten Raum.[7]

This crystallizes the point at stake here. In any novel, a strong element of chance in the plot can be a cover-up for shortcomings such as discontinuity in the narrative. In addition to this stylistic criticism, the *Zeitroman* finds its very essence threatened, it being assumed that the age portrayed is not wholly chaotic and dominated by the whims of chance. Even at the level of the structure of scenes, details small in themselves detract from any narrative tautness. After the Baroness has so perfidiously intercepted Helene's letter to Mary Burton and discussed its contents with Felix, she carelessly loses it from her pocket. Bruno is able to reclaim it for the other side of the conspiracy. The improbability of this situation, in view of the importance the Baroness attaches to the letter, renders her evil machinations almost laughable, akin to Music Hall villainry but not high intrigue by clever conspirators. Spielhagen's later attack on the veracity of *Effi Briest*[8] is vitiated by his own melodramatic gesture here.

Löwenthal's statement above also touches on that central structural issue when discussing a *Zeitroman*, the relationship between the individual and the age he lives in. We have seen that in *Die Epigonen* this relationship was a lopsided one, with the age emerging at the expense of characterization rather than through it. In *Problematische Naturen* there is a far more reciprocal relationship, with the danger, as Löwenthal implies, of the individual taking priority. It is not automatically a danger — any number of French, English and Russian novels of the 19th century testify to that. But in this particular case the result is disastrous at the conclusion of the novel, when a historical event is seemingly pasted together as a tableau-type backdrop to the resolution of individuals' fates, instead of accompanying these as an integrated narrative element. Again Spielhagen's epic powers are not the equal of his theoretical demands.[9] The diverging tendencies in *Problematische Naturen* towards a confessional [10] and a panoramic world-view are at loggerheads.

One of the clearest instances of the destructive interrelationship between the individual and his age is Oswald's penchant for ladies of noble birth despite their nobility. There is a conflict between his erotic nature and his ideological principles. In a letter to Berger, in which he also admits to revelling in the luxury of noble life (I, 126), he concedes that if his ideal-beloved insisted he renounce his principles as the price of her favours, he would not resist (I, 127). In practice, it is Oswald's fevered sensitivity to class-differences, and not that of Melitta, which undermines their relationship (I, 175, 219, 387-88). He embarks on the relationship but fails to draw its consequences in terms of self-commitment, being assailed by doubts about class-barriers that he conveniently overlooked at the beginning. With Helene, too, his consciousness of a distance never fully vanishes. These relationships do not gain any sense of tragic dignity as victims of social dictates. There is never any suggestion that an earlier revelation of Oswald's birth would have removed barriers to the relationships. Oswald's own labile nature seems to be the determining factor. The erotic strain is grafted onto the strain of anti-nobility polemics without this baneful combination seeming inevitable. This questioning of the tragic dimensions of the novel is not idle when approaching it as a *Zeitroman,* for the clash between the individual and his hostile age is seen as the crucial issue in the novel's own terms (II, 454).

Polemics can seriously obtrude on the narrative pattern. The brief chapter 12 of vol. II paints a picture of Grünwald,[11] the fictional disguise for the town Greifswald. This is consonant with references to Berlin being to the "Residenz,"[12] with transparent ciphers for its famous streets and parks such as "Unter den Akazien," etc. The thinness of the disguise seems odder still when Hamburg, Lübeck and Bremen are specifically named by way of comparison (II, 131), and when the reader's knowledge of the historical Greifswald — and not the fictionalized Grünwald — is drawn upon in an appeal such as: "[. . .] vor Allem ist Grünwald, wie jeder weiß, eine Universität" (II, 133). The chapter seems to be an interlude between the frenzied pace of action in the preceding chapters and the changed scene in the ones following it. The history of Grünwald, idealized in its more distant past, more recently declined to the level of a simple provincial town, does not even add local colour to the subsequent narrative.

However, the chapter is not simply self-indulgent nostalgia. Its point, or more accurately its barb, is kept for the last paragraph. There we hear of the country nobility's emigration for the winter period from their estates to the city. The paragraph consists of one sentence of normal length and one of mammoth proportions. The latter gathers venom as it lists the faceless droves of the noble families and their attendants, lingers briefly on the abandoned appearance of their houses in summer and finally offsets this accumulation of detail by drawing a comparison with the regular houses, "die von ordinären, Steuer zahlenden, unprivilegirten, Sommer und Winter arbeitenden Menschen bewohnt sind" (II, 133). In its position at the end of a chapter, this final comment is clearly intended to stick in the reader's throat as an exposé of all that has gone before it.

Though the resentment is sustained throughout the novel, no positive counterbalance is ever developed. In *Soll und Haben* those working summer and winter evolve an ethos of labour that in fact makes them feel privileged, capable of patronizing comments about the upper class (250-51). Here, however, they remain shadowy, and rather than being a bitter self-assertion or a plea for justice, the final comment has more the envious ring of the excluded. Elsewhere this idealized picture of the constantly diligent, self-supporting working-classes is in any case countered by the experience of Franz' prospective father-in-law. The "Geheimrat" has given his all to people in need in the hope of rehabilitating them, but has been ruthlessly exploited for his kindness and credulity. The masses are still as faceless as before, but the tone has changed radically when the debtors are described as "schlechte Subjecte" (II, 245).

Despite its black-and-white polarization, the final strident note of vol. II, ch. 12 seems to be the sole justification for the chapter, even though its invective is reiterated in the next. Spielhagen abuses the form of the *Zeitroman* both stylistically and, to use his own terms (e.g. BTT, 134), in his own lack of objectivity. Passages of this kind complicate the whole issue of the degree to which the narrator's or Oswald's verbal outbursts against the nobility are exaggerations, in which case they are more a comment on the character of the person making them than on that of the class despised. Repeatedly Spielhagen succumbs to the danger he so clearly sees at a theoretical level as threatening contemporary writers, namely

die Gefahr: tendenziös zu werden, [...] nicht mehr den Geist der Zeiten, sondern nur noch ihren eigenen Geist zu geben. (BTT, 59)

3. *Literary references*

References and allusions to other works of literature abound in Spielhagen's novels. In the following only a cross-section of examples can be cited to indicate the various purposes these references may serve. We have seen how *Die Epigonen* stood deep in the shadow of Goethe's *Wilhelm Meister* novels. Spielhagen's novel takes its title and central notion from Goethe, but little if anything else in a structural sense.[13] Even less obtrusive Goethean elements in *Die Epigonen* such as the *Mondscheinmärchen* — the *Novelle* or *Märchen* within the novel — are absent here. *Auf der Düne*, a *Novelle* originally intended as part of *Problematische Naturen,* became independent and was published separately. Other genres appear on the fringe of the novel. Oswald writes poems of a highly subjective nature, while Primula Jäger, self-styled muse of nature, perpetrates such aesthetic outrages as *Auf einen toten Maulwurf, den ich am Wege fand* (I, 73). Her efforts, like the presentation of *Wallenstein* (II, 195 ff.), clearly satirize that section of the bourgeoisie whose culture does not extend beyond reading circles. They do not belong to any serious consideration of Spielhagen's use of other works or genres in his novel.

Various ends are served by the literary references. Ch. 13 of vol. I abounds with them. It must be borne in mind that these are very early days in the relationship between Oswald and Melitta. The pair enter her house, where among other things the "Tische mit Büchern und Bilderwerken" (I, 97) impress him. Oswald begins the artistic catalogue of the chapter when he correctly identifies a sculpture as the "Rondanini'sche Meduse" (I, 98). Instructed by Melitta to be friendly to her servant Baumann, he promises to smile "wie ein Engel von Guido Reni" (I, 100). This reference is left completely in limbo. Leafing through Melitta's album, Oswald then chances on a sketch of Oldenburg. When asked for his impression, he replies with words of Goethe's Tasso (Act II, sc. I.). The Venus de Milo that Melitta has copied from the original is of course a temporary guardian of their relationship, and this reference thus has a certain direct bearing. Oswald then improvises a poem of his own on demand (II, 105), followed by the reappearance of Baumann "wie der Comthur im Don Juan" (ibid.). Oswald's erased figure on another album-leaf is likened to the "Erlkönig" (I, 106), Shakespeare's name appears in the retort to this last speech (ibid.), and finally the "Harfner" in Wilhelm Meister is mentioned (I, 110). A constellation of references fully as brilliant as in a chapter of Fontane has thus been assembled. But they are no more than passing references and add little in profile to the characters concerned, unlike the more elaborate discussions in Fontane. Here they seem largely to signal an intellectual flirtation that verges on mere names-dropping. Oswald responds to the broad experience of his aristocratic partner, while she in turn rejoices in his learnedness and brilliance, a brilliance traditionally associated with the nobility.

Though learnedness is still seen as a bourgeois virtue, Spielhagen is not as clearcut as Freytag in the matter of true Bildung. Oldenburg, admittedly a black sheep in the noble fold, cites Lessing (I, 343), Eichendorff (I, 347) and Novalis (I, 239). Melitta's tastes are seen mainly in positive terms, though not wholly, as Oswald is disappointed to find she reads Eugène Sue (I, 94). Oswald also criticizes the Baroness for squandering her chances for self-improvement by lumping together Dumas or Eugène Sue with her reading of Rousseau or Schleiermacher (I, 168). Her interest is dilettantic — she reads Schleiermacher's Reden über die Religion, but both Oswald and Jäger doubt her capacity to comprehend them. And the effect of her reading on her personal development is circumscribed by adherence to her class. "Abgedroschene, aristokratische Gemeinplätze" (I, 169), in Oswald's words, characterize her comments on general issues. She is at least versed in languages, and in this atypical of the local nobility. For Melitta tells how she managed to pass off the "braune Gräfin" as a Hungarian countess at a function by claiming she only spoke Latin beyond her native tongue — a ruse none present was in a position to test (I, 90). And Oldenburg leads Cloten a merry dance with an anecdote in which all the crucial points are in English, which he is obliged to translate for the dandy (I, 190ff.).

The bourgeoisie also provides a broad spectrum of culture, from the philistinism of Primula and her literary circle through to the cultivation that Braun or Oswald so readily exhibit. Braun's spicing of his conversation (I, 167-68) with literary references must strike a present-day reader at least as far-fetched. Their purpose seems to be to show the wide reading of the non-philistine section of the bourgeoisie. The welter of titles, figures and quotations in Problematische Naturen is not particularly differentiated or absorbed into the work. Self-education as a bourgeois virtue is taken further in Soll und Haben. Anton feels uneasy while staying on the Rothsattels' estate because of their narrowness of vision (412). He finds it tasteless that the Baroness should read "Chateaubriand und [. . .] außer kleinen Modenovellen die Romane blasierter Damen" (ibid.). In the matter of personal Bildung as with everything else in Freytag's novel, the bourgeois attitude is affirmed in strongly self-conscious terms. We read:

> Gegen die ritterlichen Künste seines Freundes verhielt er sich kühl. Nur selten überredete ihn Fink, des Sonntags sein Begleiter zu Pferde oder am Pistolenstand zu werden. Dagegen benutzte Anton Finks Bücherschrank mehr als dieser selbst. (177)

There are few direct references to works of literature in *Soll und Haben*, though Anton is found reading J. F. Cooper's *The Last of the Mohicans* one morning (107).[14] Freytag seems much surer of both his class-sympathies and the status of his chosen genre than Spielhagen. Indeed one suspects strongly that the latter's many references are largely intended to raise the tone of his novel, a suspicion lent substance by his defensiveness about the novel as a form. [15]

This whole area may seem at first to be secondary in approaching a work as a *Zeitroman*. But the novelist has clearly felt the need to lend his work a poetic framing to counterbalance depiction of a more prosaic reality. The most puzzling thing is that Spielhagen should neglect to merge the two in what would have been the most realistic, poetically least contrived, way. We never in fact see Oswald engaged in his occupation of tutoring — such a scene with a lesson chosen on literature would have positively demanded the sort of learned references we find elsewhere.

Freytag approaches the whole question from the other end by attempting to establish a kind of poetry of the prosaic. This concern had been adumbrated at the end of Tieck's *Der junge Tischlermeister*, though poetic fantasy is accorded much fuller flight in that novel:

> "Poesie!" rief Dorothea; "ei, so müßten denn auch einmal Dichter kommen, die uns zeigten, daß auch alles dies unter gewissen Bedingungen poetisch sein könnte." (538)

Anton transfigures the scene of his daily work with the Firma Schröter into "Poesie" (46, 246), while Fink extols the poetry of action above the written and read poetry of contemplation (487). Spielhagen's *Zeitroman* lacks the singlemindedness with which the bourgeois ethos is advanced in *Soll und Haben*. But since the ideals of freedom and enlightenment can only be attained outside the ranks of the decaying nobility, literary references in *Problematische Naturen* are predominantly made by bourgeois characters.

4. *The nobility*

The two main "problematische Naturen" are seen substantially in their relationship to the nobility, be it Oswald's ambiguous attitude, or Oldenburg's incisive eye for the foibles of his peers. Spielhagen has left behind Immermann's nostalgic twilight leavetaking of the nobility, but does not approach the paean to bourgeois values that ensured the continued success of *Soll und Haben* well after its author's death, in a progressively bourgeois age.[16] The nobility, whether berated or secretly imitated, is the focus of attention.

Problematische Naturen contains a continued polemic against the physical, financial and moral decay of the class, relieved only by certain touches, such as the pitiable but upright Baron von Grenwitz, designed to effect some kind of balance. The outer symbol for the internal process is established early with the descriptions of the Grenwitz' castle. While not in the same state of utter disrepair as the Schloß Schnick-Schnack-Schnurr (see p. 33), it has sufficient indications of a gradual crumbling of past glory:

Jetzt war der Thurm abgetragen, die Brücke konnte nicht mehr aufgezogen werden und aus dem Brückenkopfe hatte man längst Backöfen und andere nützliche Dinge gebaut. (I, 21-22)

There is also

ein steinernes Becken mit einer Najade [. . .] die, wahrscheinlich aus Schmerz, daß ihrem Brunnen schon seit einem halben Jahrhundert das Wasser fehlte, den Kopf verloren hatte. (I, 22)

The roots of Oswald's hatred for the despised class are to be found in his few surviving childhood memories. These show his supposed father in such a light as to rival through his own fanatic prejudice the blind hatred of other classes imputed to the nobility. For Oswald's father [17] the class as a whole is rotten; he rejects pupils of noble birth out of hand and thus simply helps maintain the unbridgeable gap he feels between the two classes (II, 8-9). His hatred is such that he steadies his aim in shooting by imagining he is aiming at a nobleman's heart (I, 195-96). This background should be borne in mind when considering Oswald's attitude to and dealings with the nobility in the course of the novel. His father's attitude is motivated late in the piece when his connection to Marie Montbert, the miserable victim of Baron Harald's dissolution, becomes clear. Berger's enmity is similarly explained (II, 56ff.), but though violent hatred is the preserve of the bourgeois, they are not the only victims of frivolousness and dishonour on the part of the nobility. For the high-born Melitta has been sold into marriage by her father to redeem a lost bet (I, 416). The Graf Julius-line in *Die Epigonen* had a similar function to the arch-villain Harald here, with a murky past generation of profligate nobles wreaking havoc right down to the time depicted. But Spielhagen's indictment of the whole class is more radical than Immermann's.

Nor is the outrage committed against Melitta a thing of the past, even if the modern refinement involves propping up waning fortunes rather than paying off concrete debts. Machinations in this direction are exposed very early. The method is through marriage by arrangement, as shown in the inhuman fate planned for Helene. Her intended's fortune is admittedly "angegriffen" (I, 40), but as he is to inherit the Grenwitz estate in the event of Malte's death, such a union would retain the family fortune within the direct circle of the family. Felix' own crumbling fortunes typify the financial decay of the aristocracy, and the whole scheme is clearly to his advantage (cf. I, 429). Spielhagen thus ruthlessly exposes those figures of the aristocracy, typified by the Baroness and Felix, who are ready to sacrifice their own flesh and blood as a pawn to the betterment of their financial position. But in his exposé, the economic forces from outside which precipitate the moral degeneracy of the aristocracy remain shadowy. We see nothing on a par with the grim business-acumen of the uncle in *Die Epigonen*, or with the Jewish usurers in *Soll und Haben*. The latter appear only on the fringe in Spielhagen's novel (see II, 138 and 267).

Caste-ideas are very strong, even with the supposedly more enlightened members of the nobility. Melitta voices preconceptions of tutors: "Er wird sein wie alle Andern: entsetzlich gelehrt, eckig, pedantisch, langweilig" (I, 43). Oswald does not conform to this stereotype, as at least Melitta recognizes. Oswald's social conduct

überraschte Melitta um so angenehmer, als sie es bei einem Manne von einer nach ihren Begriffen so untergeordneten Stellung am wenigsten erwartet hatte. (I, 47)

Her ideas are deeply ingrained but she is sufficiently openminded to revise them rather than retreat into her aristocratic shell or attack this exception to the rule as a possible threat to the security of her own class. She later sees this quality of learnedness in a more positive light when comparing it with the merely surface-deep splendour of members of her own class (see I, 93). Spielhagen does attempt to show the justification for such slogans as the one above ("von einer [. . .] Stellung"), if not as a generalization then at least as apt for certain cases, in the figure of Jäger:

> [. . .] denn der Pastor hatte sich die academische Würde durch eine grundgelehrte Dissertation über die möglicherweise vorhanden gewesenen Schriften eines bis auf den Namen verschollenen Kirchenvaters erworben [. . .]. (I, 68)

From such a caricature it is of course impossible to draw any inferences about 19th century German academics, but it does have the virtue of being considerably pithier than protracted harangues against the nobility that are often tantamount to caricature anyway. In the example of Melitta's change of opinion above, as also with Helene's letter — witness the broadening of outlook that seems to have taken place between I, 432 and I, 531-32 — it might seem as if Oswald in his tortuous path through life has at least achieved a revision of proud, caste-bound notions in two of the worthier members of the nobility. The ultimate impression, however, is not of a figure undergoing significant development in character, but of Spielhagen commenting loudly and clearly on aristocratic preconceptions of their social inferiors. The subsequent revelation that Oswald is indeed of noble blood rather works against this process of purification.

As well as the nobility, bourgeois opportunists who pander to them — like Jäger — are also the butt of Spielhagen's attacks. A self-avowed "Anhänger der Aristokratie" (I, 65), the pastor defends the principle of primogeniture (ibid.), but with such cliché-ridden language that his conservatism condemns itself as a sycophantic attitude to his noble benefactors. The condescending favour he gains thereby is shown when the Baroness speaks of Jäger and his wife:

> Die Leute haben sich stets treugesinnt und ihrer Stellung bewußt gezeigt. Ich halte es für unsere Pflicht, dergleichen Menschen zu protegiren. (II, 237)

Very early in the piece, Oswald opposes the pastor's dismissal of the Roman plebeians (I, 65) with a passionate, idealistic defence of the oppressed. But Spielhagen invests such outbursts of fire on Oswald's part with more vigour than incisiveness, an effect enhanced by the historical distancing to the Gracchi and Roman times. When the pastor draws on present conditions with a condemnation of the extravagance of the peasantry at festivals while they remain tight-fisted towards the Church, Oswald averts the issue with a counter-accusation. This the pastor in turn answers with a line of reasoning that must fail to satisfy Oswald but is clearly intended by Spielhagen to typify the attitude of the aristocracy and its toadies: "Der Adel, lieber Freund! das ist etwas ganz Anders" (I, 66). This exclusivist view is not elaborated on here, but finds a vocal champion later in Helene's princely suitor (II, 371). It is important to note the inadequacies on both sides, not only the pastor's unconvincing defence of those with whom he seeks to curry favour, but also Oswald's inability, at least here, to come to grips with the real nature of those he seeks to glorify, ready though he is to launch general broadsides (e.g. I, 174-75).

Though a champion of their cause, Oswald is in fact characterized as anything but a plebeian, but rather as one with attributes normally confined to, or held to be confined to, the aristocracy. Thus Melitta acknowledges in Oswald's nature "Schönheit der Formen, Grazie der Bewegung und Anmuth der Rede" (I, 97), precisely what she missed in Oldenburg. That is to say the external appearance of both characters belies their class, or with

Oswald, supposed class. In Oldenburg's case this paradox is all the more striking because his family is one of the oldest in the district (I, 261).

Oswald's unnatural proficiency in noble exploits is a theme laboured all too much. When Oldenburg compliments him on his horseriding ability (I, 352-53), Oswald replies:

> Es ist das um so merkwürdiger [. . .] weil ich doch eigentlich in Folge meiner plebejischen Geburt und Erziehung gar keine Ansprüche auf diese aristokratischen Vorzüge machen kann. (I, 353)

The irony of this retort does not escape Oldenburg, but the point of such laboured repetition of the class-consciousness theme may well escape the reader, with familiar catchwords such as "plebejisch," and "Ansprüche auf [. . .] aristokratische(n) Vorzüge" being repeated *ad nauseam*.

Oldenburg provides the exotic exception to the hidebound ideas of his peers. Apart from his love for Melitta, he plays a Mephistophelian role in the class he belongs to in name only. In a novel obsessed with attacking the nobility, he provides criticism from within the class to substantiate the sustained criticism coming from outside it. In this he performs a similar function to that of Fink in *Soll und Haben*,[18] with the important difference that Fink averts the financial threat to the Rothsattels by his own support (484). The motif of a noble family's financial collapse is common enough in the 19th century *Zeitroman*, but in Fink we have a rare instance of one nobleman being in the position to help another.

Just what constitutes the nobility, or its supposed superiority, is never seriously examined in Spielhagen's novel. A distinction is made by the pastor between the state of "Geburtsadel" and what he calls the true nobility of the soul (I, 62). But this is not a vehicle for examining what constitutes nobility, as the pastor sees both qualities combined in the Grenwitz household, particularly in the Baroness. This shows how little insight he has into nobility of the soul, and so a potentially inflammatory issue is skirted. It is further skirted when the pragmatist Timm pinpoints Oswald's ambiguous attitude to the nobility (II, 184). In the caste-ridden society portrayed by Spielhagen the attribute of nobility of the soul is in any case a rarity, offset even in the case of the Baron by a palpable weakness.

Oswald's rightful inheritance as the illegitimate heir of Baron Harald, ancestor of the Grenwitz', is revealed by Timm (II, 490). The hidden predilection for the nobility that Oswald frequently reveals in his tastes and tendencies does not sway him. He denies to Helene that he would ever have accepted the inheritance, least of all when its connection with the misery of his mother is made clear (II, 526). Hermann in *Die Epigonen* had accepted his new position as a depositary only; Oswald completely rejects his. Elsewhere his pride is provoked time and again because of the brittleness of his position. He consistently feels snubbed by his social superiors and sees only strained indulgence behind their efforts at accommodation. The following passage may stand for many others. Speaking to Melitta of his invitation to a ball he says:

> [. . .] man ladet mich nur ein, entweder, weil es an Tänzern fehlt, oder, um dem alten Baron eine Höflichkeit zu erweisen, in keinem Fall um meiner selbst willen. Ich werde in der Gesellschaft wie ein Mohikaner unter den Irokesen, wie ein Spion im Lager angesehen werden. Ich kenne den Adel. Der Adelige ist nur höflich und liebenswürdig gegen den Bürgerlichen, so lange er mit ihm allein ist; sind mehrere Adelige beieinander, so fließen sie zusammen wie Quecksilber und kehren gegen den Bürgerlichen den *esprit de corps* heraus. Ich sage Dir, Melitta, ich kenne die Adeligen und hasse die Adeligen. (I, 174-75)

The metaphor incorporating Cooper's Mohicans echoes the precise imagery used by Berger in his attempts to make Oswald see his entry among the ranks of the nobles in a humorous light (I, 16). In this tirade there is no longer any trace of humour, merely of bitter resentment. Oswald's final sentiment is firstly unfeeling and secondly highly questionable for being made to the woman he loves, who is after all of noble birth.

Oswald's ambiguous position — the supposed commoner endowed with noble graces, later discovered to be of noble blood — tends to work against the exposure of noble prejudices through his skills in their domain. For example, his outshining of Cloten in the art of shooting (I, 196ff.) only works as intended as long as Oswald is, and not simply is supposed to be, a commoner. As soon as it is shown that he is in fact of noble birth — corroborating the many conjectures about his physical similarity to the noble line (e.g. I, 297) — these skills shown earlier may be reinterpreted as anticipating his true status, however uncongenial he finds that status. This would tend to confirm the very equation of noble skills with noble blood that Spielhagen is trying to ridicule, and thus make his narrative design inconsistent. Such an unintended lessening of impact is avoided in *Soll und Haben*, and not merely by Anton being both born and bred a bourgeois. His prowess at dancing is not achieved by outdoing the nobility on their home ground, but "durch die bürgerlichsten aller Tugenden, durch Ordnung und Pflichttreue" (127). Furthermore, although Fink introduces his friend to noble pastimes (101), it is not in any competitive sense, and brilliance in horseriding, music or hunting is in any case relativized by Anton — in typically self-righteous vein — to more basic human values (74).

The most important idea in the passage quoted on p. 57 is associated with the nobility once they congregate.[19] When Cloten appears during a visit Oswald pays Oldenburg, the tutor is hurt in his pride by the noticeably cool treatment he receives from the dandy, and imagines a waning in his host's warmth too once the new visitor arrives and the maligned "Kastengeist" (I, 350) asserts itself. However, the latter observation is a product of Oswald's fevered hypersensitivity. Not only at this point in Spielhagen's novel are the diatribes against the nobility weakened by the tortured imagination, the "problematische Natur," of the person making them. That Oswald's suspicion towards Oldenburg is unwarranted is shown by the latter's avowal of friendship when he intervenes in the dispute at the cardtable during the social evening at the Grenwitz'. This latter incident is the sole example confirming Oswald's criticism of a caste-spirit (I, 611). His hatred thus tends to exaggeration. The nobility and Oswald's antagonistic attitude to it are seen most clearly when all are assembled at a social gathering in the following scene.

5. *The ball-scene*

The social superiority of the nobility is supposed to bring with it an elevated intellect and conversation, but clearly doesn't in cases like the trivia discussed by the Baroness on the way to the ball at Barnewitz' (I, 177-78). The ball itself crystallizes many of Oswald's class-conscious attitudes, as his pride and talents are confronted by the assembled nobility, ranging from the renegade Oldenburg to dyed-in-the-wool conservatives. Oswald's anguished feelings towards Melitta reflect a great sense of frustration at the social gap between them:

[. . .] er zürnte sich selbst, daß er sich von der Geliebten hatte bestimmen lassen, ihr in diese Gesellschaft zu folgen, diese Junkerwelt, in die er nicht gehörte, in welcher er sich nur geduldet wußte, in diese Welt frivolen Genusses und hochmütigen Dünkels, diese lärmende, blendende Welt [. . .]. (I, 207-8)

Again the tragedy here is that Oswald is so acutely aware of all this, that he is not content with the "Romantik seiner Liebe" (I, 208) to transfigure the surroundings. For Melitta does not deny this love one whit in her actions, even though she is among her social equals and not alone with Oswald, a situation which one would expect from Oswald's arguments to call forth the caste-spirit in her.

Oswald's hatred of the nobility seizes on any pretext to express itself. For instance Melitta's unsigned note bidding him to a rendezvous is misconstrued by him as a challenge to a duel, and yet again, "der ganze fanatische Haß gegen den Adel" (I, 358) fills him. He typically sees inflexibility and rejection exclusively on the noble side:

> [. . .] kann ich, der pfenniglose Abenteurer, der Freiheitschwärmer, jemals daran denken, die reiche Aristokratin zu heirathen? daran denken, mich in die Gesellschaft der verhaßten Menschen zu drängen, die den Parvenü stets über die Achsel ansehen würden? nie! nie! (I, 387-88)

His love for Melitta is incapable of surmounting the social gulf between them, because even if she were to make the further sacrifice of jeopardizing her rank through an openly-aired relationship with a tutor, Oswald for his part would never be able to look beyond the snubs, real or imagined, of the class in which he could never hope to feel at ease.

Differing greatly from Melitta's view is the exclusivism represented by the dandy Cloten when he says of Stein: "Ah! danke für ein Duell mit so einem Bürgerlichen. Partie ist zu ungleich" (I, 200), and then fails to note the keen irony of Oldenburg's fabrication of a manuscript (I, 201ff.) verifying the separation of mankind at creation into noble and bourgeois blood. When he even ventures to guess the name of the first noble pair as Cloten, we see the grounds for Oswald's complaints. However, at this level of attack, the nobility is so patently caricatured that there is no real contest between its values and others, Cloten being a ludicrous puppet in the hands of Oldenburg's superior intellect. Although Spiel-hagen's far-fetched inventiveness might be amusing, attack in the form of such distortion loses its thrust; the narrator's voice is all too strident to speak to any but the converted.

Among the twelve to fourteen noblemen at the Barnewitz' ball three were sufficiently unprejudiced to acknowledge Oswald's "ritterliches Wesen" (I, 209). This is an inadequate attempt by Spielhagen to restore a more objective perspective. Firstly the proportion of more liberal nobles is very small, and secondly even these three are treated in a rather condescending manner, their virtue consisting in the way they reflect Oswald's dazzling constellation. Baron Oldenburg is admittedly cast in an ambiguous light. Whether he is expressing his earnest conviction in championing Oswald, or whether he simply wants to irritate his young peers, is not certain. "Nathan's frommer Wunsch, daß es dem Menschen doch endlich genügen möge, ein Mensch zu sein" (I, 176) is seen by Oswald as still far from fulfilment through the rigidity of class-barriers. He laments: "Nie wird [. . .] der Adelige in dem Bürgerlichen [. . .] und umgekehrt wahrhaft seines Gleichen sehen [. . .]" (ibid.). It is important to note the fleetingly mentioned "und umgekehrt": whether through pride, an exaggerated sense of persecution or whatever, Oswald never adopts any kind of conciliatory approach to the nobility.

Spielhagen portrays with obvious relish the breakdown of formal politeness and aristo-cratic dignity as the meal progresses and with it the imbibing:

> Der dünne Firniß äußerlicher Cultur [. . .] begann [. . .] in einer erschreckenden Weise herunter-gespült zu werden, und die nackte, trostlos dürftige Natur kam überall zum Vorschein. Die jungen Herren [. . .] gefielen sich in Unterhaltungen, die scherzhaft und galant sein sollten, und die für jedes feinere weibliche Gefühl einfach plump und zweideutig waren. Indessen schienen die jungen Damen leider an diese Sorte Unterhaltung viel zu sehr gewöhnt zu sein, als daß dieselbe irgend einen unangenehmen Eindruck auf sie hätte hervorbringen können. (I, 217)

This is a truly scathing broadside, not only at the menfolk, but at the noblewomen whose sense of values they have corrupted through their habitual coarseness. Oswald on the other hand is continually showing the noble how to be noble, as when he escorts Emilie's aunt to her carriage. She asks him: "Sind Sie überzeugt, Herr Stein, daß Sie nicht von Adel sind? " (I, 234). Again his courteousness belies his supposed class. Such ungrudging recognition of Oswald's more chivalrous qualities does not however extend to all noble ladies, most emphatically not to the Baroness, whose antipathy to him never wanes.

Drawing these many strands together, then, we find the nobility is seen in this novel as an unjustly privileged class engaging in intrigues for its own preservation, e.g. the plan to marry off Helene to Felix, and vacuous pursuits of leisure such as the social evenings held by the Barnewitz and Grenwitz families. Its main opponents are the novel's three "problematische Naturen," of whom Oldenburg is the most incisive — his criticisms of the class from the inside lack the pathos-ridden fanaticism of Berger and Oswald. Oswald's attitude is in any case complicated by his own noble graces and tastes and the ultimate revelation of his birth. His claims of a noble caste-spirit are largely paranoic, and the lack of accommodation he feels on the side of the nobility applies equally to the bourgeoisie. The one exception to this is an illegitimate marriage between the two classes — Jäger's obsequiousness in currying a favour granted with great condescension for reasons of self-preservation.

The novel's polemics against the upper class are not reinforced by a consistent affirmation of the other classes. For all its at times exasperatingly repetitive diatribes against the nobility as a class, Spielhagen's work does not attempt to extol the bourgeoisie. The main bourgeois figures of the novel are Oswald and Timm. Oswald appears in anything but a uniformly positive light; Timm is exposed towards the end as the scoundrel he really is. The upper bourgeois reading circle assembled by Primula is mercilessly satirized, and its aspirations to being "wahrhaft gebildet" and "wahrhaft human" (II, 195) are shown to be absurd pretentiousness. Jäger himself is almost a parody of the enterprise and self-esteem characterizing Freytag's bourgeois figures. His professional advance is secured through the aid of his father-in-law, he is untrue to his class in his flattering praises of the nobility, and the recognition he gains comes through ludicrously abstruse scholastic pursuits (see I, 550). A certain counterbalance to these examples is provided by Braun and the Robrans, but their frequently sentimental portrayal does not have the same kind of impact — Spielhagen shows considerably more verve in negating than in affirming.

His gaze rarely extends further and the class issue thus remains a two-sided one. An inkling, but no more than that, of class realignments is given with the governmental experiment in the village of Faschwitz. Here a large estate, formerly belonging to a noble line that has since died out, is redistributed among a class of small land-owners or free farmers (I, 56), which till then had been almost completely lacking in the district. The difference between this stage and the industrialization already taking place in *Die Epigonen* reflects the difference between Pomerania and the Rhineland in terms of economic progress in the first half of the 19th century and beyond into the second half.

6. *The army*

The early Heinrich Mann had before him the examples of Germany's tardily adopted imperialism and the forewarning rumbles of World War I; Fontane's military figures have the glorious days of the 1860's and 1870's to think back to. Spielhagen's novel is set at the end of the long period of stagnation following the Wars of Liberation, and "das militärische Kraftfeld"[20] is consequently very limited. But we do receive some pointers as to the kind of spirit he saw informing the forces defending the status quo in the March Revolution of 1848.

In the following almost offhanded reference we see the same absurdly exaggerated concept of honour within the military that is to reappear in broader and more convincing form in Fontane, e.g. in *Schach von Wuthenow*. Felix tells Timm of the suicide of his former commander:

> Weil er die Schande nicht hat überleben wollen, daß bei der letzten großen Parade die zweite Compagnie mit Tuchhosen statt mit weißen Hosen angerückt kam, und er deshalb vom Commandirenden ob dieser "Schweinerei" einen fürchterlichen Rüffel besah. (I, 464)

Both in its brevity and its exaggeration, this picture belongs to the same class as Jäger's dissertation. Such patent distortions make the realism of a work problematic, for in being isolated, the thrust has this single opportunity to present its criticism and, not being substantiated elsewhere by more soberly expressed examples, sorely tests credibility. The strained conventions of honour set forth here also strain literary conventions, as the satirical element verges on the burlesque.

A glorification of the military profession comes later in the novel from the Russian prince wooing Helene. He considers the military to be the "Grundbedingung für alle übrigen Stände" (II, 370), because it alone can ensure the peace in which the other professions can thrive. "Mit diesem Stande verglichen sind alle andern niedrig und gemein" (II, 371). Because of its importance and noble function its maintenance is the domain of the nobility. Yet here too, old traditions are gradually crumbling, which cannot please the Prince:

> Daß man neuerdings auch angefangen hat, den Bürgerlichen Zutritt zu unsern Reihen zu verstatten, halte ich für einen beklagenswerthen Fehler [...]. (ibid.)

He says "neuerdings," but in Germany at least this process had gained impetus during the Wars of Liberation (see p. 33).[21] For him the difference between the two classes, their "Geist" (II, 371), is self-evident. He does elaborate with examples of specific differences, espousing an absolute inflexibility towards all hints of change and liberalism and disagreeing strongly with what he regards as the concessions made by the King to the Liberals and the "Zeitgeist" (II, 372). These amount for the Prince to an abuse of the divinely ordained office of royalty. The voicing of these sentiments by a foreign officer is but a thin façade, his origin in an even more despotic land a cover for the fact that the substance of what he says is applicable to Spielhagen's *Vormärz*-Germany. Thus in treating the military in this novel Spielhagen has chosen the isolated satiric comment, or when going into any sort of detail, he has distanced his figure by means of an alien nationality, where a more in-depth analysis of a figure modelled on contemporary reality could easily have achieved so much more. The March Revolution finally erupts against ultra-conservative elements of the Prussian nobility, elements embodying the spirit of the Prince.

The same applies to the revelation of the Prince's birth. Schmenckel's fathering of the Prince is the mirror-image of Oswald's birth across the class-barrier, and is not just symptomatic of a decline of the nobility in Russia. The Prince's mother seeks to mollify her son's horror by generalizing his plight:

> Und wähnst Du denn, daß in den Adern unseres Adels nur adeliges Blut rollt? daß Dein Fall der

einzige ist, wo ein entartetes Geschlecht durch gesundes Proletarierblut sich wieder regenerirt hat? (II, 514) [22]

Spielhagen's editorial comment is to be heard loud and clear behind the adjectives "entartet" and "gesund." Such a dénouement naturally delights Berger (II, 543), who has broken down the façade of national barriers when, in addressing Graf Malikowsky, he connects the first indications of the Berlin insurrection with revenge on the Count and his ilk (II, 505). The effect of these mixed births, as in *Die Epigonen*, is to render the more ridiculous a conservative clinging to social distinctions through blood and birth, by showing that these criteria are subject to chance and confusion.

7. The conclusion of the novel

In the last chapter of vol. 1, Oldenburg says:

Da ich für die nicht leben kann, für die ich leben möchte, und da es in unserer engbrüstigen Zeit an jedem großen Zweck gebricht, an dessen Erreichung ein Mann sein Leben setzen könnte, so will ich denn auch, ein anderer Peter Schlemihl, meinen eigenen Schatten suchen gehen. (I, 619)

At this stage a mood of *Epigonentum* prevails, the sense of an age such as Immermann had depicted, devoid of worthy ideals. The great purpose comes only later with the Berlin Revolution.

The purposeless time spoken of by Oldenburg succeeds one of fiery deeds and ideals. Berger tells Oswald of his youthful energy, how he defended his fatherland on the battlefields of Leipzig and Waterloo (II, 55ff.). After convalescing from his wounds in Fichtenau, he resumed his university studies, which the war had interrupted. He studied with great diligence and also devoted himself in what sounds like a students' organization to the cause of freedom, for which his and their blood had been shed. As reward he was betrayed by the fatherland he was so dearly trying to serve, arrested and thrown into prison without trial, where he languished for five years. Even these experiences form only the pivotal point for Berger's personal tragedy, the loss of and frenzied search for his former love, but they combine to give a damning statement on the internal politics of Germany in the period following the Napoleonic Wars.

The strands Oldenburg mentions of self-realization and historical impetus are drawn together at the end of the novel. The storm of the revolution brooding over France makes itself felt in Germany as an omen of what is to follow there too. As we see Melitta sharing with great understanding Oldenburg's hopes and fears and his decision to travel to Paris, we also see a certain equation between rational, directed activity and success in personal relationships. Oldenburg's wild, aimless wanderings had been succeeded by a zealous application to administering his estates and to following the politics of the day (II, 357). Likewise Berger considers — with apparent justification — his personal fate to be intimately bound to that of his homeland:

Der Moderdunst der Festungscasematten und die Sickluft des Polizeistaates, welche ich mein Leben lang habe einathmen müssen — das hat mich gemacht, was die Leute verrückt nennen — hatte der Professor einmal gesagt; mir ist manchmal, als ob nur ein Athemzug freier Luft im Vaterlande mir die Last wegheben würde, die hier ruht; und dabei hatte er auf die Brust gedeutet. (II, 358-59)

The relationship between the individual and the age seems to be growing in directness.

In vol. II, ch. 38, we see the atmosphere in Berlin in the early days of March 1848, in the wake of the Paris uprising and directly before the similar events in Berlin itself. This is an example of historical facts blended with the characters familiar from the novel itself, the technique of personalized history employed by many greater 19th century realists. Stendhal's description of Waterloo in *La Chartreuse de Parme* and Flaubert's framework of the 1830 Paris Revolution in *L'Education sentimentale* are famous examples. After a picture of the feverish expectancy generated by the events in Paris, we hear Oldenburg and Berger reflecting on the probable course of coming events. Timm delivers an insincere, sensational speech to a basically hostile crowd, and an initial skirmish takes place between the people and the military in which Oldenburg, Graf Grieben and Caspar Schmenckel play their parts. A little further on (II, 436-37) Franz gives another perspective on this brush and events subsequent to it. The lilting waltzes of Strauss and Lanner, displaced from the park dais by political speeches, have definitely vanished from the scene for a while, and a mood of feverish excitement grips the city. The imminence of a great upheaval is captured by Oldenburg:

> Wir stehen hier auf einem Vulkan, der jeden Augenblick zum Ausbruch kommen kann. Schon schwankt der Boden unter unsern Füßen, und ehe noch viele Tage vergehen, werden wir unerhörte Dinge erleben. Ich zittere nicht vor der Entscheidung; im Gegentheil, ich sehne sie herbei, denn sie ist nothwendig und wird für uns zum Heile ausschlagen. (II, 449)

The connection between a man as an effective political animal and the harmonious ordering of his own personal relationships receives further comment here: "[. . .] um ein ganzer Mann nach außen sein zu können, muß ich erst in mir selbst zur Ruhe kommen" (ibid.). This inner security is what Oldenburg alone has obtained in any measure by the end of the novel, and he survives, while the rootless, passionate visionaries Oswald and Berger both perish.

The issue raised here is central to any discussion of a work as a *Zeitroman*. The following question, posed by Franz and referring to Oswald, contains the kernel of the problem:

> [. . .] sollten Sie auch einen Menschen schonungslos verdammen, dessen größtes Unglück es vielleicht ist, in dieser Zeit geboren zu sein? (II, 454)

Are Oswald's restless existence and ultimate doom merely products of the age in which he lives? Did a person of Oswald's constitution have to perish in the given historical circumstances, when he may well have flourished in another era? It seems highly questionable just how far his motives and actions are to be explained merely by his historical milieu. In one respect Oswald is perhaps a victim of his age, as his three loves are noblewomen, socially inaccessible to him according to the unwritten laws of society. The one case in which scruples about such prejudices are thrown to the winds, his relationship with Emilie, ends disastrously. But overall it would appear more legitimate to see the conclusion of the novel not in terms of Oswald dying as a son of his time, but rather as a desperate and necessary end to his personal problems.

In the final pages of his novel Spielhagen brings together various thematic threads and personal fates on the barricades. Oldenburg's earlier image of the "Vulkan" is carried over first to the "Krater [. . .]" (II, 530) and then to the "Strom der Revolution" (II, 538). His appeals to his followers are couched in grandiose terms:

> Ist Einer unter Ihnen, der es süßer findet, für das Vaterland und die Freiheit leben zu bleiben, als zu sterben, der möge es jetzt sagen! (II, 536)

In Spielhagen's hands this tone all too readily declines into banality: "Jeder fühlte, daß der Würfel geworfen [. . .] sei" (ibid.). On the other hand no illusions are held as to the efficiency of the streetfighters' arms. Even the spirit moving them is cast in a questionable light when Oldenburg notes their vacillation after the Major's attempts at reconciliation. He cannot fail to notice the difference between what he considers to be the informed, firm resolve of the Paris masses and the naïve, undirected exuberance of the Berliners.

There are also more conciliatory observations on the streetfighters' opponents than earlier in the novel. Firstly comes the Major's impressive attempt to avoid violence, then we see "Damen aus der guten Gesellschaft" (II, 540) tending the wounded in the fighters' ranks. The opportunist Timm meets a dreadful end, while the divergent threads of Oswald, Berger and Oldenburg are drawn together on the side of the mass. In this final scene it is difficult to separate the elements of personal destiny and the vast significance of the historical scene being enacted. For instance, it is said of Oldenburg:

> Der Tod für die Sache der Freiheit war ihm nicht fürchterlich, ja er glaubte etwas wie eine leise Todessehnsucht in seinem Herzen zu verspüren. Schien doch die süße, fest gehegte Hoffnung, Melitta bald die Seine nennen zu dürfen, seit den letzten Tagen weiter als je hinausgerückt. (II, 553)

In other words, for all Oldenburg's admirable qualities, his motives for hurling himself into the fray with such apparent idealistic zeal are coloured by his desire to flee his personal problems. This reservation applies more strongly still to Oswald, who fought "wie Jemand, dem der Tod lieber ist, als das Leben" (II, 553-54). And for the tormented Berger peace is definitely only possible in death. When Oswald does die, his death is not seen — cannot consistently be seen — as a heroic sacrifice for a cause, but as "der letzte tiefe Athemzug einer Brust, von der die Last des Lebens für immer genommen ist" (II, 562).

This robs the final chapter's funereal tones of their effect. It is not tragic that men like Oswald and Berger should find release in death. It is a strange attempt at transfiguration when Spielhagen voices the sentiment of the 20,000 spectators (II, 563) lining the streets for the funeral procession of the 187 dead: "Der Tod für die Freiheit krönt alles Streben, sühnt alle Schuld" (ibid.). The second half of this verdict may be correct in relation to the personal lives of Oswald and Berger; the other 185 remain faceless. We neither see any final victory of "Freiheit,"[23] nor does the impression predominate that this is what has been died for. Rather does the 1848 Revolution seem a convenient device by which Spielhagen can end the fevered wanderings of two of his main figures. A sense of fusion of the historical and personal levels is certainly not achieved through a direct equation, as when Berger, but scantily characterized by flowing grey hair and glowing eyes, is elevated to become an incarnation of the Revolution — "es war, als ob die Revolution selbst Gestalt und Stimme angenommen hätte" (II, 532). The deaths of Oswald and Berger contribute by chance rather than by the successful realization of a narrative design to the cause of freedom.

Similarly the work's concluding paragraph does not emerge organically from the final chapters. The visionary quality of these utterances has not found any reflection in a sense of liberation from an impossible historical yoke, following the fighting on the barricades.[24] Little attempt has been made to lend substance to a bourgeoisie and proletariat prepared to keep at bay the powers of tyranny. Indeed we can only surmise from this passage that these powers have been overthrown already — the author focusses attention on the fate of his heroes, not the outcome of the battle. The presumed leader of the new order, Oldenburg, is there purely by chance, having survived the fray despite his death-wishes to receive his victor's laurels at the hands of his beloved (II, 561).

The novel concludes thus:

> Wir sollen arbeiten und schaffen, daß die Nacht nicht wieder hereinbreche, [. . .] die lange schmach-volle Nacht, aus welcher nur der Donnersturm der Revolution durch blutige Morgenröthe hinüber-führt zur Freiheit und zum Licht. (II, 564)

These final lines with their polarity of imagery, the darkness of the *Vormärz* being illuminated by the bloody dawning of the Revolution and yielding to the light of freedom, are little more than poetic in this context, for the novel's bounds have not extended to portraying or even preparing for this ultimate stage. In fact, the one case beyond the subtitle to vol. II where the phrase "Durch Nacht zum Licht" occurs would tend to cast a very ironic light on the visionary tones of the novel's conclusion, for it is uttered by Berger at the beginning of his incarceration (II, 58) — a period which is to extend for a further five years. *Problematische Naturen* came well after the historical March Revolution had frustrated many liberal aspirations. Clearly the Revolution is intended to be the zenith of the work and the panacea for that malady of a pre-Revolution generation expressed in the novel's title. But the author's hindsight has coloured his fonder hopes.

The view of Spielhagen's novel advanced in this chapter has been a notably negative one. Its inclusion is nonetheless readily defensible. Firstly, *Problematische Naturen* was simply the first example, and an extremely popular one, of a long line of *Zeitromane* written by Spielhagen. With the possible exception of Fontane, of whom it may be argued that his shorter narrative works are not even novels, let alone *Zeitromane*, he is the only author among those considered here to have produced by far the bulk of his output in this particular stream of the novel-genre, even if, like Wennichen in *Im Schlaraffenland* (cf. p. 119), he does not explore new territory with his subsequent works. For all its faults, *Problematische Naturen* is not some kind of object lesson in how not to write a *Zeitroman*. It is an instructive example of the genre, illustrating clearly some of its more characteristic tensions, namely between the historical reality represented and the fictitious figures, and between effective social comment and a jaundiced frontal attack.

CHAPTER IV

GOTTFRIED KELLER: *MARTIN SALANDER*

1. Introduction

With *Martin Salander* (1886) we move to Swiss soil and are confronted with the out-
growths of the progressive spirit of the *Gründerzeit* there. The relationship of the rising
bourgeoisie to the declining aristocracy is no longer the dominating issue it was in Immermann's and Spielhagen's novels. Instead we find problems wholly confined to the bourgeois sphere, in particular the financial vicissitudes of the time. The most notable German
example of this theme is Spielhagen's *Sturmflut* (1877),[1] whose title with its suggestion
of natural catastrophe is a vast allegory on the collapse inevitably attending the financial
speculation of the *Gründerjahre* in Germany.

The perspective from which the hero is treated likewise differs markedly from the
earlier novels. Just as the typifying titles *Die Epigonen* and *Problematische Naturen*
reflect the generalizing function of the hero of each, it was in accordance with the emphasis of his work that Keller chose the name *Martin Salander*, after toying with the idea of
the more ostentatious *Excelsior*. Margarete Merkel-Nipperdey sees this change in the following terms:

> Anders also als in den "Epigonen" (und im "Wilhelm Meister"), wo der Held die Funktion hat,
> verschiedene in sich verhältnismäßig geschlossene Lebensbereiche (wie Adel, Volk, gebildetes
> Bürgertum u. a.) miteinander zu verbinden, indem er in solchen verschiedenen Bereichen Eingang
> findet, selbst aber mehr oder minder passiv bleibt, anders ist die Funktion des Helden im "Martin
> Salander," wo er selbst in der Auseinandersetzung mit anderen Figuren — die Raumszenen erst
> aufbauen hilft, an diesem Aufbau selbst unmittelbar-aktiv-beteiligt ist.[2]

The spectrum in *Martin Salander* is not one of social strata, but of ethics within the
one social class — of varying susceptibility to the impact of new material abundance and
new political freedoms on timeless moral values. The panorama presented by Keller's
novel is thus far more restricted than that of Immermann's or Spielhagen's. This makes
possible a more incisive study of the one social area treated in the novel, but it also becomes more problematic when the attempt is made to derive wider, even universal significance from the relatively narrow issues treated. Martin himself may well gain in terms of
the aesthetics of the narrative by bearing a stronger stamp of individuality and direction.
However, implicit in this kind of characterization are artistic perils — finding a highly satisfying resolution in the title figure of Fontane's *Der Stechlin* — which relate to the representative quality of characters like Hermann in *Die Epigonen* or Oswald Stein in *Problematische Naturen*. This quality can easily be forfeited by a character bearing a less epoch-
bound stamp, a problem discussed in greater detail in the following sections.

2. Industrial change

Though the unaesthetic incursions of the factories in *Die Epigonen* play no part here,
certain signs of industrialization are clear, even in the opening scene of the novel when
Martin, like Leonhard Hagebucher in Raabe's *Abu Telfan*, returns to his homeland after
many years' absence. Symptomatic of the setting that is familiar to him and yet so changed
is the new railway-station, "ein weit größeres Gebäude."[3] This opening setting reappears
in the concluding paragraph of the novel, when the prime villain of the piece and negative
incarnation of the age, Louis Wohlwend, is seen leaving at the station, bound for an uncertain destination. But this redressing of the moral balance in terms of entry and exit of

characters does not obscure the change from the new station at the beginning to the "Blitzzug" at the end. These features are not merely a chance accompaniment to the individual setting of the work, but an important indicator of the social and economic factors in constant interplay with that setting.

However much the railways may exude purposeful bustle and material expansion, that is but one side of the picture. For in a novel so closely incorporating contemporary events, it is impossible to ignore the overtones deriving from the complete collapse, in 1878, of the "Nationalbahn," to which Zürich had pledged a sum in the millions.[4] It is illuminating that Keller did not exploit the Naturalistic potential of this local event, in view of the new direction taken by *Martin Salander* towards a less poetically adorned realism. The expanding network of railways makes itself felt as a new current of the age:

> Diese Nachmittagssitzung dauerte so lange, daß die Herren Volksvertreter nach Schluß derselben sofort die Bahnhöfe aufsuchen mußten, um die Heimat zu erreichen. Denn seit das Ländchen überall von den Schienenwegen durchzogen war, galt es nicht mehr für wohlanständig, die Nacht in der Hauptstadt zuzubringen, während man in einer halben oder ganzen Stunde zu Hause, und am Morgen ebenso rasch wieder da sein konnte. (117)

The railway is seen here less as a technical advance than as a dictator of fashion. Martin even entertains the following prosaic but modish idea for his daughters' wedding:

> Dem Geiste der Zeit entsprechend, wurde von allem Auffahren einer Menge Kutschen abgesehen und die Eisenbahn als Beförderungsmittel gewählt. (132)

The negative aspect looms ever in the background, as when Jakob Weidelich mentions "die Eisenbahnen, für die sich die Gemeinden und der Staat so überschuldet haben" (118). This novel avoids such abstractions as the Railway System,[5] the State, or Freedom, and their workings are seen only as they relate to the lives of individuals. Vast losses are incurred by the government through the twins' and others' financial speculations, and of course at the individual level by Martin, duped by Wohlwend. Broader themes are thus worked out through individuals — even in the former instance, the focus of interest is the twins' conniving.

A similar relationship between the individual and the historical setting holds for Martin's estrangement upon his return. He is confronted by signs of a growing orientation towards a city-existence:

> [. . .] vergeblich forschte er zwischen der rastlosen Überbauung des Bodens nach Spuren früherer Pfade, die sonst zwischen Wiesen und Gärten schattig und freundlich hügelan geleitet hatten. (7)

The pre-industrial idyll is being despoiled in the wake of the general shift of population from the land to towns and cities. This trend was not as clear in Switzerland as in Germany — nothing we see here compares even with the impression emerging from *Die Epigonen,* set so much earlier in the century. The picture here is not presented as a broad canvas, but built up as an accumulation of details. Gone are the paths Martin knew, vanished "unter staubigen oder mit hartem Kies beschotterten Fahrstraßen" (ibid.), and much as he wonders at the recent innovations, Martin is delighted to find the inn familiar to him from his earlier days there. This opening portrayal of Martin's reactions establishes his fundamental conservatism, which is allied to a deep patriotism. The despoliation that is seen in questionable terms here is positively senseless in the case of land surrounding Marie's lodgings. She tells her husband that the owner of the land had been forced to give it up:

> [. . .] da einige andere Landbesitzer den Bau einer unnötigen Straße durchgesetzt haben. Nun ist sie da, jedes schattige Grün verschwunden und der Boden in eine Sand- und Kiesfläche verwandelt; aber kein Mensch kommt, die Baustellen zu kaufen. Und seit die guten Bäume dahin sind, ist auch mein Erwerb dahin! (40)

Pointless changes that have a peculiarly modern ring; the small businesswoman is the ultimate sufferer.

The mentality behind such moves is depicted later in Salander's son-in-law Isidor. He calmly announces that the wood behind his beech-trees is to be felled shortly. Though his property will then be endangered by "Schlamm- und Schuttmassen" (178), Isidor, unmoved by any inherent beauty of the beeches, will then sell them to the wood-choppers for a tidy sum (177). With him as with many other representatives of this era, financial considerations are the ultimate ones. This motif receives more extensive treatment in Keller's *Das verlorne Lachen*, which anticipates many of the problems of his later novel. It is left to Jukundus to save the thousand-year-old oak from the greedy hands of those who had already bought up and destroyed so much woodland, a community-minded action in which he receives no support whatever from the state (V, 219-20). This negative portrayal of the age shows not simply a moral negation by the author of the values presented, but also what might be termed a negative narrative approach. Through this, the few individual examples of concern and civic-mindedness highlight by implication the general trends of the age, inasmuch as they run counter to them. These trends are occasionally embodied in a concrete example, e.g. Isidor's attitude to the beeches, but more frequently are depicted without clear substance as the object of the general lament sustained through much of the work.

Thus definite indications are present of the changing complexion of the country from a rural to an urban aspect. These changes are proclaimed in a negative light and resented as a threat to certain rather nostalgically viewed values.

3. *The cultivation of externals*

The desire to keep up often misleading appearances forms a leitmotif of the novel. It is presented in miniature in the scene with Martin's first human contact upon return from overseas. From his position as a newcomer to the prevailing social conditions he is able to see far more objectively the changes that have insinuated themselves. The scene is constructed around a semantic distinction made by the young boys. The twins, and with them their playmates, ridicule Arnold, as he is later identified, for referring to his mother as "Mutter," whereas they use the term "Mama."[6] They in fact call their mother for help when Arnold retaliates to their gibes, and she is immediately characterized by a recurring trait. She has been trying on a hat, which reappears in the story as a token of her vanity until her eyes are finally opened to her sons' unworthiness and she flings the hat away. But at this early stage she is in the prime of her ostentation, her requirements for the hat's appearance reflecting no trace of personal taste but simply the desire to take her competitive place in current fashion trends:

> [. . .] sie wolle ebenso schöne und große [Blumen], *wie andere Frauenzimmer* [. . .]. Sie wüßte nicht, warum sie nicht ebensogut weiße Bänder tragen dürfte, *wie diese und jene* [. . .]. (9) (author's emphasis)

She then makes a prophetic utterance with grim determination:

> [. . .] wenn sie auch keine Rätin sei, so werde sie dereinst vielleicht eines oder zwei solcher Stücke zu Schwiegertöchtern bekommen! (9-10)

This shows her true attitude, her inferiority complex for which she is anxious to compensate by proclaiming loudly a waiving of social barriers, and paradoxically seeking this for herself through status-symbols. Her very stridency betrays her, and what Martin admires as growing equality (11) is in fact a diversifying of signs of material prestige, not an increased social or political awareness and responsibility in those formerly ascribed to the lower middle classes. The petit bourgeois, exemplified by Frau Weidelich, seeks to compensate for inner poverty by external display.

"Mutter" is not the only word to have received emotional overtones: Frau Weidelich is incensed at Martin's reference to the people as "Volk":

> Wir sind hier nicht Volk, wir sind Leute, die alle das gleiche Recht haben, emporzukommen! Und alle sind gleich vornehm! (10)

Yet in her own eyes she can only attain this equality through such criteria as the colour of her hatbands. Her husband, addressed by their sons as "Vater," explains to Martin why this word has been retained in favour of "Papa"[7] — the menfolk would have to pay for their titles in the form of increased taxation. The women, whose presumption involves no responsibility, can thus alone indulge their vanity. Unless of course a Wohlwend is concerned; he is mortified by Marie's addressing him without that "Herr" before his name which he feels to be his due (54), a well-aimed gibe on her part.

The feudal connotations of the words "Bauer" and "Herr" in the sense of aristocratic overlord had already come under scrutiny in Gotthelf's *Zeitgeist und Berner Geist* (1852).[8] In the course of his improvised toast to his sons and their fiancées, Herr Weidelich says:

> Ich bin ein schlichter Landwirt (die Söhne hatten ihm diesen Ausdruck eingelernt, weil der alte Name *Bauer*, der immer einen *Herrn* voraussetze, im souveränen Volke nicht mehr üblich sei) [. . .] . (125)

All these instances of the emotive quality of words reflect the attitude of resentment of a self-assertive bourgeoisie towards the social barriers they are trying to eradicate. The emptiness of their efforts is demonstrated by the lack of deeds within the novel to support such claims, nor is there any question of Frau Weidelich being in the same class in personal terms as Marie Salander. Thus the quibbling over words is largely a semantic game and not the reflection of any deep change in the social make-up of the people.

The desire to keep up appearances is admittedly not confined to the Weidelichs of the story. For Marie the exposure of her poverty is to be avoided if at all possible, even if this involves her customers eating at the expense of her children. Admittedly her motivation is the reputation of her husband, who has had his luggage brought from the station by two men to hide his own suspected indigence, "eine seltsame, aber verzeihliche Selbsttäuschung" (34). These examples show rather the preservation of a sense of pride and dignity than the social-climbing of the Weidelichs, but keeping up appearances is nevertheless shown to characterize the age and not just one type of person.

The crassest example of this spirit is Louis Wohlwend, whose successive crazes of heraldry, crab-fishing and a cant-riddled religiosity are mere outer affectations of a mobile spirit to conceal his moral bankruptcy. One example will stand for many. Immediately before Martin learns of the collapse of the bank in Rio de Janeiro, Wohlwend characterizes his latest hobby thus:

"Hier lassen sich alte Fäden politischer· und kultureller Entwicklung offen legen und neue an-knüpfen im Sinne einer neuen Verteilung der Volksehren —" (44)

In Wohlwend's mouth originally lofty concepts are divested of meaning, something Salander the politician later has cause to regret with regard to the word "Republik" and its overuse. In the political sphere the desire for representation is shown at its most relent-less and destructive in the flair for titles of Kleinpeter's wife, who tries to use her hus-band's occupation as a springboard for her own social rise. This is symptomatic of the insidious, compelling force of appearances sowing discord even at the domestic level, consuming the human side of human relationships in an obsession with prestige and advancement in the public eye.

Not only words have lost their meaning. Marie visits Setti and comments on the prettiness of her dress, even though she hadn't expected visitors. Setti replies that this is the will of her husband and that she scarcely notices any more the quality of her garments (174). Thus something which would normally delight a young woman's heart has become simply a means of representing her husband fittingly to the public eye; predictably Julian imposes the same conditions on his spouse (180).

In *Das verlorne Lachen* the minister had recanted at the end. Established religion is similarly treated here as a mere gloss, church-going as churchiness. Thus Frau Weidelich makes it her business to attend

eine der Stadtkirchen, wo es immer so voll und interessant ist und die Leute ihre Visitenkarten an die Bänke nageln! (220)

Social climbing is allied here with Frau Weidelich's fanatic will to further her sons and in her turn be able to bathe in their glory:

[. . .] ich tu's meinen Söhnen zu Ehren, die gebildete Herren sind! Man soll nicht sagen, daß man ihre Mama nicht in einem gebildeten Gottesdienst zu sehen bekomme! (ibid.)

Everywhere people in the abstract ("man") are to be encountered, demanding the appear-ance of being well-bred ("gebildet"). The semblance of religiosity is also seen elsewhere. The seal is set on the true sentiments of the sanctimonious Wohlwend when he instructs his son to say grace at the very moment when Martin is raising his spoon to his mouth (203).

The Salanders' concern for appearances also recurs at different stages up till the end of the story. Arnold rejects the idea of any particular preparations for the circle of friends he has invited, but only seems to win the argument, as on the evening itself two assistants are duly installed in the kitchen. Marie reasons:

[. . .] sie habe nicht mit einem mißlungenen Wesen die Familie erst recht als Emporkömmlingsware ins Gerede bringen können! (280)

But here the more rational Arnold is seen as supplanting his mother's traditional attitude, and even the latter is harmless compared with the other examples given here. In *Martin Salander* an obsession with externals is not, as in the previous two novels discussed, an attribute of a declining aristocracy, but instead of a money-grubbing bourgeoisie.

These externals, from semantic bickerings through to hypocritically paraded religiosity, fall well within the province of this smaller-scale *Zeitroman*. Its scope is not suited to a broad presentation of wider issues, but at the same time the less spectacular examples are rarely related to a larger framework of events. The ramifications of apparent trivia that characterize Fontane are not always present in Keller's work. The individual examples in *Martin Salander* of the cultivation of externals reinforce each other in illustrating the same point, but they are seen as accompaniments to historical developments rather than as factors conditioned by them. This is to be compared with *Schach von Wuthenow*, for instance, where Schach's aesthetic sensitivity shows the decline of the old Prussia. Keller's *Zeitroman* illustrates the cultivation of externals in this age without always adequately locating them in it — abused democratization cannot always be appealed to as an explanation.

4. *Finance*

> Aber ernste Männer klagen über den reißenden Fortschritt des Geldgeistes. Monarchieen, sagt ein Schweizer selbst, ein guter Republikaner, zu mir, öffnen den menschlichen Leidenschaften mehr Abzugskanäle, zum Beispiel Titel, Adelsdiplome, Hofdienste, Orden dem Ehrgeiz, der Eitelkeit; hier aber wirft sich aus Mangel an Anderem die ganze Sinnlichkeit fast allein auf's Geld [. . .].
>
> Denn daß inmitten unserer monarchischen Großstaaten noch eine Republik besteht, auf altgesunder Grundlage, verständig, nicht ideologisch, gut konservativ: das soll sein, ist recht und in der Ordnung. Wenn sie sich nur auch vor der modernen Demokratie brav hütet! Gerade einer Republik nichts verderblicher, als der falsche, abstrakte Freiheitsbegriff![9]

The content of this extract, which might serve as something of a motto for this section, could well be taken from *Martin Salander*. In fact it comes from Fr. Th. Vischer's *Auch Einer* (1879).

The sense of appearances discussed in the preceding section is not confined to the moral and social spheres. It is carried over to the realm of finances, where fortunes are amassed, only to crumble overnight. The spread of speculation and ruin in the later stages of the novel are presaged very early in the course of Martin's narration to Moni Wighardt of his earlier family history. His constant scourge Wohlwend had secured him as the first of three guarantors for one of his enterprises. The enterprise predictably founders, and the other two guarantors disappeared before the catastrophe:

> [. . .] nicht ohne ihrerseits selbst verschiedene Bürgen oder deren Gläubiger geschädigt zu haben, insofern solche wirklich etwa bezahlten. (20)

This calls to mind part of Schiller's *Die Bürgschaft* as rendered with hair-raising accentuation by Wohlwend on an earlier occasion, an extract that sticks in Martin's mind because of its unaesthetic impact, not its thought-content:

> Ich lasse den Freund dir als Bürgen,
> *Ihn* magst du, entrinn' *ich*, erwürgen. (19)

A snowballing system is built up simulating financial security, a system which totters at the slightest prod. Money is in fact progressively enslaving rather than serving people. Salander sees this clearly when he extols to his wife "diejenige Unabhängigkeit, welche nur ein mäßiger Besitz verleiht; denn ein zu großer macht natürlich den Mann auch unfrei" (58). Such an outlook is reflected towards the end of the novel too in the very sober discussion between Martin and Arnold on whether to extend their business. Very much the exception, they are not moneygrubbers or status-seekers, preferring to further their intellectual pursuits and to stay within their relatively modest bounds.

At the other end of the scale comes Frau Weidelich. When her sons bring home the Salander girls as their betrothed, Frau Weidelich's mind boggles: "[...] die Salanderinnen, von denen das Stück erst eine halbe Million Franken gelten sollte!" (123). That is the sole criterion by which she judges the match her sons have made. Having decked herself out she turns her attention to preparing a meal for which the young people protest they have no taste. Her husband seems to be having an ironical taunt at her striving to keep up appearances beyond their station when he says: "[...] wir stellen alles durcheinander, so sieht unsere Armut um so reicher aus!" (124). Her crass materialism is exemplified by her reaction to the news that her sons' marriages are collapsing: "Der erste Gedanke war das große Erbgut, das viele Geld" (223).

Martin is a far from idealized figure, constantly shown with his foibles and weaknesses. His attitude towards the recent spate of building, which he is supporting through lending ready capital, is no exception. Rumours of an impending slump are circulating.

> Mag er kommen, dachte er, ich habe nur erste Hypotheken, und ohne das: mit geflogen, mit gefangen! Man muß mit der Zeit marschieren, sie gleicht alles wieder aus [...]. (195)

His rationalizations at the end seem reckless in the extreme, his condoning of the currents of the age seems opposed to his circumspection as a statesman. There is a sense of a financial bubble with no firm foundation, though the issue never swells to consume a whole society, as it does in Kretzer's *Meister Timpe* (1887) with depiction of the larger-scale financial speculation in Germany of the *Gründerzeit*. [10]

The disparity between appearance and reality disappears all too quickly as the swelling number of festivals is succeeded by a series of arrests and exposures of embezzlement. Martin is in fact witness to a painful scene where a reveller is led away by policemen in the midst of celebrations. So seriously does Martin take the spirit and the camaraderie of these gatherings that when the prisoner sadly removes his "Ehrenzeichen der Freude" (216), Martin likens him to an officer being dishonoured before his regiment. The folly of joining the carousing a final time is motivated with keen irony by the moralist Keller: "[...] da ja ein reinlicher Bürger auch das Unliebsame stets zu einem artigen Stammbuchverslein zu gestalten strebt" (ibid.). Thus the cloak of respectability is ripped from this man and the gay atmosphere of the festival soured.

But this is only the beginning. The same evening Martin reads in the newspaper of three similar cases, even one within his own canton, which particularly distresses him. The newspapers become progressively fuller of instances of misappropriation by people from all kinds of positions. The narrator refers to the corrupting power of money in the following moralistic tones:

> Und die schlimme Krankheit durchzog das ganze Land, ohne Ansehen der Konfessionen oder der Sprachgrenzen. Nur etwa im Gebirge, wo die Sitten einfacher geblieben und das bare Geld oder Geldwert seltener war, war nicht viel davon zu hören. (218)

To the pedagogue, parliamentarian and patriot Salander it is naturally disheartening

> daß die Übel der Zeit nicht an den Grenzen der Republik stehenblieben, deren geistigen und sittlichen Ausbau er so getreulich betrieben half. (ibid.)

Yet as we have already seen, he has himself helped nourish the false and inflated values underlying such speculation.

The peak of this trend is reached with Isidor's arrest. The sums the twins have misappropriated are colossal; it is typical of his rather naïve trust in human nature that Martin has interpreted the twins' nocturnal activities in their favour. Ermatinger [11] portrays the immediate historical background to this stage of the novel, the arrests of the notaries Koller and Rudolph, and the furore they caused. The topicality for a reader in Keller's time of the twins' historical counterparts is overlooked by Worthmann. He sees the twins as a kind of incarnation of evil who only emerge as products of the age through the author's commentary and not through the plot itself (122). The many outlets and temptations for financial ventures are to be seen in the case of Isidor as emerges from his trial: he had acted as go-between for an agriculturalists' cooperative society with its investors, and he himself invests the money he embezzles in fruitless ventures on the stock exchange (241). In a case like the following:

> Es war eben der beiden Brüdern gebliebene Anteil am menschlichen Idealismus, das Unrecht nur mit dem Vorbehalte zu üben, es mit Fortunas Hilfe rechtzeitig gutzumachen [. . .] (243),

the attitude of sheer cynicism is allowed to expose itself without any commentary, a concept like "Idealismus" already being suspect. The whole débâcle of the financial scene is not one of hard-core mercenariness, of calculating profiteering. Rather it shows the seductive lure of money, which in its all too ready accessibility misleads fairly average people into speculation, momentary success and frequent disaster.

Here again Keller's *Zeitroman* stands clearly between the more spectacular events in Immermann and Spielhagen and the complete absence of them in Fontane's last novel. While avoiding all melodrama, Keller's rather low-key approach runs the risk of making the events described seem harmless. There is little sense of waste or futility for instance when Martin, duped by Wohlwend, returns to South America, and most potential for drama or tragedy is eliminated by the frequent tone of disillusionment and resignation.

5. *Politics and education*

Martin's idealistic side appears when he is recounting to Moni Wighardt his motivation for his teaching efforts:

> Ich freute mich schon der späteren Tage, wo ich manchem Landmann zu begegnen hoffte, der es mir danken würde, wenn er eine richtige Berechnung anstellen, ein Stück Feld ausmessen, seine Zeitung besser verstehen und etwa ein französisches Buch lesen könnte, alles ohne die Hand vom Pfluge zu lassen! Allerdings hab' ich es nicht erlebt [. . .]. (17)

Martin's notions of a well-educated peasantry sound almost comical through the very images that he employs, and are in any case thwarted by that urban expansion already noted. His pedagogic trait is shown even in a brief scene when he and his family have walked to a vantage point looking out over the surrounding countryside. This serves Martin as a pretext for testing the children's geographical knowledge, and when his elder daughter answers correctly that what they see is Münsterburg(-Zürich), one of the twelve *Bezirke,* he ruminates aloud on their historical precedents and his patriotic impulses swell. That these are shared is shown by the recent introduction of *Heimatkunde* to the school curriculum.

76

Martin's visionary political opinions are gently ironized by Marie's attitude to them, though she does admire his "bürgerlichen Freisinn" (61). But the fact that Wohlwend has caused her husband to spend such a long period of his life in unforeseen, unplanned pursuits shows the brittle nature of plans for the future, such as those in Martin's last letter before his return from his second stay overseas. In this letter, Martin looks forward with great expectation to experiencing the new constitution the republics have wrought for themselves. In 1869 the new Zürich constitution replaced the legislative power of the elected councillors by the will of the people expressed through plebiscites. Martin goes on to paint a rosy picture of the increased sense of duty and responsibility which must accompany such a step. In this he is to be sadly disillusioned.

For the moment the Münsterburg constitution attracts the admiration of neighbouring statesmen, and the principles democratically introduced bring with them undreamt of changes. There is a seething political atmosphere, and the entrusting of government to such an extent to the hands of the people leads to individual enterprise of the following nature:

> Salander sah mit Verwunderung, wie im Halbdunkel eines Bierstübchens zwei Projektenmacher den Entwurf eines kleinen, Millionen kostenden Gesetzes oder Volksbeschlusses fix und fertig formulieren konnten, ohne daß die vom Volke gewählte Regierung ein Wort dazu zu sagen bekam. (73)

The succession of elections for offices of all kinds similarly keeps those entitled to vote active. Martin joins in this whirl of activity and is elected to many committees because of his known independent spirit, among his functions being that of helping explain the difficult points of their new political sovereignty to those unversed in them. This involves familiarity with many laws which he strives to assimilate. Such integrity is rarely to be observed in others in like positions, and so Martin shines as an isolated beacon of enlightenment and idealism in the midst of a sea of changes which often move too quickly for those who have effected them. A presentiment of the true state of affairs beneath the surface of hectic ferment does not escape Martin.

> Zuweilen wollte ihn eine trübe Ahnung beschleichen, als ob das Personal der politischen Ober-, Mittel- und Unterstreber gegen früher im ganzen ein klein wenig gesunken wäre, so daß die etwas geringere Beschaffenheit der einen Schicht diejenige der anderen bedinge und erkläre. (74) [12]

The people are simply not ripe in many cases for the wide-ranging powers that have been so rapidly acquired and not gradually integrated into the structure of the nation's political life. The "Gemeindammann" draws attention to the irresponsibility of those who have brought Isidor to power:

> Eigentlich müßten mir diejenigen den Schaden gutmachen, die einen solchen Menschen zu ihrem Notar wählen und das Recht dazu an sich gerissen haben! (238)

Another example is a debate in which Martin is to participate:

> Erst hörte er [...] eine Anzahl weiterer Reden an, in welchen von ungeschulten, meist jüngeren Leuten statt eingehender Gründe nur immer das Wort Republik, republikanisch, Würde des Republikaners usw. vorgebracht und geschrien wurde. (75)

This degradation to an emotional catchcry of a concept very dear to Martin's heart distresses him, and at the same time his pedagogic inclination is aroused. He administers a rebuke to the offenders in a speech in which he again dwells on historical references. These reflect his firm patriotic pride but tend to seem pedantic. He makes the timely observation, which is ill-received because of its closeness to home, "daß auch der Republikaner alles, was er braucht, erwerben muß und nicht mit Worten bezahlen kann" (ibid.).[13] Martin's keenness to remain independent changes; he realizes that the presentation of an opinion carries far more weight in the *Rat* than in other assemblies. Again he is contrasted sharply with most of his fellow-politicians: he shows exceptional reticence in simply attending the meeting without insinuating to others his desire to be elected. Whenever Martin is tacitly praised in such procedures the general state of politics and politicians of the time is equally roundly condemned by their deviations from his example.

His normally impeccable motives as a tolerant patriot are satirized when he espouses greater representation from the Old Liberals, an expedient action in view of his party's waning support.

> Namentlich war er ein Verehrer der modernen Liebhaberei der Minderheitenvertretung geworden, der nicht nur politische Philosophen, sondern auch allerlei praktische Leute anhingen, welchen der schöne Grundsatz nächstens selbst nützlich werden konnte, nachdem sie bislang keine anders gesinnte Fliege zugelassen hatten, noch ferner zuzulassen gesonnen waren. (105)

In this issue as in his financial dabblings there is no question of Martin being lumped together with the crass opportunism exposed at the end of the sentence. But the chinks in his idealistic armour do show through. This both renders the presentation of him as a character more credible — again precisely what is lacking in Arnold — and also establishes a certain continuum, so that the negative features of the age are not simply contrasted with a wholly idealized positive pole. The solid core of integrity in Martin is affirmed, but after the opening situation where his perspective as a long absent compatriot achieves a certain objectivity, his lament for the abuses of the day is far from that of a detached observer not involved in the events he is decrying. The same applies to society viewed from the other end. Julian and Isidor are not individual transgressors beyond the pale of society, but have rather been spawned by it.

There is nothing in the general tone of party politics to inspire Martin. His is an individual stance of a fervent patriot, not the pursuing of selfish or short-sighted aims with the immunity of a party label. With typical naîveté he imputes to the twins worthy motives in attending the elections (106), when in fact they seek only to impress and ingratiate themselves with the man they hope will be their father-in-law, and nominate Martin with a calculating opportunism that is countered by an unswerving integrity on his part, for he cannot accept a position under such circumstances. He himself is aware of the fact that he is not endowed with the compromising character necessary for success in politics. This quality is illustrated by the Weidelich twins; Julian's flashy sentiments are reflected by his big hat, "ein unverhohlenes Zeichen der Gesinnung" (114), which in itself earns him his candidature. Both he and Isidor — "dieser [trug] ein Hütlein wie ein Suppenteller" (113) — are very much the sons of their mother, with her own parading hat, and in all such cases the frippery betokens an inner poverty. There is no emphasis on depth of political sympathies in Julian's favour, but instead on the emotive effect of the external sign, precisely what Martin had referred to in his attack on the abuse of the word "Republik."

The political career of the Weidelich twins, brought to an abrupt end by the disgrace of their incarceration, is the most glaring indictment of the abused freedom in the Switzerland portrayed. In a particularly crass scene they throw dice to decide which party they will adhere to, having agreed upon the expediency of taking an active political interest and of not belonging to the same party. Their ruthless self-seeking, devoid of ideals and principles, is opposed to Martin's wary impartiality, which is based on strong moral sentiments. Their primitive methods of ensuring notice through hackneyed tricks — having themselves called away from meetings by telegrammes, for instance (112) — reflect their unprincipled drive for success and expose further the superficiality of an age which nurtures them and smiles indulgently on their devices. On the other hand Martin's probity is not properly recognized.

In connection with the wedding, a letter from Arnold arrives, wherein he expresses his own view and that of his friends (129ff.). These accord generally with those of an old man who has clearly impressed Arnold, and who has bemoaned successive generations restlessly undoing the work of their forebears in an excessively hasty progressive spirit. This attitude of responsible detachment is to be echoed at the end of the novel and hailed by Martin as a great hope for the future; here it meets with a certain bewilderment on his part. Indeed, it is his inability to come to grips with what he sees as his son's doctrinaire ideas that prompts him to stage "ein freiheitliches Volksfest" (128) after all as part of his daughters' wedding celebrations. This is a kind of defiance of Arnold's scepticism towards progressive trends. The girls' objections to various features planned by Martin are met halfway, though it is clearly of great importance to him that the venue of the wedding-breakfast should have "einen politischen Beigeschmack" (135). Yet he had originally been prepared, without recourse to the preferences of the girls, to sacrifice sundry features of a more conventional style of wedding through incorporating as a prime feature the railway and even the railway-station (132-33).

This headlong hurling of himself into more questionable currents of contemporary life stands at strange variance with that side of Martin that is rooted in the customs and history of his nation. His impetuosity on the one hand and fierce patriotism on the other make possible the presentation of a figure with two historical time-dimensions, with the third, the future, intended to be Arnold's domain. Martin's tendency to idealization and abstraction are offset by the gently ironic, realistic foil of Marie; there was no such norm to lend clearer contours to Immermann's or Spielhagen's figures.

At the wedding the parson proposes a toast to the newly-weds and their parents in strongly folksy tones. For him the form is of greater importance than the content, and it is symptomatic that alone of the four parents Frau Weidelich is greatly impressed. This is not the only dubious feature of the wedding. The play conceived by Martin as wedding the political ideals of the Democrats and the Old Liberals takes turns he had not expected, and democracy emerges at the expense of a ridiculed, lagging liberalism. Martin hastens to rectify the twist given to his conception, and the crowd applauds again, but is thereby shown to be very fickle. It thus seems that political opinions are to them basically a framework for the formulating of fine speeches, witty farces, etc. The political enlightenment which Salander had foreseen from abroad as the heritage of the new constitution becomes highly questionable.

The political issues raised in the play are presented in such a distorted form, more with an eye to their effect on the audience than to their intrinsic merits, that no conclusions about such merits can be drawn from the account of the play. But a more objective judgement does emerge from commentary inserted into the narrative, something essayed elsewhere to lend a general, philosophizing tone to an observation (see 29, 138). Here it ensures the reader of a more sober criticism of Liberalism which is not present for the spectator of the farce. This is achieved by the following interpolations:

[...] wobei aber der Liberalismus, *so ziemlich wie es im Leben geschieht,* ohne es zu merken, einen Satz der Demokratie nach dem andern zu dem seinigen machte [...]. (145)

and:

Es waren biedere Leute, die durch alle Ungunst der Zeit ihrer Gesinnung treu geblieben und *die im Grunde richtigen* Anspielungen auf den Wankelmut [...] nicht einmal verstanden. (146) (author's emphasis in both cases)

The narrator here adopts the pedagogic stance attributed to Martin throughout the novel. He concedes that the exaggerations of the play distance it from the conditions which form its subject-matter. At the same time he ensures that a clear verdict on those conditions does in fact emerge. Without this an uninstructed reader might have assumed from the dubious light in which both the farce and the audience's reception are cast that the satiric barb is intended to backfire, but this is not the case.

This seems a fascinating instance of that constant interplay between individual and general concerns present in the *Zeitroman.* Rather than let a more gradual and reasoned criticism of Liberalism emerge organically from his work, the novelist chooses to accentuate the individual aspect. This he does through satire which reflects, through the repeated *Hanswurst* elements and the complete lack of subtlety, more on Martin's wedding-feast and the players and spectators than on the object directly satirized. To redress this balance — since the author is also striving for a political comment — the narrator has to supply his own commentary.[14] *Martin Salander* avoids the irritating black-white scheme of characterization whereby polemical thrusts are driven home. But the above example shows the dangers with which Keller's method is fraught in balancing the colourful and satiric concerns found in his earlier works [15] with the didactic and disillusioned features of this *Zeitroman.*

Shortly after the wedding Martin is finally persuaded to become "Mitglied des Großen Rates" (150), a responsibility he takes on after much soul-searching. The irony of this lies in the immediate cause, in view of his earlier refusal to be associated with the twins' loud and vulgar nomination (106). He is later in no doubt as to this cause: "[...] die auffällige Doppelhochzeit [...], durch die ich in den Rat gekommen bin, was jedermann weiß" (233). His democratic principles are also gently ironized when shown to vanish before the beautiful presence of Myrrha: "Sie lächelte leicht [...], und er verbeugte sich bei diesem Anlaß unfreiwillig, trotz seiner demokratischen Gesinnung" (202). He discusses with his wife the recurring problem of the demands of cantons and the federal government on finances (166), but with even more enthusiasm does he expound his ideas about his hobby-horse, education. His wife is perceptive in seeing through his illusions, such as his attractive but impracticable notion of compulsory education to the age of twenty. These few pages provide an interesting comparison with *Die Epigonen.* In *Martin Salander* certain programmes and theoretical ideas are heralded, yet their presentation is consistent with character development, whether in Martin's pedagogic trait or Marie's scepticism and rather grim humour. A comparison with Wilhelmi in *Die Epigonen* must be to the latter's disadvantage — as already indicated, his pronouncements are generally outright polemics, qualified only by the hypochondria attributed to him.

A desperate and absurd attack is make on the state education system by the defence counsel for Julian. But the judge refers to the solid foundation this system has in the ideas contained in Pestalozzi's *Lienhard und Gertrud* (1781-87). His generally reasoned repudiation of the defence's claims unfortunately ends with a rhetorical flourish:

[. . .] weil es mir, wie schon öfter in neuerer Zeit, zumute war, wie wenn der Geist eines hysterischen alten Weibsbildes in unserm Ländchen herumführe, wie der Böse im Buch Hiob! (258)

This earns him many hisses as it is imputed to his Old Liberal leanings. Yet similar terms are used for the same phenomenon in a more editorial comment, when we hear of the troubles caused Martin by the "Zeitkrankheiten" (264). He himself thinks of explaining to his wife his need to worship the beauty of Wohlwend's sister-in-law Myrrha as an escape from the "Krankheiten der Zeit" (268). This rationale does not obscure the fact that from the first mention of the word "Verfall" (155) — with reference to the hapless Kleinpeter — the financial and moral bases of society have progressively disintegrated. The judge's final image in his speech above seems to be based on substance, even if it is exaggerated.

Furthermore, the verdicts of both Martin and the judge are justified in terms of integration into the narrative through being extracted from details presented. With some of Wilhelmi's utterances in *Die Epigonen*, such verdicts were often presented in lieu of these details. The same criticism applies to the end of *Martin Salander*, where Arnold's character is a vehicle for ideas rather than these emerging naturally. In the "Materialien" Keller notes: "Salander ist der Zustand der Gegenwart, Arnold der Zukunft."[16] Little more than this abstraction of Arnold's function is achieved by the novel. At the end Martin's great hope, the *Volk*, recedes and future hopes rest on the all too thinly delineated shoulders of Arnold and his friends. Except in the case of Arnold, Keller generally manages to keep the delicate balance, basic to the *Zeitroman,* between individual character representation and more generalized comment, without the characters becoming transparent ciphers and manipulated components of the fictional apparatus. Even a secondary figure like Kleinpeter, for all his function of prefiguring a strand in the main action, emerges as much more than a type.

Arnold does bring a fresh perspective from which future progress can derive its impetus in making a timely distinction between "Vaterlandsliebe" and "Selbstbewunderung" (271). Thus Martin too is brought to a realization of the relative importance of Swiss politics — cf. Arnold's maxim: "Es ist bei uns wie überall" (ibid.) — and when his infatuation with the classical beauty of Myrrha Glawicz passes, his political efforts, or at least their impulses, are greatly ironized (272).

It can be seen that the political sphere plays a dominant part, and its extensive treatment may be what Keller had in mind when he regretted the lack of "Poesie"[17] within his final work. The political currents of the age are nonetheless well integrated and a broad spectrum is achieved from the opportunism of the Weidelich twins through to the sincerity of Salander. The latter is nonetheless tempered by a tendency to idealism and by a fiasco such as the play performed at the wedding. The political changes, the adoption and initial operating of the new constitution, are just part of the series of rapid changes found also in the industrial and financial spheres, and reflect the impetuous, not always well-considered progress of this outwardly progressive stage of Swiss history.

The negative influence of Wohlwend finally disappears from the scene, after his "Gottesstaatsidee" (264) has been expounded and deflated as a solution to the governmental problems of the time. The whole tone of these concluding pages is conciliatory and confident. When his father speaks in apologetic terms of recent events in their country, Arnold points to worse excesses in the past which have not managed to hinder its development, e.g. the Napoleonic occupation. Arnold's preference for a less *engagé* attitude is not a sign of an unwillingness to shoulder responsibility, but instead is designed to preserve freedom and breadth of vision. This contrasts with Martin's persevering but perhaps somewhat narrow *engagement*, and he receives a lesson in the value of the new spirit pervading Arnold's assembled friends, "denn er war in manchen Dingen ein wenig viel zurückgeblieben" (281). It remains Arnold's lot to steer the Salanders' ship into clearer waters when threatened subsequently on the sea of life. If the high praise lavished on him by Martin were to indicate solely his suitability for this domestic role, it would be convincing. Clearly the whole future destiny of the land is seen as secure by Martin because of Arnold and his ilk; Keller thought of a sequel to this novel featuring Arnold as hero. But his emergence here as a bastion of hope does not convince because of the minor role he has played and the untestedness of his ideas as counters to Martin's. Wohlwend leaves, but the impression remaining is of the negative features of the age portrayed, with an all too insubstantial hope for the age to come.

6. *Patriotism and the "Volk"*

The worthier protagonists of ideas in this novel, such as Arnold and Martin, display a deep-seated patriotism that tends to unite them despite all diversities of outlook. This distinguishes them for instance from the hero of Spielhagen's *Problematische Naturen*, whose fevered energy is turned to the championing of political ideas without the same pride in a historical evolution already achieved. The number of German states up till Bismarck's day contrasted with the Swiss cantons, generally able to look past regional differences to a sense of federal pride formalized since 1848.

This patriotism appears in the opening scene when Salander returns to his homeland. There is a sense of national emergency and at the same time a deep expression of patriotic sentiment in his rumination:

> [. . .] schon hängt in jedem Hause, wie ich vernehme, das gezogene Gewehr und harrt der ernsten Prüfung; möge sie der Heimat lange erspart bleiben! (8)

The New World does not appeal to him:

> [. . .] die Leute sind sich gleichgültig, [. . .] denn sie haben keine gemeinsame Vergangenheit und keine Gräber der Vorfahren. Solange ich aber das Ganze unserer Volksentwicklung auf dem alten Boden haben kann, wo meine Sprache seit fünfzehnhundert Jahren erschallt, will ich dazu gehören [. . .]. (56)

The abuses of this language in his day cannot, however, be overlooked. The thriving of emigration, the lure of the New World for those not as rooted in the Old as Martin, also finds its place here.[18] There are Martin's two trips during which he is able to recoup his financial losses, while Kleinpeter's sons travel to America to seek jobs as factory supervisors (164). Arnold spends a year in Brazil to build up business connections there, while Isidor requests history and geography books about America and volumes of the travel-writer Gerstäcker to while away his time in prison. Thus the theme of emigration receives fairly extensive treatment here, though the New World simply enters the narrative in reported form and never becomes the setting.

The purest expression of the patriotic spirit is the vow made with impressive solemnity by Martin and Arnold never to leave country and people. The less exalted idealism of Arnold makes the reservation that complete degeneration of the nation they pledge their all to would nullify his vow. But he then withdraws this reservation, since then it would be *"chez nous comme partout"* (274).[19] Thus their whole national pride is relativized into something devoid of all chauvinism. The very formulation of this slogan in French, as of its inverted form (271)[20] is an illustration of its own content. That is to say, Arnold finds in another language the best means of expressing a particular truth — the very fact that this saying has become a slogan shows a breadth of application presumably reflecting a true state of affairs.[21] It is somewhat comparable in sense with the symbol of the lake in *Der Stechlin*.

The above example is of interest for the *Zeitroman* as a genre in the placing into a more general framework of the specifically Swiss conditions. These are depicted throughout the novel without drawing upon any frame of reference to conditions in other countries. This applies even to a phenomenon such as the international resonance of Darwin's *Origin of Species* (1859). The work is nowhere referred to directly, unlike the product of Swiss soil, *Lienhard und Gertrud*. The idea in this work of the individual's influence radiating out through the family to the community and state[22] has clearly influenced Keller's emphases in *Martin Salander*. But when Arnold gently ridicules his sisters' description of their wooers' earlobes as distinguishing features, he does so with terms referring to Darwin's theory of natural selection, indicating the impact of this thinker on his time (83). This is reinforced by Marie's musing on the Weidelich parents' attempts to localize the hereditary influences on their sons to one side of the family:

> Davon werde ich meinem Martin nichts sagen, sonst gräbt er ebenfalls nach und fügt seinen erzieherischen Postulaten noch eines über selektions-theoretischen Volksunterricht in sittlicher Beziehung bei, oder wie er es nennen würde! (254)

Allied to the love of country shown by Martin and Arnold comes a detailed description of the *Volk* who don't always match up to Martin's idealistic notions. The enthusiasm which the new constitution fires in Martin is not reflected in his fellow countrymen, as he finds to his disappointment in the course of a stroll amongst them:

> [...] den Hauch und Glanz aber der neuen Zeit, das Wehen des Geistes, den etwas feierlicheren Ernst, den er suchte, konnte er nicht wahrnehmen. (63)

Old songs are sung in the old imperfect manner[23] and drunken youths belie any sense of a new noble communal spirit or political responsibility. Thus Martin's naïve hope — "schon die Tatsache eines solchen Ereignisses würde Land und Himmel eine andere Physiognomie machen!" (64) — is shown to be illusory.

The immediately following scene in a restaurant sets the seal on this delusion. A Swiss tradesman flaunts his independence, the supposed superiority of his nation and his own inflated sense of importance before his South German toady. This brash boastfulness has absolutely nothing in common with the brand of patriotism espoused by Martin and Arnold. What irritates Martin at least as much is the self-abasement of the South German who spurs his companion on to ever greater excesses. Martin is sadly disappointed in his hopes of a freshly enlightened homeland. Yet his faith in the *Volk* is unshakeable, as we see in his following reaction to doubts assailing him in his political efforts: "Allein er faßte bald wieder guten Mut, auf den unverlierbaren guten Ackergrund des Volkes vertrauend" (74).

He had viewed with some scepticism the "Feste, Anlässe, Gesamtreisen, Vereinsausflüge und Begehungen allerart" (214) which constitute the people's pleasure in summer, but flushed with the élan of his late infatuation he mingles enthusiastically. The narrative takes a very sober view of the festivities, yet while virtually conceding that they amount to squandering at a time of relative financial need it does relativize even this by referring to Catholic pilgrims who were a reminder "daß früher noch mehr im Volke gewandert und geschmaust wurde, und das gerade in Zeiten der Bedrängnis" (ibid.). This achieves a historical perspective analogous to the geographical sense of *"C'est partout comme chez nous"* (271). Similarly Arnold answers Martin's apologetic tone towards the present by pointing to worse excesses in the past which have not hindered the development of the country (270). What is essayed, then, is a degree of universality radiating from a core of patriotism. But the former remains sketchy because it lacks terms of reference external to the situation portrayed, and also because the characterization and themes of the novel are far more particular than universal. Martin's patriotism seems to be based rather on the traditions and institutions preserved from the past than on the achievements of the present. The core of patriotism is far from intact by the end of the work through frequent satirization.

With its title-figure as a unifying feature and its reduced epic scope, *Martin Salander* has a much tauter narrative structure than *Die Epigonen* or *Problematische Naturen*. The other side of this coin is the restricted portrayal of the age — the relatively few figures emerge vividly, but those contemporary crosscurrents which are behind their actions are rather less substantial. Keller's only *Zeitroman* is a disillusioned reckoning with the age without the reflective wisdom and serenity sustaining Dubslav Stechlin and informing the whole tone of Fontane's last novel. *Der Stechlin* works with a still further reduced epic canvas but achieves a greater impression of breadth through tracing the subtlest gradations of that canvas.

CHAPTER V

THEODOR FONTANE: *DER STECHLIN*

> [...] der Stoff, so weit von einem solchen die Rede sein kann — denn es ist eigentlich blos eine Idee, die sich einkleidet — dieser Stoff wird sehr wahrscheinlich mit einer Art Sicherheit Ihre Zustimmung erfahren. Aber die Geschichte, das was erzählt wird. Die Mache! Zum Schluß stirbt ein Alter und zwei Junge heiraten sich; — das ist so ziemlich alles, was auf 500 Seiten geschieht. Von Verwicklungen und Lösungen, von Herzenskonflikten oder Konflikten überhaupt, von Spannungen und Überraschungen findet sich nichts.
>
> Einerseits auf einem altmodischen märkischen Gut, andrerseits in einem neumodischen gräflichen Hause (Berlin) treffen sich verschiedene Personen und sprechen da Gott und die Welt durch. Alles Plauderei, Dialog, in dem sich die Charaktere geben, und mit ihnen die Geschichte. Natürlich halte ich dies nicht nur für die richtige, sondern sogar für die gebotene Art, einen Zeitroman zu schreiben, bin mir aber gleichzeitig nur zu sehr bewußt, daß das große Publikum sehr anders darüber denkt und Redaktionen — durch das Publikum gezwungen — auch.[1]

Thus Fontane, speaking of his final novel, *Der Stechlin*. If his verdict is correct, it is clear that we are dealing here with an exceptional case in tracing the development of the *Zeitroman*, one acknowledged by its author to be at variance with what was generally considered to be "die gebotene Art, einen Zeitroman zu schreiben." Fontane had doubts about the work's appeal, but looked to the critics.[2]

Certainly the accents have shifted. Whereas in *Die Epigonen* the hero Hermann was still strongly bound to the picaresque tradition, serving as a common denominator to the various levels of society treated but not being developed as a fully-fledged character, Fontane's approach is clearly from the opposite direction. The characters emerge from the formal structuring of conversation, and through the characters such plot ("Geschichte") as there is. Wilhelmi's rhetorical reckoning with the age in his analysis of *Epigonentum* (III, 135-36) was a reflective statement on the plot to that point of the novel. Such a programmatic judgement, not relativized either by irony on the part of the author or the presentation of a contrary viewpoint, would be inconceivable in *Der Stechlin*. This is not merely because of its author's scepticism but also because of the way his novel is built up: from the succession of dialogues, the loving lingering over "Plauderei," a whole mosaic of viewpoints emerges, even if certain main lines predominate, and out of them emerges the plot that isn't one.

At the end an old man dies and two young people marry. As a summary of the action this is basically correct, but of course it does violence to the ramifications of the work, and why this objection holds again helps indicate the structure of the novel. The bare fact of Dubslav Stechlin's death does not explain its serene acceptance both by the person dying and those about him who revered him so much. Little Agnes alone weeps briefly, while Graf Barby, driving away from the burial, can exult in the natural beauty about him without this having a trace of callousness. Certainly the old Baroque motif of *memento mori* is present; Barby is conscious that he will be the next to take his earthly leave. But his response to this intimation — his joyful relish for the spring air without letting dark overtones intrude on that joy — is a worthy adjunct to the funeral of Dubslav Stechlin. The explanation of this complete lack of pathos and its absolute consistency with the novel's tone is to be found only in the gradual development of that tone, not in any details attaching to the funeral-scene itself.

Similarly, to return to Fontane's statement, two people marry. The life-cycle goes on, or as the lapidary heading of the final chapters foretells, there is the sequence "Tod. Begräbnis. Neue Tage" (764). That is altogether too glib to do justice to this novel. What is important here is the specific toning of this phenomenon — the life-cycle — as something emerging organically from the novel and therefore not merely as an extraneous note of aesthetic rounding-off. Dubslav on his deathbed is sustained by the thought of the complete dependence of the individual self on an eternal world order.

It is undoubtedly this final insight which is referred to by the beginning of the title ("Verweile doch") prefacing the concluding seven chapters of the novel. This is the moment to which Dubslav — in other respects so un-Faustian — could utter: "Verweile doch, du bist so schön!" (*Faust* I, 1. 1700) because this is his ultimate revelation. "Der Weisheit letzter Schluß" (*Faust* II, 1. 11574) also has reference to Dubslav:

> Nur der verdient sich Freiheit wie das Leben,
> Der täglich sie erobern muß. (*Faust* II, 1. 11575-76)

For Lorenzen's funeral oration includes the praise: "Er war recht eigentlich frei" (787), and Woldemar notes in his diary: "[. . .] doch kenne ich keinen Menschen, der innerlich so frei wäre wie gerade mein guter Alter" (518). The proximity of what is meant here to usage of the word "frei" elsewhere in Goethe's works is made clearer by reference to *Die Wahlverwandtschaften* ("Aus Ottiliens Tagebuche"):

> Es darf sich einer nur für frei erklären, so fühlt er sich den Augenblick als bedingt. Wagt er es, sich für bedingt zu erklären, so fühlt er sich frei. (III, 261)

That this expresses the very essence of Dubslav, his lack of illusions and false pride, his perpetual relativizing (cf. "bedingt") will emerge from a more detailed consideration of his character. Various quotations from the German literary heritage[3] have been integrated into the otherwise everyday chatter of the novel, as in the following example. Czako confides to Rex as they leave the funeral:

> "Rex, Sie sind ja wie vertauscht und reden beinah in meinem Stil. Es ist doch merkwürdig, sowie die Menschen dies Nest, dies Berlin, erst hinter sich haben, *fängt Vernunft wieder an zu sprechen.*" (793. Author's emphasis corresponds — with appropriate change of word order — to *Faust* I, 1. 1198.)

What is the function of these references to *Faust*, among other works, in this *Zeitroman*? Primarily they exemplify the Old-New leitmotif (see p. 93ff.), evoking the literary tradition in which stand both the narrator — Dubslav doesn't in fact say "Verweile doch," it remains an expression of the narrator — and his figures. For these make allusions either for learned or more ironic effect, an example of the latter being Czako's quotation from Goethe, following on from the colloquial "dies Nest." The references thus bring together ages, both in the broadest sense and in particular as stages of a continuous literary tradition. They show the interrelationship between the setting of the novel and past ages, thus achieving that breadth of vision which characterizes the Dubslavs of the novel and which is so abhorrent to Adelheid.

The idea formulated by Dubslav on his deathbed is mirrored in Melusine's letter at the end of the novel: "[. . .] es ist nicht nötig, daß die Stechline weiterleben, aber es lebe *der Stechlin*" (799).[4] Thus the novel is rounded off by repetition of its title, embracing at once the lake, whose apparent placidity conceals its connections to the external world; the essence of the Stechlin family surviving its individual members; and the family residence, constant despite its many alterations. The fantasy-ball (778) Dubslav envisages is to be held in a renovated residence, yet Melusine's final letter reports: "Morgen früh zieht das junge Paar in das alte Herrenhaus ein" (799).

The culmination of the spirit in Melusine's benediction comes with the young couple honeymooning on Capri, having been inaccessible to the world of the *Mark* for want of a fixed address. Geographically distanced though they are, and filled with a sense of union rather than the end of an existence, the contact is still preserved. They watch Vesuvius, hear a muffled omen of a fresh eruption, and Woldemar interprets that instantly in terms of its echo in Lake Stechlin.[5] Only superficial bonds are severed — those such as telegraphic services, created by a technology that proves inadequate here but is praised elsewhere (see for example 425). Individual connections are changed, a flux seen in a universal context with the fisherman's song "Tre giorni son che Nina [. . .]," but the *Stechlin*, the seismograph of impulses overriding the merely individual, remains. None of this is apparent in any bare account of the action of the novel.

Nor are the symbolic touches of the final pages. Dubslav's death coincides with the first signs of Spring. Agnes plucks snowdrops and lays them on the dying man's lap; near the church are to be seen "Holunderbüsche, die zu grünen anfingen" (785), and after the bitter cold of the morn, commented on by Molchow and von der Nonne, the weather warms and the Barbys and Berchtesgadens exult in the Spring landscape as their carriage takes them along an avenue of willows already in bud (792). These successive notes are far subtler than any "pathetic fallacy" (Ruskin). The picture is one of the rebirth of life on a scale dwarfing the potential tragedy of the morning. This rebirth is by no means restricted to the new squire of the estate and his bride, whose depiction by Lorenzen as "die blasse junge Frau" (780) parallels Dubslav's earlier musings: "[. . .] das junge, blasse Fräulein, das seine Frau werden sollte" (631). Significantly the carriage-ride is shared by mainly older members of two noble families painted in very positive terms, people whose sensitivity is such that they can perceive beauty midst the supposed "Dürftigkeit und Prosa dieser Gegenden" (792), a quality which will also enrich their lives in the sphere of human relations.

These then are the far from dismal accompaniments to Dubslav's death. The attendant circumstances of it prevail over its immediate significance, or rather transfigure this significance into natural terms. The same is true of the conclusion of the novel. The young couple does not move into the Stechlin castle immediately. The summer months — those, incidentally, when the lake could have thawed naturally — are spent in Berlin, then at Armgard's suggestion they move to the family estate. The novel's first time-setting after the introduction is October 3rd. Woldemar and Armgard move in at the same time of the year, on September 21st. Thus yet again, the action itself is of little significance, but its framing — in this case, temporal — is all-important. The older generation is paralleled with the new — with the portentous advance that the new "Herr" is greeted by the Globsower "als einer der 'Ihrigen'" (799) — and this augurs the realization of the hope expressed in Melusine's letter which rounds off the novel.

"Das 'Wie' muß für das 'Was' eintreten,"[6] an assessment of *Die Poggenpuhls* which delighted Fontane, applies equally well to *Der Stechlin*. "*Das was* erzählt wird" (author's emphasis) is dismissed here as trifling — "Die Mache!" This approach to novel-writing does however involve problems of its own. In the fourth chapter of *Stine*, Sarastro (the old Graf Haldern) introduces his nephew Waldemar and friend Papageno to the ladies gathered at Pauline's. The following quotation comes directly after his words of introduction:

In der *Art*, wie diese Vorstellung von den drei Damen aufgenommen wurde, zeigte sich durchaus die Verschiedenheit ihrer Charaktere: Wanda fand alles in der Ordnung, Pauline brummte was von Unsinn und Afferei vor sich hin, und nur Stine, das Verletzende der Komödie herausfühlend, wurde rot. (I, 496-97)

At this early stage of the work, when characters are still not particularly clearly delineated, the words of Sarastro cannot stand alone, however finely the offensive overtones sensed by Stine are blended in his hearty delivery. Thus the differentiation has to be spelt out, stridently so through the italicizing of the word "Art."[7]

In *Der Stechlin* what happens ("das 'Was' ") is at times shown to be less of subsidiary interest than outright misleading. Actions or expressions which are seemingly identical are shown on closer analysis to spring from very different motivations. Thus a *tête-à-tête* between Koseleger and Lorenzen is presented as follows:

In dünngeschliffene große Gläser schenkte Lorenzen ein, und die beiden Amtsbrüder stießen an "auf bessere Zeiten." Aber sie dachten sich sehr Verschiedenes dabei, weil sich der eine nur mit sich, der andre nur mit andern beschäftigte. (578)

Another case is when Adelheid asks Agnes for whom she is knitting the stocking. For herself, the child replies:

Dubslav lachte. Adelheid auch. Aber es war ein Unterschied in ihrem Lachen. Agnes nahm übrigens nichts von diesem Unterschied wahr [. . .] . (761)

Because of Agnes' lack of reaction a finer differentiation is uncalled for here. Only when she has left the room are we enlightened, or rather the mental picture we have of Adelheid is confirmed: "Als sie hinaus war, wiederholte sich Adelheids krampfhaftes Lachen" (ibid.). In both these examples two people perform actions that are identical on the surface but are no longer so once the reader is taken beyond that surface. The greater psychological concerns of Fontane — "das 'Wie'" — set this novel apart from the bulk of nineteenth century *Zeitromane*.

Emphasis on stylistic detail above the subject-matter as such distances Fontane from Spielhagen for instance. In Fontane's case "eine Idee, die sich einkleidet" is merely the central thread unifying many strands of comparable value, not a passionately defended *idée fixe* colouring the whole work as with Spielhagen.[8] This central thread of Fontane's novel is expressed by the title of Heiko Strech's "Theodor Fontane: Die Synthese von Alt und Neu,"[9] a synthesis favouring the Old, as we shall see. This is even hinted at in Fontane's statement on his work at the level of the nobility itself: "Einerseits auf einem *alt*modischen märkischen Gut, andrerseits in einem *neu*modischen gräflichen Hause (Berlin) [. . .] " (author's emphasis).

To return to the original assessment, Fontane emphasizes the unruffled flow of his narrative:

Von Verwicklungen und Lösungen, von Herzenskonflikten oder Konflikten überhaupt, von Spannungen und Überraschungen findet sich nichts.

This is perfectly true, and if Fontane considered these to be the criteria for a *Zeitroman* then we must seek different designations for his other prose works, for in them these elements are not absent. [10]

His last novel shows Fontane's ability in structuring conversations at its very highest. Strech writes in this context:

Die in den vorangehenden Gesellschaftsromanen aufbrechende Problematik, Fragen um Individuum, Konvention und Staat, Konfession und Politik haben sich ins Gespräch verflüchtigt, werden nicht mehr im vollen Einsatz der Existenz ausgetragen. Spektakuläre Ereignisse wie Duelle (*Effi Briest, Cécile*), Selbstmorde (*Schach von Wuthenow, Unwiederbringlich, Stine*), Ehekonflikte und ihre dramatisch-tragische Lösung (von *L'Adultera* an), Verbrechen (die Kriminalgeschichten) verschwinden gänzlich.[11]

In fact the diverging elements of the "Problematik" mentioned by Strech can be merged and, as a concerted force in the one direction, lead to the avoidance of any potential conflict. Thus in the narrator's brief biography of Dubslav in ch. 1, Dubslav's reasons for not remarrying after the death of his first wife are given as these:

> Sich eine neue zu nehmen, widerstand ihm, halb aus Ordnungssinn und halb aus ästhetischer Rücksicht. (408)

These two factors working in opposite directions are precisely what contrive to bring about Schach von Wuthenow's suicide.

The whole problem of marriage across the boundaries of social classes is bypassed in *Der Stechlin* by bringing together two people from the same class, the nobility. The agonizing issue avoided finds extensive treatment elsewhere, e.g. in the renunciation of Botho and Lene in *Irrungen Wirrungen*. Botho is obliged to marry his richer cousin Käthe to stay within the noble class but also, in a more binding sense, to repair his family's rundown fortunes. His mother's letter which seals his fate appeals to his responsibility for his family — "Du hast unser aller Zukunft in der Hand" (I, 403). And in this context Käthe's mother's professed attitude — "Herr von Rienäcker *sei* frei von dem Augenblick an, wo er frei sein wolle" (ibid.) — simulates a freedom of choice that does not exist beyond a theoretical level.

Whatever Botho might want is of no significance here. The swaying factor is the compulsion from outside his own person which is oblivious to his own preference. In this sense he explains in a letter to Lene: "Ich hatte Briefe von Haus, die mich zwingen; es muß sein, und weil es sein muß, so sei es schnell . . ." (I, 408). His mother had advised: "Ein Rückzug ist ehrenvoller als fernere Hinausschiebung" (I, 403), and once the word "ehrenvoller" appeared the whole ethical code of the nobility was brought to bear on him. Thus the apparent freedom that Käthe's mother grants him is wholly deceptive. Such predetermined alliances have only a superficial flexibility — the individuals concerned are in fact governed wholly by the dictates of their estate.

The same class-barrier leads to the suicide of the young Graf Haldern in *Stine*, while in *Frau Jenny Treibel* the border between the lower and the upper bourgeoisie proves equally rigid when Corinna Schmidt tests it in her designs on young Treibel. Schmidt assures Marcell towards the end of the novel: "In eine Herzogsfamilie kann man allenfalls hineinkommen, in eine Bourgeoisfamilie nicht" (I, 1001). In the central story of *Der Stechlin* the matter of class barriers does not arise, and furthermore the consideration which ultimately determines Botho's move in *Irrungen Wirrungen* — the restoration of the family's fortunes — is provided for into the bargain as Woldemar marries into a richer family (see 652). Financial advantage, purely an incidental result of marriage for Woldemar, is elsewhere frequently its main function for a financially declining nobility.

The question of which of the Barby daughters will become Woldemar's wife is a subject for piquant speculation, but is never a conflict. Any potential for divisiveness is removed when Melusine immediately blesses the engagement upon learning of it. The only hint of a triangle comes when Woldemar says to Armgard: "Welche liebenswürdige Schwester Sie haben" (651), to which she replies while blushing, which distinguishes her from Melusine's coquetry:

"Sie werden mich eifersüchtig machen."

"Wirklich, Komtesse? "

"Vielleicht . . . Gute Nacht." (ibid.)

And as Armgard correctly senses, these few words of parting are tantamount to a proposal, a dénouement to the jestingly sustained rivalry between the sisters that is handled by Fontane with irreducible economy. A similar device is used to similar effect in *Stine*. Throughout ch. 5 we are regaled with the inconsequential chatter and superficial brilliance of most of the company assembled at Pauline Pittelkow's. Their repartee extends for pages. In the second last paragraph they are finally brought together in the rendering of a song, harmonizing their four different parts. But the last paragraph finally turns attention to the two guests who have remained wholly outside the social banter. And though it is described in a single, short sentence, theirs is the only significant action of the whole evening: "Nur der junge Graf und Stine schwiegen und wechselten Blicke" (I, 509).

All such elements of conflict as those in *Irrungen Wirrungen*, though handled in these other works with a minimum of drama, are absent in *Der Stechlin*, and thus the relationship between the individual and the society he finds himself in is even more static, the novelist's only concern being fluctuations within that social order. Julius Petersen aptly characterizes

den Gradualismus von Typen, die keine Entwicklung durchmachen, sondern im einzelnen fest bleiben, aber in ihrer Aufeinanderfolge eine Entwicklung des sozialen und religiösen Gewissens und Gesamtbewußtseins der Zeit repräsentieren. [12]

The accents are consequently different from those in many of his other works. There is no sense here of society's dictates overriding individual volition as already observed in *Irrungen Wirrungen*. The same conflict is present in its most crystallized form in Instetten's challenge of Crampas in *Effi Briest*. This meaningless action, reluctantly taken, is required by the petrified code of morality and honour. By Fontane's last novel the theme of adultery has vanished. It recurs elsewhere in Fontane's works as a symptom of brittleness, the brittleness of marriage which, itself a microcosm of society, epitomizes the fragility of the social order. In this respect Fontane, a descendant of Jane Austen on so many counts — the primacy of manners, class conventions and conversation — stands at the opposite pole to her. For in Jane Austen marriage is the ultimate of those manners which dominate character, and marriage as an institution is affirmed without being compromised or coloured by the particular age. In *Der Stechlin* the whole issue recedes as Fontane focusses attention on the role and survival of the nobility in society. Why the nobility and not another class is explained by Paul Böckmann:

Der Adel ist nicht dargestellt, weil er als gültige Lebensform anerkannt würde, sondern weil sich an ihm die Bedeutung der geschichtlichen Wandlungen, das Verhältnis von alten und neuen Lebensformen am deutlichsten ablesen läßt. [13]

Thus Fontane's assessment of his novel can be endorsed without succumbing to the danger of blindly accepting an author's statement on his own work. From the few comparisons with earlier novels made so far, it would seem that this *Zeitroman* does represent a departure from the established methods of the genre to that time, a point to be examined further in the following, more detailed analysis of the work.

2. The Old and the New

These two concepts, each relativizing the other, form a leitmotif in the work. Their substance naturally changes. Melusine formulates this when speaking to Lorenzen:

> Ich respektiere das Gegebene. Daneben aber freilich auch das Werdende, denn eben dies Werdende wird über kurz oder lang abermals ein Gegebenes sein. (677)

Old and New are referred to so often that they almost attain the status of generally valid concepts rather than being subjectively-toned terms used by individual speakers. Why should this be so? Firstly, a perspective which emphasizes the Old, even if still surviving in many forms, and the New, even if anticipated, would seem to have reference to an age of transition.[14] This must involve a keen consciousness of the crosscurrents acting on one's own age, which has no unique identity and no developed sense of confidence such as that of the materially prospering bourgeoisie of the *Gründerjahre*. There is evidence, especially in his later letters to Friedländer, that Fontane felt the later 1890's to be just such an era, his most famous comment being the following:

> Mein Haß gegen alles, was die neue Zeit aufhält, ist in einem beständigen Wachsen und die Möglichkeit, ja die Wahrscheinlichkeit, daß dem Sieg des Neuen eine furchtbare Schlacht voraufgehen muß, kann mich nicht abhalten, diesen Sieg des Neuen zu wünschen. [15]

The rise of the Social Democrats was no meteoric, overnight affair. Some months before the introduction of Bismarck's *Sozialistengesetz* (1878), designed to thwart the party, Fontane had written to his wife:

> Millionen von Arbeitern sind gerade so gescheit, so gebildet, so ehrenhaft wie Adel und Bürgerstand; vielfach sind sie ihnen überlegen. (FLB, 383)

But twenty years later, in his final novel, Fontane is primarily concerned with Social Democracy as a part of the New, and not with its actual historical progress. This may be asserted despite the references to contemporary figures such as Bebel and Stöcker. Strech writes:

> Aus den Belegen von Petersen geht hervor, daß Fontane eine dokumentarische Darstellung der tatsächlichen politischen Verhältnisse des von ihm in den Blick gerückten ländlichen Wahlkreises völlig außer acht ließ. Die Wahl gewinnt, wer sie zu dem damaligen Zeitpunkt an dieser Stelle überhaupt nicht gewinnen konnte: die Sozialdemokratie. [16]

Thus historical evidence alone is not sufficient to explain Fontane's treatment of the New in this form.

The other possibility in considering the balance between the Old and the New is an aesthetic consideration. In most of Fontane's earlier proseworks the conclusion had been anything but harmonious, at least at the level of individual happiness. But here it is, deeply so. The central symbol from which the work takes its title stands constant and frames the novel, both opening and closing its pages. Lake Stechlin embodies the Old and the New brought together, having by repute registered the Lisbon earthquake of the preceding century and being capable — at least Woldemar is confident of the fact — of reacting to eruptions of Vesuvius (794). It registers, but also survives, all flux. This is what is sought for in all the polarities of Old and New in the novel, whether in politics, religion, or whatever — the common, lasting ground which emerges from the combination, embracing at once what is worth retaining from the past and what are valuable innovations. This whole line of argument is summarized in Melusine's words to Lorenzen:

> Alles Alte, soweit es Anspruch darauf hat, sollen wir lieben, aber für das Neue sollen wir recht eigentlich leben. Und vor allem sollen wir, wie der Stechlin uns lehrt, den großen Zusammenhang der Dinge nie vergessen. (677)

One is reminded irresistibly that in *Der Zauberberg* Hans Castorp's grandfather, Hans Lorenz Castorp, observed "den steten Zusammenhang der Dinge" (III, 40).

The aesthetic consideration is not exhausted by the title-symbol. In Fontane's other prose works — tales and novels; many of Fontane's works occupy a border-region — some particular problem or area of problems is generally emphasized. But though these other works employ to great effect conversation, *Der Stechlin* as his conversation novel par excellence produces different problems. A great range of subjects for discussion, dispute and reflection, but not the instigation of significant action, is essayed. It could be argued that Fontane's last novel favours more general, less definitive terms, as does the late Goethe. But the terms "das Alte" and "das Neue" can better be approached from the aesthetic requirements of the work. They not only lend themselves to the range of subjects treated but accord with the character of the title-figure, who sees both sides of every coin and can furthermore look back over his life with a gaze that detects general currents rather than sharp contours.

The Old-New theme appears in ch. 1 (see p. 98 ff.) and then in a discussion between Lorenzen and Woldemar in ch. 3. The former's imagery at the beginning reminds us again of the title-symbol. He expounds his ideal:

> "Einen Brunnen graben just an der Stelle, wo man gerade steht. Innere Mission in nächster Nähe, sei's mit dem Alten, sei's mit etwas Neuem."
> "Also mit dem Neuen," sagte Woldemar und reichte seinem alten Lehrer die Hand.
> Aber dieser antwortete: "Nicht so ganz unbedingt mit dem Neuen. Lieber mit dem Alten, soweit es irgend geht, und mit dem Neuen nur, soweit es muß." (430)

This establishes from the outset the balance between the two concepts which is to prevail throughout the work.[17] The dialectic can appear much less obtrusively, for example in the following description of Czako:

> [. . .] ein ganz *moderner,* politisch stark angekränkelter Mensch, der, bei strammster Dienstlichkeit, zu all dergleichen Überspanntheiten ziemlich kritisch stand. Der *alte* Dubslav nahm indessen von alledem nichts wahr [. . .] . (443-44) (author's emphasis)

Here the adjective describing Dubslav is almost passed over because it seems so trivial compared with the detailed depiction of Czako's attitude. Yet it only superficially refers to his age and summarizes with the whole concentrated force of a symbol the opposite position to Czako's.

This is the essence of Dubslav, his conservative core, yet not in the sense of a blind onesidedness. When Dubslav does criticize the New it is in comical rather than earnest terms, a momentary impatience which is checked the next moment by his sense of justice. By the lakeside he reviews his life: "Altes und Neues, seine Kindheits- und seine Leutnantstage" (631). His thoughts trace Woldemar's growth: "[. . .] und lernte bei Lorenzen all das dumme Zeug, das Neue (dran vielleicht doch was war)" (ibid.). He certainly does not rank with the post-French Revolution nobility pilloried by Ernst von

Wolzogen in his brochure "Linksum kehrt schwenkt marsch — Trab!" (1895):

> [. . .] seit der Zeit hat er in verhängnisvoller Verblendung seine Aufgabe darin gesehen, unter allen Umständen das Alte gegen das Neue zu verteidigen. [18]

Dubslav's great respect for Lorenzen as contrasted with Rex' attitude to the pastor illustrates this clearly, when the theme of Old and New [19] in religious belief is discussed by Rex and Czako. The two review their first social contacts on the Stechlin estate. Rex even overlooks Lorenzen in favour of Katzler, but when reminded of him by Czako, he describes him in terms revealing the hostility with which he views the New:

> Ja, diese von der neuesten Schule, das sind die allerschlimmsten [. . .]. Sie haben ein neues [Christentum], und das überlieferte behandeln sie despektierlich. (446-47)

In actual fact, Lorenzen alone among his longstanding friends fails to disappoint the dying Dubslav, and at no stage seeks to undermine him. In his striking dialogue with Melusine in ch. 29 he pinpoints the true source of Rex' zealousness:

> Es gibt hier um uns her eine große Zahl vorzüglicher Leute, die ganz ernsthaft glauben, das uns Überlieferte — das Kirchliche voran (leider nicht das Christliche) — müsse verteidigt werden [. . .]. (678)

Rex sees only systems that counter each other, whereas Dubslav shows a breadth of vision; for him the depth of his human contact to Lorenzen is alone decisive. This impression is strengthened when the two come together shortly afterwards and the pastor figures again in conversation. It is incidentally a turn in the conversation arising from a favouring of old jokes over new ones, showing that the springboard for a discussion of the two concepts can be found in sundry spheres. Dubslav reiterates Lorenzen's views:

> "Die aristokratische Welt habe abgewirtschaftet, und nun komme die demokratische . . ."
> "Sonderbare Worte für einen Geistlichen," sagte Rex, "für einen Mann, der doch die durch Gott gegebenen Ordnungen kennen sollte."
> Dubslav lachte. "Ja, das bestreitet er Ihnen. Und ich muß bekennen, es hat manches für sich, trotzdem es mir nicht recht paßt." (452)

Again, Rex is hopelessly cramped in his appraisal by theoretical systems, in this case a supposed divine right sanction for the status quo. He attacks Lorenzen in his professional capacity,[20] with which he associates certain inflexible notions. Dubslav on the other hand reports Lorenzen's viewpoint impartially, without any appeal to a higher order and with no hint of the moralizing and patronizing "sollte" used by Rex in the passage quoted above. And though he doesn't share it, he is sufficiently generous in outlook to acknowledge what Lorenzen's opinion has to recommend it.

These examples all show the structure of this particular formal possibility of the *Zeitroman.* Crosscurrents in contemporary politics and religion emerge not through direct depiction, nor through any action on the part of the main characters. Instead the attitudes of two characters to these matters are crystallized by reference to a third character, who in turn advances his own viewpoint later. In the playing off of opinions against each other two features emerge: firstly, a rounded analysis of the matter under discussion, and secondly, the gradual delineation of character traits moulding these attitudes. "Alles Plauderei, Dialog, in dem sich die Charaktere geben, mit und in ihnen die Geschichte."
Lorenzen is present on both occasions when the whole problem of Old and New is

grappled with programmatically. In the first instance he converses with Melusine, who speaks in almost aphoristic terms and yields before the full implication of Lorenzen's statements. After the already quoted attack against institutionalized tradition in the Church, he criticizes it in the State too, where it can appear as an unquestioning acceptance of Prussian values as the highest. He concludes in words that make perfectly concrete the restructured social foundations of the new society:

> Der Hauptgegensatz alles Modernen gegen das Alte besteht darin, daß die Menschen nicht mehr durch ihre Geburt auf den von ihnen einzunehmenden Platz gestellt werden. Sie haben jetzt die Freiheit, ihre Fähigkeiten nach allen Seiten hin und auf jedem Gebiete zu betätigen. Früher war man dreihundert Jahre lang ein Schloßherr oder ein Leinenweber; jetzt kann jeder Leinenweber eines Tages ein Schloßherr sein. (678)

This mobility of social status is described in disapproving terms by Gundermann when toasting Dubslav (598). The theme can be traced through from Immermann's *Die Epigonen*. Its implications are too great for Melusine, who replies with a laugh that it is almost possible for a lord of a castle to become a weaver too. But her laughter is hollow, her own vested interest in the nobility's status precludes any more probing elaboration of the theme, and the topic of social forms is taken up. Here too Lorenzen is relentless in his visionary utterances. He criticizes the idolization of noble norms as if they were "etwas ewig zu Konservierendes" (679). The latter undoubtedly has a second meaning with an ironic barb, as the term "einpökeln" recurs in Fontane's attacks on the nobility (see FLB, 285 and 295). For Lorenzen the primary achievement of Friedrich Wilhelm I lay not in his stabilization of the monarchy: "[. . .] er hat auch, was viel wichtiger, die Fundamente für eine neue Zeit geschaffen" (679). That new era, the glory of the nobility under Frederick the Great and then again in the Wars of Liberation against Napoleon, is past, and has left a gigantic delusion:

> Unsre alten Familien kranken durchgängig an der Vorstellung, daß es ohne sie nicht gehe, was aber weit gefehlt ist, denn es geht sicher auch ohne sie; [. . .] vorläufig [. . .] stehen wir im Zeichen einer demokratischen Weltanschauung. Eine neue Zeit bricht an. Ich glaube, eine bessere und eine glücklichere. (680-81)

It is precisely the fact that "eine Bedeutung für das Ganze"[21] is lacking in the old-style nobility which necessitates the "Synthese von Alt und Neu" (Strech). This in turn lends the novel the dimensions of a *Zeitroman* as opposed to a provincial work of purely local significance.

Lorenzen's vision admittedly tapers off, and he returns from his prophetic note to one of flattery for Melusine's sex: "Die Frauen bestimmen schließlich doch alles" (681). It is a property of this conversational mode of the novel that statements bordering on the inflammatory are left suspended, neither leading on to nor reflecting any direct action. Melusine dispels the fervour of what Lorenzen has been saying and flees before its implications into a nonetheless ironized idyllic setting:

> Und nun erlauben Sie mir, nach diesem unserm revolutionären Diskurse, zu den Hütten friedlicher Menschen zurückzukehren. (ibid.) [22]

There is another reason too why Lorenzen's ideas here cannot be further elaborated on, and that is the critical stance adopted towards the bourgeoisie in this novel (see p. 102ff.).

This feature of deeds being discussed but not enacted is not confined to Lorenzen's statements. It is not the concern of Fontane to explore the new ground frequently heralded, but to maintain an equipoise between the elements of tradition and progress. Dubslav is a very enlightened member of his class, but still inseparable from that class. Lorenzen's ideas look further forward, but in the case of his impetuously progressive fledgling, Woldemar, he counsels moderation. And Woldemar, in whose hands the future of the Stechlin estate and family lies at the novel's conclusion, is far less clearly delineated than his father or his adviser, so that the New, as in *Martin Salander,* receives no detailed exposition. Indeed the New for its own sake, an unprincipled embracing of the New, is rejected just as strongly as an empty clinging to the Old, not only by Dubslav and Lorenzen, but in Uncke's doubts about Isidor Hirschfeld (672).

The following quotation is symptomatic of the novel:

> Ich habe mit meinem Woldemar, der einen stark liberalen Zug hat (ich kann es nicht loben und mags nicht tadeln) oft über diese Sache gesprochen. Er war natürlich für Neuzeit, also für Experimente [. . .] . (716)

We only hear briefly of Woldemar's ideas here in the midst of a discussion between two venerable members of the nobility, Dubslav and Barby. The equipoise mentioned above is illustrated perfectly by the words in brackets — Dubslav is too bound to his older concepts to be able to praise his son's liberalism; at the same time he is sufficiently open to it not to want to criticize it.

The relativization doesn't always need to be so explicit. When Baruch Hirschfeld visits the ailing Dubslav, the latter introduces a nostalgic note with the words: "Aber lassen wir das schlimme Neue; das Alte war doch eigentlich besser (das heißt dann und wann)" (724). True, the brackets are there, the mental reservation, yet the illusory nature of this cosy view of the past is only shown when Baruch's true concern, namely with the ultimate takeover of the Stechlin estate, dawns on Dubslav (725-26). The Old is crumbling, with noble estates threatening to fall into the hands of Jewish usurers. Dubslav defers the New in highly ironic terms; referring Baruch to Woldemar for the transaction he suggests:

> [. . .] vielleicht können Sie gemeinschaftlich mal was Nettes herauswirtschaften, was Ordentliches, was Großes, was sich sehen lassen kann. Das heißt dann neue Zeit. (725)

So while the Old fades in beauty, the New remains distanced, the equipoise is retained in negative terms. And not only in this case — tendencies to the extreme of either pole are rejected completely, as when Sponholz' replacement Moscheles — "solchen Allerneuesten" (741) — is slated by Dubslav. Alternatively, what is seen here as a onesidedness can be viewed from a different perspective as a fusion of the two poles. This occurs when Lorenzen answers Dubslav's charge that he is proclaiming a new Christianity with the words: "[. . .] dies neue Christentum ist gerade das alte" (779).

The second major exposition of the Old-New theme comes just before Dubslav's death when he has Lorenzen summoned to his bedside. He elaborates on his hobby, "König und Kronprinz oder alte Zeit und neue Zeit" (776-77). His humour and imagination unimpeded to the last, he projects his prognostications into a fantasy-ball given by Woldemar and Armgard. Side by side with survivals from the past and the noble-caste are modern elements with which Woldemar flirts, socially cutting a count of the old line and expressing admiration for Bebel. Lorenzen assures Dubslav that his picture is at best that of an initial period of innovation before a return to familiar ways — "so halb und halb ins Alte" (779) as he puts it of Woldemar — inherited from the past. The phrase quoted further maintains the balance between the two concepts. This is enough for Dubslav, provided Lorenzen promises not to hinder any such return to the fold of the tradition-based nobility. The pastor agrees and seeks to play down the emphasis laid on his influence in any case, whatever direction it might take:

> Nicht *ich* werde ihn führen [. . .] . Die *Zeit* [author's emphasis] wird sprechen und neben der Zeit das neue Haus, die blasse junge Frau und vielleicht auch die schöne Melusine. (780)

The currents of the "Zeit" are what emerge repeatedly and are the ultimate object of the many conversations conducted. The "Zeit" becomes a prime moving force over and above the individual characters.

The one thing to transcend it is precisely Dubslav's greatest quality, present throughout the novel in his humility, tolerance and warm humour, and spelt out by Lorenzen in his funeral oration:

> Sah man ihn, so schien er ein Alter, auch in dem, wie er Zeit und Leben ansah; aber für die, die sein wahres Wesen kannten, war er kein Alter, freilich auch kein Neuer. Er hatte vielmehr das, was über alles Zeitliche hinaus liegt, was immer gilt und immer gelten wird: ein Herz. (787)

It is this attribute of Dubslav's which embodies the synthesis of Strech's title. It sets him apart from the unbalanced labours and attitudes of an Isidor or an Adelheid and from all blindness, hypocrisy and fanaticism. This principle behind the man, this lasting quality beyond the mortal individual, is extracted by Melusine in her letter at the conclusion of the novel. It is hinted at earlier by Dubslav on the broader level of the old Prussian nobility when he says they have "noch mehr Herz für die Torgelowschen im Leibe [. . .] als alle Torgelows zusammengenommen" (780). In the constant flux of temporal forces, with today's New becoming tomorrow's Old, the human heart is the one point of orientation, the essence surviving all vicissitudes.

3. *The first chapter*

The first chapter contains the bulk of the novel's concerns *in nuce.* In a novel with little plot and fewer dramatic tensions, the tranquil yet keenly observing narration opens with a description of the natural setting. It proceeds through details from the past and present in which the points of chronological orientation are drawn from Prussian history. Thus the rebuilding of the Stechlin residence is related to the accession of Friedrich Wilhelm I, while Dubslav's entry into the regiment coincides approximately with the accession of Friedrich Wilhelm IV. These parallels might have been expected anyway, but when Woldemar's birth is located as "wenig mehr als ein Jahr vor Ausbruch des vierundsechziger Kriegs" (408) the immediate correlation is less apparent. It becomes clear that the strand of personal history is to be seen in terms of history on a broader scale,[23] in this case that of the Prussian state, to which the fate of the Stechlin family is in any case inextricably bound. The constant reminder of the Prussian macrocosm alongside the noble family's microcosm also illustrates the motto of Lake Stechlin — "den großen Zusammenhang der Dinge nie vergessen" (677) — and is a further indication of the primacy of the age in this novel.

The narrator's gaze, after establishing the setting, roves deftly over a whole range of people, all of whom figure importantly in the novel, as importantly, that is, as any one individual can in accordance with the novel's concerns. Conversation as a characterizing element and the avoidance of potential conflicts are present from the outset, as is the Old-New theme in the dialogue between Hirschfeld father and son. Dubslav's "Herz" is also there immediately both in his humour and, with the slightest of touches, in the conversation with which the chapter concludes. The central symbol of the novel, Lake Stechlin, is depicted at some length in the opening paragraph. This finishes with a motif that also recurs, though in a different guise: the superstition of the red rooster. Superstition appears in humorous vein when Dubslav threatens to haunt Lorenzen (780). There is far less ironic distance in Melusine's fear of sleeping in the canopy-bed (666) — the Chinaman in *Effi Briest* being the obvious precursor — or of breaking the lake's ice lest the rooster should appear (674).

As with so much of his so-called realistic prose, Fontane concentrates meaning-laden images into his concrete descriptions. On the sloping terrace before the residence are "Kübel mit exotischen Blattpflanzen, darunter zwei Aloes" (407). Alongside one of these aloes an alien seed, the flowering rush, bursts forth each summer in a blaze of white and red, stunning all but the botanical connoisseur. The deception diverts Dubslav greatly, but again his ironic distance from this phenomenon — the false marrying of the prosaic with the exotic — strengthens his receptivity for the genuine blending of these elements in Lake Stechlin. The colours of the flowering rush seem to carry particular portents. Red and white were the colours of Kurbrandenburg. White recurs in the Prussian flag on the lookout tower; "die mit weiß und schwarzen Fliesen gedeckte Veranda" (412) reinforces its colours. Engelke wants to add a strip of red to the flag. But Dubslav opposes this suggestion with the reasoning:

> Laß. Ich bin nicht dafür. Das alte Schwarz und Weiß hält gerade noch; aber wenn du was Rotes drannähst, dann reißt es gewiß. (413) [24]

The red of the rooster is reflected in the red of little Agnes' stockings, applauded by Dubslav because of their intimidating effect on his sister Adelheid — "die sind ein Zeichen, eine hochgehaltene Fahne" (762)! There and in the case of the flowering rush he can afford a kind of playing with fire, a liberty also possible with opinions, since they are after all expressed, not implemented: "Er hörte gern eine freie Meinung, je drastischer und extremer, desto besser" (408). But the old Prussian flag is something altogether too close to home. The way he rejects the addition to it of red, quite clearly meant to represent revolutionary forces, is handled all too obviously. It is certainly a suggestive means of evoking contemporary history and incorporating a viewpoint on it. But whereas Fontane draws a great wealth of symbolic energy from Lake Stechlin, this particular symbol is contrived.

Dubslav himself is characterized in wholly sympathetic terms. His type — "der Typus eines Märkischen von Adel" (407) — is described elsewhere in scathing terms, and here the qualification follows: "[...] aber von der milderen Observanz" (ibid.). This is revealed in those qualities which so set him apart from his sister, encrusted as she is by tradition and parochialism. His pre-Hohenzollern ancestors give him a certain identity and pride, but he does not revel in them as self-justification. Even this deep-seated family tradition is exposed to the question mark he eternally places after things. This maintains his integrity before the delusion to which Adelheid succumbs, a "Wahn" Fontane describes in a letter to Friedländer:

> [...] man kann ihn [unsren Adel] besuchen wie das aegyptische Museum [...], aber das Land *ihm* zu Liebe regieren, in dem Wahn: *dieser Adel sei das Land,* — das ist unser Unglück [...]. (FLB, 310)

In Dubslav's case even his weaknesses are reckoned as merits because of his capacity for self-irony.

One of his most oft-quoted principles illustrates the ever-threatening borderland between Dubslav's healthy scepticism and sheer disorientation. "Unanfechtbare Wahrheiten gibt es überhaupt nicht" (408) is couched in the terms of a truism itself. But that form is at variance with the content of his assertion — if there are no incontestable truths, then the truth of this claim is also open to doubt — and thus follows a modification which at first glance seems to weaken the original statement: "[. . .] und wenn es welche gibt, so sind sie langweilig" (ibid.). This new form of the maxim becomes something of a programmatic utterance in the course of the novel, with its constant relativizing, suspicion towards particular one-sided directions, and frequent 180-degree turns on statements just made. To cite one example among many of what is meant by the latter — Woldemar writes in his diary of his father:

Das [a genuine *Junker* of the old school] ist er auch, aber doch auch wieder das volle Gegenteil davon. (518)

This problem of truth that resists categorizing carries over to the realm of communication. In the midst of an unspectacular biography of Dubslav, following him through his unheroic days of military service to his retirement to the Stechlin estate, the narrator inserts the following quotation from his subject:

"Wir glauben doch alle mehr oder weniger an eine Auferstehung" (das heißt, er persönlich glaubte eigentlich nicht daran) [. . .] . (408)

What seemed to be a revelatory credo is immediately retracted through the incursion of the narrator, whose sovereign manipulation of the characters throughout the work repudiates any naïvely realistic tendencies claimed for Fontane. At this early stage of the work we are not yet in a position to make the mental reservations contained in the narrator's insertion, but through such qualifications of the meaning expressed we become critical towards subsequent statements claiming any generality of validity. Such a radical dissection of the devices and actual import of communication is no great distance from confusion and ever-diminishing circles of meaning. But Fontane never oversteps the dividing line, and his scepticism achieves an injection of new energies in uncovering new sides of the object in question, instead of the dissipation of those already present.

Another aspect of this whole communication problem, the symbolic quality of names, also receives detailed exposition here. On the one hand there is the accumulation of associations behind the word "Stechlin" as this is applied in turn to the lake, the wood surrounding it, the village, the castle and the family. All bear the one name, all become organic components of the symbol with which the novel begins in its title and ends in the letter of Melusine. In other cases, names of people or names assigned to objects have no such harmonious effect. Dubslav is critical of his own Christian name as not reflecting the area into which he was born. The import of names — there is never a suggestion that they are arbitrary — is further elaborated in this chapter as a springboard for subsequent development. When Dubslav receives Woldemar's telegramme with the news that Rex and Czako are accompanying him, he ponders on whom to invite to a welcoming dinner:

Czako, das ginge vielleicht noch. Aber Rex, wenn ich ihn auch nicht kenne, zu so was Feinem wie Rex paß ich nicht mehr [. . .] . (414)

Thus the two officers are first introduced with a certain prejudgement on the basis of their names. These afford subsequent material for conversation too, or at least Czako's does, as it is on this note that both ultimately depart the scene before the novel's concluding pages. Czako is clearly smitten by Melusine but, being conscious of gradations within the nobility, is afflicted by doubts, which are revealingly related to his name: "Und dazu diese verteufelt vornehmen Namen: Barby, Ghiberti. Was soll da Czako? " (793). But Rex will have none of this evasion: "Italienisieren Sie sich und schreiben Sie sich von morgen ab Ciacco" (ibid.). This infuses Czako with fresh hope, and his final words, couched in two foreign languages, show him belying that background he seeks to escape: "Sapristi, Rex, c'est une idée" (ibid.). The issue thus evaporates on a light, playful note, but has been both a conversational strand and one of the vehicles for a reckoning with language.

A further example of this reckoning in the first chapter is found in the various appellations of the erstwhile castle. For Dubslav, "Schloß" is an inflated term; he writes at the head of letters "Haus Stechlin" and even uses the words "ein alter Kasten" (410). Rex combines the two sides of the building in the ironic epithet "Schloßkate" (420). Another case is the progression in the titles with which Dubslav vainly tries to approach the peculiar being and status of Katzler's wife:

> [. . .] und die Frau, das heißt die Gemahlin (und Gemahlin is eigentlich auch noch nicht das rechte Wort) [. . .]. (414)

The former example speaks eloquently of that freedom imputed to Dubslav by Woldemar and Lorenzen. A man-made edifice is no cause for conceit in his eyes. His pride is confined to the lake — "Das andere gibt es woanders auch, aber der See . . ." (454) — and in this he glories in a connection with the outside world to an extent probably not even enjoyed by the much-travelled Graf Barby. The connection between this tiny neck of the woods and the outside world, present in the symbol of Lake Stechlin, occurs in other instances too as when Lorenzen's Christian-Socialist tendencies are related to those of Stöcker in Berlin (429).

The polar opposite to Dubslav's breadth of outlook is his sister Adelheid, a crabbed survival of the obsolete caste-spirit. Her attitude also receives its exposition in the first chapter. Thus her financial aid to Dubslav is rendered

> nicht aus Liebe zu dem Bruder [. . .], sondern lediglich aus einem allgemeinen Stechlinschen Familiengefühl. Preußen war was und die Mark Brandenburg auch; aber das Wichtigste waren doch die Stechlins, und der Gedanke, das alte Schloß in andern Besitz und nun gar in einen solchen übergehen zu sehen, war ihr unerträglich. (411)

Prussia is the absolute limit of her field of vision, and even it is most decidedly secondary to family interests. At no stage does she escape the confines of her narrowness in response to the more liberal perspectives around her. She belongs to those contrasted with Graf Barby in the following extract from Woldemar's diary:

> Er weiß — was sie hierzulande nicht wissen oder nicht wissen wollen —, daß hinterm Berge auch noch Leute wohnen. Und mitunter noch ganz andre. (518)

His sister's caste-spirit is not to be found in Dubslav himself: he does not match the "gute Partie" (410) sought by his father in his three wives. At least we do not hear of such an economic rationale in Dubslav's case, only of the brief happiness shared by him and his wife. Both father and son are disposed of in this connection in a few lines, so that the whole issue of arranged alliances, treated in such ironic detail in *Frau Jenny Treibel,* is skirted here. Dubslav's financial need is met instead by his sister and by the Jewish usurer,

Baruch Hirschfeld. Unlike his more radical son, he is content to bide his time and wait for the estate to fall into his hands in due course. This threat to the Stechlin family — ever there, though never as great as that posed by Veitl Itzig in *Soll und Haben* — would seem to have been removed by the end of the novel with Woldemar's assured backing from his richer father-in-law. Thus the static quality of the novel implied by Fontane's verdict on it — the life-cycle of the family as the only real event — is somewhat misleading, as Woldemar will not be dependent on financiers.

As a final observation on ch. 1 of the novel, the Prussian flag is not alone in its tattered state:

> Eine große, etwas schadhafte Marquise war hier herabgelassen und gab Schutz gegen die Sonne, deren Lichter durch die schadhaften Stellen hindurchschienen und auf den Fliesen ein Schattenspiel aufführten. (412)

These signs prefigure Dubslav's fantasy at the end of the novel of the newly-married couple entertaining in a renovated residence. It places the novel in the long line we have already seen represented by Immermann's *Die Epigonen* and *Münchhausen,* with the rotting of the exterior mirroring the financial decline of the nobility. The notable difference here is that external decay is not symptomatic of an inner one, at least not in the case of the Stechlins and Barbys.

The novel begins as it ends, with Lake Stechlin and its feelers going out into all the world. The first chapter of the novel has a similar function — and for this reason it has received such detailed attention — in introducing almost all important elements of the succeeding work. The characterizations are in miniature form and yet so economically direct. Consider the following first mention in a conversation between Dubslav and Engelke of a couple to play no mean part in the subsequent story:

> "Was meinst du, ob die Gundermanns wohl können?"
> "Ach, die können schon. Er gewiß, und sie kluckt auch bloß immer so rum."
> "Also Gundermanns. Gut." (414)

The matter of inviting the Gundermanns is settled, but we already have a clear picture of husband, anxious to gain social acceptance, and wife, a fussy chatterbox.

4. Social classes

a) Bourgeoisie

The bourgeoisie certainly does not emerge as anything like a dominant force, as for instance in *Frau Jenny Treibel,* but the attitude adopted to it shows a similar disenchantment. Czako asks Dubslav in frivolous vein how the carp in Lake Stechlin reacts to the legendary red rooster:

> [...] ist er [...] ein Feigling, der sich in seinem Moorgrund verkriecht, also ein Bourgeois, der am andern Morgen fragt: 'Schießen sie noch?' (427)

Here a comment on the social standing of the bourgeois is couched in witty conversational tone. There is no elaborated discussion, and in fact the class which had figured prominently with Immermann and Spielhagen is of minimal interest here.

Certainly Gundermann, though recently ennobled, is to be regarded as bourgeois at heart in his crass materialism and vain attempts to gain full acceptance in noble circles. In a terse, atypically harsh verdict, Lorenzen describes him thus: "Gundermann ist ein Bourgeois und ein Parvenu, also so ziemlich das Schlechteste, was einer sein kann" (579). Yet Gundermann's dubious status within the nobility does not always reflect on him. It does when he advocates doing away with the *Reichstag* and is criticized by von Molchow:

> Es ist doch 'ne Wahrheit, daß sich [...] die Stände jedesmal selbst ruinieren. Das heißt, von 'Ständen' kann hier eigentlich nicht die Rede sein; denn dieser Gundermann gehört nicht mit dazu. (599)

But not, or at least not exclusively on him, when his reservations about Lorenzen's funeral oration for Dubslav are patronizingly observed by the " 'Alten und Echten' (die wohl *sich,* aber nicht *ihm* ein Recht der Kritik zuschrieben)" (788). Here the authentic noblemen's caste-spirit rebounds on their heads.

Familiar attitudes emerge again in Frau Gundermann's following criticism of the local nobility:

> [sie] legen alles auf die Goldwaage. Das heißt, vieles legen sie nicht auf die Goldwaage, dazu reicht es bei den meisten nicht aus; nur immer die Ahnen. (431)

The oft-observed financial decline of the nobility and their recourse to family tradition — applicable to Adelheid, but certainly not to Dubslav — are coupled with an odd sublimation of materialism by imputing that to them too, until the succeeding spiteful observation, contradicting this claim, gives the speaker even more pleasure. Frau Gundermann expresses pride in her husband's business acumen in building up a timber empire. Yet the true state of his splendour is exposed when Woldemar, Rex and Czako are passed by his cart:

> [...] eine ziemlich ramponiert aussehende Halbchaise, das lederne Verdeck zurückgeschlagen [...] die Sitze leer, alles an dem Fuhrwerk ließ Ordnung und Sauberkeit vermissen; das eine Pferd war leidlich gut, das andre schlecht, und zu dem neuen Livreerock des Kutschers wollte der alte Hut [...] nicht recht passen. (470-71)

Frequently Fontane inserts wry authorial comments on people but rarely at any length. The above is quoted extensively to show the sustained indictment of the owner through a merciless description of his vehicle. The rub lies in the final touch of the coachman's new coat not matching his old hat, mirroring in a single image the half-baked nature of Gundermann himself, trying to blend his newly-attained status with his long-held one and failing dismally. There is no synthesis of the Old and the New here. But he is presumably as unaware of this self-ridicule as of the self-irony contained in his favourite catchcry, "Wasser auf die Mühlen der Sozialdemokratie," harking back as it does to his own mills, all seven of them. A possibility for genuine advancement, politics, is for him no more than an object for dilettantic dabbling, just as Treibel never became really involved and entrusted his hapless campaign to Lieutenant Vogelsang. Gundermann lacks all pretension to culture and does not even look at the pictures in newspapers.

His wife is a fitting soul-mate, finding "gelehrig" (435) Czako's lengthy story of a rat-hunt in the sewers of Paris. This is the only time Czako lapses into such an eccentric tale in the novel, undoubtedly a commentary on his assessment of his table-companion and what degree of taste he can presuppose in her. He has gauged her ignorance of the

French language in translating the phrase "Oeil-de-Boeuf" (ibid.) for her, and it was she who broached the topic of rats with sufficient detail, midst her protested distaste, to give herself away. The whole episode seems to be a consciously grotesque distortion of the novel's title-symbol. Instead of dwelling on the characteristic features of a city undoubtedly unfamiliar to Frau Gundermann, Czako chooses to expand this curious item of conversation. Lake Stechlin brings together world crosscurrents: Czako's guide through Paris ignores the city's truly notable features or distorts them. "Oben drei Millionen Franzosen, unten drei Millionen Ratten" (434), and the seething metropolis "oben" remains faceless. Among art-treasures the Venus de Milo alone is mentioned, and that as a calculated appeal to Frau Gundermann's feigned prurience. Czako's dismissal of Paris' attractions — "Und das alles haben wir schließlich auch, und manches haben wir noch besser" (ibid.) — is likewise guaranteed to reinforce her chauvinist core.

It is characteristic of this novel that the damning picture of Frau Gundermann emerging above is relativized first to her social milieu and then to other classes. Dubslav excuses her own dubious story about rats as "Berliner Stil" (441), reinforcing the narrator's toning-down of her individuality:

> Denn eigentlich hatte sie für gar nichts Interesse, sie mußte bloß, richtige Berlinerin, die sie war, reden können. (438)

Dubslav's breadth of vision does not fail him, even here. Having called her in conversation with Czako "eine Vollblutberlinerin," he adds:

> Aber wir von Adel müssen in diesem Punkte doch ziemlich milde sein [. . .]. Unser eigenstes Vollblut bewegt sich auch in Extremen [. . .]. (441)

This is a genuine striving for a balanced perspective. The person of Frau Gundermann recedes behind the type, a type not confined to any one level. The characterization of her as speaking for the sake of hearing her own voice is also of course of particular significance. For the debasing of conversation to an end in itself is ample comment on a figure in a work where conversation is the vehicle of character-exposition.

A further strong criticism of the bourgeoisie comes from Onkel Hartwig, cited by the domestic Hedwig to support her own complaints about employers' hospitality: "[. . .] der Bourgeois tut nichts für die Menschheit. Und wer nichts für die Menschheit tut, der muß abgeschafft werden" (550). This dissatisfaction is reflected but never voiced in such class-conscious terms by Hedwig, who misses a proper "Schlafgelegenheit" (549) in her place of employ, even with upper bourgeois families; "bei Hofrats" (550) she was quartered in a cluttered-up bathroom. Her complaint does not assume political dimensions — she expresses loyalty to the state — but is simply against the inhuman working conditions. These are described in graphic detail, the now proscribed "Hängeböden" (ibid.)[25] among them, but the economic causes are not examined. It is significant that Hedwig finally finds satisfactory and settled conditions when employed by Armgard and Woldemar at the end of the novel — Engelke and Jeserich are instances of exemplary service under the patronage of exemplary masters.

b) *Social Democracy*

Unlike the bourgeoisie, the proletariat receives considerable attention in the novel, still as something rather amorphous. But if its implications are as yet unforeseeable to most, the few of Graf Barby's vision see the most burning issue of their time to be ob sich der vierte Stand etabliert und stabiliert (denn darauf läuft doch in ihrem vernünftigen Kern die ganze Sache hinaus) [. . .]. (545)

Such a sober appraisal is, however, rare. For Gundermann the bogey of Social Democracy is forever having grist brought to its mills, while for Schulze Kluckhuhn it is likened to the spectral bane of the Danish warship "Rolf Krake." Gundermann's criticism in particular loses all incisive thrust through repetition *ad nauseam,* while his own shortcomings are never very far away. Thus his reasons are given for defending the new possibilities of telegraphy in an outburst against innovations which are, predictably, "Wasser auf die Mühlen der Sozialdemokratie": "Und dabei das beständige Schwanken der Kurse. Namentlich auch in der Mühlen- und Brettschneidebranche . . ." (425). Dubslav interrupts him before his Mammonism can take fuller flight.

Even beyond its unworthy opponents Social Democracy never loses its suspect nature in this novel. Woldemar's "Schimmer von Sozialdemokratie" (420) is branded by Czako as "Freiheitsluxusse" and seen as running counter to his position in the army. Granted that at the end he leaves his army post and is greeted warmly to his estates by the Globsower, the Old is at best waning rapidly, the New has still not emerged in any clear form. Lorenzen, who is sympathetic to their cause, does not seem to expect a Social Democrats' victory in the local election.

The winds of change are crystallized in a conversation between Hirschfelds senior and junior on voting in the election. Dubslav's personal stature is never questioned, even by his opponents, but Isidor Hirschfeld prefers to the venerable old man's spotless character a platform in which he sees the correct principle and the interests of humanity (567). The sordid reality behind these lofty-sounding notions becomes apparent all too soon. Dubslav's carriage stops to take on the drunkard Tuxen, prostrate from the excesses of the Social Democrats' victory celebrations. Dubslav presses him — with amusement, not resentment — as to his political choice, and this proves to be based on no concrete grievances but on hopes, above all for a patch for potato-growing in a juster land distribution (606). This platform is cast in a very dubious light by being presented at two removes, coming firstly not from the campaigner but from one of his less impressive supporters, and secondly with that supporter not being in full command of himself. Lorenzen sums up the sad mobility of the "Volk": "Denn auf das arme Volk ist kein Verlaß. Ein Versprechen und ein Kornus, und alles schnappt ab" (579). The harrying of Bennigsen elsewhere elicits a similarly pessimistic comment from him on the lack of imagination of the electorate:

Jedes höher gesteckte Ziel, jedes Wollen, das über den Kartoffelsack hinausgeht, findet kein Verständnis, sicherlich keinen Glauben. (776)

Uncke questions the integrity of Isidor's principle and also tells Dubslav that Torgelow is making an uncertain start to his parliamentary career. Even his own supporters find him "zweideutig" (671), a quality which Uncke sees as the besetting sin of modern change. It is the negative correlate of Dubslav's capacity to see an issue from various sides. Dubslav reiterates his interest in Torgelow's doings when talking again with Uncke shortly before his death. This follows his assessment: "Und die Sozialdemokratie will auch hoch raus" (774). But these unmellowed aspirations of the eruptive political force do not cause Dubslav concern, in fact he says:

Nu kann Torgelow zeigen, daß er nichts kann. Und die andern auch. Und wenn sie's alle gezeigt haben, na, dann sind wir vielleicht wieder dran [. . .]. Vorläufig aber müssen wir abwarten und den sogenannten 'Ausbruch' verhüten und dafür sorgen, daß unsere Globsower zufrieden sind. (ibid.)

The terms in which Dubslav speaks here have a direct bearing on the question of the meeting of Old and New in a historically transitional era. These are admittedly the visionary utterances of a man on his deathbed, steeped in the traditions of a class experiencing a decline he feels to be temporary. They imply an answer in the negative to the burning question of the time posed by Barby (see p. 105). But this is a wholly organic work, and Dubslav's idea here has been anticipated in his comments to Barby:

> Das Junkertum [. . .] hat in dem Kampf dieser Jahre kolossal an Macht gewonnen, mehr als irgendeine andre Partei, die Sozialdemokratie kaum ausgeschlossen, und mitunter ist mirs, als stiegen die seligen Quitzows wieder aus dem Grabe herauf. Und wenn das geschieht, [. . .] so können wir was erleben. Es heißt immer: 'unmöglich' [. . .]. Nichts ist unmöglich. (715)

c) Class-relationships

For all his smiling indulgence towards Tuxen's hopes, Dubslav himself has advanced a similar idea elsewhere. In a tirade against the evil designs he sees behind the Globsowers' glass factory, he says he would prefer to avert "die große Generalweltanbrennung" (469) by meeting their basic economic needs. Lorenzen smilingly retorts: "[. . .] das ist ja die reine Neulandtheorie. Das wollen ja die Sozialdemokraten auch" (470). But this brings a rather impatient reaction from Dubslav, who doesn't continue the topic. It can possibly be said that Dubslav appreciates progressive ideas but still recoils when a tag is put on them, disliking such constrictions. On the other hand it may be a realization that his own pronouncements can only sound liberal and disinterested from within his own sphere, having a progressive ring but only relatively so, until for instance the Social Democrats are mentioned. At all events the incident, as well as furthering the Old-New theme, hints at a phenomenon to be examined further in this novel and to be discussed also in connection with *Im Schlaraffenland,* namely the fading of class boundaries.

The most striking instance of this here — striking, admittedly, because of its rarity — is the marriage of the Princess of Ippe-Büchsenstein with the bourgeois Katzler. The real-life precedent of this was the marriage between the Prinzessin von Hohenlohe-Schillingsfürst and the bourgeois portrait-painter Richard Lanchert.[26] The Princess' efforts to conform to her new station are intriguing in the contrast they form to the far more common case of bathing in past or reflected glory. This is of course the prerogative of the more debilitated nobility such as von der Nonne (see 589), but also of prestige-seekers like Koseleger, of whom Dubslav says: "Er war Galopin bei 'ner Großfürstin; das kann er nicht vergessen" (585). It is consonant with this novel's emphases that the Katzlers' marriage is presented as a *fait accompli* and primarily as a touchstone for other people's verbal reactions to it.

Thus Rex finds the alliance, and above all its prodigious progeny, beyond his comprehension. He immediately expresses his disgust: "Diese Ausgiebigkeit [. . .] ist doch eigentlich das Bürgerlichste, was es gibt" (476). Then after hearing more details of the Princess' attitude he changes his own completely and rationalizes her action as "andauernde Opferung eines Innersten und Höchsten" (477). He admires her — "Welch ein Maß von Entsagung" (ibid.) — and to further what seems to be a conscious parody of Classical concepts, the Princess' highest value in life is "Pflicht," which she explicitly contrasts with "Neigung" (582). Rex views her action positively, although in point of fact she divests herself of noble ties through a strenuous adherence to the moral imperative of Duty.[27]

106

Lorenzen assesses her aptly: "Alles an ihr ist ein wenig überspannt" (586), and this verdict applies to her sense of duty, which can be warped to the point of contravening nature. For while lying in childbed she sends her husband off to the elections "mit der Bemerkung, daß im modernen bürgerlichen Staate Wählen so gut wie Kämpfen sei" (588). Her behaviour thus does not reflect an outlook which has simply adapted to a new station in life, but forever shows self-consciousness and self-moulding.

In short, this marriage is a mistake. This is shown symbolically in the death in childbirth of four of their seven children and the fact that although with each child they hope for a son, the survivors are all daughters, so that there is no male heir to continue the new hybrid line. It is also shown in Dubslav's verdicts. In congratulating Woldemar on his choice of a bride, he writes: "[. . .] höher hinauf geht es kaum, Du müßtest Dich denn bis ins Katzlersche verirren" (652). And then after an attempt by the Princess to minister to Dubslav's soul while he lies sick, the old man reflects:

> Es ist doch nicht gut, wenn Prinzessinnen in Oberförsterhäuser einziehn. Sie sind dann aus ihrem Fahrwasser heraus und greifen nach allem möglichen, um in der selbstgeschaffenen Alltäglichkeit nicht unterzugehn. (739-40)

Dubslav's ultimate disillusionment comes when the Princess and Koseleger plan founding a refuge for neglected children (781) and suggest Agnes as their first charge. This draws from him an indictment of pious princesses, which is another instance where a reaction to an action or attitude is more important than the action itself.

Further light is cast on the nobility from a completely different direction by Adelheid:

> Was ich Adel nenne, das gibt es nur noch in unsrer Mark und in unsrer alten Nachbar- und Schwesterprovinz, ja, da vielleicht noch reiner als bei uns. (563)

The following genealogy of other German nobility and its inadequacies, her gross conceit — "und dann haben wir hier noch zweierlei: in unserer Bevölkerung die reine Lehre und in unserm Adel das reine Blut" (564) — her feigned dismissal of money as a factor in considering an alliance, everything here and elsewhere brands her as the antipole to her brother's broad, undogmatic, generous outlook.

The ultimate confrontation between Dubslav and Adelheid comes when he takes young Agnes into his house both as a diversion and as an insurance against visitation by Adelheid. She in turn stands on the tradition she feels to be slighted by such a move, and transmits her own standards to Dubslav, though he himself never makes any great issue of family or of noble connections to throne and empire (763). She holds an ambiguous position, and again it is an élitist one, on the matter of waning social distinctions. She deplores Agnes' stockings: "[. . .] sie sind ein Zeichen davon, daß alle Vernunft aus der Welt ist und alle gesellschaftliche Scheidung immer mehr aufhört" (762). Yet she can mass the opposition under one banner: "Torgelow und Katzenstein (was keinen Unterschied macht)" (763). In other words, class differentiation applies for her only when her all-consuming preoccupation, the nobility, is involved. Attwood interprets the conclusion of this scene in the following terms:

> Und es ist in höchstem Maße symbolisch, daß Dubslav die kleine Agnes [. . .] angesichts des nahenden Todes ins Haus ruft [. . .]. Die überlebten Vorstellungen nachhängende Adlige geht, die junge, frische Vertreterin des vierten Standes kommt, und der alte Dubslav, der ja den Aufzug selber inszeniert hat, schaut in lächelnder Zustimmung zu.[28]

This would make of Dubslav an arbiter of social class relationships, an all too explicit interpretation of the playing with Adelheid's class prejudice that is undeniably there. The episode with Agnes and Adelheid is a clear and humorous victory for that freedom which characterizes Dubslav, the fact that he is superficially prepared to snub his own class and flirt with the proletariat. But Agnes' role is also inadequately described by Attwood, sounding as it does like the heroine of a party-line DDR novel.[29] She belongs to a long tradition of outsider or gypsy children robbed, or here borrowed, from their parents, something seen already in *Problematische Naturen* (see p. 50). She is hardly to be taken as representative of the fourth class, whereas Adelheid is of a certain sector of the nobility. And Dubslav's action is certainly not a championing of this class, of which he has written to Woldemar: "Die Proletarier — wie sie noch echt waren, jetzt mag es wohl anders damit sein" (653).

The character of Adelheid is probably the only one other than that of the less-developed Gundermanns to receive a consistently negative portrayal apart from some concessions to her social savoir-faire. In a novel concerned with the survival of a humane, enlightened form of the nobility, she represents many of the faults of the class which have led to its decline as an ethical force. She is not involved at the more basic level of its financial decline. Her whole being is totally opposed to, and uncomprehending before, the spirit of the title-symbol. Significantly this is fêted at the end by Melusine, Adelheid's pet aversion.

5. *Contemporary history*

Various references to contemporary life, especially that in Berlin, add depth to the work by lending local colour and situating it further in the age being portrayed. This applies to the "Pferdebahn" described by Tante Adelheid (500), as it does to the string of place-names tracing Woldemar's journey to the Barbys' (527).

There is frequent mention of Wagner in Fontane's works. The Conservative supporters move to their meal after the elections to the ironically exalted strains of the march from Tannhäuser (596). Wrschowitz' scorn for Niels Gade grows from his developing enthusiasm for Wagner. Yet again the real force of such references emerges from the following characteristic one, in which Melusine expresses her regrets to Woldemar:

> [. . .] daß wir in einer halben Stunde fort müssen, Opernhaus, 'Tristan und Isolde.' Was sagen Sie dazu? Nicht zu Tristan und Isolde, nein, zu der heikleren Frage, daß wir eben gehen [. . .]. (515)

Melusine squashes in advance any comments on Wagner's music possibly ensuing from a misunderstanding of her question. Similarly the performance in *Cécile* of *Tannhäuser*, attended independently by Gordon and Cécile, is commented on by the former as a thin veil for his own thwarted feelings, not in any sense as an aesthetic judgement. The fact that this particular opera is being performed simply reinforces the atmosphere of febrile eroticism never far beneath the surface of *Cécile*.

There is much talk in *Der Stechlin* of London and England and some too of Italy, but this is far from being a travelogue. It can indicate the open nature of the Stechlins as expressed most tellingly in the central symbol of the lake. This openness is preserved through Woldemar's trip to London and then Armgard's stimulating impressions of their honeymoon in Italy, which contrast with Käthe's gushing in *Irrungen Wirrungen* (I, 439-41). It can further define character — Adelheid hears of Armgard's Italian impressions with boredom and expresses ludicrous prejudices against life in England which she bases entirely on hearsay. On the other hand more informed opinion, such as Lorenzen's in the following quotation, can give important information about contemporary attitudes to England:

> Sie sind drüben schrecklich runtergekommen, weil der Kult vor dem goldenen Kalbe beständig wächst; lauter Jobber und die vornehme Welt obenan. Und dabei so heuchlerisch; sie sagen 'Christus' und meinen Kattun. (630)

The picture presented of London, those features which the speaker deems worthy of special comment, also tell by implication something about Berlin as presumably lacking in those features. Typically for the novel we hear less of institutions and buildings and more of human features of rare colour, such as the Chinese acrobat grinning in through the window at Herbstfelde, or Koseleger's anecdote of the duchess' unsuccessful court case against a beautician charging an exorbitant fee. He draws the following conclusion from the story, comparing the mentality of the country with his own state:

> In unserm guten Preußen, und nun gar erst in unsrer Mark, sieht man in einem derartigen Hergange nur das Karikierte, günstigstenfalls das Groteske, nicht aber jenes Hochmaß gesellschaftlicher Verfeinerung, aus dem allein sich solche Dinge [. . .] entwickeln können. (664)

The extensive discussion of England centring of Koseleger's tale is preceded by a very brief reference to a closer to home instance of contemporary history. The Berlin-Stralsund line had led to the insolvency or suicide of many investors:

> Zunächst wurde von der Nordbahn gesprochen, die, seit der neuen Kopenhagener Linie, den ihr von früher her anhaftenden Schreckensnamen siegreich überwunden habe. (660)

The epic dimensions of this reference, so condensed, are realized in Spielhagen's *Sturmflut*. But the cursory mention here is wholly consonant with Fontane's work, whose domain excludes the elaboration of such epic potential.

6. Social manners, customs

In the novels already discussed, some picture of the general social background of an era emerged almost incidentally in details such as etiquette, fashion, etc. In Fontane's case it is attention to details such as these which is at the very core of the novel. These details reflect the much broader concerns of the world beyond, a world whose panoramic depiction is not Fontane's task.

Thus the fourth chapter begins:

> Frau von Gundermann schien auf das ihr als einziger, also auch ältester Dame zustehende Tafelaufhebungsrecht verzichten zu wollen [. . .]. (435)

Throughout Fontane's works great emphasis is laid on table-manners and social forms. Tante Adelheid's otherwise proficient hostessing is deficient in one respect: "[. . .] aber *eine* Gabe besaß sie nicht, die, das Gespräch, wie's in einem engsten Zirkel doch sein sollte, zusammenzufassen" (491). Even language itself is subjected to formal requirements, not merely in such conventions as correct forms of address. The following comments of the Baronin Berchtesgaden, in which she imagines a Japanese painting with a stork, testify to

Victorian restrictions of propriety in not talking of certain unmentionables, even in a context where they could not possibly have this connotation: "In meinen Jahren darf ich ja von Storch sprechen. Früher hätt ich vielleicht Kranich gesagt" (634). The word "Storch" seems particularly loaded; when Agnes uses it quite naturally in talking about the Berlin *Tiergarten*, Dubslav's servant-maids instantly congregate about her (764). In a similar scene Professor Cujacius begins a Schiller quotation, "Das ist der Fluch der bösen Tat. . ." (644), but declines to finish it out of deference to the ladies present, because it includes the word "gebären."[30]

The formal demands of convention largely survive the mobility of social status witnessed in the novel. At the same time such details tend to set the characters in their age at a more basic level of existence than, say, the election campaign or theoretical wranglings about issues. The electoral procedure and results are described in personalized terms, not as the operating of some abstract system, but as the rather lightweight accompaniment to vignettes of character. Political and religious powers may be questioned and rejected, but social conventions remain more constant and they are thus a far more effective instrument, from the viewpoint of the technique of the *Zeitroman*, in relativizing the most individualistic character to the overriding demands of his age. The priorities are even made quite explicit, with an appropriate dash of humour, when the following thought is imputed to Dubslav's political supporters: "Siegen ist gut, aber Zu-Tische-Gehen ist noch besser" (594). There follows a wealth of loving detail as this wish is realized. Firstly the occupying of the table is pictured, with due attention devoted to the important question of whether Dubslav or "der Edle Herr von Alten-Friesack" (595) should sit at the head of the company.

The possibilities of interweaving comments of far greater implication than the specific details given, are brilliantly shown in the following. The assembled company raise their glasses in a toast to the King:

> [. . .] und während der junge Lehrer abermals auf den auf einer Rheinsberger Schloßauktion erstandenen alten Flügel zueilte, stimmte man an der ganzen Tafel hin das "Heil dir im Siegerkranz" an, dessen erster Vers stehend gesungen wurde. (596)

The information about the piano's background, at first sight gratuitous, throws a highly ironic light on the whole proceedings. For here are Conservatives expressing their loyalty to their monarch. They do so to the musical accompaniment of an object auctioned at what would have been regarded as a bastion of their cause, but one which has obviously seen more prosperous days. It is possible to read a similar satiric thrust in their singing a song first published in 1790 which, in addition to being the Prussian national anthem, in 1793 underwent changes and became known as the "Berliner Volksgesang" (see 998 – Anm. to 596). At all events the accumulation of colour and atmosphere is never arbitrary and frequently conceals a barb such as the superficially harmless piano. The barb can also be elaborated far more explicitly, as in the following comment on the music accompanying the end of the meal of the same company:

> [. . .] unter den Klängen des "Hohenfriedbergers" – der "Prager", darin es heißt: "Schwerin fällt", wäre mit Rücksicht auf die Gesamtsituation vielleicht paßlicher gewesen – kehrte man in die Parterreräume zurück [. . .]. (599)

7. Art

Works of art are another touchstone for reactions revealing more of the person concerned without direct authorial comment, at the same time as they lend another dimension to the age being portrayed. Subtle shades are lent to characterization through discussions of tastes. Thus Lorenzen's copy of a Rubens Crucifixion is contrasted by Koseleger with the art tastes to be encountered in the locality around him. Koseleger almost pesters Lorenzen to get away from this provincial atmosphere; he himself is transported in memory back to Antwerp, where he had seen the original years before. But Koseleger is not to be reckoned among those exhibiting the true spirit of openness contained in the title-symbol; what seems to be his progressiveness is exposed as sheer ambition by the end of the section, and his dissatisfied restlessness contrasts sharply with Lorenzen's mildness. Lorenzen's taste emerges as all the more creditable for lacking immediate contact with the outside world. The pile of newspapers he removes from the sofa table (575) may be understood as a further testimony to his keen mind seeking to remain informed.

In this case their titles are not mentioned, but newspapers are a further indicator of cultural tastes. When Engelke brings Dubslav the mail and his newspapers, "zuunterst die 'Kreuzzeitung' als Fundament, auf diese dann die 'Post' " (746), this gives a touch of contemporary history in citing two examples of papers circulating in noble circles, and simultaneously, a further indication of Dubslav's foundations in those circles for all his occasional championing of more progressive viewpoints. Admittedly the weight carried by such a title as the "Kreuzzeitung" is not to be gauged by the modern reader from this work alone; its mere mention should have conveyed sufficient implications to a reader who was a contemporary of Fontane. This problem of elements bound to a particular age becomes intensified when veiled references are made to contemporary figures, however thin this veil might have been for contemporaries. Thus the professor who enthuses for Peter Cornelius is apparently a reference to Karl Pfannschmidt (998 — Anm. to 609). From this figure we hear a detailed account of one of Cornelius' "Kartons" in particular, but the absolute terms he uses expose his enthusiasm as fanaticism, and also provide the springboard for Melusine's wry reference: "Mir persönlich ist die Böcklinsche Meerfrau mit dem Fischleib lieber" (610), a reflection in the artistic sphere of her own nature. These hints about the character of people in a discussion are Fontane's real concern over and above the individual work discussed.

This is also the case in a discussion between Baronin Berchtesgaden and Melusine. The Baroness mentions the painter Skarbina. Melusine then describes another of his pictures and more details of his style, but all this is a mere springboard for what follows. For the perspective then shifts in turn to Italian paintings of the Ascension and the simplicity of the Japanese style, showing the title-symbol at work in yet another sphere, with crosscurrents of art being brought together. The focal point of the whole episode comes with Melusine's reflection: "Ach, daß doch das Natürliche wieder obenauf käme" (634). The Baroness assures her this process is already under way, by which stage the conversation goes far beyond the issue of realism in art and refers to the whole domain of social relationships calcified by unnatural conventions, so antipathetic to the freely soaring spirit of Melusine.

The impression made earlier by Professor Cujacius is confirmed by Melusine's dismay at his arrival and her harsh judgement once he has left. His condescension seems unlimited, his verdicts allow no other viewpoint — "Ein überwundener Standpunkt" (643), "Es gibt nur ein Heil" (645). The self-important manner — again the "Wie" for the "Was " — in which he speaks of Millais, Millet or Turner is of more importance than what we incidentally learn of their art. Discussion of these painters and more so the way his own contribution is introduced — "Woldemar, der einsah, daß irgendwas gesagt werden müsse" (644-45) — point up a dilettantism in the latter's appreciation of art.

The ultimate exposure of Cujacius comes when he draws swords with a similarly intractable nature, Wrschowitz, over the worth of Niels Gade. A dispute about the musician deteriorates rapidly into scathing personal broadsides. All rational elements of criticism, "Krittikk" (534) being after all Wrschowitz' highest value, recede before an invective that throws a very dubious light on critical capabilities when basic human graces are lacking. Mention of a current cultural figure, Niels Gade, does not simply lend a flavour of the contemporary cultural scene. The main aim is to allow fanaticism in art to exhibit and destroy itself, just as fanaticism on other levels, e.g. Adelheid's fantastic notions of grandeur for her caste, is exposed in the novel as contrary to the spirit of the title-symbol.

8. *Religion*

In treating this area as part of the material of a *Zeitroman*, attention must be directed not so much at individual answers to the *Gretchen-Frage* as at aspects of religious debate or of church history. Unlike the musty delving into oddities of the past in *Cécile*, church history in *Der Stechlin* is current, interesting, and of direct bearing on characters. Through Lorenzen's affiliation with the Christian-Socialist movement we hear Rex talk of the movement's founder, the court preacher Adolf Stöcker (cf. FLB, 294). This in turn leads Lorenzen on to mention of Sebastian Kneipp, "dieser Wörishofener Pfarrer" (429). For all their similarity of outlook, the differences in manner between the fiery Stöcker and the composed Lorenzen are emphasized. Current church history receives an airing in relation to a key figure in the novel, but the individuality of that figure is carefully preserved from eclipse by his more illustrious contemporary. Lorenzen still embodies certain currents of the age but is far more than a mere vehicle for the exposition of these.

This is not the case with Rentmeister Fix, who never appears in person anyway but only in Adelheid's observations, and then always as a source of authority for her. His views on the "Wortlaut" (498) are important for their influence on Adelheid and for broaching an issue of considerable controversy in religious circles of the time. Another current idea receives passing mention here too, when Fix, as reported by Adelheid, speaks of the necessity of an "Umwertung" (499). Nietzschean concepts reappear when Dubslav voices his dissatisfaction with the notion of the "Übermensch" (701). These are no more than fleeting references, and a more systematic appraisal of Nietzsche's influential ideas is excluded, but again the idea of the title-symbol is there with crosscurrents drawn from many sources. The extreme form in this possibility of the *Zeitroman*, the cursory, unelaborated reference, occurs in cases such as the following, where Rex is speaking at first of Stöcker and then of Lorenzen:

> [. . .] aber der 'neue Luther', der doch schon gerade bedenklich genug ist — Majestät hat ganz recht mit seiner Verurteilung —, der geht ihm gewiß nicht weit genug. (446)

What would normally be seen as a mere expanding of Rex' line of thought, in appearing in parenthesis, is of considerable importance to the *Zeitroman*, referring to the dismissal of Stöcker by Wilhelm II in 1890, a breach strengthened by a telegramme from the Kaiser in 1896. Rex passes an opinion and then has recourse to the Kaiser's judgement to verify that opinion. A reference to an historical event is thus introduced in terms that are neither laboured nor in any sense a mere tabulation of events. This priority of emphasis is appropriate to the *Zeitroman* in Fontane's hands, whereas a historical novel for instance would almost certainly have lingered over the Kaiser's judgement and not left the full import of Rex' reference — as he does — to be gained from sources outside the novel.

One other feature deserving brief mention here is Rex as a nonconformist (474). "Er hat [. . .] einen Verein gegründet für Frühgottesdienste" (448), on which account Czako playfully (474) and Dubslav much more earnestly (448) upbraid him. But the freshly-emerging sects which also appeared in *Cécile* (I, 200) and *Irrungen Wirrungen* (I, 426) remain on the fringe of *Der Stechlin* because of the disposition of speakers. For Adelheid broaches the topic of proliferating sects with Rex and makes clear her own disapproval (487). Though about to become an "Irvingianer" (ibid.) himself, he is too much a man of the world to dispute her views. The dictates of polite conversation are here supreme. The people expressing facts and opinions, and even more so the social conventions moulding their behaviour, prevail over the facts and opinions themselves, just as in *Irrungen Wirrungen* Mormons are "ein Thema, wie geschaffen für Frau Dörr" (I, 427).

9. *The army*

The greatness that Prussia has known is frequently mentioned in *Der Stechlin*, and the Prussian army, both in its present form and in reflections on its past, receives detailed attention. Very early in the piece Czako expresses doubts about Woldemar's suitability for his position in his regiment. These lead him to expand on the topic of the progressive refinement of the army (420) through the presence of more and more princes in its ranks. The Marwitz', the Bredows and the other venerable Prussian families which provided the backbone of the army till 1806 no longer do so:

[. . .] der Adel gab den Ton an, und die paar Prinzen mußten noch froh sein, wenn sie nicht störten. Damit ist es nun aber, seit wir Kaiser und Reich sind, total vorbei. (420)

This thesis of an over-refinement in the army as opposed to that of about a century earlier is questionable within the bounds of the novel. Czako's credentials to make such a judgement are qualified when Woldemar says of him almost exactly what he had said (419) of Woldemar: "[. . .] er paßt nicht so ganz zu uns und eigentlich auch kaum zu seinem Regiment" (500). The brittle state of the whole pre-Jena Prussian military tradition had in any case been portrayed by Fontane in his *Schach von Wuthenow*, where significantly an over-refinement of the title-figure is a main issue.

In conversation with Czako, Dubslav advocates a form of enlightened despotism in accordance with the Friderician concept of the State. He says the instruments of support for such a ruler are still at hand in the nobility, the army, and particularly in Czako's regiment (443). But such a régime does not come to power and Dubslav's comment is less a programmatic statement than a springboard for his following reminiscing and warming to the theme of Russia with delvings into its history and that of his own state. This demonstrates another problem of the conversational-style *Zeitroman*, namely to what degree statements are made to stimulate further discussion, especially given the openness of a Dubslav to all sides of a viewpoint, and to what degree they can be understood as an expression of the convictions of the character concerned.

The whole concept of heroism is thrown into doubt in this novel. Dubslav philosophizes to Czako:

"Heldentum ist Ausnahmezustand und meist Produkt einer Zwangslage. Sie brauchen mir übrigens nicht zuzustimmen, denn Sie sind noch im Dienst."

"Bitte, bitte", sagte Czako. (427)

It is as if the façade required by the upholding of institutions is seen through by both, the need to maintain the fiction of heroism in the army overriding rationality. The theme occupies Dubslav and Lorenzen at length in their last conversation but one of the book. Dubslav asks to be told a heroic military anecdote, but Lorenzen retorts: "*Mein* Heldentum [. . .] ist nicht auf dem Schlachtfelde zu Hause" (750), and proceeds to tell the tale of the North Pole adventurer, Lieutenant Greeley. He is obscure only by popular standards; to Lorenzen he embodies a true heroism, heedless of all demands of convention in assessing the needs of an exceptional situation. The whole bygone glory of the military has passed to inventors like James Watt and Siemens. The reactionary endeavours of Wilhelm II to ignore this fact earn him Lorenzen's criticism (680).[31] Even without considering the further guidance of Woldemar entrusted to Lorenzen, Woldemar's withdrawal from the army and retirement to the family estate at the novel's conclusion are no mere repetition of his father's move several years before. For the two events lie at opposite ends of the novel, and in the intervening pages the whole fabric of the military has received a searching examination and a new, more individual order of heroism has been proclaimed.

Nevertheless, the signs of the old one are still very much in evidence. In the company of Dubslav's supporters gathered before the election, both Katzler and Kluckhuhn wear their military medals (569). When they are returning from their outing to the *Eierhäuschen,* Woldemar conjectures to Melusine that the rocket they have just seen is part of celebrations for Sedan or Düppel or the crossing to Alsen. Reminders of Prussia's recent victories and its emergence as a leading power through its army's achievements are thus a constant background.

But even Sedan lies several years back in the past, and these military victories are perpetuated by the older generation. The younger one fluctuates. At first Armgard shows a predisposition to what is "preußisch-militärisch" (698), as Woldemar observes with satisfaction, preferring to be wed in the Berlin Garrison Church rather than the old family church. She also favours Woldemar's remaining in service: "[. . .] ich bin sehr für Freiheit, aber doch beinah mehr noch für Major" (ibid.). But when they return to Berlin after their honeymoon, the big city and the military world no longer hold the same attraction for her, and she echoes Woldemar's own sentiments in suggesting they move to the Stechlin estate: "Die Scholle daheim, die dir Freiheit gibt, ist doch das Beste" (798). So that "Freiheit," secondary in Armgard's earlier preferences, wins the day after all, echoing Dubslav's inner freedom so extolled by Lorenzen in his funeral oration, and rounding off one of the most important concepts running through the novel.

It is in this light that this particular thematic area of Fontane's work is to be seen. The military historical background is there, ingrained in the older characters and still lending colour to the present. But the ultimate consideration, which again represents a jump from the more stratified society depicted elsewhere in his works, is the human level of heroism and freedom. So that once Woldemar feels the latter to be lacking in the confines of his military career, he seeks it — as one of the highest values posited in the work — on the old estate.

10. *Conclusion*

Als erster hier hat er [Fontane] wahrgemacht, daß ein Roman das gültige, bleibende Dokument einer Gesellschaft, eines Zeitalters sein kann; daß er soziale Kenntnis gestalten und vermitteln,

Leben und Gegenwart bewahren kann noch in einer sehr veränderten Zukunft, wo, sagen wir, das Berlin von einst nicht mehr besteht. Alles vermöge richtig gesehener, stark gezeichneter Personen, einer Welt von Personen oder einzeln ausgesuchter, die dasselbe tun: standhalten, sich selbst unverletzt überbringen den weiten Weg von damals her. [. . .] Nach *Effi Briest* sagte er: "Das kommt nicht wieder." Er wußte, was er gemacht hatte, war übrigens alt. Er schrieb noch *Der Stechlin,* da wird sein herber Realismus geisterhaft, wie nach dem Leben das Ende; sein eigenes spricht verhalten mit. [32]

Heinrich Mann's evaluation, fifty years after Fontane's death, serves firstly as a convenient bridge to the next chapter, which deals with one of Heinrich Mann's own novels, and also as an acute assessment of the older author's work. It brings us back to Fontane's own verdict at the beginning of this chapter. For we see here the vindication of the method outlined by Fontane.

He had claimed his characters evolve from conversation, *"mit und in ihnen* die Geschichte" (author's emphasis). These are the accents that cannot be stressed too strongly. They are respected by Heinrich Mann, when after his first broad statement about the social documentation in Fontane he goes straight to the narrative means whereby this is achieved: "Alles vermöge [. . .] Personen." This is what ensures the life of the work, life in both senses of its immanent vitality and its literary survival long after the passing of the age depicted. Far from characters being tacked on to arguments to lend them a certain plasticity, ideas and facts — whether historically actual, or 'facts' in terms of the narrative reality — are subsidiary to the purely human dimension of the characters associated with them. This contrasts Fontane's treatment with that of Immermann or Spielhagen. With Spielhagen, the decline of the nobility on any one level was symptomatic of a wholesale decline. But not so with Fontane. Petersen can correctly see the election "als Symptom eines politischen Niederganges des Adels,"[33] but it is only a political decline; the humour and warmth of the members of the nobility remain unimpaired.

The problem of transience, inherent in the genre of the *Zeitroman*, is overcome by this deceptively obvious device. Long after minute details of local colour have passed, effective though they are at one level, the broad attitudes of the characters remain, as do the historical forces in interplay with them. And these forces survive not as abstract props but in a subtly constructed panorama of the age. Before Fontane, a like emphasis on the individual was in Germany the preserve of the *Bildungsroman* if one excludes the lesser success of Raabe with more eccentric figures removed from the mainstream of life. Indeed, the whole issue is seen most clearly in a letter from Keller to his publisher Vieweg in 1850. Speaking of the hero of *Der grüne Heinrich,* Keller specifically relates "die Verhältnisse seiner Person und seiner Familie" to those "im bürgerlichen Leben," the moral of his work being that failure in the one sphere necessarily implies failure in the other.

Die Schuld kann in vielen Fällen an der Gesellschaft liegen, und alsdann wäre freilich der Stoff derjenige eines sozialistischen Tendenzbuches. Im gegebenen Falle aber liegt sie größtenteils im Charakter und dem besonderen Geschicke des Helden und bedingt hierdurch eine mehr ethische Bedeutung des Romans. [34]

To Keller it seemed a matter of choice, whereas Fontane succeeded in merging the two. In *Der Stechlin* at least, he encompasses both society and the individual in his individuality, and furthermore the interaction between the two. In doing so he creates something transcending the pejorative sense Keller conveys with his phrase "sozialistisches Tendenzbuch." At the same time, the method of characterization differs from the *Bildungsroman*; there is no process of development and the depiction of character is static, but not stagnant, rather calm like the surface of Lake Stechlin.

How are we to understand Heinrich Mann's assessment of *Der Stechlin*: "[. . .] da wird sein herber Realismus geisterhaft"? Various critics [35] have spoken of the "Verklärung" of this novel, and this is what Heinrich Mann seems to be implying too. Is a "verklärter Zeitroman" a contradiction in terms? If one thinks only of Keller's postulated "sozialistisches Tendenzbuch," the answer will be 'yes.' But if one considers the theoretical abstraction by Fontane (p. 87) of what has been shown in this chapter as fully achieved — an achievement finding its due appreciation in Heinrich Mann's assessment — then the answer must be 'no.' Fontane is in fact an outright negation of those tendencies bedevilling the German *Zeitroman* of the 19th century. Polemics, mere provincialism, and a clinging to alien traditions are all absent from his work, quite apart from his stylistic superiority. "Verklärung" in Fontane's last novel does not mean a distancing from reality through artistic manipulation, but an enhancement of reality through artistic mastery. If the resulting realism seems "geisterhaft," it is so not in any sense of remoteness or insubstantiality, but rather it parallels little Elfriede's "wehmütigen Zauber":

Ihr zarter, beinahe körperloser Leib schien zu sagen: "Ich sterbe." Aber ihre Seele wußte nichts davon; die leuchtete und sagte: "Ich lebe." (767)

CHAPTER VI

HEINRICH MANN: *IM SCHLARAFFENLAND*

1. Introduction

Mit fünfundzwanzig Jahren sagte ich mir: 'Es ist notwendig, soziale Zeitromane zu schreiben. Die deutsche Gesellschaft kennt sich selbst nicht.'[1]

Thus Heinrich Mann in 1926, a retrospective judgement that throws a rather different light on his estimate of Fontane mentioned in the last chapter. For it becomes clear from other sources that Mann — at least in the 1920's — saw himself as a pioneer in the field of the social novel. Either he did not class Fontane's novels as social novels,[2] or he had still to reach close acquaintance with Fontane or his high opinion of him — just which is not clear. For the very virtues he later sees in the older writer were overlooked in statements like the following in 1924:

[. . .] ich hoffe aber doch, [. . .] daß meine Arbeiten Anfänge einer sozialen Roman-Literatur sind. Wir haben keine, wie Sie bemerken [. . .].[3]

Or the following in 1927:

Ne croyez pas que la formule du roman social fût si facile à faire accepter. On ne connaissait pas cette manière. Il y eut surtout une résistance de *mentalité*. [. . .] Pour le roman et jusqu'à la fin du siècle, rien de très sérieux, rien du moins qui fût en même temps de quelque portée sociale et de grande valeur littéraire.[4]

In the latter case he does refer to the post-1848 essays at a social novel in Freytag and Spielhagen — he mentions *Problematische Naturen* — but sees this attempt to establish a tradition as petering out, and points to the psychological and sociological limitations of their works. He then mentions Hauptmann's early plays and in particular the anti-capitalist protest of *Die Weber* (1894) — the same play that is mercilessly satirized in the guise of *Rache* in *Im Schlaraffenland* (1900). But that was drama; the novel had yet, in his opinion, to produce such a work.

It is clear that if we accept this last verdict of Mann, the emergence of a social novel tradition is far from a smooth linear development, but rather one of relatively isolated contributions in different directions, despite the many cross-references which have offered themselves among the works treated. There is certainly no close connection between Spielhagen and Freytag on the one hand and Fontane on the other, while H. Mann rejects the former writers and only acknowledges the latter late in his career. This rejection is given plastic shape in the novel under discussion with the doddering remnant of the 1848 Revolution, Wennichen. It is probably not of primary importance whether it is Freytag or Spielhagen[5] whom Wennichen is meant to represent. What is important is the lack of a tradition of the *Zeitroman* to do justice to the particular era described in the novel. Mann's comments to Lefèvre, quoted above, help explain the picture presented of Wennichen:

Wennichen bezog nur noch halbe Honorare, da er seit fünfzig Jahren immer dieselben Romane verfaßte, die niemand mehr las [. . .]. Er sah nichts von den Veränderungen der Zeit seit achtundvierzig [. . .].[6]

Wennichen's slogans — "Ehre des Handelsstandes [. . .] Errungenschaften der bürgerlichen Revolution" (ibid.) and so on — are clearly dated in approaching the reality of Berlin of the 1890's, distorted though that reality becomes in H. Mann's novel.

With this point we have reached the crucial difference between Mann's work and others treated here, namely its strongly satirical bias. The problems raised by this approach were crystallized by the contemporaneous critic Josef Ettlinger:

> Die Personen sind zumeist echt, die Art, wie der Verfasser ihren Jargon in allen Spielarten beherrscht, erregt Staunen; in den Vorgängen aber und ihren Voraussetzungen steckt viel mehr groteske Übertreibung als die satirische Absicht rechtfertigt. Auch tritt die gewollte Ironie bisweilen in der Darstellung zu unverblümt hervor, als daß man geneigt sein möchte, den Roman als glaubhaften Spiegel tatsächlicher Naturzustände gelten zu lassen. Es sollte wohl so etwas wie der blutrote Feuerschein einer nahenden kapitalistischen Götzendämmerung über diesem Zeitgemälde liegen; aber es zeigt sich nur die grellweiße Beleuchtung eines künstlichen Scheinwerfers. [7]

The main point raised here — the grotesque exaggeration of the satire and the resulting distortion of reality — will be returned to later. The satirical thrust need not exclude a realistic basis, but implies this is viewed in a negative light. Mann's use of satire is not to be compared with the occasional heavyhanded use of the same device by Spielhagen, nor with the gentler tones of a Fontane.

Through its more extreme tone, it would be fair to claim that *Im Schlaraffenland* bears more overtly than the other novels discussed the imprint of its author's personal style. There are programmatic statements on the age and its tendencies in *Die Epigonen*, but the degree to which they are coloured by the personality of the person expressing them is not significant, and a fairly uniform editorial comment emerges from the aggregate of such pronouncements. In H. Mann's novel the chapters "die deutsche Geisteskultur" (25ff.), "ein demokratischer Adel" (54ff.) and "Politik und Volkswirtschaft im Schlaraffenland" (145ff.) are not springboards for rounded appraisals of the concepts they introduce, but fuel for Mann's satiric fire. High-sounding concepts that they are, they are stripped of any lofty veneer and exposed in their true colours as catchcries of charlatanism when applied to this society, the subtitle "ein Roman unter feinen Leuten" being laden with irony.

As a narrative device, reflection is absent from this work, the only perspective being that of the novel's characters. Considerable intellectual reflection and juggling within the authorial viewpoint are nevertheless implied by the distanced, dissecting perspective of satire. This novel thus calls for a different approach when statements reflecting the age are related to the age itself. Satire need not necessarily have the radically negative effect it has here. Both Grimmelshausen's *Der Abentheurliche Simplicissimus* and Gogol's *Dead Souls* employ it as a basis for attacking contemporary society, while at the same time being brilliant evocations of those societies. However, in neither is the overall impression one of wholesale debunking as in H. Mann's novel, which distances it completely from the attitude of mid-19th century Realists[8] that satire was a non-artistic, dogmatic device. For all its strengths as a critical medium, Mann's satire has brought criticism that his figures are largely caricatures.[9] This returns us to the central issue of the individual and his age, for a truly severe indictment of the latter seems in this case to have been achieved at the expense of the former. Alongside the other works, written in a straight narrative vein despite touches of irony, *Im Schlaraffenland* has been included as an example of the satiric potential of the *Zeitroman*, first realized in Immermann's *Münchhausen* (1838), and also by way of contrast. For the claim has been made: "Nichts ist den Romanen Fontanes ferner als der Roman *Im Schlaraffenland.*"[10]

Another problem of Mann's novel is its scope. Though its characterization has been described as a "Nebeneinander von Menschen,"[11] *Im Schlaraffenland* is only a "Roman des Nebeneinander" within a limited sphere, namely "unter feinen Leuten." This framework is, however, flexible to the point of including the venal worker Matzke and the last male scion of a debilitated noble line, von Hochstetten. But basically it is the upper-bourgeois realm which dominates. This question of scope is not solely one of social stratification, but also one of breadth of the milieu. When "der ganze Berliner Ton" (19) impresses Andreas with its shallowness, "Berliner" is primarily a contrast to the Rhenish homeland from which Andreas has just come, but it is frequently specified elsewhere too (see 129-30). Chapter 3 bears the heading: "Die *deutsche* Geisteskultur" (author's emphasis), an even more comprehensive generalization from the particular.[12] Liebling traces the progression from the particular to the general, although we never see the latter, when at the end of the novel he speaks of Andreas' former standing:

> Als ein geachtetes Mitglied der feinsten Kreise, als einer der beliebtesten Dramatiker Berlins, und ich darf wohl sagen ganz Deutschlands [. . .]. (352-53)

Liebling's assessment raises a serious problem. In striving for more breadth in his novel, H. Mann really works against the reflection of reality in it through the supposed fame of one of his own fictional creatures, who is furthermore not a key-figure ("Schlüsselfigur") for any dramatist of the day.[13] We can accept unexceptional figures in the *Zeitroman* as chiffres of the age in a situation which, while invented, seems historically feasible, whereas exceptional figures suspend credibility in their particular fields of achievement. If Andreas were really one of the most popular dramatists in Berlin and even Germany we might expect to hear for instance of Hauptmann taking offence at the misrepresentation of his own play in Klempner's *Rache*. Even in such a confrontation it would be a "Kunstfigur" Hauptmann and not the historical person, and any such reference would be a breach of the novel's character-scheme, its figures being inventions of H. Mann.

This problem draws attention to the awkward middle region between historical and fictional reality. When a key-figure is employed in a novel, both levels are blended in a clear relationship — the figure X in the novel is modelled on figure Y in reality and takes the significant features of his own fictional reality from those of Y. When clearly fictitious characters are employed they can still be used as representatives of an age, and an aura of more immediate reality can be added, as so often in Fontane's works, by reference to actual historical events or persons in conversations, newspaper reports, etc. But the co-existence of the historical and fictional levels is strained in a *Zeitroman* in a case like the above one: for Andreas to be such an acclaimed dramatist almost demands that he be a key-figure.

The perspective within the novel remains uniform, everything is seen in its relationship to the Türkheimer empire. No rounded picture is presented despite the above-mentioned devices, which simulate one. The same phenomenon is present, even if we allow for his exaggeration, when Kaflisch tells Andreas: "So tief ins Volk dehnt das Schlaraffenland seine Grenzen aus, sehr geehrter Herr, und alle wollen hinein" (184). Here Mann attempts to generalize from his own fictional structure — or rather the transposition of a familiar concept to his own setting — by having the *Schlaraffenland* extend its feelers. This is important for H. Mann's *Zeitroman* in attempting to lend a certain general validity to the author's own satiric creation.

The expansion of the novel's scope from a single group to a whole society makes it difficult, as Ingeborg Meister has pointed out,[14] to fit the work into German novel traditions existing at the time, especially since the framework of an *Entwicklungsroman* is retained. It is in fact for the post-1929 reader a kind of negative *Entwicklungsroman* in view of Andreas' letter prefacing the whole novel, H. Mann's answer to the request for a preface to the 1929 edition (7-9). Here it is clear, even before the reader approaches the novel proper, that Andreas will not undergo any positive development. At the same time the traditional format is turned upside down in that Andreas' career is traced in its external course, not as a basically inward-looking spiritual saga.[15] This is of course in line with the emphases of the *Zeitroman*.

A further complicating dimension is to be seen already in the novel's title, with its legendary aspect. When he first goes to the Türkheimers' residence clutching Bediener's note of reference, Andreas is described as "einsam wie der Märchenprinz, der ein verwunschenes Schloß erobert" (36). This overlapping of the worlds of the social novel and the fairytale is further evident in Bienaimée's weakness for a fairytale prince (278 et passim). However, her sentimentalized illusions recede before the harsh bourgeois reality of her arranged marriage with Andreas. This is undoubtedly a parody of arranged alliances in aristocratic circles and also an inversion of the kind of dénouement we have seen in *Die Epigonen* and *Problematische Naturen,* with the revelation of the noble blood of the hero hitherto presumed to be bourgeois.

The worlds of the social novel and the fairytale are merged in the metaphorical description of Türkheimer's empire, with Türkheimer as king, the *Schlaraffenland* as his court, and Andreas as court jester. The choice of this image also reflects the lack of a positive alternative within the novel to its depiction of Berlin of the 1890's. There is no change in the feudal order, despite temporary inroads made by the likes of Andreas and Bienaimée. Türkheimer and Adelheid remain the real king and queen. The elaborate metaphor of royalty and courtiers blends the novel's title and subtitle, with the satiric invention of the legend of the *Schlaraffenland* transposed to this particular society, whose economic power-structures parallel the hierarchies of the feudal kingdoms. Money, and the power accruing from its possession, are at the very base of this society. But this core is described primarily in terms of the legend:

> Das Geld rollte hier unter den Möbeln umher. Gewiß tat keiner etwas anderes, als sich die Taschen zu füllen. Welch ein Wohlleben in diesem Schlaraffenland! (49)

The stock exchange is described in similar terms to those above. Its economic basis is not probed further, responsibility for its processes is abdicated: "[...] man lebte unter der Hand einer höheren Fügung" (189). The puppeteer behind the scenes is acknowledged in equally shadowy terms in Andreas' reaction to his winnings on the stock exchange:

> Die Einrichtung in der Lützowstraße, die gepreßten Ledermöbel, das geschnitzte und vergoldete Louisquinze-Bett wurden in diesem Augenblick gleichsam aus einer höheren Sphäre an Fäden zu ihm herabgelassen [. . .] . (252)

The legendary strand is continued to the end of the novel, where Andreas rues his lost grace in the eyes of the "Sagenkönig" (367). Türkheimer's last triumphal procession fades away, "gleich der Apotheose am Schluß eines Feenmärchens" (ibid.). The basic reality the novel is concerned with still emerges clearly. But the fairytale quality of its satirical framework causes those elements of naturalism which would seem to be inherent in the genre of the *Zeitroman* to dissolve in insubstantiality. In fact, in the distortions of *Rache*, such naturalistic elements become in turn the butt of satire. This tension does not threaten the social commentary of Thackeray's *Vanity Fair*, where a cross-section of a particular society is simultaneously seen as the contemporary actors in a timeless morality play.[16] Thackeray achieves this partly through repeated appeals to the reader and to the narrator's own professed acquaintance with Vanity Fair, implicating reader and narrator as having had experience of what is being discussed.

What the fairytale element also achieves in Mann's novel is that the fictitious framework never disappears completely, whereas the Spielhagen *Zeitroman* had attempted to bely its fictitious nature through striving for objectivity. Through such an elaborate metaphorical frame of reference to familiar stock-figures, a certain timelessness is also lent to the age portrayed. This in turn enables the work to transcend the purely localized follies of Berlin W. in the 1890's, since the follies are simultaneously those of the Türkheimer circles and of the universal figures of the *Schlaraffenland*, their fictional archetypes. This is a major part of that "different approach" referred to on p. 120: the device contributes to a universality that has been seen as one of the most vexed issues of the genre.

The degree of timelessness would be inappropriate to a more dynamic *Zeitroman*. But it accords with Mann's novel, whose conclusion is a testimony precisely to a cyclical pattern.[17] The *Schlaraffenland* has returned unruffled to its state before Andreas' brief irruption into its ranks, Türkheimer's financial power is being wooed by the Großfürst of Walachei — but the exotic nature of his title shows his arbitrariness as a figure dependent on Türkheimer's financial constellation — and Adelheid has a new lover. Andreas' benediction: "Dumm, ruchlos und glücklich. Meinen Segen haben sie" (369), is a final testimony to his dubious gift for seeing through people, but is also a reflection on the static, timeless quality of the *Schlaraffenland*.

2. Art and Society

a) The metaphor of the theatre

Central to this novel is the experience of the theatre, both as an external component of the cultural scene and as a source of images for the author which are designed to accentuate the role-acting of the society he portrays. The interweaving of the two is established very early when Andreas seeks advice from Köpf as to how to go beyond the "Café Hurra" in his entry to Berlin society. Köpf says there are three ways, "nämlich die Presse, das Theater und die Gesellschaft" (22). In literature — "in der eigentlichen Literatur" (23) as Köpf puts it, thereby dissociating the theatre from literary pretensions and allowing it solely social ones — no way of acceptance is to be found among a wilfully non-literary public.

Köpf's comments here on his own novel-writing activity raise a problem, as does the sentence on the very first page of the novel, referring to the local patron of arts:

> Es war der alte Herr, den es in jeder kleinen Stadt gibt, und der bei seinen Mitbürgern als harmloser Sonderling gilt, weil er sich mit Literatur befaßt. (11)

In both cases the voice of editorial irony is loud and clear. They are neat comments, valid from the author's own viewpoint, but can they be regarded in any sense as a legitimate comment on the state of literature and its reception at that time? Köpf's comment apparently can be taken at face value, to judge by Fontane's two essays of 1881 and 1891 entitled "Die gesellschaftliche Stellung des Schriftstellers in Deutschland."[18]

Köpf continues:

> Das Theater hat zweifellos auch eine literarische Seite, aber die gesellige ist wichtiger. Beim Theater hat man es stets mit Menschen zu tun [. . .]. Hier kommt es vor allem auf die gesellschaftlichen Verbindungen an. (23)

The last sentence refers to the theatre specifically but is equally applicable to the whole

Schlaraffenland, as Andreas is to find out. In the same speech Köpf denies theatre, or at least dramatists, the qualities of "Ernst, Abgeschlossenheit und Rücksichtslosigkeit" (ibid.), and whenever a serious situation arises in life it can be conveniently stripped of any threatening genuineness of feeling through reference to the theatre. Thus Klempner describes to Andreas the financial ruin of one of Türkheimer's debtors, suddenly transfigured by the debt-collector's suing for his daughter's hand: "Der ruinierte Mann [. . .] fällt [. . .] vor seinem Retter auf die Knie. Stellen Sie sich die Szene auf der Bühne vor!" (69)

In a description of Claire Pimbusch occupying almost a page, the effect of her ghastly appearance is repeatedly described in theatrical terms:

> Es lag über ihr [her forehead] ein künstlicher grüner Schimmer, wie über der schlecht aufgeklebten Stirnhaut einer Theaterperücke. (98)

But for all her ugly features, Claire Pimbusch does not make an impression of ugliness on Andreas:

> Es war ihm, als habe er, zum erstenmal in seinem Leben, die Ehre, einer großen, sehr teuren Kokotte gegenüberzusitzen, nach deren Loge die jungen Leute auf ihren Parkettplätzen sich erblassend umwenden. (ibid.)

Thus in close succession this figure is described in terms assigning her to the stage and to the audience of a stage performance; she is at once actress and spectator, so that the relationship between the theatre and society proclaimed by Köpf is reinforced. For while the connection in Köpf's speech referred to social advancement, the roles of protagonist and spectator are fused here. In this, Claire Pimbusch typifies the inhabitants of the *Schlaraffenland,* as theatrical images are used again and again. In the midst of the adulation drawn to him by the reading of his play and Türkheimer's attention, Andreas is described as "der junge Mann, dessen Clowngesicht alle erheiterte" (203), and it is this mask, this role of providing general amusement, that Andreas is obliged to sustain to please Türkheimer, the producer of the whole life-play that constitutes the *Schlaraffenland* — "Wenn Sie Trübsal blasen, fallen Sie aus der Rolle" (245). As well as consciously repeating phrases used by others, calculated to draw attention to himself, Andreas shows long before his final hybris that he is a far from harmless Pulcinello in miming people maliciously in their absence.

At the level of personal relationships the histrionic props are indulged or even cultivated, whereas at the more fundamental, rarely probed level of the realities underlying the *Schlaraffenland,* they can be viewed negatively. Andreas is an exception in assigning power to the person who really wields it, Türkheimer, even though the latter does not display all the panoply of his position.

> So aber traut der blöde Pöbel sie [die Macht] noch immer jenen anderen, Buntgekleideten zu, die bloß Theater spielen. (254)

The whole dissembling apparatus of this society leads to a Macchiavellianism of the emotions and of viewpoints. In talking with Duschnitzki and Klempner, Andreas makes the mistake of openly admiring Jekuser. This offends not so much his companions' own views as an unwritten law proscribing such genuineness, which runs counter to the whole fabric of polite conversation in this realm. On the other hand:

> Frau Türkheimer gegenüber war es vielleicht etwas anderes? Da, wo er einen ungewöhnlichen Eindruck machen wollte, durfte er doch nicht den Allerweltsgeschmack nachahmen. Dort war es vielleicht hohe Politik, sich so zu zeigen, wie er wirklich war? (60)

The sheer boldness of discarding all masks is thus itself unmasked as a calculated, "hohe Politik" to be employed effectively in making a certain kind of impression. Even Asta's acerbity is seen in terms of theatre. Türkheimer's daughter, who goes around "à la Ibsen frisiert" (40), explains to her sister-in-law: "[. . .] es muß irgendwo stehen, daß eine Frau sich von einem Manne scheiden lassen darf, der keine Lackschuhe trägt" (225). Such self-assertion is related by Andreas to Ibsen's *Nora*. He whispers his revelation to Adelheid, his accomplice in eavesdropping, which is itself a highly theatrical kind of activity.

This excursion into the theatre-images which permeate the novel has been fairly detailed as an attempt to disclose its metaphorical foundations. For it will be seen that this basic metaphor of the theatre, of acting, masks, and a cosily distanced audience, underlies many themes in the work. It becomes a motif of paramount importance for H. Mann, witness the extended performance in *Die kleine Stadt* (1909). Mann had examples of opera from his French models, as in the performances of *Lucia di Lammermoor* in *Madame Bovary* and of *Manon Lescaut* in *Le Rouge et le noir*. The self-effacing taunts about the novel in the latter are akin to Köpf's comments. In a German context, Wilhelm Meister had experienced aesthetic awakenings in the theatre; the performance of *Rache* shows Andreas what is expected of him in this art form that is now externalized in both effect and success.

b. *"Die deutsche Geisteskultur"*

At the beginning of the novel, before Andreas has been assimilated into the society of his new city, he observes with more detached shrewdness, not as yet being caught up himself by the façades he can see through. Georg, in Paul Lindau's *Der Zug nach dem Westen* (1886), also comes to Berlin from the Rhineland, studies, and becomes the fêted darling of society after the success of his opera. However, he and Lolo alone stand outside the social superficiality — he doesn't play along, or mimic, like Andreas — and their stand challenges society's conventions.

Andreas at first shares the general admiration evoked by Dr. Libbenow's glib assertion that he has not read a book for ten years. Through a process of inverted snobbery, being uninformed has assumed a positive value. But he quickly comes to recognize such dilettantism in its true colours as an expression of ignorance and impotence. "Aber der ganze Berliner Ton kam schließlich bloß von Mangel an Tiefe" (19). With "impotence" the tone is set for the decadence encrusting the whole society, in a quite literal sense in a representative of the nobility such as Hochstetten.

Apart from the generalizing function of a chapter-heading like "Die deutsche Geisteskultur," the lofty concept contained is laden with irony. Doktor Bediener uses the high-sounding phrase: "Im übrigen betrachten wir uns als ein Organ der deutschen Geisteskultur" (29) — in the same chapter Kaflisch assesses from Andreas' reception that the time is ripe to ask Bediener for the commission to report a "Lustmordprozeß"! Bediener's words are echoed twice subsequently, once by Andreas in a display of mimicry for Adelheid's benefit, and then when Adelheid and Lizzi are engaged in a dispute over their protégés. Kaflisch explains to Türkheimer that their quarrel is over German culture ("Geisteskultur" — 163). The man of might is signally unimpressed by the bone of contention: "Wenn es sonst nichts ist —" (ibid.) is his reply. This is directed rather against the hollowness of the concept as here expressed than against the arts themselves as a sphere for Türkheimer's attention. For he himself, pragmatic in his patronage as in all else, adds: "Wir müssen was für die Kunst tun, wer soll es sonst? Immer bloß Abfütterung, das ist ja wie beim Mittelstand" (ibid.). Fontane's *Frau Jenny Treibel* had already shown that the gradations within the middle class could be greater than those separating it from the class above, a view to which Türkheimer would clearly subscribe.

An instance of Türkheimer's patronage has been seen earlier in the novel in the art of Claudius Mertens. What proportion love of the arts and self-aggrandizement respectively constitute in Türkheimer's patronage emerges from the fact that Mertens works exclusively for a few houses such as Türkheimer's, destroying models of his creations for a fittingly large reward.[19] Works of art in the *Schlaraffenland* are the preserve of financial aristocrats such as Türkheimer, art is a ware that can be bought and treated with exclusiveness. The artist's attitude to his work is similarly pragmatic. His talents are sacrificed to his venality, though of course a society of artistic philistines is also responsible, people prepared to encourage panderings to their own poor taste. Thus from his beginnings, which would have done credit to Michelangelo, Mertens has declined to creating elaborate *Kitsch* — a roulette-wheel in which ivory horses serve as spokes, their riders "in meistens durchaus intimen Stellungen" (75) — or figures distantly reflecting the features of some of Türkheimer's own circle of friends, in monstrous postures. His creations on the one hand pamper the narcissistic impulses of his protectors[20] and on the other externalize the thwarted Dionysian impulses which they are simply incapable of generating (65).

This then is the sad reality behind the lofty phrase: "Die deutsche Geisteskultur."

c. *The theatre as a social institution*

In this novel H. Mann employs a feature which recurs in later works. He portrays the production of a play or opera, less as a comment on the aesthetic side of the art itself than as a device whereby he can bring together his main figures. These are generally seen in smaller groups within the larger one, even in such cases as a grand function at the Türkheimers' residence. This serves a similar artistic purpose to the ball at the Barnewitz' in *Problematische Naturen* in bringing together a range of social types, manners etc., without differences in social levels being accentuated by H. Mann. With a theatrical production at which the bulk of the novel's figures are present, the one central interest attracts their varying reactions, which are what most interest the writer. We find this on a larger, more finely delineated scale in *Die kleine Stadt* with the performance of the opera *Die arme Tonietta*, and with much less epic sweep in the *Lohengrin* episode of *Der Untertan*. The element of literary criticism is also present, in this case a broadside at Hauptmann's *Die Weber* as the representative of Naturalist drama. H. Mann had expressed his distaste for this work in 1894:

> [. . .] ouvrage foncièrement antipathique [. . .]. Le drame manque de toute beauté morale, la misère *en révolte* n'offrant pas, à mon sens, ce charme de pitié et de commisération duquel est imbue la résignation [. . .], c'est le manque de tout contenu moral qui me choque le plus [. . .].[21]

It is ruthlessly pilloried here in a performance of Klempner's *Rache*.

Claudius Mertens' figures were a debasement of his models in the *Schlaraffenland*, yet these revelled in what they saw as a perpetuation of themselves. Similarly do they respond to the potential mirror held before them on the stage. When the factory owner's wife is forced by the abuse of the workers' wives to drop the veneer of respectability she answers them "mit der gleichen schmutzigen Beredsamkeit" (115), comparable to the confrontation between Adelheid and Frau Levzahn (231). This scene reduces the audience to a frenzy of acclaim. Just as Claudius Mertens has lost his affinity to Michelangelo through the selling-out of his art, so does the reverse process of evaluation apply when

Pimbusch as the spokesman for the aesthetically bankrupt audience calls the tastelessness of the drama "Michelangelesk!" (117).

Kaflisch sees the task of the social dramatist thus:

Kräftige volkstümliche Instinkte, Wollust und Grausamkeit, die sonst eher im Panoptikum befriedigt werden, in 'ne gewisse höhere Sphäre erheben. (119)

For Türkheimer the cathartic side of theatre has a more direct function. At the end of the performance the "Arbeitermarseillaise" is intoned by the remnants of the audience. "In der Loge der exotischen Diplomaten sah man Türkheimer wohlgefällig lächelnd den Takt schlagen" (129).[22] For him the theatre provides a legitimate outlet for substitute ardour, for feelings that could otherwise undermine his position if transferred from the grotesque emotionality of simulated reality to his reality.[23] Nor are revolutionary feelings the only ones sublimated here. The sensationalism and lack of art of the play are rivalled only by the avid response of most of the audience, as when the ladies stand up to follow the abduction of two of the female characters behind stage-prop scrub, transported by their most sensuous desires to which they give full rein, albeit by proxy. But then the people of the Schlaraffenland show no capacity to experience any genuinely strong emotions other than at second hand. The only two spectators not caught up in the enthusiasm are the blithely innocent Frau Blosch and the venerable Wennichen, whose comprehension of politics has remained static since 1848. The critics are duped or bribed too, witness Abell's absurd eulogies:

Ein neuer Stern ist aufgetaucht, der manchen unserer dramatischen Epigonen aus dem Feld schlagen dürfte . . . Geniale Synthese einer differenzierten Gesellschaftspsychologie . . . Napoleonische Bewegung der Massen . . . Überlegener sozialer Gerechtigkeitssinn . . . (135)

This supposed "Gerechtigkeitssinn" is lauded by the spectators in their wilful blindness to its possible application to their own position, so blinded is their judgement by the play's sensationalism. Earlier somebody had on the other hand objected to the censorship of the desecration scenes: "Darf man nur uns auf der Bühne vergewaltigen und die Pfaffen nicht?" (43). But by the end there is no sense of offence, and Adelheid is astonished and full of admiration when Andreas draws the logical inference that Klempner has bitten the hand that has been feeding him. The audience's acclaim is, ideologically speaking, suicidal. If we take the "Schnapswirt" (114) as being an oblique reference to Pimbusch, then the latter's rhapsodic reaction to the play (117) is in keeping with his self-destructive outlook. Not that he penetrates the transparent veil. Parallel to his is his wife's reaction to the treatment meted out to Mesallina, the wife of the "Schnapswirt" (119).

The whole spectacle is symptomatic of the cultural appreciation of the Schlaraffenland. Not only does it lack all vestige of taste. But for it the theatre is purely a social institution, a point of convergence of fashions, carefully chosen platitudes and the indulging of emotions, not a vehicle for ideas or for any direct criticism of contemporary society. For this audience, even social drama with far greater pretensions than Rache could ultimately only be a sociable evening's entertainment. At the same time the title of the play is symptomatic of the Schlaraffenland. The words "Rache" and "sich rächen" appear repeatedly with respect to a whole range of characters and situations (see for example 171, 198, 218, 246, 265, 349 et passim). They demonstrate in each case a display of power.[24] The revenge exacted frequently only ruffles the surface of the society momentarily, but can go beyond this harmless level in threatening the very foundations of a hierarchy built up on fear (cf. 249) — thus Türkheimer is disconcerted when Andreas envisages for him death at the hands of anarchists.

The audience present at *Rache* is later criticized by Lizzi Laffé. But here as elsewhere the problem is raised which André Banuls, speaking of another episode, formulates as follows:

> [. . .] die Ironie ist, vor allem dadurch, daß die Kritik oder das Lob von selbst lächerlichen Gestalten formuliert werden, derart vielschichtig, daß man sich fragt, ob die Satire nicht alle Parteien trifft. [25]

Certainly "unser dünkelhaftes Berliner Publikum" (161) is attacked by Lizzi alone, but not through any genuine insight into its deficiencies. Rather is she motivated by spite and jealousy, and she makes the ludicrous counter-assertion that true cultivation is to be found in provincial outposts like Posemuckel and Meseritz, where her protégé's play has met with success.

The final incisive satire of the writer's role comes in inflated, meaningless terms when Andreas is riding on the crest of his wave:

> "Ich besitze ein zu empfindliches Organ für den kaum erst wahrnehmbaren Hauch des Zeitgeistes. Ah! wie wenige sind wir im Grunde, in ganz Europa verstreut, die es besitzen. Wir bilden sozusagen einen Geheimbund, mit der Absicht, zu fühlen, was keiner fühlt, die erst zu erfindenden Verfeinerungen, den noch ungeborenen Kitzel einer hohen geistigen Korruption. Fühlen, das ist alles! Was bedeutet es, Gedichte zu verbrechen oder einen Roman zu schreiben?"
> Er schrieb keinen. (313-14)

In the laconic editorial sequel to Andreas' exalted nonsense we see that the wheel has turned a full cycle, another attribute of the *Schlaraffenland*. Dr. Libbenow's glib assertion in the "Café Hurra" that he had read no books for ten years finds its echo here in Andreas' scorning of further literary activity after his one play has found for him a niche in this society. The credo of the young Goethe: "Gefühl ist alles!" (*Faust* I, 1. 3456-57) has been debased here to an emasculated obscurantism. In place of the upsurge of creative energy untrammelled by the intellect, Andreas' slogan is a justification of his inactivity. [26] The "Geheimbund" is also an allusion to coteries of ages past, modernized here as the preserve of a decaying society.

Andreas makes further literary references. On one occasion he endows himself with a Faustian "Zweiseelenleben" (261). On another, Klempner sympathizes with him on account of his fresh fame, which involves so many social obligations. Andreas agrees and professes a desire to dedicate his energies exclusively to work. But the insubstantiality of this desire is shown by the farfetched concepts he uses:

> Ganz zur Arbeit zurück! In einem fünften Stockwerk, mitten in einem Proletarierviertel Berlins, oder in irgendeiner fernen Waldeinsamkeit. (212)

The seamier side of Berlin is just as distant from this darling of its society as the "Waldeinsamkeit" of a Tieck. The remoteness from true poetry is symptomatic of the novel. The genuine idyll of a Romantic "Waldeinsamkeit" is the exact counterpart of the self-indulgent and superficial community living *Im Schlaraffenland*.

3. *Politics*

The tone for the shallowness of political opinion is set early in the piece in the course of Andreas' apprenticeship in the ways of Berlin society:

> Zum Lohn dafür durfte er Meinungen, die er nicht einmal hatte, sogar dem strengen Doktor Pohlatz gegenüber vertreten. Einmal ließ er sich einfallen, den Sozialismus, der ihm durchaus gleichgültig war, nur darum herauszustreichen, weil er dies für etwas Besonderes hielt. (17)

Here we see two variations of the central image of the theatre. Andreas voices opinions as if reading a part; they are not his own. We shall see (p. 140) how it also occurred to him to feign strong Catholic views to impress Adelheid. Both causes he ostensibly champions are something out of the ordinary, their espousal purely designed to attract attention. In this novel there is no possibility of suggesting any concrete alternative as none of the main and few of the secondary characters are endowed with the sincerity to express an opinion that can be considered on its merits. This *Zeitroman* exposes mercilessly but does not proclaim.

Andreas goes on to learn the origin of the name "Café Hurra":

> Die Herren von der Tafelrunde hatten früher staatsumwälzenden Grundsätzen gehuldigt, bis im März 1890[27] sich die Sozialdemokratie als nicht mehr zeitgemäß herausstellte. Damals hatten alle einem Bedürfnis der Epoche nachgegeben, sie waren ihren freisinnigen Prinzipalen ein Stückchen Weges nach rechts gefolgt und bekannten sich seither zum Regierungsliberalismus und Hurra-patriotismus. (17)

The gentlemen so described seem to have been motivated solely by what was "zeitgemäß" in their earlier upholding of social-democratic principles. Their "Hurrapatriotismus" is later echoed in Liebling's fanatical championing of all that is "deutsch" (see p. 140).

Political capriciousness has emerged as something of a topos of the *Zeitroman* from Immermann through to H. Mann, with the exception of the swansong to Prussian conservatism in *Der Stechlin*. Political opinions can be cast off like clothes in the Berlin of *Im Schlaraffenland,* witness the story behind the name of the "Café Hurra." At one historical remove we have seen the opportunistic twins Julian and Isidor throwing dice to determine their political allegiance in *Martin Salander.* Still further back, some sixty years earlier, Mann's image was prefigured by Wilhelmi in *Die Epigonen* to decry the shifting sands of opinion of his own generation. With Immermann the lack of stability arises from the historical fate of *Epigonentum,* having no firm present identity to confront the multiplicity of fragmented inheritances from the past. With H. Mann it is a tendency to drift dictated by expediency. It is simply not good business to run a newspaper along politically committed lines, as Andreas learns from Doktor Bediener (29). Going beyond expediency is complacency, a wilful lack of involvement as proclaimed by Ratibohr before an admiring audience (47). It is a reflection of the *Schlaraffenland,* the final stages of an over-refined society slowly subsiding into ruin. Common to both Immermann's and Mann's ages, at least as seen by these two literary seismographs, is their lack of historical identity. Wilhelmi says of his age: "Sie spielt Komödie wie keine andere" (III, 55), and of his generation:

> Abwechselnd kriecht sie in den frommen Rock, in den patriotischen Rock, in den historischen Rock, in den Kunstrock und in wie viele Röcke noch sonst! (ibid.)

Parallels offer themselves: Andreas' "Marotte" (see p. 140) as an example of the first coat, the "Café Hurra" and Liebling in connection with the second, Türkheimer's Renaissance-style palace (36) with the third, and the admirers of Claudius Mertens' art with the fourth.[28] Because, like coats, they are changeable at will, political opinions are arbitrary. This fact impresses itself strongly on Andreas at the Türkheimers' soirée, where opposed viewpoints forwarded by Liebling and Wennichen are discounted by Ratibohr's clinching remark: "Es ist ja Nebensache, wie regiert wird" (47). The ineducability of these circles is registered, the political apathy and the accompanying penchant for self-destruction of the upper bourgeoisie.

Türkheimer's domain, where power truly resides, is described correspondingly in terms of the apparatus of the state. Images from the sphere of government predominate in Andreas' impression (26) of the vast power of Bediener and of Jekuser, a constitutional monarch with even greater powers. It is a metaphor developed on a grand scale, showing the state being surpassed by an empire on the scale of Türkheimer's. Andreas' appraisal of Jekuser continues:

> Und er war reicher als sie [andere gekrönte Häupter] , denn von den Abgaben seines Volkes, von den fünfzehn Pfennigen, die Hunderttausende von Lesern täglich erlegten, blieb der größere Teil in seiner Tasche zurück. (ibid.)

This picture of a monopolistic capitalism is only slightly modified later by Türkheimer-style Communism, which involves supporting all those in his immediate circle. But it of course doesn't benefit the countless readers of the "Nachtkourier," and these subjugated readers, or rather the system they imply, still inspire awe in Andreas (208) when he has gained acclaim through his play and is tending to treat his wellwishers very condescendingly.

4. Class-barriers

Jürgen Zeck sees an affirmation of class-barriers in this novel. Referring to H. Mann's articles for the journal *Das zwanzigste Jahrhundert,* Zeck writes:

> Die revolutionären, demokratischen, liberalen und besonders sozialistischen Ideen seiner Zeit lehnt Heinrich Mann entschieden ab und stellt ihnen sein Bild des hierarchischen Staates, der sich aus einer traditionellen Ständegesellschaft zusammensetzen soll, entgegen. Nach Thema und Inhalt muß der Roman 'Im Schlaraffenland' dieser ersten Phase seines politischen Denkens zugeordnet werden.[29]

In fact, consideration of the text will show that this is not the case and that boundaries between the classes are becoming very fluid indeed in this novel.

This is seen from the heading of chapter 5, "Ein demokratischer Adel" — alluding to the forthcoming marriage of Asta and Hochstetten — a combination of concepts unthinkable in any society that is hierarchically constructed in the traditional sense. The tendency, already observed, to paint a negative, satirical picture without any positive counterbalance, is carried through consistently. An indictment of one class applies equally well to another. For example, Goldherz coins the phrase "Müde Rasse!" (61) to capture the debilitated nobility. But this is not symptomatic only of the nobility, and in the next chapter Kaflisch uses the same term to describe Frau Pimbusch, wife of the spirits merchant (74). Although in this he is consciously mimicking Hochstetten and his detractor Goldherz, the parallel remains. Hochstetten's impotence is countered by Claire Pimbusch's frigidity, a situation which draws together Hochstetten and his imitator (297). Indeed, so representative is the figure of Claire meant to be that she alone of the figures from *Im*

Schlaraffenland is carried over into *Die Göttinnen* and mentioned as a subject for painting in the same breath as "die Hysterie und das *ohnmächtige* Laster"[30] (author's emphasis).

Class-barriers further vanish before the power of money. Just as Türkheimer can buy the art of Claudius Mertens, so can Asta, backed by her father's colossal wealth, buy herself into the nobility. Klempner sums it up thus:

> So 'nen Baron und gar 'nen Geheimrat vom neuen Kurs kann sich doch jetzt schon der gute Mittelstand leisten, seit der Adel sich den Liberalismus anschafft, den wir abgelegt haben! (63)

There is thus a mutual interdependence. The bourgeoisie, in this case Asta, still pays homage to the old order by acknowledging a noble title as something worth attaining, although from Duschnitzki's offhanded words — "Sie kauft sich einen Namen! Was ist denn so'n abgetragener Name heute wert? " (ibid.) — it is clear that this name is but a hollow shell of its former substance. On the other hand the nobility, here Hochstetten, needs the financial reserves of the bourgeoisie to prop up its crumbling fortunes. This situation is far more radical than in Fontane's works. In *Irrungen Wirrungen,* for instance, the fortunes of one noble family are still restored by marrying into another, while in *Die Poggenpuhls* a marriage between Leo and either of two rich Jewesses is averted by a legacy inherited from his uncle. Class-distinctions are, on the other hand, transgressed in *Im Schlaraffenland.* Türkheimer's fêting of Matzke's daughter draws from Köpf the comment:

> Oh, keine Frau gehört einer bestimmten Klasse an [. . .]. Vornehmsten Anstand und tiefste Canaillerie, alles besitzen sie von Hause aus. Man zieht ihnen ein neues Kleid an, und flugs entdecken sie in sich die dazu passenden Sitten. (264)

This makes a complete mockery of notions of an earlier age that certain qualities such as social deportment were solely possessed by the upper class, their inherited birthright. At the same time it exposes the hollowness of such assumed "Anstand" — the two-edged sword is ever H. Mann's satirical weapon.

The blurring of contours between the bourgeoisie and the nobility is furthered in the character of Pimbusch, who consciously models himself on Hochstetten. Like Hochstetten, Pimbusch has inherited his position and the fame associated with his name. "Der träge Zug der Proletarier" (94) ensures his continued commercial success, and he despises those whose misery he cultivates. The extent of his influence is described in mock apocalyptic tones: "Ein giftiger Duft zog durch die Stadt, die in einem Meer von Schnaps zu ertrinken trachtete" (95). He steeps the masses in deeper degradation while ostensibly providing them with a panacea. The figure of Pimbusch alone is sufficient to contradict the following thesis of Zeck. Citing Matzke's and Hochstetten's venality before the all-consuming wealth of Türkheimer, Zeck concludes:

> Heinrich Mann will damit den destruktiven Einfluß der jüdischen Hochfinanz auf die niederen wie die höheren Volksschichten zeigen. Diese antisemitische Tendenz darf in diesem Roman nicht übersehen werden. [31]

The first sentence of this quotation is demonstrably onesided — there could be little more ravaging abuse of power and position towards the lower classes than that exhibited by the Gentile Pimbusch. The second sentence, while true, is developed by Zeck into a regular witchhunt of antisemitism:

> Das von Juden regierte 'Schlaraffenland' läßt die Entfaltung eines deutsch empfindenden Menschen nicht zu, der negative Einfluß auf den Adel wie auf das Proletariat wird gezeigt.[32]

The claim that Jewish finance is responsible for, and not simply contemporaneous with, the ethical decline of both nobility and proletariat is not substantiated. Moreover, Zeck's assertion that Jewish sentiments are swamping Germanic ones ignores the figure of Liebling, ever in the background, who is proselytised at the end in the opposite direction, abandoning his Zionist sentiments for an insidious chauvinism.

To return to Pimbusch, Kaflisch's descriptions of him — "Schnaps*feudalen*," "*Feudaljobber*" (95 — author's emphasis) — strengthen the impression of his self-styled affinity to Hochstetten. Again the picture presented is unrelievedly prophetic of doom, because Pimbusch's motives in modelling himself on Hochstetten are not a misguided attempt to emulate a grandeur that is absent: "[. . .] es war Pimbuschs zehrender Ehrgeiz, als letzter Ausdruck einer an Überfeinerung zugrunde gehenden Gesellschaft zu gelten" (ibid.). The final parallel between the two classes comes with the following appraisal of their fate:

> Und obwohl er von der Herkunft seines Großvaters durchaus nichts wußte, kam dieser Sproß des kräftigen Bürgertums dem Ideal des vollkommenen Kretinismus mindestens ebenso nahe wie der Freiherr von Hochstetten, dessen Vorfahr mit dem Burggrafen von Nürnberg in Brandenburg eingezogen war. (ibid.)

The ironic "Sproß des kräftigen Bürgertums" is in itself enough to undermine the hope Wennichen places in the class. Here the trust in the revitalizing effect of bourgeois blood on inbred noble circles — as expressed by the mother of the Russian Prince in Spielhagen's *Problematische Naturen* — seems remote indeed. H. Mann's portrayal is of course too exaggerated to be a general comment on the age; it is part and parcel of the distortion of his satire. But the tendency he is pointing to cannot be dismissed as easily — the figure of Pimbusch would seem monstrous and not simply overdrawn in a novel set in the Berlin of a slightly earlier period.

For all Hochstetten's pathetic weakness and insignificance as an individual, the class to which he belongs still retains certain privileges which outsiders can only aspire to through connections such as Hochstetten. Thus does the parasitic Pimbusch trail after his model wherever he goes.

> Denn Pimbusch hegte den wahnwitzigen Ehrgeiz, durch Vermittelung von Türkheimers Schwiegersohn in den hocharistokratischen Jeuklub aufgenommen zu werden. (97)

And Türkheimer himself, colossus of power that he is, finally induces his son-in-law to gain an honour for him through his position as "Geheimrat." He gains the "Kronenorden vierter Klasse" (368), an honour that is laughably insignificant compared with the store he sets by it and is outside his own power to achieve.[33] This motif is developed with Diederich Heßling's ultimate award of the "Wilhelmsorden" at the end of *Der Untertan*.

Im Schlaraffenland blurs the distinctions between classes through elaborate parallels, e.g. Pimbusch and Hochstetten, and the actual crossing of class borders, e.g. Asta's marriage into the nobility. Bienaimée's status as daughter of a worker is only really changed when she marries Andreas and they are both assured of stultifying bourgeois mediocrity. Though a higher jump, her position as mistress of the finance-giant Türkheimer was always tenuous. Fontane, in *Stine*, portrays the partners each one step higher on the social ladder with the bourgeois Pauline Pittelkow as mistress to a nobleman. Despite the fluidity of social boundaries, the examples of Pimbusch and Türkheimer have shown that a certain level of social prestige, however empty that prestige may seem, is attainable only through noble connections. This assures even such a weakling as Hochstetten of a certain power, for when Asta no longer provides her husband with an adequate allowance, he can confidently find support in Pimbusch, ever nurturing his hopes of acceptance into the aristocratic "Jeuklub." These last vestiges of noble power protect Hochstetten and his ilk from the state envisaged by Andreas: "Alles Bestehende ist heutzutage unsicher, und kein Mensch weiß, ob er nicht eines Tages wird arbeiten müssen" (100). Like so many of his utterances, this is admittedly said less with earnestness than to create an effect. Instead of being a verdict on the times it becomes a foretelling of Andreas' own end.

For all its decline the nobility still ultimately retains its superiority through its rootedness in tradition, its natural right to those signs of taste and refinement almost violently trumpeted forth by a bourgeoisie that is suffering from an inferiority complex as historical upstarts. Bourgeois pretensions are no more ruthlessly exposed than in what Griseldis von Hochstetten's scornful gaze seems to Andreas to be saying at the Türkheimers' soirée. It is almost substantiation of her criticisms that the symbols she seizes on as embodying bourgeois pretensions and the meanness she detects behind them are to be found in some cases verbatim in Fontane's anti-bourgeois prose works. Here belong the "Zimmer voll echte Gobelins" (106), the "Meißner Porzellan" (ibid.) and the "Trödelläden" (105), [34] while her final broadside strikes the bourgeoisie at its most vulnerable point, which no amount of imitation can ever redeem:

Ihr [. . .] prahlt mit diesen und anderen historischen Erinnerungen, als ob ihr Erinnerungen haben könntet, und als ob in den Zeiten, als jene Herrlichkeiten erfunden wurden, euresgleichen existiert hätte! (106)

Griseldis' diatribe, almost a page in length, is not even an explicit comment — "Sie schien zu sagen" (105) — but rather what Andreas reads into her severe expression, and thus it reflects his attitude to the bourgeoisie's weaknesses as much as hers. It is a further device employed by H. Mann which diminishes the binding quality of what is said, however much truth it is meant to contain from the viewpoint of the character concerned, the author behind the novel or actual history. This distancing seems to overcome a problem otherwise encountered in the *Zeitroman,* where either the author can intrude with some statement on the times or such a statement can be expressed through one of the characters. The dry sententiousness of some of Wilhelmi's pronouncements in *Die Epigonen* shows the dangers inherent in the latter approach.

For all its poetic devices, Mann's novel does capture the main crosscurrents of the age. This can best be seen by drawing on an economic historian — the following quotation sounds almost like an abstraction of Mann's novel, combining as it does so many of the work's features:

Das Großbürgertum trennte sich vom übrigen Bürgertum und wurde feudalisiert. Es suchte in seinem Streben, zur Spitze der gesellschaftlichen Pyramide aufzusteigen, nach einer Lebensform, die ihm die Zugehörigkeit zur Elite bestätigte, und es glaubte diese Form in dem durch lange Tradition gefestigten Lebensstil des Adels zu finden. Man sieht diese Übernahme aristokratischer Lebensformen an der Entwicklung der Fabrikantenwohnungen vom kleinen Haus unmittelbar neben dem Betrieb über die Villa zum ländlichen Herrensitz [. . .] und schließlich im Streben nach der Nobilitierung oder wenigstens einem auszeichnenden Ratstitel. Die Feudalisierung des Großbürgertums entsprang nicht nur gesellschaftlichem Ehrgeiz, sondern auch einem gemeinsamen sozialpolitischen und allgemeinpolitischen Interesse mit dem Adel. Diese politische Interessengemeinschaft beruhte darauf, daß *beide* einen *gemeinsamen Gegenspieler* hatten: die Arbeiterbewegung. [35]

5. Finance

Lest Griseldis' standing on noble pride (331) should be seen as a potentially positive value, it in turn is demolished. In a vicious scene with Asta, the latter expresses her disappointment in her husband, with a neat inversion of class roles:

> Schon während der ganzen Reise hat er mir durch seine unnobeln, wie soll ich sagen — bürgerlichen Gewohnheiten das Leben unmöglich gemacht. (224)

Despite her expressed wish he fails to wear patent leather shoes, which rouses her indignation and her desire to divorce him — a feature perhaps comparable with Bienaimée's stubborn search for her fairytale prince, and one which at once renders her ridiculous. But for all this, her attack on Griseldis loses none of its venom. When she protests Hochstetten's inability to present her with an heir, Griseldis hypocritically objects:

> Sprechen Sie doch nicht von einem Erben Ihres Geldes, liebe Asta, sondern von einem Stammhalter des Hauses Hochstetten! (225)

Asta then proceeds to unmask Griseldis and at the same time the reasons for Hochstetten's waning finances: — he passes the pocket money received from Asta on to Griseldis, who invests it in Gold Mounts shares. The latter objects all too loudly and stands stripped of her superior veneer. Money has exercised its lure on her too, and she does not content herself with sending gifts to Palestine, "zur Bekehrung von Judenkindern" (226). Even in the completely unprincipled *Schlaraffenland* it is a grotesque piece of satire that the money of the Jewish financier Türkheimer should find its way via Asta, Hochstetten and Griseldis to the Holy Land to proselytise his co-religionists.

Money, not religious, cultural or moral values, stands at the core of this society: [36]

> Gutes Essen, feine Weine, Weiber, Witze, Kunst und Vergnügen, es ist alles da. Man langt eben zu, wie im Schlaraffenland. (87)

Thus muses Andreas. Directly before, he has questioned the origin of all the money, a single time. Manfred Hahn draws attention to this and registers the following, somewhat tendentiously expressed criticism:

> Insgesamt beschränkt also die Unkenntnis der ökonomischen Prozesse die Breite der erfaßten Wirklichkeit und die Tiefe ihrer Analyse. Reife der Weltanschauung und des Realismus korrespondieren. [37]

In fact statements on the financial bases of the *Schlaraffenland* seem contradictory. When Andreas hears that Ratibohr has more millions than he, Andreas, has marks, Duschnitzki claims: "Hier sind wir Millionäre oder Schubbejacks" (57), to which Klempner adds: "So ist es. Der Mittelstand stirbt aus" (ibid.). Andreas himself, in trying to fathom the functioning of the *Schlaraffenland,* says later: "Die einen haben schauderhaft viel Geld, die anderen gar nichts" (86). But this financial polarization is not the whole picture. Klempner's statement is not valid, as the bulk of the novel is concerned with the financial "Mittelstand." At most those people in the middle range of wealth might be dying out as wealth becomes concentrated in the hands of tycoons like Türkheimer. But even that is an oversimplified picture because according to the tenets of Türkheimer-style Communism all within his far-reaching domain receive some of the benefits of his accumulated fortunes.

However artificial their wellbeing might be, there are no absolute have-nots.

This is seen in the bitter satire of Matzke's swaying convictions; his anti-nobility views are temporarily quietened by his daughter's rise to wealth and reappear with her fall from Türkheimer's grace. His views are seen to be without revolutionary substance, as springing purely from the jealousy of the non-possessing, and they are thus without hope of enforcing a change in the system because they can be bought by the system. The proletariat, a rising force in Fontane's *Der Stechlin*,[38] holds no keys to the future in this novel. Nor does the narrative dwell on their material misery. Reference to the poorly ventilated back room (172) in which Sophie Levzahn has been raised, brings only a slight touch of social criticism. What interests Mann is the hopelessly confined manners and morals of the Levzahns. But if the proletariat is not yet ripe for revolution, the bourgeoisie is atrophied in its wellbeing, and the following glimmering appreciation of social problems is a lonely voice in the wilderness: "Geben wir dem Volke nicht Brot und Feste, so kommen wir selbst früher oder später an den Galgen" (46).

Türkheimer's role as the centre of this financial solar system[39] requires closer consideration. A typical example of his operations on a smaller scale is given early in the novel as the background to Blosch's marriage. Blosch, Türkheimer's man-of-straw in shadier transactions on the stock exchange, travels to the provinces to settle amicably a bankruptcy case involving an industrialist, Türkheimer having assured through mortgages his eventual ownership of the factory. More spectacular instances of Türkheimer's power are the Puerto Vergogna affair and the Texas Bloody Gold Mounts shares. These show his wide-ranging influence and business acumen. In the former, Türkheimer emerges with a gain of seventy million, while the republic of Puerto Vergogna is financially ruined and furthermore reaps the enmity of the German government. To show its attitude, a cruiser is despatched to defend the interests of the duped creditors and to show the world how far the strong arm of Germany extends (83-84). The incident is of course fanciful and yet a very pertinent statement on Germany's policy at the time[40] of developing naval power overnight to vie with England's, and exhibiting this in brash and belligerent fashion. Indeed it is highly prophetic, foreshadowing Wilhelm II's landing at Tangiers on March 31st 1905.[41] This coup of Türkheimer's earns him the following eulogy from Kaflisch: "[. . .] für uns moderne Literaten geht nichts über das Genie der Tat. Napoleon, Bismarck, Türkheimer!" (ibid.). Exaggerated as this comparison is, it does show Türkheimer's span of influence, setting off reactions not only on the local stock exchange but also in international politics. The parallel to Bismarck in supposed grandeur, never in historical terms, is reinforced later when Türkheimer consciously adopts one of the Iron Chancellor's more famous terms, offering to mediate in a quarrel between his wife and Lizzi Laffé "als ehrlicher Makler" (163). Such historical *geflügelte Worte* tend to reinforce the ideas of Türkheimer's might. Removed from a historical context, they also suggest hybris on the part of the fictional character.

The incident of the Texas Bloody Gold Mounts shares shows Türkheimer's power extending from the stock exchange to the sphere of journalism, in contriving the removal of his rival Schmeerbauch and gaining into the bargain the admiration of the masses who have been his suffering pawns. This he achieves by offering them a scapegoat when their resentment threatens to become ugly. Schmeerbauch suicides and the *Volk*, their bloodthirstiness whetted by the policeman's account of the editor's end, are appeased by the false sacrifice. Just as Türkheimer had occasion to smile indulgently at the misdirected venting of revolutionary zeal at the performance of *Rache*, so does he regard this interlude as greatly diverting. Türkheimer speaks of the duped masses either in platitudes of incredible distance and hollowness — "Das Volk ist doch das einzig Wahre" or "Für das

Volk muß was geschehen" (259) — or with a far more direct, scandalously patronizing cynicism:

> Denken Sie bloß an all die Dummen, [. . .] meist kleine Leute, die ihre Groschen in ihrem saueren Schweiß aufbewahren wie Rollmöpse in Essig. Heutzutage muß man schließlich 'n paar soziale Gefühle haben , [. . .] und Dumme sind auch Menschen. (245)

Those he can crush under his thumb either remain ignorant of this, pitting their resentment against the far less significant Schmeerbauch, or they are ineffective in their protests. Thus Matzke's vulgar denunciation of Adelheid and her affluence as she drives past — "Dicket faulet Aas, [. . .] *fährt uff Jummirädern*" (257)[42] — remains no more than a bold expletive, moreover one which amuses Türkheimer greatly, because Matzke's resentment can be bought off.

Yet there are other threatening signs which throw into partial relief Türkheimer's most triumphant moment. Andreas concludes his praise of the great man by saying his ilk meet their deaths at the hands of anarchists (254), which alarms Türkheimer into hastily changing the subject. This is not the end accorded Türkheimer in the novel, indeed he meets no end, though progressively ravaged by his increasing blood-sugar level, and Andreas does prepare his obituary. But the exposure to publicity that is Türkheimer's lot, the masses thronging the street who see Andreas bathing in the reflected glory of the great man, all this sets the scene for such a deed if sufficient resentment were fostered. There are signs of this, too. Kokott, whose talent has been purchased and debased like Claudius Mertens', lives from Türkheimer's bribes not to divulge his master's devious business methods. That alone shows the precariousness of Türkheimer's position, that and the resentment harboured by his hireling: "Kokott schnitt in Türkheimers Rücken eine rachgierige Fratze." Kokott concludes:

> Kriege ich ihn aber mal zufällig mit auf ein Gerüst hinauf, dann soll er bedeutend plötzlicher unten wieder ankommen, als ihm lieb ist! (256)

But these are mere omens in the novel. Concerted opposition by the exploited is nowhere evident. Such opposition as they do offer is misdirected, ineffective. The end of the chapter summarizes both this impotence and also the self-destructive trait present in Türkheimer. He entreats his vassal: "Machen Sie mal Ihre Judenfratze!" (260); Kokott complies and Türkheimer congratulates him. Thus Türkheimer only gets to see the grimace he has demanded and not the other, dangerous one made behind his back.

Andreas, though not one of the oppressed, does see the far-reaching implications of Türkheimer's system of power:

> Eine Laune, ein Wink von Ihnen, und der oder jener ist ruiniert, eine Unmasse Familien geraten ins Elend oder werden glücklich, je nachdem es Ihnen gefällt; notleidende Stände gehen ganz zugrunde oder dürfen ihr Dasein fristen, und die soziale Unzufriedenheit nimmt ab oder wächst. (253-54)

The stock-exchange is entirely at the whim of the few main speculators. It slumps when Türkheimer declares he can no longer take champagne. The wellbeing of its few key figures forms the whole tenuous foundation of the *Schlaraffenland*. Andreas, for all his insight, succumbs to the imposing grandeur of Nietzsche-like "Herrenmenschen" (248) in the Türkheimer mould. He enumerates Türkheimer's crimes but abdicates judgement:

> Von gefälschten Pressenachrichten, Irreführung der öffentlichen Meinung und ausgeplünderten

Bevölkerungsmassen zu faseln, das überlasse ich den Moralisten. (251)

For him the most important factor is "das Ästhetische" (ibid.) embodied in Türkheimer, his example of Renaissance-like greatness to a weak generation.

H. Mann's satire is directed against two qualities combined in Andreas here, his kinship with Diederich Heßling in the face of power, however much abused, and his furthering of the Nietzsche-cult of turn-of-the-century writers in asserting the primacy of the aesthetic over the moral, a problem that is at the heart of *Die Göttinnen*. Even more significant than this aspect of Andreas' eulogies is his exposure of the hollowness of aristocratic symbols (253). This is actually a result of his adoration of power; he sees no substance behind the outward display of pomp presented by the nobility and attributes its lack of power quite simply to the stratification of the classes. Speaking of any prince, he says: "Er steht ja in gar keiner Verbindung mit uns und unserem bürgerlichen Leben" (ibid.). Real power does not reside with those who wear uniforms adorned with orders, but with the moneyed, the moneyed bourgeois, exemplified by Türkheimer.

Not that Türkheimer can afford to keep his amassed fortunes to himself:

[...] wenn ein einzelner Mann so blödsinnig viel gestohlen hat wie Türkheimer, dann kann er keinem mehr weismachen, daß ihm das wirklich alles alleine gehört. (183)

Communism is acceptable to Türkheimer when interpreted as the supporting of the people in the many and varied branches of his financial empire. On such a simple basis — benevolent despotism in the administration of finances instead of government — does the economic system of the *Schlaraffenland* rest, or, as the grandiose title of ch. 9 terms it: "Politik und Volkswirtschaft im Schlaraffenland." Within the confines of the novel this basis seems to suffice.

In the final pages we witness the triumphal procession of Türkheimer and the "Großfürst der Walachei," who, as Andreas ruefully observes, is simply a follower in the footsteps of the president of Puerto Vergogna. So the novel ends on a familiar note with a new celebrity committing himself to Türkheimer's powerful clutches and a cheering, unenlightened crowd reinforcing the cyclical quality of the *Schlaraffenland*. Despite the blatant abuses of Türkheimer's power, the oppressed masses remain blinkered and apathetic. But the land is after all only seemingly impregnable; Türkheimer's health is deteriorating fast and he has no heir. Manfred Hahn summarizes the situation at the end thus:

Die Gesellschaft der großen Bourgeoisie ist durch Stagnation, mehr: durch Verfall gekennzeichnet [...]. Am nächsten liegt durchaus nicht eine revolutionäre Vernichtung durch die Arbeiter, sondern eher ein Prozeß der Selbstzersetzung. [43]

6. *Social manners, customs*

Much is made of Andreas' being a newcomer to the salons of Berlin, his origins in the Rhineland counting very much in his favour. Köpf admonishes him:

Bedenken Sie nur Ihre ältere Kultur! Jeder seßhafte Bauer bei Ihnen zu Hause ist ein Aristokrat gegen die Landstreicher aus dem wilden Osten, die hier in Palästen wohnen. (88)

Köpf's statement refers to the parvenus,[44] especially Jews, who with progressive industrialization swarmed from eastern regions to the capital Berlin.[45] This pattern of migration and the further one of social-climbing from the east to the west of Berlin itself are embraced by the title of Paul Lindau's novel, *Der Zug nach dem Westen*. Because of the lack of a firm basis in tradition for self-respect among the Berliners, they tend to respect Andreas' background. He exploits its potential to the full. It enables him for example to stage successfully his "Marotte" of Catholicism, calculated to be of great curiosity value in nominally Protestant Berlin W. The Rhenish peasant extolled by Köpf reappears in highly ironized form with reference to Andreas' supposed earthy vitality as a lover:

> Zuweilen rächten sich seine natürlichen Anlagen, der bäurische Drang nach ungeheurer fleischlicher Fülle übermannte ihn. (307. Cf. too 140)

Or else he seeks to explain the wild anti-establishment urges roused in him by the performance of *Rache* in the following terms: "Vielleicht waren es uralte Bauerntriebe, die ihn gegen den verhaßten, überfeinerten Stadtbürger aufbrachten" (130).

Certainly the fact of having one's origin in the east is a taint that cannot be thrown off. When Liebling adopts a pedagogic tone towards Bienaimée in his transaction on Türkheimer's behalf, she knows how to hit him below the belt:

> Nanu? Sie langen woll eben von Ihre hinterpommerschen Rittergüter an, Herr Graf, un sind eklig uff die feinen Manieren? (356)

Andreas finds the theme of emancipated womanhood has been degraded by writers from Posen and Schlesien: "Diese besaßen eben die Schwerfälligkeit und den Fanatismus niedriger Kulturstufen" (189-90). When he says: "Die neudeutsche Kultur hat nun mal was Östliches" (189), his comment is to be understood both at a quantitative level — the permeation of culture by the many easterners — and at a qualitative one.

The ultimate example of deference to Andreas comes with the hailing of his play *Die Verkannte*. As Köpf said in the first chapter, the theatre is primarily a social, not a literary, institution, and its successes must be acclaimed accordingly. A steady flow of admirers files before Andreas, the darling of the moment, jumping on the bandwaggon of his success and fêting his supposed qualities as a writer. But the depth of their praise is shown when Türkheimer appears and Andreas is but the protégé of his mighty patron, to whom honour has to be accorded as the only constant hero of the *Schlaraffenland*. This is all conveyed in a scene reminiscent of that in which Andreas' reading of Griseldis' glance is given at length. Here it is the gaze of each person looking towards Türkheimer and seeking approval for his act of devotion. The description is couched in almost prayerful tones in accordance with Türkheimer's supremacy (cf. 209).

Greed, extortion and hypocrisy are exposed at all levels of society, not simply the higher ones. Frau Levzahn and her daughter are primarily interested in the money they can extort from Adelheid as the price of silence, not in offended moral principles. Andreas, who has witnessed Adelheid's humiliation at the whim of their sharp tongues, is offended at an aesthetic level — such baseness is the opposite of his concept of Macchiavellian magnificence. It is thus another instance of the misunderstood Nietzschean *Übermensch*. Andreas even manages to win Bienaimée's respect and love a single time when in a moment of rage he produces his riding-whip! [46]

A particularly crass example of pretentiousness comes towards the end of the novel when Andreas is at the height of his arrogance. He changes the nameplate on his door to read "Andreas zum See" (312), a motif borrowed directly from Maupassant's *Bel-Ami*. [47] "Er fand, daß dieser Name, wenn noch nicht aristokratisch, doch kaum mehr bürgerlich klinge" (312-13). This could stand as a motto for the whole *Schlaraffenland*, seeking to break with one's identity but never quite achieving a new one.

7. Morality and religion

Apart from Liebling, none of the figures of the *Schlaraffenland* strikes a moralistic pose. Far more important than morality are the possible permutations and combinations of money, power and prestige. Religion also plays a marginal role, though an important one, in its adoption by Andreas as his "Marotte." A hierarchy of values is established by the gathering assembled at Türkheimers', Andreas' first contact with this society. It is reported that Hochstetten, who has used his influence at Türkheimer's behest, has managed to have *Rache* passed for performance largely intact: "Bloß das bißchen Kirchenschändung und die Benutzung der geweihten Gefäße zu unsauberen Zwecken muß weg" (43). Objections to this prerogative of the church are countered by a lady and by Andreas, who typically expresses an opinion behind which lies no personal conviction but the need to make his impression on the course of the conversation. The group concurs, allowing the mishandling of a whole range of hallowed concepts, "die Ehre des Bürgertums [. . .] unser ruhmreiches Heer [. . .] die allerhöchsten Personen! [. . .] den Ruf einer Frau! [. . .] sogar die Börse" (43-44), but drawing the line finally, after scaling these giddy heights, at ridiculing God. This is the limit of iconoclasm. It is drawn not only hypocritically, but unrealistically. A truer appraisal of the hierarchy here postulated is given later by Kaflisch:

> Majestätsbeleidigungen und Gotteslästerungen kann sich bei dem Fortschritt heutzutage der Ärmste leisten; aber haben Sie schon mal jemand gekannt, der an Türkheimer klingelt? [. . .] Das ist nämlich beträchtlich kitzliger. (184)

There is one crime even more terrible than blasphemy. And it is in this context that the hybris of Andreas and Bienaimée is to be seen when they throw the power structure into question.

Genuine moral indignation is virtually unknown where lovers and mistresses are not merely tolerated but expected; indignation about financial matters is far more to be feared.

> Türkheimer ist ja ein sehr verständiger Mann, um die Privatangelegenheiten seiner Frau kümmert er sich nicht. Aber wenn die Geschäfte ins Spiel kommen, dann wird er strenge. (50)

These then are the priorities. The above verdict on Türkheimer refers to the following ticklish situation:

> Dem Bankier Ratibohr zu Gefallen war sie [Adelheid] zur Spekulantin geworden und hatte ihren Gatten nicht nur im Schlafzimmer, sondern was schlimmer war, an der Börse betrogen. (141)

As with so many cases this is an instance of the cyclical nature of the *Schlaraffenland*, presaging Andreas' unforgivable crime. Indeed, it cannot be pretended that his being cuckolded disturbs the potentate at all. Adelheid warns the unversed Andreas: "[. . .] es gibt hier nichts, was man nicht um eines guten Geschäftes willen verraten würde!" (52). Liaisons are wholly subservient to finance and can be used as means towards financial ends, the accepted lovelessness of this society making reactions like jealousy seem ludicrous anyway. But Andreas is far from naïve in his view of their relationship, calculated for his advancement (62, 307).

Nevertheless, morality is observed at a certain level. Köpf warns Andreas against underestimating the womenfolk of the *Schlaraffenland*, at the same time exposing the hollowness of their risqué jokes, their appearance of liberality:

> Vergessen Sie nicht das Moralische! Bei Türkheimers steckt man, so viel Zynismus der gute Ton auch vorschreibt, im Grunde doch voll moralischer Bedenken. Es sind schließlich nur Bürgers-frauen. (87)

The conclusion to Klempner's play, devised by him to answer the aesthetic requirements of his audience, further illustrates the fundamental morality of the *Volk* after all the bloody excesses which have gone before.

The image of play-acting is encountered again in this context, further exposing as a sham such religiosity as is expressed. It is of great curiosity value to have a "Marotte," some whim like Liebling's Zionism which is never taken completely seriously and yet commands respect both for its inherent beliefs and for the singular position of interest it assures its holder. Andreas initially rejects Adelheid's invitation to the performance of *Rache*, seizing upon the inspiration of the moment that he, as a devout Catholic, has to go to church instead. This achieves the desired effect, though Andreas threatens to over-play his hand. It is after all a role, however clever a one, and Adelheid reflects: "[. . .] er durfte seine religiösen Pflichten nicht gar zu ernst nehmen, sonst verdarben sie das Spiel" (110). This characterizes precisely the nature of Andreas' religiosity and further qualifies the hierarchy of absolutes established by Süß, Duschnitzki and the others (see p. 139), making a mockery of Andreas' own protestations in the same scene. He pursues his self-composed role to the extent of arranging his room to resemble a cell and receiving Adelheid's visit in the apparel and pose of a monk. This apparition evokes "Schreckens-vorstellungen [. . .] , die sie der langjährigen Lektüre des 'Nachtkouriers' und des 'Kabel' verdankte" (133). Readers of these papers have learnt to regard the Catholic Church as a dangerous relic of the past. This is possibly a barb by H. Mann against Bismarck's earlier anti-Catholic legislation of the *Kulturkampf* and is at all events an indictment of the insular anti-Catholicism bred by influential Berlin papers such as those owned by Türk-heimer.

The person most overtly concerned with morality is Liebling, for whom "der sittliche Gedanke" is the ultimate criterion of assessment. Yet in an unmasking of what lies behind his assumed moral rectitude at the end of the story, we gain a horrifyingly familiar pro-phetic look into the near future. Cloaked in the guise of moral excellence lies an insidious chauvinism, not for his earlier espoused Zion but for Germany. When a dejected Andreas describes his own actions as "Hybris," Liebling doesn't immediately comprehend, and then exhorts him: "Sprechen Sie übrigens doch deutsch! Wir Deutsche verstehen jetzt nur noch deutsch und sind stolz darauf" (354). Consistently with this he berates Bien-aimée:

> Ich liebe es nicht, wenn Frauen rauchen. Das Weib sollte seinem natürlichen Berufe als Familien-mutter treu bleiben, besonders das deutsche Weib. (356)

It is all there, the ideals of purity and morality in the hypocritical sense of a following generation, the relegation of womanhood to the function of childbearing and -rearing, and the ever-recurring yardstick, "deutsch." In less sinister but equally fanatic mantle a corresponding nationalism is found in Abell's accolades to the fêted dramatist An-dreas.[48] Liebling's moralistically toned pronouncements, often reflecting in the falseness of the language used their falseness of content (see 357), are ultimately debunked in a way even more telling than the clash between his Zionist convictions and his Germanic ideals. In the final passing parade through the *Schlaraffenland* it is he who sits by Adelheid's side as Andreas' successor, which demolishes with one blow his pretence of morality. It also relativizes his efficient mediating work for Türkheimer in arranging the expedient of Andreas' marriage to Bienaimée, since this not only relieves Türkheimer but clears the field for Liebling himself.

Ethics and religion are basically a further possibility for exposing the hypocrisy of the society depicted here. No clearly-contoured picture of religious crosscurrents of the day appears — unlike references to sectarianism and Stöcker in *Der Stechlin* — simply because no one really takes religion seriously. Culture at least had a social value; religion does not even have that, and in any case a *Schlaraffenland* presupposes an existing state of paradise.

8. *Conclusion*

H. Mann's devices in portraying Berlin in the 1890's are largely witty repartee and satiric barbs rather than detailed analysis of social conditions. This has led to a certain uniformity in the spheres considered, for the prevailing impression in all is a combination of emptiness, hypocrisy and theatricality. The society portrayed is basically homogeneous — a calcified upper bourgeoisie — and the traits of the one character can recur in any sphere. This inbred quality of the *Schlaraffenland* works against the novel as a *Zeitroman*. It lacks some variation of the title-symbol in *Der Stechlin* to relate the rather limited epic arena to a more general context, and such efforts as are made to generalize from the particular have been seen as not wholly successful (cf. pp. 120-21).

The novel is, however, important in showing the development in issues common to most other novels treated, notably the relationship between nobility and bourgeoisie. With Immermann and Spielhagen this was a conflict. Here it is a matter of coexistence, though the bourgeoisie has made huge strides in effective power, directed by its financial supremacy. The *Schlaraffenland* of legend, where one simply reaches out for what one wants without worrying about where it has come from, is reflected here in the unreal aura surrounding the whole — the foundations are never clarified. Yet even the fantasies of the author, e.g. the Puerto Vergogna affair, have such direct reference to the social events of the day that the novel can be regarded as a *Zeitroman*, and a very telling one at that, which shrouds the harsh realities in an imaginative veil.

CHAPTER VII

CONCLUSION

The *Zeitroman,* an ill-defined and inadequately researched genre, has found less resonance than the other main novel stream in 19th century German literature, the *Bildungsroman,* and still less than the social novel in other European literatures. This is partly because of the quality of the *Zeitroman* before Fontane and partly because of the slow development of a traditional basis of the genre. The form can be established in broad terms as a novel whose main concern lies in depicting the age contemporary with the writer as an agglomeration of historical and social forces. In doing this the *Zeitroman* exemplifies in a very particular way the tension between the temporally limited and spatially expansive world of the novel. As well as other works treated more cursorily, five novels have been analyzed in detail as representing possibilities of the *Zeitroman.*

The novels chosen span some seventy years' development within German history and literature. This period saw dramatic changes at the historical level, changes reflected in the concrete settings of successive eras of *Zeitromane.* These changes — and not merely greater artistry — are also responsible for a notable feature in Keller's and Fontane's works considered here; this feature might best be termed 'radiation.' In the phrase *"c'est partout comme chez nous"* and Lake Stechlin, we have a relativizing, an application of the particular case portrayed to a more general context. This ensures that the narrowed scope of the fictional worlds in Keller's and Fontane's novels is nonetheless located in a broader framework. The aesthetic device reflects a historical progression: such a radiation would have been unthinkable in the fragmented world of pre-unification Germany depicted in *Die Epigonen* and *Problematische Naturen.*

Thomas Mann wrote to Julius Bab in 1925: "Sicher, Roman, das heißt Gesellschaftsroman [...]."[1] Such an emphasis would have been inconceivable without the gradual evolution of the frequently ignored *Zeitroman.* The nineteenth century novel, in particular the social novel, is popularly held to have been both a democratic form and one feeding substantially on the metropolis, e.g. with Dickens and Balzac. If this view is correct, then the *Zeitroman* evolved under historically blighted augurs in the Germany of the period. Disappointed hopes after the 1848 Revolution, ignored by Spielhagen in *Problematische Naturen*, plus Bismarck's *Kulturkampf* and repeated renewal of the *Sozialistengesetz* (1878-1890) are the most striking examples of the thorny progress of German democracy in the nineteenth century. Furthermore, Berlin was still relatively provincial when it became a capital city. It figures but briefly in Immermann — its salons, a side considerably more developed in H. Mann's scathing satire — and Spielhagen, basically as the setting for the Revolution.

However, it should be noted that there was a turning away from Idealism earlier in the century, at the latest with writers of the *Junges Deutschland.* That is, the aesthetic presuppositions for the form were there, even if the substance of the political and social reality was insufficient to sustain these with much epic sweep. Immermann was still caught up in older aesthetic traditions, even though his novel represents a considerable thematic change. Freytag's clear propagandistic aims make possible a certain breadth within an intact closed system, an illuminating and extolling of the bourgeoisie from all sides, with the nobility, the Poles and the Jews as negative counterpoles. These three groups are not explored or differentiated, and are not even presented as threatening bogeys, but form a negative basis of comparison with German bourgeois virtues. All this of course implies a strongly flavoured view of the age, but also a manageable epic compass. Spielhagen's more complicated political and aesthetic sympathies combine with a more ambitious dissection of society at various levels to produce a novel which uses a spectacular event from contemporary history to draw together its many threads. The elements *Zeit* and *Roman* of the *Zeitroman* are not balanced here.

The Swiss example included sets off the German ones to a degree, Switzerland having a more developed democratic tradition and lacking the *Zeitroman* leitmotif of the decline of the nobility. *Martin Salander* directly relates financial and political currents to individual existences, i.e. as crucial events within those existences. It does not always show the wider communal bases of these individuals, their daily lives, the feel of their environment. These factors are ever-present in Fontane's *Zeitromane*, whose epic dimensions, other than in *Der Stechlin*, are still further reduced.

With the late Fontane and the early H. Mann we have a realization of the historically more favourable preconditions for the genre within Germany, and at the same time a link between the historically distant stature of Goethe's novels and the substantial German contributions to the novel of the twentieth century. *Der Stechlin* is furthermore a consummate resolution of the problems of individualization inherent in the genre. Fontane's personalized *Zeitroman* makes no formal sacrifices for the sake of breadth of subject-matter, but presents figures which are unmistakable and unforgettable in their individuality. He does not develop a natural phenomenon into a large-scale historical analogy, as Spielhagen had done in *Sturmflut*, but transforms a lake actually existing in the Mark Brandenburg into a central symbol. This approach answered that need which had not been met by earlier writers of *Zeitromane* in satisfactory fashion, namely the desirability of combining the individual example with the larger frame of reference. Fontane does not manipulate reality for his own poetic ends, but goes beyond the firm realistic base that is present to an aesthetically satisfying symbolic level, which assures the poetic dimension of the *Zeitroman* its due. His work is neither a historical document nor an artistic fiction but both; it is truly a *Zeit-Roman*. From his position at the end of the century he surveys the subsequent development of those issues which had been too confusing for Immermann and too compelling for Spielhagen, and blends them with characters who really do live out and live in the particular historical period instead of being chance, faceless accompaniments.

From the variety of features observed it is clear that in the nineteenth century the *Zeitroman* was not a static form, as is implied by any normative approach such as Hasubek's in taking Gutzkow as a yardstick. It nevertheless exhibited problematic areas that remained constant and were naturally held in common with those genres whose concerns were also primarily with a panorama of the present or the immediate past. Büchner's view[2] of the historical dramatist being bound in material to historical reality but remoulding that reality in artistic form, could be a statement on the same tension within the *Zeitroman*, and it returns us to Thomas Mann's description of the *Zeitroman* as portraying the inner picture of an era.

Another tension characteristic of the genre is that between ephemeral and more universal elements, the ephemeral which result from exploring an age in considerable depth, and the universal arising from locating the particular age within a broader historical span. This tension relates directly to that between individuals and types in characterization, which is in turn bound up with relative emphases laid on the individual and his age. Too often in the *Zeitroman* the figures are no more than chiffres of the age, manipulated embodiments of abstract ideas and historical forces. Before Fontane these areas of emphasis were in any case often separated into the *Bildungsroman* and the *Zeitroman*: only with him are the individual and his social background combined satisfactorily. The historical basis of the *Zeitroman* is nowhere more apparent and nowhere more clearly external to the novel's fictional entity than in the dilemma confronting the author of a *Zeitroman* at the conclusion of his work. For while a historian of the nineteenth century has definite historical boundaries to his investigation and the writer of a *Bildungsroman* had only to concern himself with the resolution of his hero's fate, the author of a *Zeitroman* had to combine both elements of the individuals and their historical age.

The significance of the social background, not merely as narrative colour but as the very basis of the work, complicates the application of aesthetic criteria to the *Zeitroman*. Extra-literary factors play a greater role in shaping this genre than most others. Aesthetically the *Zeitroman* advanced from somewhat faltering beginnings to complete self-sufficiency, from the trammels of a Classical tradition evident in Immermann and still present in Spielhagen, to Fontane's novels on the threshold of the new century. Very different tones emerge, from the elegy of Immermann's creation through the polemics and idealism of Spielhagen to the disillusionment of Keller, the serenity of Fontane and the grotesquely drawn features of Heinrich Mann's world. Fontane's predecessors tackle the problems of the *Zeitroman* from different directions and make progress in different areas: the scene at the beginning of *Martin Salander* where the children quibble over the distinction between the words "Mutter" and "Mama" is one of the first successful transferences of the theme of social distinctions to a naturally portrayed human context.

These then are some of the main problem-areas of the *Zeitroman*. This investigation has aimed to eliminate at least some of the perplexity evident in the two extreme viewpoints cited on p. 13. For only from a more precise concept of the *Zeitroman* can future research approach the problem-areas summarized above.

1   Elida Maria Szarota, *Lohensteins Arminius als Zeitroman: Sichtweisen des Spätbarock* (Bern, 1970); *Von Buch zu Buch. Günter Grass in der Kritik: Eine Dokumentation,* hrsg. v. Gert Loschütz (Neuwied u. Berlin, 1968), S. 61.
    So unambiguous did the term seem to Szarota that *Zeitroman* does not appear in the extensive *Namen- und Sachregister.*

2   Hartmut Steinecke, "Die 'zeitgemäße' Gattung. Neubewertung und Neubestimmung des Romans in der jungdeutschen Kritik," *Untersuchungen zur Literatur als Geschichte. Festschrift für Benno von Wiese,* hrsg. v. Vincent J. Günther et al. (Berlin, 1973), S. 341.

3   Thomas Mann, *Gesammelte Werke in zwölf Bänden* (Frankfurt/Main: Fischer, 1960), XI, 611-12. Cf. too *Der Zauberberg,* III, 748-50; Ulrich Karthaus, " 'Der Zauberberg' – ein Zeitroman (Zeit, Geschichte, Mythos)," *DVjs,* 44, Heft 2 (1970), 269-305.

4   Manfred Windfuhr, *Immermanns erzählerisches Werk: Zur Situation des Romans in der Restaurationszeit* (Gießen, 1957), S. 74.

5   Klaus Jeziorkowski (Hrsg.), *Dichter über ihre Dichtungen. Gottfried Keller* (München, 1969), S. 531.

6   Peter Hasubek, *Karl Gutzkows Romane 'Die Ritter vom Geiste' und 'Der Zauberer von Rom': Studien zur Typologie des deutschen Zeitromans* (Diss. Hamburg, 1964). Future references to this work will be in the form: a, plus page no.
    Peter Hasubek, "Der Zeitroman: Ein Romantypus des 19. Jahrhunderts," *ZfDPh,* 87, Heft 2 (Mai, 1968). Future references to this article will be in the form: b, plus page no.

7   Joachim Worthmann, *Probleme des Zeitromans: Studien zur Geschichte des deutschen Romans im 19. Jahrhundert* (Heidelberg, 1974).

8   Gerhard Gräfe, *Die Gestalt des Literaten im Zeitroman des 19. Jahrhunderts,* Germanische Studien, Heft 185 (Berlin, 1937).

9   Viktor Klemperer, *Die Zeitromane Friedrich Spielhagens und ihre Wurzeln* (Weimar, 1913), S. 111.

10 Ivo Braak, *Poetik in Stichworten: Literaturwissenschaftliche Grundbegriffe. Eine Einführung,* 4. Auflage (Kiel, 1972), S. 195. This amorphousness of terminology is present when Majut calls Laube's *Der deutsche Krieg* a "Zeitroman." The novel was written in 1865-66 and set in the period 1619-1648.
    See Rudolf Majut, "Der deutsche Roman vom Biedermeier bis zur Gegenwart," *Deutsche Philologie im Aufriß,* Bd. II, hrsg. v. Wolfgang Stammler, 2. Auflage (Berlin, 1960), Sp. 1455.

11 "Er [der Dichter] sieht aus der Perspektive des in den Lüften schwebenden Adlers herab." Karl Gutzkow, *Die Ritter vom Geiste,* 2. Auflage (Leipzig: Brockhaus, 1852), I, 8 (Vorwort).

12 "Der neue Roman ist der Roman des *Nebeneinanders."* (I, 7)

13 Rudolf Krämer-Badoni, "Der Topos von der Zeitkritik," *Der Monat,* 12, Heft 138 (März, 1960), 5-11.

14 See E. M. Forster, *Aspects of the Novel,* Pelican Books A557 (1927; rpt. Harmondsworth: Penguin, 1968), p. 53.

15 Friedrich Schleiermacher, "Ästhetik 1819/33," in *Romantheorie und Romankritik in Deutschland: Die Entwicklung des Gattungsverständnisses von der Scott-Rezeption bis zum programmatischen Realismus,* hrsg. v. Hartmut Steinecke (Stuttgart, 1975), II, 17.

16 Op. cit., Sp. 1408.

17 Ibid., Sp. 1385.

18 Ibid., Sp. 1437.

19 Sir Walter Scott, *Ivanhoe,* Everyman's Library (London: Dent, 1975), p. 19 (from "Dedicatory Epistle To The Rev. Dr. Dryasdust, F. A. S.").

20 See Heinz Eugen Greter, *Fontanes Poetik* (Bern, Frankfurt/Main, 1973), S. 130, for Wolzogen's view. See too H. Mann's verdict on Fontane (pp. 114-15), and Hans Mayer's Introduction to Ehm Welk's *Die Heiden von Kummerow* (Rostock: Hinstorff, 1956), VIII-IX.

21 Leo Tolstoy, "Preface to Von Polenz' Novel 'Der Büttnerbauer,' " in *What is Art? and Essays on Art,* trans. Aylmer Maude (London, 1962), p. 316.

22 Cf. Majut, op. cit., Sp. 1385;
   Lucien Goldmann, *Soziologie des Romans*, trans. "Ingeborg Fleischhauer, Paris, gemeinsam mit dem Autor" (Darmstadt und Neuwied, 1972), S. 239-40.

23 J. P. Stern, *On Realism* (London and Boston, 1973), p. 104.

24 Karl Konrad Polheim, "Novellentheorie und Novellenforschung (1945-1963)," *DVjs,* 38 (1964), Sonderheft, S. 312.

25 Worthmann places Raabe on a par with Fontane (9 et passim) in transcending the limitations of this particular novel-type, but the present author does not consider him to have equalled Fontane's achievement. Not only are Raabe's figures generally more limited in a geographical sense — provincials without connections with the outer world such as those found in *Der Stechlin* — but they are also frequently more encrusted in their individuality, making them odd though colourful personalities rather than individuals firmly located in the crosscurrents of their age. Lesser figures than Raabe receive more attention in the present text through being more important for the development of the genre.

26 He calls this novel-form "den psychologischen und tendenziösen Gesellschaftsroman." Fritz Martini, *Deutsche Literatur im bürgerlichen Realismus 1848-1898,* Epochen der deutschen Literatur, Bd. V/2 (Stuttgart, 1962), S. 409.

27 Achim von Arnim, *Armut, Reichtum, Schuld und Buße der Gräfin Dolores: Eine wahre Geschichte zur lehrreichen Unterhaltung armer Fräulein,* in Achim von Arnim, *Sämtliche Romane und Erzählungen* (München: Hanser, 1962), I, 318, 382 et passim.

28 Op. cit., S. 205.

29 Op. cit., Sp. 1371-72.

30 Joseph von Eichendorff, *Ahnung und Gegenwart,* in Joseph von Eichendorff, *Eine Auswahl* (München: Hanser, 1949), II, 193, 214.

31 Cf. Walter Killy, "Der Roman als romantisches Buch: Über Eichendorffs 'Ahnung und Gegenwart,' " in *Interpretationen, Band III: Deutsche Romane von Grimmelshausen bis Musil,* hrsg. v. Jost Schillemeit (F./M., Hamburg, 1966), S. 140.

32 Similar examples:
   Die Dinge selber, zumal die Naturphänomene, bedeuten Eichendorff nur so viel, als sie die Fähigkeit haben, auf das in ihnen wirkende Absolute hinzuweisen. (28)

   Eichendorff stellt die Welt nur in den Vermittlungen seiner Religiosität dar und errichtet so in seiner Dichtung eine Formel-Welt reiner Poesie. (ibid.)

33 Ludwig Tieck, *Der junge Tischlermeister,* in Ludwig Tieck: *Werke in vier Bänden* (München: Winkler, 1966), IV, 355-56 et passim.

34 Die Zeit-Dimension eröffnet sich nicht im konkreten Schicksal der Personen, das sich als Handlung vollzieht, sondern in ihren Äußerungen. (43)

35 In his discussion of Worthmann's book, Jeffrey Sammons writes:
   'Die Ritter vom Geiste' sind an sich ein beachtenswertes literarisches Experiment, das für kurze Zeit viel Aufmerksamkeit auf sich zog; in der Romangeschichte aber sind sie ein fast folgenloses Kuriosum geblieben.
   "Buchbesprechungen," *ZfDPh,* 95/2 (Juni, 1976), S. 302.

36 Schmidt's "Berichterstatter" advances three reasons why the novel is supposedly still worth reading: 1) the concept expressed in the title, the "Organisation der Élite"; 2) the "lupenrein fotografierten 'Dias' der Einzelbilder"; 3)
   [. . .] daß die *Prosaform überhaupt* mit Gutzkow einen gewaltigen Schritt nach vorn tat — leider damals *ohne Nachfolger & Fortsetzer* (author's emphasis). Er schuf nämlich sich den Begriff, *und das Ding=selbst* nicht minder: den *'Roman des Nebeneinander'* [. . .].
   Arno Schmidt, "Zur Literatur des 19. Jahrhunderts," in *Nachrichten von Büchern und Menschen,* Bd. 2 (Frankfurt am Main, 1977), S. 104-6.

37 This can be uneasily interwoven with a character's viewpoint:
   Siegbert konnte bei seinem jeweiligen Zusammentreffen aller dieser reaktionären Elemente die Gefahr ermessen, der bei uns die bessere Begründung der Zukunft noch zu lange ausgesetzt ist. (VII, 382)
   The breadth of the perspective is imposed on the reader rather than emerging organically from the work.

38 At a ball a conversation is struck up among young men, lawyers, painters, officers:
   Den Austausch dieser Ansichten schildern wir nicht. Nennt diese Streitenden Söhne der Zeit,

nennt sie Dioskuren auf den weißen Lichtrossen der Legitimität, nennt sie die gefesselten Titanen der Opposition; sie erörtern nur Das, was wir vorziehen, durch die Hebel des Volkes und an ihm selbst zu schildern durch eine allmälige Entwickelung von Persönlichkeiten, deren Bedeutung für den modernen Volksgeist im späteren Verlaufe sichtbarer hervortreten wird. (IV, 369)

[39] Chapter 15 of *Die Ritter vom Geiste,* "Die 'Gesellschaft' und die 'kleinen Cirkel, ' " clearly belongs to a *roman à clef,* with a satire of the whole court and successive monarchs, their followers, and fads in fashion.

[40] See Jeziorkowski, op. cit., S. 126, 131.

[41] See the subtitles to Stendhal's *Le Rouge et le noir (Chronique du XIXe siècle)* and Flaubert's *Madame Bovary (Moeurs de province).* These works appeared in 1830 and 1857 respectively.

[42] Raymond Williams, "Realism and the Contemporary Novel," in *The Long Revolution* (London, 1961), p. 280.

[43] Ibid., p. 287.

[44] Gerhard Friesen, *The German Panoramic Novel of the 19th Century* (Berne and Frankfurt/Main, 1972), pp. 63-64.

[45] Op. cit., S. 610.

[46] Margarete Merkel-Nipperdey, "Gottfried Kellers 'Martin Salander': Untersuchungen zur Struktur des Zeitromans," *Palaestra,* 228 (Göttingen, 1959), S. 38, Anm. 4.

CHAPTER II

[1] Ludolf Wienbarg, "Wanderungen durch den Thierkreis. Faule und frische Romane" (Hamburg, 1835), in *Romantheorie: Dokumentation ihrer Geschichte in Deutschland 1620-1880,* hrsg. v. Eberhard Lämmert et al. (Köln/Berlin, 1971), S. 298.

[2] For the genesis of the novel, see Windfuhr, op. cit., esp. S. 49-58, 133-35.

[3] Fritz Böttger (Hrsg.), *Karl Immermann. Im Schatten des schwarzen Adlers: Ein Dichter- und Zeitbild in Selbstzeugnissen, Werkproben, Briefen und Berichten* (Berlin, 1967), S. 403.

[4] *Immermanns Werke,* hrsg. v. Harry Maync (Leipzig u. Wien: Bibliographisches Institut, 1906), III, 15.

[5] Cf. Immermann' s verdict in a letter to Tieck:
> Früh fühlte ich mich mit der Zeit und Welt in einem gewissen Widerspruche, oft überkam mich eine große Angst über die Doppelnatur unsrer Zustände, die Zweideutigkeit aller gegenwärtigen Verhältnisse, in diesem Werke legte ich dann alles nieder, was ich mir selbst zur Lösung des Rätsels vorsagte.

Harry Maync, *Immermann: Der Mann und sein Werk im Rahmen der Zeit- und Literaturgeschichte* (München, 1921), S. 383.

[6] Published in 1840 under the pseudonym of Friedrich Oswald in Gutzkow's "Telegraph für Deutschland." See Hans Mayer, "Karl Immermanns 'Epigonen,' " in *Von Lessing bis Thomas Mann* (Pfullingen, 1959), S. 253.

[7] This lament is echoed some 30 years later by the "Heimkehrer" in Raabe's *Abu Telfan,* with even the most atrocious external conditions still being preferable to those in Germany.

[8] Ernest K. Bramsted, *Aristocracy and the Middle-Classes in Germany,* revised ed. (Chicago and London, 1964), p. 59.

[9] J. H. Clapham, *The Economic Development of France and Germany 1815-1914,* 4th ed. (Cambridge, 1955), p. 92, n. 1.

[10] Cf. Friedrich Sengle, *Biedermeierzeit: Deutsche Literatur im Spannungsfeld zwischen Restauration und Revolution, 1815-1848,* 2 vols. (Stuttgart, 1971-72), II, 295-98, 634.
Cf. too Werner Hahl, *Reflexion und Erzählung: Ein Problem der Romantheorie von der Spätaufklärung bis zum programmatischen Realismus,* Studien zur Poetik und Geschichte der Literatur, 18 (Stuttgart/Berlin/Köln/Mainz, 1971), S. 9, 73.

[11] See for instance Hippolyt's observations on the Parisians (III, 10). Worthmann says of some works of the *Jungdeutschen,* including Laube's novel:
> Im Medium der zeittypischen Briefschreiber spiegelt sich Realität als eine abstrakte, gleichsam literarische Größe. Zeit-Wirklichkeit ist hier kein konkretes Sein, sie wird nicht im Leben der Menschen veranschaulicht, sondern zum Zwecke propagandistischer Wirkung unmittelbar in Reflexion verwandelt. (60)

[12] Benno von Wiese, "Zeitkrisis und Biedermeier in Laubes 'Das junge Europa' und in Immermanns 'Epigonen,' " *Dichtung und Volkstum,* 36 (1935), 178-79.

[13] Konrad Hecker, *Mensch und Masse: Situation und Handeln der Epigonen gezeigt an Immermann und den Jungdeutschen* (Diss. Leipzig, 1933), S. 19.

[14] Cf. Steinecke, op. cit., I, 85.

[15] Cf. Sengle:

Immermanns *Epigonen,* welche die schauerempfindsamen Motive nicht konsequent vermeiden, sind vor allem mit den Mitteln des Salonromans an die wesentlichen Probleme der Gesellschaft herangekommen. (op. cit., II, 888)

[16] In the space of a few lines we read: "[. . .] wollen wir grade nicht billigen" and then:

Denn darin war er glücklich zu preisen: kein Zweifel, kein Leid versenkte ihn unnütz grübelnd in sein Ich, wo so viele Menschen fruchtlos die Auflösung ihrer Bedrängnisse suchen — fruchtlos, weil alle Selbstbetrachtung nur tiefer zerstört. (III, 285)

[17] Windfuhr, op. cit., S. 141. Cf. too Sengle, op. cit., II, 917 ff.

[18] Ibid., S. 142.

[19] It is still a powerful factor in Gutzkow's *Die Ritter vom Geiste,* where the Wildungens' legal claim is seen in the following terms:

Freimüthige Seelen und solche, die am Neuen und Seltenen Gefallen fanden, [. . .] fanden in dieser [. . .] Verhandlung eine höhere Symbolik und erklärten, diese durch zwei Jahrhunderte herrenlos gebliebene, nur dem Stärkeren anheim gefallene Hinterlassenschaft eines geistlichen Ritterordens wäre ja ein Bild der Verwirrung unserer Zeit überhaupt [. . .]. (V, 94)

[20] Bramsted, op. cit., p. 54, n. 1.

[21] Wilhelm Raabe, *Die Akten des Vogelsangs* (Berlin: Ullstein, 1969), S. 26-27. Cf. too S. 93-94, 106-7.

[22] See Hippolyt's attempt to trace the stages of the nobility's decline in *Die Poeten:*

[. . .] man fing an, die Bestandteile der Gesellschaft zu prüfen, der Adel war genötigt zu glänzen, weil sein Kern verdorrt war.

Heinrich Laube, *Das junge Europa,* Vol. 1-3 of *Heinrich Laubes gesammelte Werke in fünfzig Bänden,* hrsg. v. H. H. Houben (Leipzig: Hesse, 1908), I, 112. Wilhelmi uses similar imagery but takes it a step further in reproving Hermann for the naïveté of his outburst:

Ja freilich ist der Adel im Kern verwest; aber das Gehäuse steht noch aufrecht, und man kann sich daran noch immer die Stirn einrennen. (III, 158-59)

[23] Bramsted, op. cit., p. 37.

Cf. also the deacon's words in *Münchhausen:*

Gegenwärtig ist durch die Errettung des Vaterlandes, welche von allen Ständen ausging, die höchste Ehre ein Gemeingut geworden [. . .]. (I, 241)

[24] Walter Höllerer, "Karl Leberecht Immermann," in *Zwischen Klassik und Moderne: Lachen und Weinen in der Dichtung einer Übergangszeit* (Stuttgart, 1958), S. 447-48 (Anm. 36 to S. 236).

[25] Stendhal, *Le Rouge et le noir* (Paris: Editions Garnier Frères, 1957), p. 357.

[26] In *Die Ritter vom Geiste,* Leidenfrost gives a kind of negative answer to this hope. He says of poets and composers:

Alle leiden daran, daß unsere Zeit erst zu einer neuen Herrschaft großer Thatsachen im Durchbruch liegt, Alle klammern sich an Vergangenes und machen sich eine künstliche Bildung, weil für eine natürliche und zeitgemäße die Anknüpfungen fehlen. (III, 302)

[27] The qualification: "Sie sagen, wer ein Stück Blei — aber es muß nicht von einer Kirche sein" (IV, 209) would seem gratuitous unless it refers to the plot of Weber's opera. If this is the case, two ideas seem to have been condensed into one, as Kaspar in fact includes the following in his brew:

Hier, erst das Blei! Etwas gestoßenes Glas von zerbrochenen Kirchenfenstern; das findet sich! (*Der Freischütz,* Act II, Scene II)

[28] A fact not recognized by many of Immermann's contemporary critics. See his exasperation in a letter to his brother Hermann:

[. . .] Wilhelmi ist der Druckurteiler Leitstern; was der sagt, das ist ihnen Tendenz des Buches, der Verfasser mag ihn noch so krank und hypochondrisch hingestellt haben, an seinen Worten läßt sich wie an einem guten Henkel das Gefäß am besten ergreifen. (Böttger, op. cit., S. 417)

[29] Cf. Sengle, op. cit., I, 97.

Leonhard, the title-figure in Tieck's *Der junge Tischlermeister,* describes very similar symptoms and goes beyond mere description to an analysis, connecting role-playing with exclusion from political activity:

Ich glaube in der Tat, daß die Masse der übertriebenen und krankhaften Eitelkeit unserer Tage, die Sucht, eine lügenhafte Rolle vor der Welt und vor sich zu spielen, dieses Heucheln von süßlicher Bildung, unechter Frömmigkeit, affektierter Liebe zur Natur und dergleichen mehr, nur möglich geworden ist, seitdem es dem Menschen untersagt ist, eine Rolle von Staats wegen zu spielen, seitdem er so ganz auf die Haushaltung in seinen vier Pfählen, und auf sein Herz in seinem sogenannten Innern angewiesen ist, denn ich fühle es, daß der Trieb, sich zu entfliehen, sich selbst fremd zu werden, und als ein anderes Wesen wieder anzutreffen, mächtig in uns ist. (264-65)

[30] See Windfuhr, op. cit., S. 71 ff, and by the same author the article "Der Epigone: Begriff, Phänomen und Bewußtsein," *Archiv für Begriffsgeschichte*, Bd. 4 (1959), S. 182-209.

[31] As in poems by Hofmannsthal (*Epigonen*, 1891) and Keller (*Ghasel* I, 1847) cited by Windfuhr, "Der Epigone," ibid., S. 190.

[32] Cf. Harry Haller's words to the editor in Hesse's *Der Steppenwolf:*

Es gibt nun Zeiten, wo eine ganze Generation so zwischen zwei Zeiten, zwischen zwei Lebensstile hineingerät, daß ihr jede Selbstverständlichkeit, jede Sitte, jede Geborgenheit und Unschuld verlorengeht. Natürlich spürt das nicht ein jeder gleich stark. Eine Natur wie Nietzsche hat das heutige Elend um mehr als eine Generation voraus erleiden müssen, — was er einsam und unverstanden auszukosten hatte, das erleiden heute Tausende.

Hermann Hesse, *Gesammelte Dichtungen,* Vierter Band (Berlin: Suhrkamp, 1958), S. 205-6.

[33] Claude David, "Über den Begriff des Epigonischen," in *Tradition und Ursprünglichkeit* (Akten des III. Internationalen Germanistenkongresses 1965 in Amsterdam), hrsg. v. Werner Kohlschmidt und Herman Meyer (Bern, 1966), S. 73.

[34] Cf. Sengle, op. cit., II, 929.

[35] The conventional aura of grandeur surrounding a duel is counterpointed against a stark view of the absurd reality:

[. . .] daß Helmuth von einem unabänderlichen Fatum der Ehrenhaftigkeit, aus dem es kein Entrinnen gab, tragisch erfaßt worden sei. Bertrand dagegen sagte: "Das Merkwürdigste ist es doch, daß man in einer Welt von Maschinen und Eisenbahnen lebt, and daß zur nämlichen Zeit, in der die Eisenbahnen fahren und die Fabriken arbeiten, zwei Leute einander gegenüberstehen und schießen."

Hermann Broch, *Pasenow oder die Romantik,* Bibliothek Suhrkamp, 92 (Frankfurt/Main: Suhrkamp, 1969), S. 63.

[36] Cf. the following section of a letter from Konstantin to Hippolyt in Laube's *Das junge Europa,* where the "epigonenhaft" nature of the age emerges in terms similar to Immermann's and argumentation is seen as supplanting heroism:

Es wird und muß sich eine neue Zeit bilden, wir leben freilich in keiner, sondern in dem Zwischenraume auf der Brücke zweier Zeiten. Individualitäten, plastische Figuren, mit einem Worte, *Helden* verschwinden, und an die Stelle der Helden tritt die *Meinung.* (I, 61)

[37] It is impossible to draw from this the following inference, whose terms ("Aristokratie des Geistes und der Menschlichkeit") go well beyond the confines of this novel:

[. . .] die Zukunft gehört also keinem Stande als solchen, sondern einer kleinen Gruppe von mäßigen, vielseitigen, selbstbeherrschten, klassenlosen Mittelmenschen, mit anderen Worten der *Aristokratie des Geistes und der Menschlichkeit,* den kulturtragenden Denkern.

J. F. T. Hope, *Epigonentum und Biedermeier: Karl Immermanns Verhältnis zur Biedermeierzeit.* M. A. Melbourne, 1967, S. 648. Nor is Rumler's view of the synthesis in a wholly positive light acceptable. See Fritz Rumler, *Realistische Elemente in Immermanns 'Epigonen,'* Diss. München, 1964, S. 133.

[38] Cf. Jacob Korg, "Society and Community in Dickens," *Politics in Literature in the Nineteenth Century,* ed. Janie Teissedou et al., Paris, 1974, p. 87:

In Dickens' Communities [. . .] there are no values higher than the immediate satisfactions appreciable by every member. They are reversions to a pre-industrial period, when daily life was likely to be organized on rural and familial lines and isolated from external influences. [. . .] The Communities are typically set off from the outside world [. . .] not as a claim of superiority, but for the sake of safety and freedom.

[39] A letter from the statesman Friedrich v. Gentz to Amalie Imhoff puts the conservative view very sympathetically, while realistically accepting the inevitable. Written in 1827, it is nearly contemporaneous with the novel's conclusion (1829) and gains further interest through the striking similarity of its terms of reference:

Die Weltgeschichte ist ein ewiger Übergang vom Alten zum Neuen. Im steten Kreislaufe der Dinge zerstört alles sich selbst, und die Frucht, die zur Reife gediehen ist, löst sich von der

Pflanze ab, die sie hervorgebracht hat. Soll aber dieser Kreislauf nicht zum schnellen Untergang alles Bestehenden, mithin auch alles Rechten und Guten führen, so muß es notwendig neben der großen, zuletzt immer überwiegenden Anzahl derer, welche für das Neue arbeiten, auch eine kleinere geben, die mit Maß und Ziel das Alte zu behaupten, und den Strom der Zeit, wenn sie ihn auch nicht aufhalten kann noch will, in einem geregelten Bette zu erhalten sucht. In Epochen gewaltiger Erschütterungen, wie die unsrige, nimmt der Streit zwischen diesen beiden Parteien einen leidenschaftlichen, überspannten, oft wilden und verderblichen Charakter an [. . .].

Golo Mann, *Friedrich von Gentz: Geschichte eines europäischen Staatsmannes* (Zürich/Wien, 1947), S. 364.

[40] Helmut Böhme, *Prolegomena zu einer Sozial- und Wirtschaftsgeschichte Deutschlands im 19. und 20. Jahrhundert,* edition suhrkamp, 253 (Frankfurt/Main, 1968), S. 85.

[41] Op. cit., S. 270.

[42] Ibid., S. 271.

[43] It is also undoubtedly an attempt to restore the poetic to an unpoetic era. Cf. Steinecke:

Das wichtigste "Surrogat für die verlorene Poesie" sieht Vischer wie bereits Hegel in der Liebe, der "Poesie des Herzens." (op. cit., I, 227)

Cf. too Dankmar's musings as he feels drawn to Melanie in *Die Ritter vom Geiste*:

Wo ist auch noch ein Trost für unbefriedigte Gemüther, wenn sie die Söhne unserer Zeit sind, als allein in der Liebe? Wo ist die Bürgschaft noch, daß in den Schrecken der Empörungen und Kriege, in den schaudervollen Gerichten der Reaction und der Rache noch etwas vom Ewigen und Menschlichen sich erhält, als in der Liebe? (II, 356)

CHAPTER III

[1] Friedrich Spielhagen, *Problematische Naturen,* 2 vols., 22. and 21. Auflage resp. (Leipzig: Staackmann, 1900), I, 344. These two vols. are nos. 1 and 5 of "Friedrich Spielhagen's sämmtliche Romane."

[2] Friedrich Spielhagen, *Beiträge zur Theorie und Technik des Romans,* Faksimiledruck nach der 1. Auflage von 1883, Deutsche Neudrucke, Reihe Texte des 19. Jahrhunderts, hrsg. v. Walter Killy (Göttingen, 1967), S. 180. Future references to this work are abbreviated to BTT plus the page no.

[3] Gustav Freytag, *Soll und Haben* (München: Knaur, 1960), S. 94.

[4] Cf. Günter Rebing, *Der Halbbruder des Dichters: Friedrich Spielhagens Theorie des Romans,* Literatur und Reflexion, 8 (F./M., 1972). Speaking of Spielhagen's novel technique in general, he says:

Nicht nur die zahlreichen Dialoge, sondern der ganze Roman bekommt dadurch ein forciert dramatisches Gepräge. Dieser Effekt wird verstärkt durch inhaltliche Eigentümlichkeiten: Häufung erotischer Konflikte, moralische und soziologische Schwarzweißmalerei (Adlige zum Beispiel sind zumeist völlig korrupt und gewissenlos), Spannungserzeugung durch Hintanhalten der wahren (unweigerlich ganz verblüffenden) Identität geheimnisumwitterter Figuren und ähnliches mehr. (S. 215)

[5] But compare Siegfried Kohlhammer, *Resignation und Revolte. Immermanns 'Münchhausen': Satire und Zeitroman der Restaurationsepoche* (Stuttgart, 1973), S. 195 (Anm. 7 to S. 121).

[6] G. W. F. Hegel: Aus *Vorlesungen über die Ästhetik*, 1818/29.

Eine der gewöhnlichsten und für den Roman passendsten Kollisionen ist deshalb der Konflikt zwischen der Poesie des Herzens und der entgegenstehenden Prosa der Verhältnisse, so wie dem Zufalle äußerer Umstände [. . .]. (Steinecke, op. cit., II, 16)

Fr. Th. Vischer: Aus *Aesthetik oder Wissenschaft des Schönen*, 1857.

Hier [in der Erfindung auffallender, überraschender Begebenheiten] ist es nun allerdings ganz in der Ordnung, daß im Roman der *Zufall* als Rächer des lebendigen Menschen an der Prosa der Zustände eine besonders starke Rolle spielt [. . .]. (ibid., II, 260)

J. W. v. Goethe, *Werke*, 4 Bde. (Berlin und Darmstadt: Tempel, 1962), III, 727.

So vereinigte man sich auch darüber, daß man dem Zufall im Roman gar wohl sein Spiel erlauben könne [. . .].

[7] Leo Löwenthal, *Erzählkunst und Gesellschaft: Die Gesellschaftsproblematik in der deutschen Literatur des 19. Jahrhunderts,* Sammlung Luchterhand, 32 (Neuwied und Berlin, 1971), S. 175.

[8] He criticized Effi's failure to destroy the letters compromising her. Friedrich Spielhagen, *Neue Beiträge zur Theorie und Technik der Epik und Dramatik* (Leipzig, 1898), S. 109 (in ch. III: *Die Wahlverwandtschaften und Effi Briest*).

[9] Cf. BTT, 48 and 73. Spielhagen himself admits the ideal, unattainable nature of his demand for epic portrayal of a hero who is representative of the whole of humanity:

> [...] da [...] ein Menschenleben [...] doch immer nur ein Einzelnes bleibt, an welchem immer nur ein aliquoter Teil des allgemeinen Menschenloses illustriert werden kann, so kann auch [...] das Abbild das Urbild nicht völlig decken. (BTT, 74)

[10] Cf. Friedrich Spielhagen, "Die Geschichte des Erstlingswerks. Wie die 'Problematische Naturen' entstanden," *Deutsche Dichtung*, 17. Bd. (Okt. 1894-März 1895), S. 2. Cf. too Rebing, op. cit., S. 174-75.

[11] Also referred to in some editions as "Sundin" by virtue of the sound on which it lies (II, 131). See the Volksausgabe of 1909, 51-55. Auflage (Leipzig: Staackmann), S. 630.

[12] Similarly the opening of *Die Ritter vom Geiste* coyly avoids actually naming the setting:

> Kirche und Friedhof lagen auf einer [...] Anhöhe, die eine Fernsicht auf diejenige große und berühmte deutsche Hauptstadt erlaubte, welche der Schauplatz der nachfolgenden Mittheilungen sein wird. (I, 14)

[13] It surprises a reader of today that "wirklich Goethesche Kraft und Anschaulichkeit" were ascribed to the work by — the young Nietzsche (1865)! See Winfried Hellmann, "Objektivität, Subjektivität und Erzählkunst: Zur Romantheorie Friedrich Spielhagens," in *Deutsche Romantheorien: Beiträge zu einer historischen Poetik des Romans in Deutschland*, hrsg. u. eingeleitet von Reinhold Grimm (Frankfurt/Main und Bonn, 1968), S.165.

[14] On Cooper's popularity in Germany, see Karlheinz Rossbacher, *Lederstrumpf in Deutschland: Zur Rezeption James Fenimore Coopers beim Leser der Restaurationszeit* (München, 1972).

[15] See BTT, 134 (from *Der Ich-Roman*, written in 1882):

> [daß] ein Produkt der epischen Dichtkunst, auch das höchste, an absolutem Kunstwert immer hinter den höchsten Produkten der beiden Schwesterkünste zurückbleiben muß.

[16] Cf. T. E. Carter, "Freytag's 'Soll und Haben': A Liberal National Manifesto as a Best-seller," *GLL*, XXI (1968), 328. Carter produces astonishing sales figures for the periods between World War I and the Weimar Republic and then again after World War II.

[17] For convenience M. d'Estein, who has protected the deserted Marie Montbert (Oswald's mother) and raised Oswald as if he were his own son, will be referred to as Oswald's father rather than supposed father.

[18] As noted already by Julian Schmidt. See his article "Friedrich Spielhagen," *Westermanns Jahrbuch der Illustrirten Deutschen Monatshefte*, 29. Band (Okt. 1870 - März 1871), S. 430.
See too the contemporary critic Arthur Levysohn, speaking of comparisons drawn by critics with *Problematische Naturen*:

> Unsere Leser werden begreifen, daß diese Vergleiche meist mit Bezug auf Freytag's "Soll und Haben" statthatten. (*BLU* [1863], 906)

[19] "Diese sonderbare geheime Verbindung" and "dieser geschlossene Bund" are phrases used by Dankmar for the same phenomenon in *Die Ritter vom Geiste* (I, 265).

[20] Hasubek, a, 66-67.

[21] For the historical perspective following Spielhagen's novel, see Otto-Ernst Schüddekopf, *Herrliche Kaiserzeit. Deutschland 1871-1914* (F./M., Berlin, 1973), S. 138:

> War das Verhältnis zwischen adligen und bürgerlichen Offizieren 1860 noch 65 zu 35 Prozent, so bestand es bereits 1913 aus 70 Prozent Bürgerlichen und nur noch 30 Prozent Adligen.

For examples of the aggressive overcompensation of the new breed and the bewilderment of the old order at this change, see Arnold Zweig, *Der Streit um den Sergeanten Grischa*, 16. Auflage (Berlin und Weimar: Aufbau, 1973), S. 342, 499-500.

[22] The same issue is broached by Fontane. In *Stine*, Baron Papageno reports Waldemar's uncle as having said to him:

> Glauben Sie mir, Baron, ich kenne Familien und Familiengeschichten, und, mein Wort zum Pfande, wo das alte Blut nicht aufgefrischt wird, da kann sich die ganze Sippe begraben lassen. Und behufs Auffrischung gibt es nur zwei legitime Mittel: Illegitimitäten oder Mesalliancen.

Theodor Fontane, *Werke in drei Bänden*, hrsg. v. Kurt Schreinert (München, 1968), I, 533. All future references to page nos. (alone) relate to Vol. II of this edition, other vols. are referred to by I or III.

When the uncle is required to turn from the general to the particular, close-to-home case, he cannot consent to the misalliance between Waldemar and Stine (*Stine*, ch. 12).

For a further example of the greater procreativity of the bourgeois implied in *Problematische Naturen* by the Prince's mother, cf. *Der Stechlin*, ch. 6. Here Frau Katzler, born in the noble Ippe-Büchsenstein line, answers Dubslav's hint that she already has enough offspring with the following: "Wenn ich diesen Segen durchaus nicht wollte, dann mußt ich einen Durchschnittsprinzen heiraten [. . .] " (477).

[23] Nor really, from within the confines of the novel, of this being a stage along the way, as Spielhagen envisaged it in the following:

> Und [Gott] weiß [. . .] daß, wie verfehlt auch sonst dein Leben war und du [Oswald] selbst bankerott an Glauben und Hoffnung und Liebe, du wenigstens sterben durftest mit vielen hunderten [cf. the 187 in the novel!], die braver waren als du, für eine Idee, die, tausend-mal blutig gegeißelt und schmählich ans Kreuz geschlagen, immer wieder aus dem Grabe er-stehen und endlich die Welt besiegen wird. ("Die Geschichte des Erstlingswerks," op. cit., S. 7)

[24] Cf. Schmidt, op. cit., S. 434-36. Schmidt rejects the ending on historical grounds (S. 436), and without specifically drawing the comparison, clearly plays off Spielhagen against Freytag to the advantage of the latter:

> Auf die Revolution zu rechnen, ist so viel als auf ein Hazardspiel zu rechnen. Die bürgerliche Arbeit, die unablässig Tag aus, Tag ein schafft, bringt keinen glänzenden, aber einen sicheren Erwerb [. . .] . (Ibid.)

Cf. the motto for *Soll und Haben* — "Der Roman soll das deutsche Volk da suchen, wo es in seiner Tüchtigkeit zu finden ist, nämlich bei seiner Arbeit" — taken from Julian Schmidt.

For further objections, see the Hart brothers' "Friedrich Spielhagen und der deutsche Roman der Gegenwart," *Kritische Waffengänge*, Sechstes Heft (Leipzig, 1884), esp. S. 32 and 44.

CHAPTER IV

[1] For the connection between this novel and the ending Keller planned for his work, see J. M. Ritchie, "The Place of 'Martin Salander' in Gottfried Keller's Evolution as a Prose Writer," *MLR*, 52 (1957), 221.

[2] Op. cit., S. 108-9.

[3] Gottfried Keller, *Gesammelte Werke in acht Bänden* (mit einer biographischen Einleitung von Max Rychner), Achter Band (Leipzig: Philipp Reclam jun., o.J.), S. 7. All future references to page nos. alone refer to Vol. VIII of this edition, other works are referred to by vol. no. as well.

[4] See Emil Ermatinger, *Gottfried Kellers Leben, Briefe und Tagebücher*, Bd. I (Stuttgart u. Berlin, 1916), S. 634.

[5] Cf. the personalized locomotive, "Die schwarze Suse," in Sudermann's *Frau Sorge* (1887).

[6] Cf. Karol Szemkus, *Gesellschaftlicher Wandel und sprachliche Form: Literatursoziologische Studie zur Dichtung Gottfried Kellers* (Stuttgart, 1969), S. 21.

[7] The distinction is clear too in Ehm Welk's *Die Heiden von Kummerow*, which appeared in 1937 but is set round the beginning of the century. Martin, asked by a superintendent for his father's Christian name and then what his mother calls his father, answers in both cases "Papa." Thereupon the superintendent observes to the pastor:

> "Das wundert mich übrigens, in Bauernfamilien ist es doch nicht üblich."
> "Ach," erwiderte der Pastor laut, "der Grambauer, der will hoch hinaus. Dem gefiel auch sonst sein Vorname nicht." (120)

[8] Jeremias Gotthelf, *Zeitgeist und Berner Geist* (Basel: Birkhäuser, 1951):

> "Es ist nicht mehr die Zeit, wo zwischen Herr und Bauer ein gesetzlicher Unterschied war, wir sind einer so gut als der Andere, es gibt keine Sklaven und Landvögte mehr, es kann ein jeder daherkommen, wie es ihm gefällt und wie er es vermag." (I, 60)
> Der Zweite [Jäger] frug, ob der Herr vom Hause daheim sei. Lisi sagte, obschon es die Redens-art recht gut verstand, sie hätten hier keinen Herr, der Bauer aber sei fort [. . .]. (II, 185)

[9] Friedrich Theodor Vischer, *Auch Einer: Eine Reisebekanntschaft* (Stuttgart u. Leipzig: Hallberger, 1879), II, 247-48.

[10] Man schrieb das Jahr 1873. Ein industrieller Schwindel hatte die gesamte Gesellschaft erfaßt, die Gründungen auf Aktien schossen wie Pilze aus der Erde. Kapital und Arbeit standen sich schroff gegenüber. Die Koalitionsfreiheit der Arbeiter feierte Triumphe, denn eine seltene Einigkeit beseelte die unteren Massen. Die Ansprüche der Niederen und Enterbten steigerten sich mit dem Golddurst der Reichen und Begüterten. An Hunderten von Bauten Berlins wurde nur zeitweise gearbeitet.

Max Kretzer, *Meister Timpe* (Berlin: Das neue Berlin, 1949), S. 103.

[11] Op. cit., S. 635-37.

[12] Cf. Jakob Baechthold, *Gottfried Kellers Leben. Seine Briefe und Tagebücher. Dritter Band: 1861-1890* (Berlin, 1897), S. 641 (Materialien zu "Martin Salander"):

Das gesunkene Niveau der politischen Sitte und Moral hatte auch den Stand des Strebertums hinabgezogen, so daß im allgemeinen die Ober-, Mittel- und Unterstreber je um einige Grad niedriger als früher gegriffen waren.

[13] Not an abuse of particular words, but a propensity to wordiness is seen at the beginning of *Auch Einer*, set late in 1865. When A. E. has been interrupted three times, he retorts:

Da haben wir wieder das Menschenvolk! Und darunter sind erst noch Schweizer, Republikaner? Selbstregierung bei Menschen, die nicht einmal warten können, bis ein Mitmensch ausgeredet hat? Reif für Tyrannenstock! (9)

[14] This scene is a clear exception to Ritchie's verdict:

There is no longer a story-teller between the reader and the story [. . .]. No personal opinion on the events related is ever expressed [. . .]. The facts speak for themselves. (op. cit., p. 221)

For more exceptions, see Merkel-Nipperdey, op. cit., S. 25.

[15] E.g. *Das Fähnlein der sieben Aufrechten* and *Die drei gerechten Kammacher* respectively.

[16] Baechthold, op. cit., S. 641.

[17] See Jeziorkowski: "Es ist nicht schön! Es ist zu wenig Poesie darin!" (op. cit., S. 531). This verdict is belied by occasional descriptions such as that of the setting sun, the chalice and the red wine (215).

[18] The issue must have been particularly relevant when Keller wrote his novel:

In 1883 the all-time maximum was reached when 13,500 persons went overseas, but the tide remained high throughout the 1880's — the more so since an industrial depression in 1885-86 made the effects of the agricultural depression cumulative.

Kurt B. Mayer, *The Population of Switzerland* (New York, 1952), p. 203.

[19] The duality of this motto was well formulated by Otto Brahm: "*C'est partout comme chez nous. Das ist eine bittere Erkenntnis, aber auch ein Trost.*"

Otto Brahm, "Gottfried Keller 1882-1890," *Meisterwerke deutscher Literaturkritik*, 2. Band: *Von Heine bis Mehring*, hrsg. u. eingeleitet v. Hans Mayer (Berlin, 1956), S. 812. Keller expressed the second aspect in a letter to Julius Rodenberg of 5./7. August 1885:

Der Umstand jedoch, daß es am Ende lohnt zu zeigen, wie man keine Staatsform gegen das allgemeine Übel schützt, und ich meinem eigenen Lande sagen kann *voilà, c'est chez nous comme partout*, läßt mich über jenes Bedenken hinwegsehen und ausharren.

Jeziorkowski, op. cit., S. 512.

[20] Cf. too Martin's ruminations on the slogan "*l'amour est le vrai recommenceur!*" (215).

[21] See Baechthold, op. cit., S. 606 for Keller's appreciation of the question of internal and external success of his work, and the hope that the latter will produce the former. Later he laments to Ida Freiligrath:

In meinem Lande ist es wohl verstanden und unter großem Gebrumme gelesen worden. Draussen aber haben nur wenige gemerkt, was es sein soll, und daß es sie auch etwas angeht. So geht es, wenn man tendenziös und lehrhaft sein will. (ibid., S. 614)

[22] With Gotthelf the family domain is emphasized above all others:

Nicht die Regenten regieren das Land, nicht die Lehrer bilden das Leben, sondern Hausväter und Hausmütter tun es, nicht das öffentliche Leben in einem Lande ist die Hauptsache, sondern das häusliche Leben ist die Wurzel von allem, und je nachdem die Wurzel ist, gestaltet sich das andere.

Jeremias Gotthelf, "Geld und Geist," *Sämtliche Werke in 24 Bänden*, hrsg. v. Rudolf Hunziker u. a., 7. Bd. (München und Bern: Eugen Rentsch, 1911), S. 366. The pastor's words here show the avowed limitations of Gotthelf's panorama, his repeated didactic concerns and his inversion of the more usual emphases in a *Zeitroman*.

[23] With Arnold's friends it is a different matter:

> Sie sangen dort mit resoluten frischen Stimmen ein lebensfrohes Lied, rasch und taktfest, kurz und gut [. . .] . (282)

CHAPTER V

[1] "Theodor Fontane an Adolf Hoffmann. Berlin 1897 (Entwurf)," in *Theodor Fontane 1819.1969. Stationen seines Werkes*, Eine Ausstellung des Deutschen Literaturarchivs im Schiller-Nationalmuseum Marbach a.N. (Stuttgart, 1969), S. 210-11.

[2] Letter to Friedrich Fontane, "Karlsbad 4. Sept. [18] 98":

> [. . .] so hat sich mir doch auch wieder die Frage aufgedrängt "ja, wird, ja *kann* auch nur ein großes Publikum darauf anbeißen? " Ich stelle diesmal meine Hoffnungen auf die Kritik.

"Ein bisher unveröffentlichter später Brief von Theodor Fontane," *Die Zeit*, 1. 5. 70. S. 31.

[3] There are also quotations, or at least adaptations of them, from other sources, e.g. Luther, as is pointed out by Herman Meyer, *Das Zitat in der Erzählkunst* (Stuttgart, 1961), S. 174-85.

[4] It seems incontestable that this is to be regarded as a benediction, as a final statement on the theme of the passing of individuals being offset by the survival of the principles they represent and the spirit they embody. Thus the following interpretation cannot be supported:

> In dem Rückzug auf das Elementare wird der Mangel Melusines als "Herz" deutlich, so, wenn sie in dem den Roman abschließenden Satz meint, es sei nicht nötig, "daß die Stechline weiterleben, aber es lebe der Stechlin."

Vincent J. Günther, *Das Symbol im erzählerischen Werk Fontanes* (Bonn, 1967), S. 128.

[5] Cf. Fontane's letter to Joseph Viktor Widmann (Berlin, 19. 11. 1895):

> Ich kenne zwei Seen in unserer Mark, in denen sich Springflut und Trichter bilden, wenn in Italien und Island die Vulkane losgehen.

Richard Brinkmann (Hrsg.), *Dichter über ihre Dichtungen: Theodor Fontane Teil II* (München, 1973), S. 470.

[6] Siegmund Schott, "Die Poggenpuhls," in *Beilage zur Allgemeinen Zeitung vom 3. Februar 1897*, ibid., S. 469.

[7] For the perils with which *Der Stechlin* is fraught, cf. Peter Demetz, *Formen des Realismus: Theodor Fontane*, 2. Auflage (München, 1966), S. 182-85.

[8] Cf. one of Fontane's criticisms of Zola: "c) Fehler in der Tendenz (große Kunstwerke müssen tendenzlos sein)."

"Aus Entwürfen zu einem Aufsatz über Zolas 'La Fortune des Rougon,' " in *Theorie und Technik des Romans im 19. Jahrhundert*, hrsg. v. Hartmut Steinecke (Tübingen, 1970), S. 68.

For what Fontane understood by "Tendenz," cf. Greter, op. cit., S. 49ff.

[9] In *Philologische Studien und Quellen*, Heft 54, hrsg. v. Wolfgang Binder, Hugo Moser u. Karl Stackmann (Berlin, 1970).

[10] There is however nothing apologetic about Fontane's appraisal of this difference. Demetz' curious assessment must be discounted:

> [. . .] er selbst neigte ja dazu, den *Stechlin* an seinen früheren Arbeiten zu messen und war beunruhigt, daß sich nichts von "Verwicklungen [. . .] Überraschungen" fand. (op. cit., S. 180)

[11] Op. cit., S. 13.

[12] Julius Petersen, "Theodor Fontanes Altersroman," *Euphorion*, 29 (1928), 67.

[13] Paul Böckmann, "Der Zeitroman Fontanes," *Deutschunterricht*, 11, Heft 5 (1959), 75-76.

[14] The corresponding position when there is no sense of a new age, weighed down by the Old to a degree stifling the possible emergence of the New, is that of *Epigonentum*.

[15] Letter of 6. 5. 1895 to Friedländer. In *Theodor Fontane. Briefe an Georg Friedländer*, hrsg. u. erläutert von Kurt Schreinert (Heidelberg, 1954), S. 284. Future refs. are to FLB.

[16] Op. cit., S. 70. The reference to Petersen is to S. 32ff.

[17] Reuter makes the following comment on this interchange between Woldemar and Lorenzen:

> Der Roman bietet genug eindeutige Belege dafür, daß es für Lorenzen [. . .] mit dem Neuen gehen *muß*, weil es mit dem Alten nicht mehr gehen *kann*.

Hans-Heinrich Reuter, *Fontane* (München, 1968), S. 809-10. He repeatedly insists on this clear rejection of the Old in favour of the New (see S. 61, 96, 636 [referring to earlier works] , 848), even though he says the following about the old flag:

> Die Flagge wird zu einem Symbol voller hintergründiger "Bedeutungen." Enthalten ist darin der "Degout" des märkischen Landedelmannes gegen die sozialistische Bewegung, gegen das "Rote," [. . .] . (ibid., S. 465)

For a fair assessment of the baffling mixture of scholarship, insight and distortion contained in Reuter's work, cf. Karl Heinz Gehrmann, "Der Stechlin und die klassenlose Gesellschaft: Notizen zur neuesten Fontane-Interpretation," in *deutsche studien*, 35 (1971), 293-302.

[18] Quoted by Petersen, op. cit., S. 34. The work enthused Fontane, who called it "ganz vorzüglich" (FLB, 285).

[19] Drawing on the title of David Friedrich Strauss' "Der alte und der neue Glaube" (1872). See 981, footnote.

[20] In a diatribe against the nobility Fontane wrote to Friedländer on 14. 8. 1896:

> Sie verlangen *Dienste*, man ist, immer mehr oder weniger, Pastor, Hauslehrer oder Inspektor; sie sind ganz unfähig *Individuen* richtig einzuschätzen [. . .]. (FLB, 300-01)

[21] Just before the passage quoted on p. 93 ("Mein Haß [. . .] "), Fontane had written:

> Die Welt wird noch lange einen Adel haben und jedenfalls *wünsche* ich der Welt einen Adel, aber er muß danach sein, er muß eine Bedeutung haben für das Ganze, muß Vorbilder stellen, große Beispiele geben und entweder durch geistig moralische Qualitäten direkt wirken oder diese Qualitäten aus reichen Mitteln unterstützen. (FLB, 284)

In his next letter to Friedländer, Fontane finds these "Vorbilder" elsewhere among the flourishing Berlin bourgeoisie.

[22] "Krieg den Palästen, Friede den Hütten" was a battlecry from Paris Commune days.

[23] The reverse technique can show the self-preoccupation of a character in the midst of world-shattering events. In *Vanity Fair*, a lengthy passage on Amelia concludes:

> So imprisoned and tortured was this gentle little heart, when in the month of March, Anno Domini 1815, Napoleon landed at Cannes, and Louis XVIII. fled, and all Europe was in alarm, and the funds fell, and old John Sedley was ruined.

W. M. Thackeray, *Vanity Fair* (Dent: London, 1975), p. 167.

[24] Bei Bismarck repräsentiert sich der revolutionäre Nationalstaat gegenüber den alten Monarchien in der Reichsfahne. Dubslav überträgt dieses Verhältnis ins Konkret-Sinnbildliche, indem er das Rot der Fahne als das Rot der Revolution (das Rot des Hahnes, das Rot als revolutionäres Flammenzeichen), als die Zerstörung des sowieso schon hinfälligen Alten nimmt.

See Günther, op. cit., S. 107.

[25] For documentation of servant-girls' quarters in turn-of-the-century Berlin see *Deutsche Sozialgeschichte. Dokumente und Skizzen Band II: 1870-1914*, hrsg. v. Gerhard A. Ritter und Jürgen Kocka (München, 1974), S. 258-59.

Nor were these primitive conditions confined to Berlin of the *Gründerzeit*. In *Tonio Kröger* we hear of the following:

> Der Küche gegenüber [. . .] sprangen wie vor alters in beträchtlicher Höhe die seltsamen, plumpen, aber reinlich lackierten Holzgelasse aus der Wand hervor, die Mägdekammern, die nur durch eine Art freiliegender Stiege von der Diele aus zu erreichen waren. (T. Mann, *Ges. Werke*, VIII, 312)

For a general survey of living conditions in Berlin at the time, see Friedrich Mielke, "Studie über den Berliner Wohnungsbau zwischen den Kriegen 1870/71 und 1914-1918," in *Jahrbuch für die Geschichte Mittel- und Ostdeutschlands*, Bd. 20, S. 202-38.

[26] See 985 (Anm. 476). It was with this marriage in mind that Fontane wrote to Friedländer:

> Die Prinzessinnen höchster Häuser können einem leid thun; *wie* schwer muß es sein, was Paßliches zu finden und wie richtig handeln *die*, die einen Maler oder einen Professor heirathen. Wenn ich denn schon mal aus meiner Sphäre 'rausfalle, dann auch ordentlich. (FLB, 316)

Despite this, the presentation of the Princess in *Der Stechlin* is not affirmative on balance.

[27] But the noble ties cannot be forgotten, witness the embarrassment experienced by Dubslav (414) and Woldemar (476) in finding words adequate to her hybrid state. Her bearing also belies her new social level:

> Sie war nicht schön, dazu von einem lymphatisch sentimentalen Ausdruck, aber ihre stattliche Haltung und mehr noch die Art, wie sie sich kleidete, ließen sie doch als etwas durchaus Apartes und beinahe Fremdländisches erscheinen. (580)

[28] Kenneth Attwood, *Fontane und das Preußentum* (Berlin, 1970), S. 239-40. Cf. Strech's more restrained interpretation, op. cit., S. 56-57.

[29] This criticism is far from applicable to the rest of his argumentation, and his own irony above can admittedly not be overlooked.

[30] Cf. Meyer:

> Das völlig nutzlose Abbrechen des ohnehin allbekannten und grundanständigen "Wallenstein"-

Zitats wirkt als lächerliche Prüderie und entbehrt dennoch nicht eine gewisse schneidige Eleganz, die für des Professors gesamte Redeweise charakteristisch ist. (op. cit., S. 182)

A similar example is to be found when Adelheid speaks of England:

[. . .] die Frauen, bis in die höchsten Stände hinauf, sind beinah immer in einem Zustand, den ich hier nicht bei Namen nennen mag. (661)

[31] And elsewhere Fontane's — cf. FLB, 309-10.

[32] "Theodor Fontane, von Heinrich Mann," in *Fontane und Berlin,* hrsg. v. Hans-Dietrich Loock (Berlin, 1970), S. 84-85.

[33] Op. cit., S. 33.

[34] Löwenthal, op. cit., S. 221.

[35] E. g. Reuter, op. cit., S. 740.

CHAPTER VI

[1] Klaus Schröter, *Heinrich Mann,* Rowohlts Monographien (Hamburg, 1967), S. 41.

[2] This would seem unlikely from the qualities he emphasizes in them. He does claim in 1948 to have known Fontane in the 1890's:

Was ich büße, ist mein Sinn für das öffentliche Leben, die Voraussetzung jedes einzelnen. Damit befremdete man, als ich anfing, in Deutschland; trotz Fontane, der da war. Ihn kannte ich, zugleich mit den Franzosen, seinen Zeitgenossen. (An Karl Lemke, 10. 12. 1948)

Reuter, op. cit., S. 533.

[3] Letter to Félix Bertaux of 24. 11. 1924. In *Neue Deutsche Literatur,* 19, Heft 3 (1971), 22.

[4] Frédéric Lefèvre, "Heinrich Mann," *Une heure avec. . .,* VIme Série (Paris, 1933), pp. 31-32.

[5] Thus Roberts assumes it is Freytag (p. 29), as does Weisstein in the body of his text (S. 30), though he modifies this and acknowledges features of Spielhagen as well in a footnote (Anm. 69, S. 36).

See David Roberts, *Artistic Consciousness and Political Conscience: The Novels of Heinrich Mann 1900-1938,* Australisch-Neuseeländische Studien zur deutschen Sprache und Literatur, hrsg. v. Gerhard Schulz und John A. Asher in Verbindung mit Leslie Bodi, Bd. 2 (Berne and Frankfurt/M., 1971).

Ulrich Weisstein, *Heinrich Mann: Eine historisch-kritische Einführung in sein dichterisches Werk* (Tübingen, 1962).

[6] H. Mann, *Im Schlaraffenland* (Hamburg: Claassen, 1966), S. 45.

[7] J. Ettlinger, "Ein satirischer Roman," *Das litterarische Echo,* 3. Jg., H. 5 (1900), Spalte 335. See Ingeborg Meister, *Traditionen des französischen Gesellschaftsromans in Heinrich Manns "Im Schlaraffenland,"* Magisterarbeit (Berlin, 1971), S. 2.

[8] As in *Die Grenzboten.* See Sengle, op. cit., I, 271-72.

[9] Klaus Günther Just, *Von der Gründerzeit bis zur Gegenwart: Geschichte der deutschen Literatur seit 1871,* Handbuch der deutschen Literaturgeschichte. Erste Abteilung — Darstellungen, Band 4 (Bern und München, 1973), S. 192.

[10] Ibid.

[11] Hans W. Rosenhaupt, "Heinrich Mann und die Gesellschaft," *The Germanic Review,* 12 (1937), 271.

[12] For the representative nature of Berlin in considering German conditions, cf. *Das zwanzigste Jahrhundert* (6.1.179).

N. B.: References to H. Mann's contributions to this journal will be in the form of three numbers. The first indicates the year, the second the half-volume and the third the page no. (Jg. 6, 1. Halbband = Okt. 1895-März 1896).

[13] Weisstein sees Diederich Klempner as a key-figure representing Gerhart Hauptmann ("Heinrich Mann. Besichtigung eines Zeitalters," *Zeitkritische Romane des 20. Jahrhunderts: Die Gesellschaft in der Kritik der deutschen Literatur,* hrsg. v. Hans Wagener (Stuttgart, 1975), S. 22).

The drastic parody of Hauptmann's *Die Weber* in Klempner's *Rache* does not justify a direct parallel between the two authors. Klempner is initially called a "Dramatiker" (S. 41) without having written anything; *Rache* remains his only work to be performed before his fame passes and he is consigned to a fringe-position in the *Schlaraffenland,* working on a newspaper but not plays. None of this accords with Hauptmann's career. Klempner's rise and fall serve to presage Andreas' in the cyclical *Schlaraffenland.*

[14] Op. cit., S. 13.

[15] Ibid., S. 13-14.

[16] The term "Vanity Fair" goes back to Bunyan's *Pilgrim's Progress* and reappears, for instance, in ch. XXXIX of Scott's *The Heart of Mid-Lothian*.

[17] Though with the clear indication that the bases of the *Schlaraffenland* are threatened. Cf. Manfred Hahn, "Zum frühen Schaffen Heinrich Manns," *Weimarer Beiträge*, Heft 3 (1966), S. 385.

[18] For the 1881 essay, see Theodor Fontane, *Aufzeichnungen zur Literatur*, hrsg. v. H.-H. Reuter (Berlin, 1969), S. 177-90.

For the 1891 essay, see Theodor Fontane, *Sämtliche Werke; Aufsätze Kritiken Erinnerungen I*, hrsg. v. Walter Keitel (München, 1969), S. 573-77.

[19] This is still a hallowed practice. In the *Zeit-Magazin*, advertisements like the following frequently appear:

> Einmalige Auflage von 400 Exemplaren handsigniert, datiert und numeriert [. . .]. Die Druck-platten wurden nach dem Druck vernichtet. (Issue of 25. 10. 1974, S. 9)

[20] See Just, speaking of the depiction of nudes in sculpture of the era:

> Das berühmteste Beispiel aus dem wilhelminischen Zeitalter ist der Brunnen mit fünf knieen-den, in sich versunkenen Jünglingen, den George Minne 1898 schuf. Die Spiegelung des Nar-ziß in der Quelle, also das Tun eines Einzelnen, wird hier vervielfacht und gibt damit vor, für die Epoche insgesamt verbindlich zu sein. (op. cit., S. 131)

[21] Quoted (as "Privatnotizen") in André Banuls, *Heinrich Mann* (Stuttgart, 1970), S. 27.

Cf. too Fontane's critique of *Die Weber*:

> Hier aber, am Schluß des vierten Aktes, hätte der abschließende Sieg nichts bedeutet als – was eben zu wenig ist – den Sieg der Rache (!).

(*Aufsätze*, op. cit., S. 858-59)

[22] Cf. the visionary tones of the following, the non-staged reality, the conclusion to the "Parteitag der Sozialdemokratie in Hannover 1899":

> Die Arbeitermarseillaise brauste durch den Ballhof. Hörte niemand die Dissonanz? Es waren nicht die Geister der Vergangenheit, die Prinzessinnen, die Kurfürsten und die Könige, die sie hervorriefen. Es war der Geist der Zukunft.

Lily Braun, "Memoiren einer Sozialistin, Kampfjahre," in *Historisches Lesebuch 2: 1871-1914*, hrsg. v. Gerhard Ritter, Fischer Bücherei (F./M., 1967), S. 155. In *Die Epigonen* the would-be knights, drunkenly celebrating, are likewise oblivious to the undertones of the original, the "Mar-seillaise" itself, when played by the musicians entertaining them (III, 249).

[23] Here the 'king' of the *Schlaraffenland* does react differently from the historical Kaiser. See Barbara W. Tuchman, *The Proud Tower: A Portrait of the World Before the War 1890-1914* (London, 1966):

> The Kaiser himself had removed the imperial coat of arms from the Deutsches Theater when it performed Hauptmann's *Die Weber* to a cheering Socialist demonstration in the mid-nineties. (p. 324)

[24] See Lefèvre:

> Mes romans sont généralement consacrés à la connaissance du pouvoir et de ses conditions dans une société donnée, de ses déplacements à l'intérieur de cette société.
>
> Dans mon premier roman berlinois, *Au pays de cocagne*, le pouvoir demeurait encore ferme aux mains du souverain et des possédants. A côté seulement et inofficiellement, fonctionnait la grande force sociale du capital. (op. cit., p. 32)

[25] Op. cit., S. 74.

[26] A similar doctrine, though without the same negative overtones, is proclaimed by Violante in *Die Göttinnen*. She writes to her friend, the old Garibaldi disciple San Bacco: "[. . .] unter uns kommt es auf Gesinnungen an, nicht auf Werke" (I, 239). And later: "Ich kenne nur eine Aristokratie, die der Empfindung. Gemein nenne ich jeden, der häßlich empfindet" (II, 129). See Roger A. Nicholls, "Heinrich Mann and Nietzsche," *Modern Language Quarterly*, 21 (1960), 168. The second quo-tation of course involves far more than the content of what Andreas is saying, but both are expres-sions of an effete society.

[27] Bismarck's *Sozialistengesetz* of 1878 had been largely countered by the time of his deposition on 21. 3. 1890. The government did in fact call an international conference for the protection of workers which took place from 15.-29. 3. 1890 (see *Historisches Lesebuch 2*, op. cit., S. 264-65).

[28] The three goddesses of H. Mann's next novel *Die Göttinnen*, as dominating aspects of the Herzogin von Assy, show a somewhat different changing of coats and roles, each one being lived out to the exhaustion of its possibilities.

[29] Jürgen Zeck, *Die Kulturkritik Heinrich Manns in den Jahren 1892 bis 1909*, Diss. Hamburg, 1965, S. 66. Hahn justifiably criticizes the linear connection Zeck draws between Mann's contributions to

Das zwanzigste Jahrhundert and the novel *Im Schlaraffenland*. See Manfred Hahn, "Heinrich Manns Beiträge in der Zeitschrift 'Das zwanzigste Jahrhundert,' " *Weimarer Beiträge*, Heft 6 (1967), S. 1015, Anm. 4.

[30] H. Mann, *Die Göttinnen oder Die drei Romane der Herzogin von Assy* (Hamburg und Düsseldorf: Claassen, 1969), S. 389.

[31] Op. cit., S. 64.

[32] Ibid., S. 70.

[33] Fontane discusses the lowliness of the order and at the same time the miserable position of German writers in a letter of 29. 4. 1890 (FLB, 123).

Cf. too Lamar Cecil, "Jew and Junker in Imperial Berlin," *Leo Baeck Institute Year Book*, XX (1975):

> Some Jews introduced variations on this basic pattern [entry to aristocratic clubs] in order further to reduce the gulf which separated them from the Prussian nobility. Bleichröder, Schwabach and Friedländer received titles from the Prussian sovereign — some whispered that they bought them — as did several Goldschmidt-Rothschilds. (p. 51)

> [. . .] the brisk market in titles and the intensity with which such distinctions were sought after [. . .] was only one sign of the vulgarisation that had set in with the last Kaiser. Aristocratic comment invariably drew invidious comparisons between the elegance and exclusiveness of the court of William I and of Berlin society in his reign with the theatrics and tinsel glory as well as the democratisation of society under his grandson. (p. 52)

[34] The equivalents of Gobelins corresponding to the wealth of Pauline Pittelkow are to be found in her front room, "die Fransen des vor dem Sofa liegenden Brüsseler Teppichs." From *Stine*, ch. 4 (I, 495).

Hildegard Munk no sooner arrives in Berlin than she gushes:

> Eure Berliner Muster schlagen jetzt alles aus dem Felde [. . .]. Scheltet mich übrigens nicht, daß ich in einem fort von Dingen spreche, für die sich ja morgen auch noch die Zeit finden würde: Grecborte und Sèvres und *Meißen* und Zwiebelmuster [author's emphasis].

From *Frau Jenny Treibel*, ch. 14 (I, 987).

The following quotation applies to the motley collection of elegance, pretentiousness and trivia in Pauline Pittelkow's front room:

> All dies Einrichtungsmaterial, Kleines und Großes, Kunst und Wissenschaft, war an ein und demselben Vormittage gekauft und mittels Handwagen [. . .] von einem *Trödler* in der Mauerstraße nach der Invalidenstraße geschafft worden. (I, 494 - author's emphasis)

[35] Karl Erich Born, "Der soziale und wirtschaftliche Strukturwandel Deutschlands am Ende des 19. Jahrhunderts," *VSWG*, 50 (1963), 375.

[36] This holds true of München as well as Berlin. In *Was die Isar rauscht*, Drillinger says to Weiler: "[. . .] die wirtschaftlichen Fragen beherrschen alles. Die Lebenslinie bewegt sich aufwärts mit der Kraft des Wohlstandes." M.C. Conrad, *Was die Isar rauscht: Münchener Roman* (Leipzig: Wilhelm Friedrich, o. J.), I, 158.

[37] Hahn, "Zum frühen Schaffen," op. cit., S. 383.

[38] In the *Reichstag* elections of 20. 2. 1890, the Social Democrats had for the first time gained more votes than any other party.

[39] Cf. Cecil:

> Without wealth they [the Jews] would never have succeeded in penetrating society, yet it was the very emblem of riches that made them objects of noble derision and fuelled the resentment of those who had in better times been the standard by which elegance had been measured. The collapse of aristocratic fortunes was due largely to international agricultural competition and bad capital investments, and for both misfortunes Jewish bankers, speculators and grain traders were blamed. (op. cit., p. 53)

[40] The first *Flottengesetz* was passed by the *Reichstag* in 1898.

[41] Cf. Wolfgang Mommsen, *Das Zeitalter des Imperialismus*, Fischer Weltgeschichte, Bd. 28 (Frankfurt/Main, 1969), S. 174, Böhme, op. cit., S. 100.

[42] Cf. Akt V of *Die Weber*, satirized in *Rache*:

> Chirurgus Schmidt: [. . .] ich meechte kee Fabrikante sein, und wenn ich gleich uf Gummirädern fahr'n keente.

Gerhart Hauptmann, *Die großen Dramen* (Berlin: Propyläen, 1965), S. 74.

[43] Hahn, "Zum frühen Schaffen," op. cit., S. 385.

[44] Cf. Hans Herzfeld, "Berlin als Kaiserstadt und Reichshauptstadt 1871-1945," *Jahrbuch für die Geschichte Mittel- und Ostdeutschlands*, hrsg. v. Wilhelm Berges et al., Bd. 1 (Tübingen, 1952), S. 144.

See too H. Mann in *Das zwanzigste Jahrhundert*:

> Berlin [. . .] schließt trotz allem noch soviel glücklich Kleinstädtisches in sich, es enthält so viele nicht abgeschliffene, proviziale Elemente und bewahrt in seiner groben Emporkömm-lings-Physiognomie im Grunde einen so einheitlichen Charakter. (6.1.201)

[45] Cf. Herzfeld, ibid., S. 161; Böhme, op. cit., S. 85; Wolfgang Köllmann, "Industrialisierung, Binnen-wanderung und "Soziale Frage": Zur Entstehungsgeschichte der deutschen Industriegroßstadt im 19. Jahrhundert," *VSWG*, 46 (1959), 60.

[46] "Du gehst zu Frauen? Vergiß die Peitsche nicht!"

Friedrich Nietzsche, *Werke in drei Bänden*, hrsg. v. Karl Schlechta (München, 1960), II, 330.

[47] See Weisstein, *Heinrich Mann: Eine historisch-kritische Einführung*, op. cit., S. 27 (Anm. 49). Cf. too the *Materialien zu 'Martin Salander.'* "Der reiche Emporkömmling, welcher sich auf schlauem Wege adelig machen will" is described thus:

> Dann legt er mit Bezug auf das Haus seiner Adresse die Bezeichnung "zum" bei und **verläßt** sich darauf, daß der Sprachgebrauch ein "von" daraus machen werde [. . .] .

Baechtold, op. cit., S. 645.

Cf. too FLB, 381-82 (Anm. 4 to S. 276):

> Ehrendoktor Fontane.
>
> Fontane ist nun wohl fein 'raus,
> Er ist jetzt ein gelehrtes Haus,
> Und will er bürgerlich nicht bleiben,
> Kann er sich auch *von Tane* schreiben.

(Beilage des Berliner Tageblatts "Der Ulk," Jahrgang 23, 1894, Nr. 49 vom 7. Dezember)

[48] Abell extols "unsere nationale deutsche Tingeltangelpoesie" (204) at the expense of others: "Welch ein Mangel an Tiefe in den französischen Chansons!" (205). It is characteristic of H. Mann's editorial use of irony to expose his characters that "eine napoleonische Miene" (206) concludes Abell's tirade against the French.

CHAPTER VII

[1] Hans Wysling, *Einführung zum Briefwechsel T. Mann-H. Mann 1900-1949* (Frankfurt/Main, 1968), S. XLII.

[2] "An die Familie," Straßburg, den 28. Juli 1835:

> Der dramatische Dichter ist in meinen Augen nichts als ein Geschichtschreiber, steht aber *über* letzterem dadurch, daß er uns die Geschichte zum zweiten Mal erschafft und uns gleich unmittelbar, statt eine trockene Erzählung zu geben, in das Leben einer Zeit hinein versetzt, uns statt Charakteristiken Charaktere und statt Beschreibungen Gestalten gibt.

Georg Büchner, *Werke und Briefe*, dtv-Gesamtausgabe, 3. Auflage (München, 1968), S. 181.

SELECT BIBLIOGRAPHY

I

PRIMARY SOURCES

Arnim, Achim von.

Armut, Reichtum, Schuld und Buße der Gräfin Dolores: Eine wahre Geschichte zur lehrreichen Unterhaltung armer Fräulein. Bd. 1 of *A. v. A.: Sämtliche Romane und Erzählungen.* Hrsg. v. W. Migge. München: Hanser, 1962.

Broch, Hermann.

Pasenow oder die Romantik. Bibliothek Suhrkamp, 92. Frankfurt/Main: Suhrkamp, 1969.

Büchner, Georg.

Werke und Briefe. München: dtv, 1968.

Conrad, M. C.

Was die Isar rauscht: Münchener Roman. Leipzig: Wilhelm Friedrich, o. J.

Eichendorff, Joseph von.

Ahnung und Gegenwart. Bd. II of *J. v. E.: Eine Auswahl.* Hrsg. v. E. Roth. München: Hanser, 1949.

Fontane, Theodor.

Werke in drei Bänden. Hrsg. v. Kurt Schreinert. München: Nymphenburg, 1968.

Sämtliche Werke. Abt. III: *Aufsätze, Kritiken, Erinnerungen,* I. Hrsg. v. Walter Keitel. München: Hanser, 1969.

Aufzeichnungen zur Literatur. Hrsg. v. H.-H. Reuter. Berlin und Weimar, 1969.

Briefe an Georg Friedländer. Hrsg. u. erläutert von Kurt Schreinert. Heidelberg, 1954.

Letter of 24/9/1895 to Polenz. *Sinn und Form,* 21 (1969), 1290-91.

Letter of 4/9/1898 to Friedrich Fontane. *Die Zeit,* 1.5.70, S. 31.

Theodor Fontane 1819. 1969. Stationen seines Werkes. Eine Ausstellung des Deutschen Literaturarchivs im Schiller-Nationalmuseum Marbach a. N. Stuttgart, 1969.

Brinkmann, Richard (Hrsg.). *Theodor Fontane,* Teil II. Dichter über ihre Dichtungen, 12. München, 1973.

Freytag, Gustav. *Soll und Haben.* München und Zürich: Knaur, 1960.

Gotthelf, Jeremias. *Zeitgeist und Berner Geist.* Basel: Birkhäuser, 1951.

Geld und Geist. München und Bern: Eugen Rentsch, 1911.

Goethe, Johann Wolfgang von. *Werke.* 4 Bde. Berlin und Darmstadt: Tempel, 1962.

Gutzkow, Karl. *Die Ritter vom Geiste.* 2. Auflage. Leipzig: F. A. Brockhaus, 1852.

Hauptmann, Gerhart. *Die großen Dramen.* Berlin: Propyläen, 1965.

Hesse, Hermann. *Der Steppenwolf.* Bd. IV of *H. H.: Ges. Schriften.* Frankfurt/Main: Suhrkamp, 1958.

Hofmannsthal, Hugo von. *Ges. Werke in zwölf Einzelausgaben: Gedichte und lyrische Dramen.* Hrsg. v. H. Steiner. Stockholm: Bermann-Fischer, 1946.

Immermann, Karl Leberecht. *Werke.* Kritisch durchgesehene und erläuterte Ausgabe. 5 Bde. Hrsg. v. Harry Maync. Leipzig und Wien: Bibliographisches Institut, 1906.

Keller, Gottfried. *Ges. Werke in acht Bänden.* Mit einer biographischen Einleitung von Max Rychner. Leipzig: Philipp Reclam jun., o. J.

Jeziorkowski, Klaus (Hrsg.). *Gottfried Keller.* Dichter über ihre Dichtungen. München, 1969.

Laube, Heinrich. *Das junge Europa.* Bd. 1-3 of *Heinrich Laubes ges. Werke in fünfzig Bänden.* Hrsg. v. H. H. Houben. Leipzig: Hesse, 1908.

Mann, Heinrich. *Im Schlaraffenland. Ein Roman unter feinen Leuten.* Hamburg: Claassen, 1966.

Die Göttinnen oder Die drei Romane der Herzogin von Assy. Hamburg und Düsseldorf: Claassen, 1969.

Das zwanzigste Jahrhundert: Blätter für deutsche Art und Wohlfahrt. Hrsg. v. H. M. 6. Jahrgang, 1. Halbband; Okt. 1895-März 1896.

Thomas Mann Heinrich Mann Briefwechsel 1900-1949. Hrsg. v. Hans Wysling. Frankfurt/Main, 1968.

Letter to Félix Bertaux of 24/11/1924. *Neue Deutsche Literatur,* 19, Heft 3 (1971), 22-25.

Lefèvre, Frédéric. "Heinrich Mann." *Une heure avec . . .,* VIme Série. Ed. Ernst Flammarion. Paris, 1933, pp. 25-37.

Mann, Thomas.
Ges. Werke in zwölf Bänden. Frankfurt/Main: Fischer, 1960.

Nietzsche, Friedrich.
Werke in drei Bänden. Hrsg. v. Karl Schlechta. München: Hanser, 1960.

Raabe, Wilhelm.
Die Akten des Vogelsangs. Berlin: Ullstein, 1969.

Scott, Sir Walter.
Ivanhoe. London: Dent, 1975.

Spielhagen, Friedrich.
Problematische Naturen. 2 Bde., 22. and 21. Auflage resp. Bd. 1 and Bd. 5 of *Friedrich Spielhagens sämmtliche Romane.* Leipzig: Staackmann, 1900.

Problematische Naturen. Volksausgabe, 51.-55. Auflage. Leipzig: Staackmann, 1909.

"Die Geschichte des Erstlingswerks. Wie die 'Problematische Naturen' entstanden." *Deutsche Dichtung,* 17 (Okt. 1894-März 1895), 1-7.

Beiträge zur Theorie und Technik des Romans. Faksimiledruck nach der 1. Auflage von 1883. Mit einem Nachwort von Hellmuth Himmel. Deutsche Neudrucke: Reihe Texte des 19. Jahrhunderts. Göttingen, 1967.

Neue Beiträge zur Theorie und Technik der Epik und Dramatik. Leipzig: Staackmann, 1898.

Stendhal.
Le Rouge et le noir. Paris: Editions Garnier Frères, 1957.

Thackeray, W. M.
Vanity Fair. London: Dent, 1975.

Tieck, Ludwig.
Der junge Tischlermeister. Bd. IV of *L. T.: Werke in vier Bänden.* Hrsg. v. Marianne Thalmann. München: Winkler, 1966.

Vischer, Friedrich Theodor.
Auch Einer: Eine Reisebekanntschaft. Stuttgart und Leipzig: Hallberger, 1879.

Welk, Ehm.
Die Heiden von Kummerow. Rostock: Hinstorff, 1956.

Zweig, Arnold.   *Der Streit um den Sergeanten Grischa.* 16. Auflage. Berlin und Weimar: Aufbau, 1973.

II

SECONDARY LITERATURE

a. Historical background

Balfour, Michael.   *The Kaiser and his Times.* London, 1964.

Benjamin, Walter.   *Berliner Kindheit um Neunzehnhundert.* Bibliothek Suhrkamp, 2. Frankfurt/Main, 1962.

Böhme, Helmut.   *Prolegomena zu einer Sozial- und Wirtschaftsgeschichte Deutschlands im 19. und 20. Jahrhundert.* edition suhrkamp, 253. Frankfurt/Main, 1968.

Born, Karl Erich.   "Der soziale und wirtschaftliche Strukturwandel Deutschlands am Ende des 19. Jahrhunderts." *VSWG*, 50 (1963), 361-76.

Cecil, Lamar.   "Jew and Junker in Imperial Berlin." *Leo Baeck Institute Year Book*, 20 (1975), pp. 47-58.

Clapham, J. H.   *The Economic Development of France and Germany 1815-1914.* 4th ed. Cambridge, 1955.

Dawson, W. H.   *The German Empire 1867-1914 and the Unity Movement.* 2 vols. London, 1966.

Dietrich, Richard.   "Von der Residenzstadt zur Weltstadt: Berlin vom Anfang des 19. Jahrhunderts bis zur Reichsgründung." *Jahrbuch für die Geschichte Mittel- und Ostdeutschlands,* 1 (1952), 111-39.

Enzensberger, Hans Magnus et al. (Hrsg.).   *Klassenbuch 1: Ein Lesebuch zu den Klassenkämpfen in Deutschland 1756-1850.* Sammlung Luchterhand, 79. Darmstadt und Neuwied, 1972.

                                     Klassenbuch 2: Ein Lesebuch [. . .] 1850-1919. Sammlung Luchterhand, 80. Darmstadt und Neuwied, 1972.

Feuchtwanger, E. J.   *Prussia. Myth and Reality: The Role of Prussia in German History.* London, 1970.

Hamerow, Theodore S.   *Restoration, Revolution, Reaction: Economics and Politics in Germany, 1815-1871.* Princeton, 1958.

Herzfeld, Hans.

"Berlin als Kaiserstadt und Reichshauptstadt 1871-1945." *Jahrbuch für die Geschichte Mittel- und Ostdeutschlands*, 1 (1952), 141-70.

Köllmann, Wolfgang.

"Industrialisierung, Binnenwanderung und 'Soziale Frage': Zur Entstehungsgeschichte der deutschen Industriegroßstadt im 19. Jahrhundert." *VSWG*, 46 (1959), 45-70.

Mann, Golo.

Friedrich von Gentz: Geschichte eines europäischen Staatsmannes. Zürich und Wien, 1947.

Deutsche Geschichte des neunzehnten und zwanzigsten Jahrhunderts. Frankfurt/Main, 1959.

Mayer, Kurt B.

The Population of Switzerland. New York, 1952.

Mielke, Friedrich.

"Studie über den Berliner Wohnungsbau zwischen den Kriegen 1870/1 und 1914-1918." *Jahrbuch für die Geschichte Mittel- und Ostdeutschlands,* 20 (1971), 202-38.

Mommsen, Wolfgang J.

Das Zeitalter des Imperialismus. Fischer Weltgeschichte, Bd. 28. Frankfurt/Main, 1969.

Pöls, Werner.

"Bismarckverehrung und Bismarcklegende als innenpolitisches Problem der Wilhelminischen Zeit." *Jahrbuch für die Geschichte Mittel- und Ostdeutschlands,* 20 (1971), 183-201.

Pöls, Werner (Hrsg.).

Deutsche Sozialgeschichte: Dokumente und Skizzen, Bd. I: *1815-1870.* München, 1973.

Pollard, Sidney and Holmes, Colin (ed.).

Documents of European Economic History. 2 vols. London, 1972.

Ritter, Gerhard A.

Historisches Lesebuch 2. 1871-1914. Fischer Bücherei, 834. Frankfurt/Main und Hamburg, 1967.

Ritter, Gerhard A. und Kocka, Jürgen (Hrsg.).

Deutsche Sozialgeschichte: Dokumente und Skizzen, Bd. II: *1870-1914.* München, 1974.

Sagave, Pierre-Paul.

1871: Berlin, Paris — Reichshauptstadt und Hauptstadt der Welt. Frankfurt/Main, Berlin, Wien, 1971.

Schüddekopf, Otto-Ernst.

Herrliche Kaiserzeit: Deutschland 1871-1914. Frankfurt/Main und Berlin, 1973.

Schwarz, Dietrich W. H.

Die Kultur der Schweiz. Handbuch der Kulturgeschichte, I/11. Frankfurt/Main, 1967.

S

Stürmer, Michael (Hrsg.). *Das kaiserliche Deutschland: Politik und Gesellschaft 1870-1918.* Düsseldorf, 1970.

Treue, Wilhelm. "Wirtschafts- und Sozialgeschichte Deutschlands im 19. Jahrhundert." *Handbuch der deutschen Geschichte,* **Bd. 3:** *Von der Französischen Revolution bis zum Ersten Weltkrieg.* Hrsg. v. Bruno Gebhardt. 8., vollständig neubearbeitete Auflage. Stuttgart, 1960.

Tuchman, Barbara W. *The Proud Tower: A portrait of the world before the War 1890-1914.* London, 1966.

b) Approaches to the Novel and Literary History of the 19th Century

Bisztray, George. "Literary Sociology and Marxist Theory: The Literary Work as a Social Document." *Mosaic,* V/2, 47-56.

Braak, Ivo. *Poetik in Stichworten: Literaturwissenschaftliche Grundbegriffe. Eine Einführung.* 4. Auflage. Kiel, 1972.

Bramsted, Ernest K. *Aristocracy and the Middle-Classes in Germany: Social Types in German Literature 1830-1900.* Revised ed. Chicago and London, 1964.

Forster, E. M. *Aspects of the Novel.* Pelican Books A557. 1927; rpt. Harmondsworth: Penguin, 1968.

Friesen, Gerhard. *The German Panoramic Novel of the 19th Century.* Berne and Frankfurt/Main, 1972.

Fügen, Hans Norbert. *Die Hauptrichtungen der Literatursoziologie und ihre Methoden: Ein Beitrag zur literatursoziologischen Theorie.* Abhandlungen zur Kunst-, Musik- und Literaturwissenschaft, 21. Bonn, 1964.

Goldmann, Lucien. *Soziologie des Romans.* 2. Auflage. Übersetzt v. Lucien Goldmann und Ingeborg Fleischhauer. Darmstadt und Neuwied, 1972.

Gräfe, Gerhard. *Die Gestalt des Literaten im Zeitroman des 19. Jahrhunderts.* Germanische Studien, 185. Berlin, 1937.

Hahl, Werner. *Reflexion und Erzählung: Ein Problem der Romantheorie von der Spätaufklärung bis zum programmatischen Realismus.* Studien zur Poetik und Geschichte der Literatur, 18. Stuttgart/Berlin/Köln/Mainz, 1971.

Hasubek, Peter. *Karl Gutzkows Romane 'Die Ritter vom Geiste' und*

'Der Zauberer von Rom': Studien zur Typologie des deutschen Zeitromans im 19. Jahrhundert. Diss. Hamburg, 1964.

"Der Zeitroman: Ein Romantypus des 19. Jahrhunderts." *ZfDPh*, 87, Heft 2 (1968), 218-45.

Hermand, Jost.   "Gründerzeit und bürgerlicher Realismus." *Monatshefte*, 59, No. 2 (1967), 107-17.

"Zur Literatur der Gründerzeit." *DVjs*, 41, Heft 2 (1967), 202-32.

Jaeggi, Urs.   *Literatur und Politik: Ein Essay.* edition suhrkamp, 522. Frankfurt/Main, 1972.

Just, Klaus Günther.   "Von der Gründerzeit bis zur Gegenwart: Geschichte der deutschen Literatur seit 1871." *Handbuch der deutschen Literaturgeschichte: Erste Abteilung — Darstellungen*, Bd. 4. Bern und München, 1973.

Klein, Johannes.   "Ästhetische und soziologische Literaturbetrachtung." *Archiv für Sozialgeschichte*, I. Hrsg. v. der Friedrich-Ebert-Stiftung. Hannover, 1961, 19-25.

Klotz, Volker.   *Die erzählte Stadt: Ein Sujet als Herausforderung des Romans von Lesage bis Döblin.* München, 1969.

Krämer-Badoni, Rudolf.   "Der Topos von der Zeitkritik." *Der Monat,* 12, Heft 138 (März 1960), 5-11.

Kunisch, Hermann.   "Zum Problem des künstlerischen Realismus im 19. Jahrhundert." *Festschrift Helmut de Boor.* Tübingen, 1966, S. 209-40.

Lämmert, Eberhard.   *Bauformen des Erzählens.* Stuttgart, 1955.

Lämmert, Eberhard et al. (Hrsg.).   *Romantheorie: Dokumentation ihrer Geschichte in Deutschland 1620-1880.* Köln und Berlin, 1971.

Langenbucher, Wolfgang R.   "Der Roman als Quelle geistesgeschichtlicher Forschung." *Zeitschrift für Religions- und Geistesgeschichte*, 3 (1968), 259-72.

Laurenson, Diana and Swingewood, Alan.   *The Sociology of Literature.* London, 1972.

Löwenthal, Leo.   *Erzählkunst und Gesellschaft: Die Gesellschaftsproblematik in der deutschen Literatur des 19. Jahrhunderts.* Sammlung Luchterhand, 32. Neuwied und Berlin, 1971.

Lukács, Georg.

Die Theorie des Romans: Ein geschichtsphilosophischer Versuch über die Formen der Großen Epik. 2. Auflage. Neuwied und Berlin, 1963.

"Ein Briefwechsel zwischen Anna Seghers und Georg Lukács." *Georg Lukács Werke. Probleme des Realismus*, I. Bd. 4. Neuwied und Berlin: Luchterhand, 1971. S. 345-76.

Mc. Innes, Edward.

"Zwischen 'Wilhelm Meister' und 'Die Ritter vom Geist': zur Auseinandersetzung zwischen Bildungsroman und Sozialroman im 19. Jahrhundert." *DVjs*, 43, Heft 3 (1969), 487-514.

Magill, C. P.

"The German Author and his Public in the Mid-Nineteenth Century." *MLR*, 43, No. 4 (1948), 492-99.

Majut, Rudolf.

"Der deutsche Roman vom Biedermeier bis zur Gegenwart." *Deutsche Philologie im Aufriß*, Bd. II. Hrsg. v. Wolfgang Stammler. 2. überarbeitete Auflage. Berlin, 1960.

Martini, Fritz.

Deutsche Literatur im bürgerlichen Realismus 1848-1898. Epochen der deutschen Literatur, V/2. Stuttgart, 1962.

"Spätzeitlichkeit in der Literatur des 19. Jahrhunderts: Überlegungen zu einem Problem der Formengeschichte." *Stoffe, Formen, Strukturen: Studien zur deutschen Literatur.* Hrsg. v. Albert Fuchs und Helmut Motekat. München, 1962, S. 440-70.

Mayer, Hans.

"Der deutsche Roman im 19. Jahrhundert." *Von Lessing bis Thomas Mann: Wandlungen der bürgerlichen Literatur in Deutschland.* Pfullingen, 1959, S. 297-316.

Mielke, Hellmuth.

Der deutsche Roman. Berlin, 1898.

Pascal, Roy.

The German Novel: Studies. Manchester, 1956.

From Naturalism to Expressionism: German Literature and Society 1880-1918. London, 1973.

Platz-Waury, Elke (ed.).

English Theories of the Novel: Nineteenth Century. English Texts, 9. Hrsg. v. Theo Stammler. Tübingen, 1972.

Ritchie, James M.

"Realism." *Periods in German Literature.* Ed. James M. Ritchie. London, 1966, pp. 171-95.

Sagarra, Eda.	*Tradition and Revolution: German Literature and Society 1830-1890.* London, 1971.
Sagave, Pierre-Paul.	*Recherches sur le roman social en Allemagne.* Aix-en-Provence, 1960.
Sammons, Jeffrey L.	Review of *Joachim Worthmann: Probleme des Zeitromans* [. . .] . *ZfDPh*, 95 (1976), 299-303.
Schwarz, Egon.	"Grundsätzliches zum literarischen Realismus." *Monatshefte*, 59, No. 2 (1967), 100-6.
Schwerte, Hans.	"Deutsche Literatur im Wilhelminischen Zeitalter." *Wirkendes Wort,* 14 (1964), 254-70.
Sengle, Friedrich.	"Der Romanbegriff in der ersten Hälfte des 19. Jahrhunderts." *Arbeiten zur deutschen Literatur, 1750 bis 1850.* Stuttgart, 1965, S. 175-96.
	Biedermeierzeit: Deutsche Literatur im Spannungsfeld zwischen Restauration und Revolution, 1815-1848. 2 Bde. Stuttgart, 1971-72.
Stanzel, Franz K.	*Typische Formen des Romans.* 5. Auflage. Göttingen, 1970.
Steinecke, Hartmut (Hrsg.).	*Theorie und Technik des Romans im 19. Jahrhundert.* Deutsche Texte, 18. Tübingen, 1970.
	"Die 'zeitgemäße' Gattung: Neubewertung und Neubestimmung des Romans in der jungdeutschen Kritik." *Untersuchungen zur Literatur als Geschichte.* Festschrift für Benno von Wiese. Hrsg. v. Vincent J. Günther et al. Berlin, 1973, S. 325-46.
	Romantheorie und Romankritik in Deutschland: Die Entwicklung des Gattungsverständnisses von der Scott-Rezeption bis zum programmatischen Realismus. 2 Bde. Stuttgart, 1975.
Stern, J. P.	*On Realism.* London and Boston, 1973.
Tolstoy, Leo.	"Preface to Von Polenz's Novel 'Der Büttnerbauer.' " *What is Art? and Essays on Art.* Trans. Aylmer Maude. London, 1962, pp. 313-22.
Wagner, Reinhard.	"Die theoretische Vorarbeit für den Aufstieg des deutschen Romans im 19. Jahrhundert." *ZfDPh,* 74 (1955), 353-63.

Werenberg, W.

"Der deutsche Tendenzroman." *Blätter für literarische Unterhaltung* Nr. 3, 15. Januar 1853, S. 49-53.

Williams, Raymond.

Culture and Society, 1780-1950. London, 1958.

"Realism and the Contemporary Novel." *The Long Revolution.* London, 1961, pp. 274-89.

"Literature *in* Society." *Contemporary Approaches to English Studies.* Ed. Hilda Schiff. London, 1977, pp. 24-37.

Worthmann, Joachim.

Probleme des Zeitromans: Studien zur Geschichte des deutschen Romans im 19. Jahrhundert. Probleme der Dichtung, 13. Heidelberg, 1974.

Zéraffa, Michel.

Roman et société. Paris, 1971.

c) Individual authors

1. Immermann

Böttger, Fritz (Hrsg.).

Karl Immermann. Im Schatten des schwarzen Adlers: Ein Dichter- und Zeitbild in Selbstzeugnissen, Werkproben, Briefen und Berichten. Berlin, 1967.

David, Claude.

"Über den Begriff des Epigonischen." *Tradition und Ursprünglichkeit* (Akten des III. Internationalen Germanistenkongresses 1965 in Amsterdam). Hrsg. v. Werner Kohlschmidt und Hermann Meyer. Bern, 1966, S. 66-78.

Gadamer, Hans-Georg.

"Zu Immermanns Epigonen-Roman." *Kleine Schriften II: Interpretationen.* Tübingen, 1967, S. 148-60.

Grütter, Emil.

Immermanns 'Epigonen.' Ein Beitrag zur Geschichte des deutschen Romans. Diss. Zürich, 1951.

Guzinski, Elisabeth.

Karl Immermann als Zeitkritiker: Ein Beitrag zur Geschichte der deutschen Selbstkritik. Neue deutsche Forschungen, 142. Berlin, 1937.

Hecker, Konrad.

Mensch und Masse: Situation und Handeln der Epigonen gezeigt an Immermann und den Jungdeutschen. Diss. Leipzig, 1933.

Höllerer, Walter.

"Karl Leberecht Immermann." *Zwischen Klassik und Moderne: Lachen und Weinen in der Dichtung einer Übergangszeit.* Stuttgart, 1958, S. 212-39.

Hope, J. F. T.

Epigonentum und Biedermeier: Karl Immermanns Verhältnis zur Biedermeierzeit. M. A. Melbourne, 1967.

Kohlhammer, Siegfried.

Resignation und Revolte. Immermanns 'Münchhausen': *Satire und Zeitroman der Restaurationsepoche.* Stuttgart, 1973.

Kommerell, Max.

"Immermann und das neunzehnte Jahrhundert." *Essays, Notizen, Poetische Fragmente.* Hrsg. v. Inge Jens. Olten, Freiburg/Br., 1969, S. 187-222.

Kuczynski, Jürgen.

"Immermann und die industrielle Revolution." *Gestalten und Werke: Soziologische Studien zur deutschen Literatur.* Berlin und Weimar, 1969, S. 141-62.

L[aube], H[einrich].

"Immermanns Epigonen." *Mitternachtzeitung für gebildete Stände,* 11, 137 (22. August, 1836), 545-48. (Athenäum Reprints, *Die Zeitschriften des jungen Deutschland,* hrsg. v. Alfred Estermann. Frankfurt/Main, 1971.)

Mayer, Hans.

"Karl Immermanns 'Epigonen.' " *Von Lessing bis Thomas Mann.* Pfullingen, 1959, S. 247-72.

Maync, Harry.

Immermann. Der Mann und sein Werk im Rahmen der Zeit- und Literaturgeschichte. München, 1921.

Moritz, Anita.

Die Raumstruktur in Immermanns 'Epigonen': Eine Untersuchung zur epischen Raumgestaltung am Beispiel eines Zeitromans. Diss. Göttingen, 1955.

Mundt, Theodor.

"Zwölfte Vorlesung." *Geschichte der Literatur der Gegenwart.* Berlin, 1842, S. 451ff.

Rumler, Fritz.

Realistische Elemente in Immermanns 'Epigonen.' Diss. München, 1964.

Sammons, Jeffrey L.

Six Essays on the Young German Novel. University of North Carolina Studies in the Germanic Languages and Literatures, 75. Chapel Hill, 1972.

Wiese, Benno von.

"Zeitkrisis und Biedermeier in Laubes 'Das junge Europa' und in Immermanns 'Epigonen.' " *Dichtung und Volkstum,* 36 (1935), 163-97.

Windfuhr, Manfred.

Immermanns erzählerisches Werk: Zur Situation des Romans in der Restaurationszeit. Gießen, 1957.

"Der Epigone: Begriff, Phänomen und Bewußtsein." *Archiv für Begriffsgeschichte,* Bd. 4, 1959, S. 182-209.

Anderson, Alexander R.   *Spielhagen's Problematical Heroes.* Ph.D. thesis, Brown University, 1962.

Brahm, Otto.   "Friedrich Spielhagen." *Kritische Schriften,* Zweiter Band: *Literarische Persönlichkeiten aus dem neunzehnten Jahrhundert.* Hrsg. v. Paul Schlenther. 2. Auflage. Berlin, 1915, S. 77-86.

Geller, Martha.   *Friedrich Spielhagens Theorie und Praxis des Romans.* 1917; rpt. in Bonner Forschungen. Schriften der literarhistorischen Gesellschaft, Bonn. Hrsg. v. Berthold Litzmann. Neue Folge, Bd. 10. Hildesheim, 1973.

Goessl, Frank.   *Die Darstellung des Adels im Prosaschaffen Friedrich Spielhagens.* Diss. 1966, Tulane University.

Hart, Heinrich und Julius.   "Friedrich Spielhagen und der deutsche Roman der Gegenwart." *Kritische Waffengänge,* Sechstes Heft. Leipzig, 1884.

Hellmann, Winfried.   "Objektivität, Subjektivität und Erzählkunst: Zur Romantheorie Friedrich Spielhagens." *Deutsche Romantheorien: Beiträge zu einer historischen Poetik des Romans in Deutschland.* Hrsg. u. eingeleitet von Reinhold Grimm. Frankfurt/Main und Bonn, 1968, S. 165-217.

Hochfelder, Hermann.   *Die Kritik der Gesellschaft in den Romanen Friedrich Spielhagens.* Diss. Erlangen, 1954.

Klemperer, Viktor.   *Die Zeitromane Friedrich Spielhagens und ihre Wurzeln.* Forschungen zur neueren Literaturgeschichte, 43. Weimar, 1913.

Kuczynski, Jürgen.   "Vom möglichen Nutzen unschöner Literatur: Friedrich Spielhagen." *Gestalten und Werke: Soziologische Studien zur deutschen Literatur.* Berlin und Weimar, 1969, S. 194-203.

Levysohn, Arthur.   Review of *Friedrich Spielhagen: Problematische Naturen. Blätter für literarische Unterhaltung,* 1863, S. 904-6.

Rebing, Günter.   *Der Halbbruder des Dichters: Friedrich Spielhagens Theorie des Romans.* Literatur und Reflexion, 8. Frankfurt/Main, 1972.

Schierding, Hermann.

Untersuchungen über die Romantechnik Friedrich Spiel-hagens. Diss. Münster, 1914.

Schmidt, Julian.

"Friedrich Spielhagen." *Westermanns Jahrbuch der Il-lustrirten Deutschen Monatshefte,* 29 (Okt. 1870-März 1871), 422-49.

(Spielhagen-Album).

Friedrich Spielhagen. Dem Meister des deutschen Ro-mans zu seinem 70. Geburtstage von Freunden und Jüngern gewidmet. Hrsg. auf Veranlassung der Verlags-handlung vom Festausschuß der Spielhagen-Feier. Leip-zig, 1899.

3. Keller

Ahl, Herbert.

"Martin Salander." *Deutsche Rundschau,* 76 (1950), 579-84.

Baechtold, Jakob.

Gottfried Kellers Leben: Seine Briefe und Tagebücher, Dritter Band: *1861-1890.* Berlin, 1897.

Benjamin, Walter.

"Gottfried Keller." *Schriften,* II. Frankfurt/Main, 1955, S. 284-96.

Boeschenstein, Hermann.

Gottfried Keller. Sammlung Metzler, M. 84. Stuttgart, 1969.

Brahm, Otto.

"Gottfried Keller 1882-1890." *Meisterwerke deutscher Literaturkritik,* 2. Band: *Von Heine bis Mehring.* Hrsg. u. eingeleitet von Hans Mayer. Berlin, 1956, S. 747-821.

Ermatinger, Emil.

Gottfried Kellers Leben, Briefe und Tagebücher auf Grund der Biographie Jakob Baechtolds, Bd. 1. 2. Auf-lage. Stuttgart und Berlin, 1916.

Dichtung und Geistesleben der deutschen Schweiz. Mün-chen, 1933.

Grolman, Adolf von.

"Gottfried Keller — 'Martin Salander.' " *Europäische Dichterprofile,* 1. Reihe. Düsseldorf, 1947, S. 93-106.

Kaiser, Michael.

Literatursoziologische Studien zu Gottfried Kellers Dichtung. Abhandlungen zur Kunst-, Musik-, und Literaturwissenschaft, 24. Bonn, 1965.

Kohlschmidt, Werner.

"Louis Wohlwend und Niggi Ju: Eine vergleichende Studie zum Zeitgeistmotiv bei Keller und Gotthelf." *Dichter, Tradition und Zeitgeist: gesammelte Studien zur Literaturgeschichte.* Bern, 1965, S. 337-48.

"Der Zeitgeist in Gottfried Kellers 'Martin Salander.' "
Orbis Litterarum, 22 (1967), 93-100.

Lindsay, J. M. *Gottfried Keller — Life and Works.* London, 1968.

Lukács, Georg. "Gottfried Keller." *Die Grablegung des alten Deutschland: Essays zur deutschen Literatur des 19. Jahrhunderts; Ausgewählte Schriften I.* Reinbek bei Hamburg, 1967, S. 21-92.

Merkel-Nipperdey, Margarete. "Gottfried Kellers 'Martin Salander': Untersuchungen zur Struktur des Zeitromans." *Palaestra*, 228 (1959).

Ritchie, James M. *Martin Salander: Eine Untersuchung von Kellers Alterswerk.* Diss. Tübingen, 1954.

"The Place of 'Martin Salander' in Gottfried Keller's Evolution as a Prose Writer." *MLR*, 52 (1957), 214-22.

Szemkus, Karol. *Gesellschaftlicher Wandel und sprachliche Form: Literatursoziologische Studie zur Dichtung Gottfried Kellers.* Germanistische Abhandlungen, 26. Stuttgart, 1969.

Weber, Werner. "Verbindende Kleinwörter: Marginalie zu 'Martin Salander.' " *Forderungen: Bemerkungen und Aufsätze zur Literatur.* Zürich und Stuttgart, 1970, S. 147-50.

Zäch, Alfred. *Gottfried Keller im Spiegel seiner Zeit.* Zürich, 1952.

4. Fontane

Attwood, Kenneth. *Fontane und das Preußentum.* Berlin, 1970.

Barlow, D. "Symbolism in Fontane's 'Der Stechlin.' " *GLL,* 12 (1959), 282-86.

Beaton, K. B. "Theodor Fontane and Karl von Holtei: The Tradition of the 'Adelsroman' in Nineteenth Century Germany." *Proceedings of the 11th AULLA Congress.* Sydney, 1967, pp. 145-65.

Behrend, Erich. Theodor Fontanes Roman 'Der Stechlin.' Marburg, 1929.

Böckmann, Paul. "Der Zeitroman Fontanes." *Deutschunterricht,* 11, Heft 5 (1959), 59-81.

Brinkmann, Richard. *Theodor Fontane: Über die Verbindlichkeit des Unverbindlichen.* München, 1967.

Brüggemann, Diethelm.   "Fontanes Allegorien." (I) — *Neue Rundschau, 82*, Heft 2 (1971), 290-310; (II) — *Neue Rundschau, 82*, Heft 3 (1971), 486-505.

Buscher, Heide.   *Die Funktion der Nebenfiguren in Fontanes Romanen unter besonderer Berücksichtigung von 'Vor dem Sturm' und 'Der Stechlin.'* Diss. Bonn, 1969.

Demetz, Peter.   *Formen des Realismus: Theodor Fontane; Kritische Untersuchungen.* 2. Auflage. München, 1966.

Gehrmann, Karl Heinz.   "Der Stechlin und die klassenlose Gesellschaft: Notizen zur neuesten Fontane-Interpretation." *deutsche studien,* 35 (1971), 293-302.

George, E. F.   "The Symbol of the Lake and Related Themes in Fontane's 'Der Stechlin.' " *Forum for Modern Language Studies,* IX, No. 2 (1973), 143-52.

Gilbert, Mary-Enole.   "Das Gespräch in Fontanes Gesellschaftsromanen." *Palaestra,* 174 (Leipzig, 1930).

Grawe, Christian.   "Fontanes neues Sprachbewußtsein in *Der Stechlin.*" *Sprache im Prosawerk.* Bonn, 1974, S. 38-62.

Greter, Heinz Eugen.   *Fontanes Poetik.* Bern, Frankfurt/Main, 1973.

Günther, Vincent J.   *Das Symbol im erzählerischen Werk Fontanes.* Bonner Arbeiten zur deutschen Literatur, 16. Bonn, 1967.

Hayens, K.   "A Liberal Conservative: 'Der Stechlin.' " *Theodor Fontane: A Critical Study.* London, 1920, pp. 248-72.

Hofmiller, Josef.   "Stechlin-Probleme" (1932). *Die Bücher und Wir.* Zürich, o. J., S. 67-75.

Loock, Hans-Dietrich (Hrsg.).   *Fontane und Berlin.* Berlin, 1970.

Lübbe, Hermann.   "Fontane und die Gesellschaft." *Literatur und Gesellschaft vom neunzehnten ins zwanzigste Jahrhundert.* Hrsg. v. H. J. Schrimpf. Bonn, 1963, S. 229-73.

Lukács, Georg.   "Der alte Fontane." *Die Grablegung des alten Deutschland: Essays zur deutschen Literatur des 19. Jahrhunderts; Ausgewählte Schriften i.* Reinbek bei Hamburg, 1967, S. 120-59.

Meyer, Herman.   *Das Zitat in der Erzählkunst: Zur Geschichte und Poetik des europäischen Romans.* Stuttgart, 1961.

Minder, Robert.   "Über eine Randfigur bei Fontane." *Dichter in der Gesellschaft: Erfahrungen mit deutscher und französischer Literatur.* Frankfurt/Main, 1966, S. 140-54.

Mittenzwei, Ingrid.   *Die Sprache als Thema: Untersuchungen zu Fontanes Gesellschaftsromanen.* Frankfurter Beiträge zur Germanistik, 12. Bad Homburg, Berlin, Zürich, 1970.

Müller-Seidel, Walter.   "Theodor Fontane. Der Stechlin." *Der deutsche Roman vom Barock bis zur Gegenwart,* II, Hrsg. v. Benno von Wiese. Düsseldorf, 1963, S. 146-89.

Theodor Fontane: Soziale Romankunst in Deutschland. Stuttgart, 1975.

Osiander, Renate.   *Der Realismus in den Zeitromanen Theodor Fontanes: Eine vergleichende Gegenüberstellung mit dem französischen Zeitroman.* Diss. Göttingen, 1953.

Petersen, Julius.   "Theodor Fontanes Altersroman." *Euphorion,* 29 (1928), 1-74.

Preisendanz, Wolfgang.   *Humor als dichterische Einbildungskraft: Studien zur Erzählkunst des poetischen Realismus.* Theorie und Geschichte der Literatur und der schönen Künste, 1. München, 1963.

Remak, Joachim.   *The Gentle Critic: Theodor Fontane and German Politics, 1848-1898.* Syracuse, 1964.

Reuter, Hans-Heinrich.   *Fontane.* 2 Bde. München, 1968.

Richter, Wilfried.   *Das Bild Berlins nach 1870 in den Romanen Theodor Fontanes.* Diss. Berlin, 1955.

Roch, Herbert.   *Fontane, Berlin und das 19. Jahrhundert.* Berlin-Schöneberg, 1962.

Rowley, Brian A.   "Theodor Fontane: A German Novelist in the European Tradition?" *GLL,* XV, No. 1 (1961), 71-88.

Rychner, Max.   "Theodor Fontane: Der Stechlin." *Deutsche Romane von Grimmelshausen bis Musil. Interpretationen,* III. Hrsg. v. Jost Schillemeit. Frankfurt/Main, 1966, S. 218-29.

Samuel, Richard H.   "Theodor Fontane." *Selected Writings.* Ed. D. R. Coverlid et al. Melbourne, 1965, pp. 112-21.

Schäfer, Renate.   "Fontanes Melusine-Motiv." *Euphorion*, 56 (1962), 69-104.

Schillemeit, Jost.   *Theodor Fontane: Geist und Kunst seines Alterswerkes.* Zürcher Beiträge zur deutschen Literatur- und Geistesgeschichte, 19. Zürich, 1961.

Schmolze, Gerhard.   "Wie 'realistisch' war Fontane? Beobachtungen bei ost-westlichen Fontane-Interpretationen." *Zeitwende*, 42 (1971), 40-51.

Schulz, Eberhard Wilhelm.   "Fontanes Gesellschaftsbild." *Wort und Zeit.* Kieler Studien zur deutschen Literaturgeschichte, 6. Hrsg. v. Erich Trunz. Neumünster, 1968, S. 60-83.

Sommer, Dietrich.   "Probleme der Typisierung im Spätwerk Theodor Fontanes ('Der Stechlin'). " *Fontanes Realismus. Wissenschaftliche Konferenz zum 150. Geburtstag Theodor Fontanes in Potsdam: Vorträge und Berichte.* Berlin, 1972, S. 105-19.

Strech, Heiko.   *Theodor Fontane: Die Synthese von Alt und Neu; 'Der Stechlin' als Summe des Gesamtwerks.* Philologische Studien und Quellen, 54. Hrsg. v. Wolfgang Binder, Hugo Moser und Karl Stackmann. Berlin, 1970.

Turk, Horst.   "Realismus in Fontanes Gesellschaftsroman: Zur Romantheorie und zur epischen Integration." *Jahrbuch der Wittheit zu Bremen,* 9 (1965), 407-56.

Vincenz, Guido.   *Fontanes Welt — Eine Interpretation des Stechlin.* Zürich, 1966.

Wandrey, Conrad.   *Theodor Fontane.* München, 1919.

Wegner, Hans-Gerhard.   "Theodor Fontane und der Roman vom märkischen Junker." *Palaestra,* 214 (Leipzig, 1938).

5. H. Mann

Banuls, André.   *Heinrich Mann.* Sprache und Literatur, 62. Stuttgart, 1970.

Benn, Gottfried.   "Heinrich Mann zum sechzigsten Geburtstag." *Gesammelte Werke in acht Bänden.* Hrsg. v. Dieter Wellershoff. Wiesbaden: Limes, 1968. III, 691-701.

Hahn, Manfred.   "Zum frühen Schaffen Heinrich Manns." *WB*, 3 (1966), 363-406.

"Heinrich Manns Beiträge in der Zeitschrift 'Das Zwanzigste Jahrhundert.' " *WB*, 6 (1967), 996-1019.

Jhering, Herbert.

Heinrich Mann. Berlin, 1951.

Kantorowicz, Alfred.

"Heinrich Manns Vermächtnis." *Text + Kritik*, Sonderband. Hrsg. v. Heinz Ludwig Arnold. München, 1971, S. 15-33.

Kirchhoff, Ursula.

Die Darstellung des Festes im Roman um 1900. Münstersche Beiträge zur deutschen Literaturwissenschaft, 3. Münster, 1969.

König, Hanno.

Heinrich Mann: Dichter und Moralist. Tübingen, 1972.

Kunnas, Tarmo.

Das Werden des Humanismus bei Heinrich Mann. Suomalaisen Tiedeakatemian Toimituksia (Annales Academiae Scientiarum Fennicae), Series B, Nr. 178. Helsinki, 1973.

Lehnert, Herbert.

"Die Künstler-Bürger-Brüder: Doppelorientierung in den frühen Werken Heinrich und Thomas Manns." *Thomas Mann und die Tradition*. Hrsg. v. Peter Putz. Athenäum Paperbacks: Germanistik, 2. Frankfurt/Main, 1971, S. 14-51.

Lemke, Karl.

Heinrich Mann. Köpfe des XX. Jahrhunderts, 60. Berlin, 1970.

Linn, Rolf N.

Heinrich Mann. Twayne's world author series, 27. New York, 1967.

Meister, Ingeborg.

Traditionen des französischen Gesellschaftsromans in Heinrich Manns 'Im Schlaraffenland.' Magisterarbeit, Berlin, 1971.

Nerlich, Michael.

"Der Herrenmensch bei Jean-Paul Sartre und Heinrich Mann." *Akzente*, 16, Heft 5 (1969), 460-79.

Nicholls, Roger A.

"Heinrich Mann and Nietzsche." *MLQ*, 21 (1960), 165-78.

Rehm, Walter.

Der Dichter und die neue Einsamkeit: Aufsätze zur Literatur um 1900. Hrsg. v. Reinhardt Habel. Kleine Vandenhoeck Reihe, 306. Göttingen, 1969.

Roberts, David.

Artistic Consciousness and Political Conscience: The Novels of Heinrich Mann 1900-1938. Australisch-Neuseeländische Studien zur deutschen Sprache und

	Literatur (hrsg. von Gerhard Schulz und John A. Asher in Verbindung mit Leslie Bodi), 2. Berne and Frankfurt/Main, 1971.
Rosenhaupt, Hans W.	"Heinrich Mann und die Gesellschaft." *GR,* 12 (1937), 267-78.
	Der deutsche Dichter um die Jahrhundertwende und seine Abgelöstheit von der Gesellschaft. Sprache und Dichtung, 66 (Bern und Leipzig, 1939).
Schröter, Klaus.	*Anfänge Heinrich Manns: Zu den Grundlagen seines Gesamtwerks.* Germanistische Abhandlungen, 10. Stuttgart, 1965.
	Heinrich Mann in Selbstzeugnissen und Bilddokumenten. rm, 125. Reinbek bei Hamburg, 1967.
Trapp, Frithjof.	*"Kunst" als Gesellschaftsanalyse und Gesellschaftskritik bei Heinrich Mann.* Berlin, New York, 1975.
Urbanowicz, Mieczyslaw.	"Das Bürgertum und die Arbeiter in den Romanen von Heinrich Mann." *Germanica Wratislaviensia,* 6 (1960), 97-113.
Weisstein, Ulrich.	"Bel-Ami im Schlaraffenland: Eine Studie über Heinrich Manns Roman 'Im Schlaraffenland.' " *WB,* 3 (1961), 557-70.
	Heinrich Mann: Eine historisch-kritische Einführung in sein dichterisches Werk. Mit einer Bibliographie der von ihm veröffentlichten Schriften. Tübingen, 1962.
	"Heinrich Mann. Besichtigung eines Zeitalters." *Zeitkritische Romane des 20. Jahrhunderts: Die Gesellschaft in der Kritik der deutschen Literatur.* Hrsg. v. Hans Wagener. Stuttgart, 1975, S. 9-36.
Werner, Renate.	*Skeptizismus, Ästhetizismus, Aktivismus: Der frühe Heinrich Mann.* Literatur in der Gesellschaft, 11. Düsseldorf, 1972.
Winter, Lorenz.	*Heinrich Mann und sein Publikum: Eine literatursoziologische Studie zum Verhältnis von Autor und Öffentlichkeit.* Kunst und Kommunikation, 10. Köln, 1965.
Zeck, Jürgen.	*Die Kulturkritik Heinrich Manns in den Jahren 1892 bis 1909.* Diss. Hamburg, 1965.

OTHER WORKS CITED

Carter, T. E.

"Freytag's 'Soll und Haben': A Liberal National Manifesto as a Bestseller." *GLL*, 21 (1968), 320-29.

Karthaus, Ulrich.

" 'Der Zauberberg' — ein Zeitroman (Zeit, Geschichte, Mythos)." *DVjs*, 44, Heft 2 (1970), 269-305.

Killy, Walter.

"Der Roman als romantisches Buch: Über Eichendorffs 'Ahnung und Gegenwart.' " *Interpretationen, Bd. III: Deutsche Romane von Grimmelshausen bis Musil*. Hrsg. v. Jost Schillemeit. Frankfurt/Main, Hamburg, 1966, S. 136-54.

Korg, Jacob.

"Society and Community in Dickens." *Politics in Literature in the Nineteenth Century*. Ed. Janie Teissedou et al. Paris, 1974, pp. 83-111.

Loschütz, Gert (Hrsg.).

Von Buch zu Buch: Günter Grass in der Kritik; Eine Dokumentation. Neuwied und Berlin, 1968.

Polheim, Karl Konrad.

"Novellentheorie und Novellenforschung (1945-1963)." *DVjs*, 38 (1964), Sonderheft, 208-316.

Roßbacher, Karlheinz.

Lederstrumpf in Deutschland: Zur Rezeption James Fenimore Coopers beim Leser der Restaurationszeit. München, 1972.

Schmidt, Arno.

"Der Ritter vom Geist." *Nachrichten von Büchern und Menschen, 2: Zur Literatur des 19. Jahrhunderts*. Frankfurt/Main, 1977, S. 84-113.

Szarota, Elida Maria.

Lohensteins Arminius als Zeitroman: Sichtweisen des Spätbarock. Bern, 1970.

I often tell the story of the irritable monk: the Abbot posted him one day at the door of the monastery, ordering him to welcome every inhabitant or visitor of the monastery with this sentence: *"I am happy to see you!"* At first he was seething. It is hypocrisy, you will say? Oh no! The hypocrite is he who conceals his game, without any desire to change his heart, he wants to appear good; whereas this monk acted consciously, wanting to be good. And at the end of several months, our porter was transformed. Such is the virtue of working from the exterior to the interior, work united to prayer.

Perseverance: the three steps

Persist, sustain it, and the prayer will expand the reality of your desire for peace, love and joy. See how excellent this tactic is: the prayer introduces a fifth column, spies, parachutists, who infiltrate into the core of your heart. From inside we blow up the bridges of our adversary and, at the same time, we encircle him with our outward attitudes. To pray is to parachute, to bombard the inner works, to attack the enemy 'from behind.' From the two sides, inner and outer, he is crushed. And suddenly our external gestures, with their theatre and desire, reunite with the patient prayer. They have united together; the compulsion is gone, the kingdom of peace is within our grasp; we live in the kingdom of joy. Even if counterattacks assail us, they will be accidental. The invader is driven out; the Spirit reigns.

Another remark will take us further. It happens frequently that those who wish to do better, to pray more and more easily, do not get there; they feel a violent deception. We see people who are active, energetic in business, steeped in goodwill to enter into the spiritual life, but getting no result. And they cry out: if I do nothing, how can I deserve heaven! I am not going forward, I am not budging! This statement suffers from our lack of will, from the absence of that 'something' which pushes towards the goal; were it only a push, the idea could arise that we have no grace, and this could make us sink into a greyness, a spiritual nonchalance.

The Lord's Prayer warns us: my 'will,' the very fact of being able to pose the question of will, of obedience to the divine will, can only be envisaged after having been through the three stages of the soul:

Our Father who art in heaven
hallowed be thy Name,
thy Kingdom come.

One *can* obey God only after having lived through these three periods. Before this, our attempts fail and will continue to fail; either they will be nourished by ambition or they will not be spiritual and will manifest our extreme weakness: I wish but I am not able!

NOTES

[118] It is the *Codex Bezae Cantabrigiensis* (fifth and sixth centuries) which contains the lesson *eletheo to pneuma sou to agion eph'emas* (that your Holy Spirit come upon us) instead of *elthato he basilea sou* (that your Kingdom Come). But this lesson is very old, as attested by the famous heresiarch Marcion, of the second century, by Tertullian in the third, and by Saint Gregory of Nyssa in the fourth.

[119] See Matthew 6:33 and Luke 12:31.

[120] See Luke 6:46.

[121] This expression of the author is so specific as to be almost obscure. He wished to say that, paradoxically, virtues do not demand an effort of will: that they are as much natural to us — that is to say part of our nature — as are our vices. This links with statements made by Saint Theophan the Recluse that, taken together, appear paradoxical: he once said that Christianity is natural to man, and at another time he said that Christianity demands that we struggle against our nature.

[122] Ezekiel 11:19 and 36:26.

CHAPTER THIRTEEN

"THY WILL BE DONE:"
OBEDIENCE

"Thy will be done, " which follows the three first verses of the Lord's Prayer, poses the problem of our obedience to the divine Will.

Psychological meaning of the first three verses

Let us simplify to the extreme — if one can say so — the three first phrases and descend together to the psychological plane, very close to our soul, for if on this plane we discern clearly what they mean, the fact that we were living much more by our 'psyche' than by our spirit confers on us a possibility of realizing the Lord's Prayer in its depth, practically and not only on an intellectual plane.

What then is their psychological meaning?

Our Father is in heaven, He is *heavenly* and we are his children. Psychologically, this is the elevation of the soul. The first attitude will therefore consist in being an idealist, in desiring something great. Children of a heavenly Father, we cannot be worms clinging to the earth. All that lowers and diminishes the human being, all the false humility, will be abolished. I shall call the first impulse a psychological raising of the soul: greatness, idealism, a notion of the divine sonship of man through grace. To see as great: life, and even the enemy! The least 'leveling' is an obstacle to this attitude. How can we fulfill God's Will when we see small? Those who see large are not yet sons of God, but almost.

As soon as the soul is open to greatness, to space, *"Hallowed be thy name"* requires us to accept a style of life appropriate to this elevation. The vulgar, I do not at all say poor, is avoided.

Finally, *"Thy kingdom come"* corresponds to the environment. We may be great and noble in style, but if we still do not create a spiritual climate around us, we are not ready.

Acceptance of the divine will

Let us go a little further. The three first verses reflect the Father, the Son and the Holy Spirit. *"Thy will be done"* dogmatically confesses the creative will of God and at the same time reflects the Virgin Mary — and in her the whole of humanity — arriving, by her acceptance of the divine will, at the second birth. It is, in reality, the response of the world, through the human Mother of God, to the appeal of the Lord and to His Incarnation.

I want to draw your attention to these two meanings of the terms 'earth' and 'heaven': *"Thy will be done on earth as it is in heaven."* We can first understand that the divine Will should be realised on earth, that is to say, in the visible world as it is done in heaven, that is, in the invisible and angelic world. But we can also see it in another way — and some Fathers explain it in this way — that it should be done on earth and in heaven. In this view, it is interesting to note that this accomplishment begins with the external attitude and not the interior. Anyone who thinks that he can begin by interior obedience is mistaken. Obedience in external conduct, acceptance of such and such a test, of such or such a condition, progressively brings interior obedience.

The paradox of obedience

It is evident that this request introduces us to the realm of obedience, the paradox of not begging to receive what we need, for if we pray: *"Thy will be done,"* why pray? That becomes a kind of passive state, leaving it to the divine will. Nevertheless Christ declares: *"Ask and you shall receive... knock and it will be opened to you,"* [123] and if I address myself to God, this is so that my will should be accepted by Him. Does not this verse of the Lord's Prayer contain an apparent contradiction?

Yes, a great effort of will, and a violent battle with oneself, are necessary to yield to Him and to obey Him. Furthermore, the Church teaches us, alongside these words, that we have to almost tear away from God what we desire. On the one hand, our ardent prayer demands; on the other hand, it bows its head: *"Nevertheless, I cannot judge, thy Will and not mine!"* [124] The antinomy arises in our consciousness.

Obedience and inner listening

Obedience is in general poorly understood. Philologically the term obedience in Greek, Latin, and Slavonic signifies: *listening.* Its roots go into 'listening.' Obedience opens the *inner ear.* It is a state which is particularly attentive, not passive. Often, the fraud of the authorities appears here. They mingle obedience to the Spirit with administrative obedience: "You must obey!" This discipline, far from disposing the inner ear, moves the mouth more than in rebellion. All authority which crushes, whatever it may be, the authority of science, of the state, or of the Church, kills the possibility of hearing. People have played on words. Certainly it is normal to obey in the army when it is a question of winning a battle; it is necessary to obey when it is a question of the success of a collective piece of work, but this is in view of a result, of something concrete. The fraud begins the moment religion and the priests use the word obedience in a 'military' way. They destroy the essential, which is to develop the interior ear to be ready always to hear. Obedience frees us, giving us the possibility of being that recipient in whom the Will of God can flow, while external discipline closes the opening.

Thus a monk will obey his Abbot, even if he commands him to go round a table 80 times without reason. First, he gets rid of useless cares: it will be a *positive-negative* obedience; then, he will be freed externally and that will permit him to think of something else. Finally, going round the table — an absurd act — he will rid himself of his prejudices, and, perhaps, of his 'opinions', opening himself to listen, because... not having ever before gone round a table, the position set him seems an absolute 'dogma,' and here the dogma is broken in his soul, preparing him to be available.

But when the religious hierarchy commands us: *"Do not concern yourself about it; obey; dogmas are the concern of theologians; do this and you will be saved,"* then what are they freeing us from? The cares of the world? Not at all! They are freeing us — if one may say so — from God, even from spiritual experience, precisely from what they should bring us to.

It may be that a doctor who is taking care of our body does not describe our illness to us, for the important thing is our healing; but obedience, on the contrary, is the escape from all that could prevent us from hearing. How often this word is dishonestly exploited! Whatever your preferences, when Karl Marx proclaims that religion is the "opium of the people," his words contain a measure of truth. Under the pretext of revelation, under the pretext that the truth has come from on high, we are commanded to obey parents, priests, the State, this person and that; and to await the reward after death. Here, I should affirm, the greatest crime is perhaps to have distorted a number of Christian words; we begin by applying to them a little inexact shading, and suddenly, one day, we perceive that their meaning has changed entirely.

Obedience and liberty

Christian obedience is not disinterestedness; we free ourselves from all we can possibly be freed from so *that we can 'listen'* better and better to the Word.

Why is the Church in the West so occupied with social work just now? Is it afraid that we were beginning to think, beginning to see ourselves falling into heresy? Ah! If the admirable Roman organization suppressed material worries — taxes, for instance — I would be the first to say to them: "Bless you!" For now we could truly obey, and return to the monastic plane again, whose goal is to give man back freedom of spirit and soul.

Personally I have never tasted freedom as well as behind the barbed wire of my captivity in Germany. Like an Archangel Michael, Hitler had organized those little paradises. We were housed and fed; badly housed and badly fed, but all expenses paid, with a great expanse of sky over our heads. And to preserve us from the wicked world, he had stretched barbed wire and posted his angels: the sentries. It was remarkable...

Alas! *obedience*, admirable in its religious meaning, this word has become irreligious, a spiritual deception. It is urgent to restore to it its original powerful and Christian meaning.

NOTES

[123] Luke ll: 9 and Matthew 7:7.

[124] This was the attitude of Jesus at Gethsemane: Matthew 26:39, Mark 14:36 and Luke 22:42.

CHAPTER FOURTEEN

"THY WILL BE DONE":
SYNERGY

Let us try to explain the apparent paradox which we touched on in the last chapter: the union of our resignation to the divine will, on the one hand, with the persistence of our requests taught by Christ on the other. We implore; we insist: *"Knock and it will be opened to you"*; we pray for the sick, to stop trials, to obtain joys; and, on the other hand, we say with a certain fatalism: *"Thy will be done."*

Choosing the divine will

Are we in fact faced with a contradiction? There are three phases: thy will, my will, and *"thy will be done."* God is so powerful that I can do nothing when faced by Him. His will transcends all my possibilities. But then my will enters into play, (my desire that the divine will be done), for it will not be done *if I do not ask Him.* It is not just abandonment to divine will; it is our will which comes to wish it and beg for it.

What do these words mean: *"Thy will be done,"* if not the existential knowledge [125] in our soul, in our whole being, that God is more intelligent, better than we! You will reply to me: this is obvious. No, it is not as obvious as you think. This evidence is revealed in the intellect, but in the human psyche it is not at-all obvious. Let us make a curious, honest experiment: let us rely on God's will, as soon as fear arises, beyond our strength, and if the hand of the Lord will be heavy, if he demands of us something beyond our capabilities, and if, and if... We are afraid that He does not take into account our little desires, our little will, our little impossibilities. To recognize His all-powerfulness and our incapacity, it seems to us, is fatalism, the result of a broken heart.

"Thy will be done" is precisely the opposite of resignation, it includes the movement of an active human will which *wishes* and *chooses* God's will as best for itself.

Voluntary acceptance, the opposite of resignation

Let us try to get to the bottom of this so-called contradiction, for the process of the human soul presents an immense difficulty. How many times in my life I have avoided saying wholeheartedly: *"Thy will be done,"* in apprehension of hearing God ordering me to do something painful, to make a disagreeable effort of psyche. Did He not call Abraham to sacrifice his only son? [126]

And here we are: the moment when we accept voluntarily, not through passivity in the face of His power, but through confidence in His goodness, at the moment when we are ready to give our son, that is to say, what is dearest to us, when we are disposed to respond to the Lord: everything which happens to me, I take it without sacrifice, I abandon myself to Thee, for I am not a servant submitted to a capricious master; my will meets Thy will; at that moment, at the last minute, appears the hand which stops the knife. And we receive a gift superior to all that we could have hoped.

Let us know how then to distinguish resignation from the recognition by our 'psyche' of the very good will of "our Father who art in heaven". Let us insist: man can cry: *"God is good!"* As soon as man enters into conscious contact with Him, doubts rise, the divine greatness takes on a transcendent and dread face as it views our weakness.

I would say that the attitude of *"Thy will be done"* is not even that of a son towards his father (frequently the human father is a master for his child), but that of a small child before his mother, or still more: towards a grandmother who pampers and forgives. The 'pampering' of our God is at the end of the narrow passage, and a superabundance of grace followed Isaac's sacrifice. Have no reservations toward Him, and He will have none toward us.

My will and 'Thy will': One will as one

Finally, my will and 'thy will' are only one will, a synergy, one will as one.

What does one generally ask of God? A thousand things, money, love, prayer, power, intelligence. We begin by demanding: *"give, give,"* then approaching Him we come to murmer: *"nevertheless, thy will!"* And an unexpected phenomenon takes place. The soul, sensing that it realizes the divine will, prays more and more ardently, the two wills become communicating receptacles, the ineffable mixture is established because we will it. This stream of water, this circulation of flame become ours progressively, and ours becomes that of God. We express this, for example, in the Eucharist: *"Thine own of Thine own we offer Thee; in all and for all."* [127] We offer God what is God's, God Himself, but it is we who offer Him!

The meaning of unanswered prayer

When prayer is unanswered, what does this mean?
It is admirable! It is always the beginning of something greater. A prayer

answered by divine condescension, although outside the divine plane, is not always the best solution and can produce unsuspected difficulties. I have known people who, praying unceasingly for years, finally obtained the object of their desires; they sometimes paid a heavy price for it... On the contrary, unanswered prayer is, in principle, a step towards a blossoming out. At one time in my life I almost lost my sight; for three or four days I was in a state of blindness. A friend advised me to have myself healed through anointment with the holy oil of the Archangel Michael. I did not do it, because I felt clearly that this trial of losing my sight could give me something new, a distance between the world and my thought, a separation from a multitude of useless things, an increase of inner attention, a fresh and perpetual vision of the invisible, etc... It is necessary to understand — every request not answered: for money, health, affection — conceals a superior wealth that is within our reach.

Recapitulation of the Lord's Prayer

Let us recapitulate the Lord's Prayer in another way. *"Our Father who art in heaven:"* we enter into the reality; we exist, not for ourselves, but as children of the Father; *"Hallowed be thy name:"* we are known by God; *"Thy rule come:"* loved by God, we are alive; *"Thy will be done:"* we are wanted by God, desired by Him... to be desired by God! *"Thy will be done on earth as it is in heaven:"* here we are the object of the divine will and desire.

And also:

"Our Father who art in heaven:" our heavenly sonship, the pledge of our immortality. We cannot disappear: but, being sons of the Father, calling Him "Father," Him, the eternal living One; rooted in Him, we are eternally, not through immortality of the soul, but through Himself. *"Hallowed be Thy name"*; our immortality is conscious, we have consciousness of it. *"Thy rule come:"* the rule of the Holy Spirit; our conscious immortality will be more and more alive. *"Thy will be done on earth as it is in heaven:"* our conscious, living immortality will be creative; for if rebellion and disobedience lead to sterility in man, acceptance and desire for the will of God open anew the domain of creation. This justifies the thought of Archimandrite Sophrony [128] that we shall create in the ages to come, God being in us. These words do not indicate a road from below upwards, but the mysterious *afterlife*, a post-transfiguration road of the world.

Let us finish this picture of the Lord's Prayer.

"Give us this day our supersubstantial bread:" our conscious immortality, living, creative blossoms in the supersubstantial Bread: the communion. *"Forgive us our debts as we forgive our debtors:"* our conscious immortality,

living, creative, blossoming, will be in common, in participation with our debtors. *"Lead us not into temptation:"* our conscious immortality, living, creative, blossoming, common, fraternal, will not show any fissures of hesitation. *"But deliver us from the Evil One:"* no further possibility of a fall.

NOTES

[125] Here the word in the French is *reconnaissance* - recognition.
[126] See Genesis 22:1-18.
[127] Liturgy of Saint John Chrysostom.
[128] See P. 63 note 69.

CHAPTER FIFTEEN

"GIVE US THIS DAY OUR DAILY BREAD"

We reach the heart of the Lord's Prayer, the fifth request: *"Give us this day our daily (or supersubstantial bread.)"*

As children of God we identify ourselves with the Son through the sanctification of the divine name within us. We become a temple of the Spirit, calling for the coming of the kingdom. We realize synergy through our voluntary entry into the world of the deification of our being. One could think that this says everything! But no, we have reached the domain of the sacrament: of God as food.

The mystery of food

Food is granted to man to nourish his life. It is certain that the organism which does not eat dies. Nevertheless, food has become a safeguard only since the original sin. Its role in the "world before sin," or in the transfigured world, is one of development, not of conservation. To feed oneself and so develop oneself and so blossom out into eternity — *"He who eats my flesh and drinks my blood has eternal life, and I will raise him up on the last day."* [129] This is a communion with lasting progress, an enrichment without end of all that is in us.

God does not feed himself; He nourishes his creature. To understand the meaning of all the mysteries (I use the word 'mystery' in the Greek sense, that is: sacrament) is always to rediscover the mystery of food.

The food mystery, the communion mystery, is revealed in two forms.

I repeat, God cannot feed Himself, since He is the Source: the Being; on the contrary, the creation, itself non-being, can be only through communion in God. From the African to the Hindu, all the ancient mysteries are basically a banquet.

The devil's food

There exists a second manifestation of the mystery, very widespread, in which man tries to nourish the divinity, whether by an offering of rice, honey, flour, milk, whether by immolation of animals, bulls, oxen, he-goats or even virgins. This so-called food presented to the divinity is, in reality, feeding the devil. Realize this, that in their underlying meaning these sacrifices to divinities are not offerings to the Almighty, who has no need of them, but to him who is always hungry.

Why the devil? Because the devil is a pure spirit whose power over the world lacks one thing; and haven't you noticed that what we do not possess seems in general the most precious? This feeling is pushed to the extreme in the father of lies; he is tortured by a constant jealousy: he can be neither man nor matter.

This rage is so acute that on the one hand he tries to convince us by every means that matter is detestable and, on the other hand, he is pleased to devour with a gaze the carnal delicacies which it is impossible for him to consume. His hatred of the Incarnation is such that he struggles to prove that Christ is not really man. His thirst for blood, which he does not possess, runs throughout the history of humanity; he is hungry, for having refused the divine grace, the food of the angels, he is greedy, above all, for the world. And in the world, he is greedy above all for the tenth angel which is humanity, that strange being, neither flesh nor spirit, a small part beast, a small part vegetable, a small part angel, a small part God, not knowing very well himself who he is. Furthermore, Christ came for such a being: a completely unbearable thought for the demon, hence his pathologically vital need to obtain blood sacrifices. He is nourished only spiritually, without doubt, since, lacking flesh, he will not know how to eat, but he feeds on both psychic and spiritual substance.

This state is comparable to the enjoyment of the sight of sin committed by another; *sin-watching* is much more serious than an evil action. From this angle, imagination wrongly oriented is more destructive than the act of sin. The Satanic eucharist is the foundation of the devil's food and forms the basis of all the religions desirous of appeasing, of 'buttering up' the principle of iniquity who reigns over men.

God, taking into account human infirmity, progressively substituted himself for the adversary. When, in the Old Testament, He accepts bulls, he-goats and oxen on His altar, it means: "Otherwise, O men, you would bring them to the devil; so at least offer them to my wrath." And men, having begun to sacrifice to the True God, became accustomed to turning their hearts towards Him. After this, God sends out His prophets, crying: *"I abominate your bloody sacrifices!"* [130]

Finally, Christ abolishes them, becomes incarnate, and replaces the food brought by man to the divinity, by the divine food given to man by God.

I have gone on to this brief statement, which deserves to be studied in greater depth, to introduce you to the sacraments and to the sacrament par excellence: the Eucharist.

The Word teaches us: *"Give us this day our daily (or supersubstantial) bread."*

Bread, at least for the West, is the essential food. The East would say: "rice." To ask for bread is not a luxury, but a necessity without which we could not live. In recent times people have taken these words in the literal sense. This is not a mistake: give us what maintains life, so that material problems will not disturb us beyond measure; in other words; free us from the useless cares of this world. We should take this attitude into consideration. We frequently hear it said that it is easier to live in a monastery than in the world: no more taxes, no children, no fear for the future, etc., etc. I will reply, without dwelling on the spiritual difficulties which monks encounter, that one of the goals of the monastic life is precisely to be freed from cares, for difficult sacrifices have no 'a priori' value. A man who makes his life especially painful is impossible for himself and others to live with. Social reforms, Christian socialisms, consist not in procuring justice or comfort above all, but in making life easier; all else is false romanticism. That a shock can release the flavour of the spiritual life is, I agree, beneficial, but the Christian life cannot depend on daily electro-shocks. That it is indispensable to overcome obstacles is true, but we should always applaud and collaborate as far as possible in the efforts which make life easier. The modern danger resides in the fact of creating and adding useless needs, confusing that which lightens the burden of existence with that which excites it. Thus, selling on credit is questionable, for example, as while it makes things easier, it often engenders new demands.

The divine thought is: Lord, *"give us today the essential."* This fifth request is indispensable. It envelops also another reality: the Church sees in it communion with God. This communion is manifested doubly: Christ answers the devil: *"Man does not live by bread alone, but by every word which comes from the mouth of God."* [132] Communion is then expressed both by the Word and by the Eucharist.

The food of the word

The West has undergone a curious phenomenon: the Protestants in practice do not want to feed on anything but the Word, while the Roman Catholics do not take sufficient account of it. Although they preach and read the Gospel, they remain centred on the Host, forgetting that the teaching is double: word and communion.

When I say that Protestants feed only on the Word, this is only half true. I remember a conference which I held before a number of pastors at the protestant Institute of Theology at Montpellier. The subject was the place of Holy Scripture in the Orthodox Church. When the conference was over, several listeners said to me: we thought that you would speak of icons, of the Fathers of the Church, of the liturgy, of Dostoyevsky, and you dealt with our subject, the Holy Scripture in itself. Yet we had the impression that you were speaking of a Holy Scripture which we did not know! Since then I have realised the cause of this reaction. I said, for example, that it was necessary to read the Psalms without wanting to comment on them at once; reading them will first *leave its mark* in us and work to transform the interior. Now Scripture is, for most people, a text which is commented on as soon as it is read. This allows one to adopt an attitude immediately. The words, the Word, have not had enough time to go deep into the heart, to be eaten, to be drunk; they are not assimilated. Holy Scripture is no longer a spiritual food, but more of a directive, a master teaching from outside.

No! My friends, we do not have to grasp it at once; we should receive the Word as we take in food. It will work in us and clarify our intelligence. Let us listen to the reading of the Gospel 90% and reflect 10%. And our reflection should not depend on our comprehension in that moment. We are on the threshold of a mysterious kingdom: the food dispensed by Holy Scripture. Here is the meaning of the canonical books: if you read them as books of external law, you run the risk of making all sorts of heresies spring up, for inevitably you will underline what pleases or impresses you. Your soul will register or reject this or that psychological aspect. The food of Holy Scripture should imperceptibly inform the intelligence and release the antennae which will pick up the 'true gnosis.' It is this motif which made the Fathers of the Church avoid calling the Scriptures 'authorities.' The Canon[133] is first a nutritious inspirer, then a master, then, if one can say so, a 'supervisor.'

The eucharistic food

The eucharistic food is veiled in symbol, and we commune then with God, and with the world transfigured as it is. Experience proves it: the more a person communes, the more he is organically strengthened in the spiritual life. The best attitude with respect to communion is to consider it as daily bread, but divine: a simple daily necessity. Its effects are not immediate. I would rather say that it is like homeopathy, or a medicine like penicillin. The consequences of communion are observed in the course of an entire life, in groups, and it is interesting to see how much the spiritual sense diminishes in periods of the history of the Church when communion is almost non-existent. This phenomenon is concrete to the point where it materializes in statistical data.

As to the term *"this day,"* the Fathers agree in saying that is refers to daily communion. Communion with God should never be a project, but an act of "this day."

NOTES

[129] John 6:54.

[130] Isaiah 1:11 and following. (In one translation one phrase says: *'Stop bringing meaningless offerings.)'*

[132] Matthew 4:4.

[133] 'Canon' is a Greek term that signifies 'rule' and defines the rules put into operation by the Church for its own use. The 'canonical' books are those which the Church has selected as essential as a vehicle for the Revelation; they are inspired by the Holy Spirit.

CHAPTER SIXTEEN

THE LAST THREE REQUESTS
"FORGIVE US OUR DEBTS AS WE
FORGIVE OUR DEBTORS"

With mercy and humility

If I am strong and fair, God will be strong and fair with me... I fear this category of virtues because of my weakness; they give me a power, but they are opposite to the divine Virtues! Christ said: *"Judge not that you shall not be judged."*[134] *"Forgive us our debts as we also have forgiven our debtors"*;[135] I prefer to treat people with mercy and humility so that they treat me in the same way.

A man deceived me for two years. Until now I have wanted to ignore it and act as if he had not abused me, in the hope of seeing our Lord adopt similar conduct towards me. For if the laws disappear some day, one alone will remain: as you have forgiven, God will forgive you.[136] Here is the kernel of the angelic revelation, immense, dread, imposing; this revelation is linked, tied to the relationships with 'others'; it is social. Do not forget that when we are told to be good to our brothers, it is not at all because they need it, but to call forth God's goodness upon us; God, being identified with each person, is our neighbour. I will then leave the great and virtuous people to judge their neighbour since they will be capable of enduring the judgement of God. Myself, I cannot. Excuse me, I will have pity on myself; I will be weak. Do not imagine that it would be impossible for me to know, for example, the instinct of an Ivan the Terrible. (Perhaps I could kill.) During a shipwreck one simply holds onto a plank, bent on not sinking; me, I clutch hold of one single certainty: to have extreme indulgence towards my brother in order to find this indulgence between the hands of our Father. You will respond: *"You run the risk of losing souls!"* I will answer you that I am not strong enough, not great enough to save souls. Now it is enough for me not to lose my own completely, the one which God has entrusted to me! Our soul is not our property; it is a precious vessel which must be transported.

This is a confession, but beyond my personal attitude, which is not indispensable, one can be great and not forgive: the majority of people consider that they have the right not to forgive debts... I doubt this.

Forgiveness of debts: the foundation of the church

This supplication: *"Forgive us our debts,"* is the basis of the Church as a society, which is the reason for all the injunctions of the Gospel; it also indicates the Second Coming[137] which is now being realized.

We could never judge our neighbour if the Second Coming of Christ were present to our spirit, for who will be the judges of this ultimate tribunal? Our conscience, that is to say our conduct towards our brothers, and God with respect to our conduct towards them. Besides, all will be visible, our sins as well as our virtues. So it is not necessary to be ashamed of discovered sins, only to do penance. Besides, the Last Judgement is not the end of time, it occurs in the present, conditioned by ourselves.

Our steps weave theologies. Are we fair? We trace the theology of a just God. Are we people of sacrifice, a little tragic? Our God takes on the look of sacrifice. Are we indifferent? God will be indifferent.

When this legend spreads that in our parish of Saint Irenaeus we 'feel' community, and that it is less so in others, I would cry: *"My friends! Community or not, I do not know, but there is one real thing: true community grows where every member progresses in forgiveness, and every time we progress in not reclaiming debts, we are increasing the Church, we are building it."* To build without forgiving debts is to summon the judgement of God.

"And lead us not into temptation":
Trials are not possible unless God allows them

Let us first put a principle: evils and temptations cannot arise if God does not permit it. We read in 2 Kings that the Lord will deliver Jerusalem to Nebuchadnezzar,[138] in chapter 42 of Isaiah, verse 24: *"Who has delivered Jacob to pillage, and Israel to the spoilers? Is it not the Lord? We have sinned against Him."*[139] We all know, in the Book of Job, the passage in which Satan comes near the Throne of the Lord and asks Him to deliver Job to him, and God replies: *"Here is everything which belongs to him, I deliver it to you; only do not lay your hand on him."*[140]

When Jesus is summoned before Pilate, does He not declare to him: *"You would have no power over Me if it had not been given from on high?"*[141] Thus temptations require divine permission.

Then why this phrase in the Lord's Prayer? Do not trials really purify us? And he who has not known temptation, says Ecclesiastes, has not passed his trials.[142] Theoretically speaking we can, of course, grow without suffering, but in practice we find that it is when we go through the wine-press that we are strengthened. By failing a hundred times with a picture, we make a masterpiece. And Saint James in his first General Epistle develops it: *"My brothers, regard as a subject of complete joy the different trials to which you can be exposed."*[143] Finally, in the Psalms, God *"tries the minds and hearts"*[144] and plunges us into the crucible, into the fire, and into the water in order to take us out again and give us happiness.[145] What saint, what man of the Church is seen to go through life without trials?

"Lead us not into temptation." Certain people practice a false doctrine: *hoping* for trials; we should not look for them. Saint Cyril of Jerusalem gives us an explanation of this seventh phrase of the Lord's Prayer: "tempt," in Greek, and still more in Hebrew, almost corresponds to *'submerge.'* Lord, make it that we should not be submerged by temptation. We ask to be good swimmers, says the same Cyril, knowing how to swim through the waves to arrive at the port. Do not let us founder; do not let us sink! This request has no other meaning.

Call on divine assistance

Nevertheless here we come to another question: if God permits temptations, he never tempts us beyond our strength, say the Scriptures.[146] So why ask not to succumb?

Surely this is an external and superficial logic! We can only be good swimmers on the express condition that we ask for divine help. It is the same in the liturgy: the Word wants the consecration of the bread and wine; nevertheless all we do is obey his order: *"Do this in remembrance of me,"* then we ask: *"Send thy Spirit."*

Yes, God gives us trials because He knows that we can swim, and yet we should ask Him to help us: God, not as goal, God, not as cause; God always as our help, our collaborator!

Christ emphasises: *"Watch and pray lest you enter into temptation."*[147] The Apostle Peter, who walked on the waters — the waters are the temptations — began to sink, and if Christ had not reached out his hand to him, he would definitely have sunk.[148] Peter was animated by a great desire to go towards God; Peter was moved by a great faith, he lacked prayer. At that moment he lacked that state of prayer in which we need divine help for the least thing, that help which makes our soul walk on the waters of grace.

The formulation of Calvin and of Ignatius of Loyola: "To the greater glory of God," is inexact, in the sense that the motive of the glory of God is insufficient; it has no need for us. God loves us to work with Him, in Him. I will even say that He appreciates a piece of work whose aim is not always exceptional, if it is executed with prayer: help me; lead me not into temptation, I am weak. I would propose to you an image: God places His immaculate lips on the lips of our soul. That is why we must always pray, and when we discern His Will, there is nothing else to do but bend to it: we will have the strength necessary to realize it.

The Love of God, and Perfection

It is evident that in praying to God to free us from temptations, we are asking Him to free us from all that could separate us from Him. Invisibly Christ puts two weights in balance: love of God, and our own perfection. For perfection it is better for us to go through the crucible and conquer ourself; to love God, it is better not to be perfect. How much better it is to be with Him than to compose one's perfection. I have seen souls slow their spiritual ascent because they wanted to be perfect. The construction of the marvellous temple around them prevented the Word from getting in. I will go further: to become a saint, give up the taste for holiness.

"And deliver us from the Evil One:"
Evil does not exist

Evil does not exist. What exists is not evil; it is different aspects of being. Evil is a personal state of consciousness. The Evil One is; the bad deeds are; evil in itself is not.

The evil one falsely combines truths

When the evil one acts, he makes use of a multitude of falsely assembled truths. In Genesis the devil speaks the truth malignantly: "*You will be like God.*"[149] It is true. You will have knowledge, it is true, he did not lie. He emphasised these truths in order to turn Adam and Eve away from God and make them lose his friendship. Does the evil one slip us into traps by lies? No, by truths arranged in such a way that they become deadly; this is why he is called the evil one. False things break down of themselves. Thus, he wants to convince us, as he tried to convince the Living God, through the words of Scripture;[150] the way he puts them together is such that they detach us from our divine sonship. He tries to make us his children. Christ, in a moment of anger, thunders: *"You are not children of Abraham but of Satan."*[151] To reach his goals he cooks up all the truths; through a little crack he introduces a virulent virus; insensibly he turns us away from the "Father who is in heaven." He communicates to us the impression that we are divinities; he does this by means of despair or pride, it does not matter which!

"Deliver us from the Evil One" comes in when we are already on a level with the luminous perspective of the children of God. Never forget that our life has fissures in it. We are full of interior joy, free from all fetters, vibrant with grace, at the door of life eternal, united to God; even then let us never forget, at the door of life eternal, until the end of time, there is a possible crack through which the Evil One's seduction can slip in.

NOTES

[134] Matthew 7:1.

[135] Matthew 6:12.

[136] See Luke 6:37-38.

[137] Of Christ at the last judgement: Matthew 25: 31-45.

[138] 2 Kings 24:1-4.

[139] Isaiah 42:24.

[140] Job 1:12.

[141] John 19:11.

[142] Reference to Ecclesiastes 34:10 untraceable

[143] James 1:2.

[144] Psalm 7:9.

[145] Psalm 66:10-12.

[146] See Saint Paul, I Corinthians 10:13.

[147] Matthew 26:41.

[148] See Matthew 14:28-31.

[149] Genesis 3:5.

[150] An allusion to the temptation of Christ in the desert: Matthew 4:1-11 and Luke 4:1-13.

[151] See John 8:39-44.

CHAPTER SEVENTEEN

CONCLUSION TO PART TWO

What is remarkable in the Lord's Prayer is that Our Lord does not teach us to begin with *"Deliver us from the Evil One"; "Forgive us our sins,"* but with the more positive: *"Our Father,"* that is, with a total confession of our divine sonship; then, as soon as we have sanctified the name of the Word, and have lived this sanctification which transforms us; after we have implored the Spirit to fill the smallest atom of our being, and accepted with the Virgin all the Will of God; then we ask for the Eucharist, the daily Bread; our attitude towards the neighbour only comes after that. How much easier it is to forgive debts when one has fully lived what goes before. It is only at the last, steeped, armed, and protected, that we add: *"But deliver us from the Evil One."*

In pronouncing the Lord's Prayer, persist one thousand times with *"Our Father who art in heaven, hallowed be thy Name, thy Kingdom come"*; 700 times with *"thy Will be done"*; 500 times with *"Forgive us our debts as we forgive our debtors"*; fifty times with *"Lead us not into temptation,"* and ten times with *"But deliver us from the Evil One."*

The supplications of this prayer should not be lived equally: let the first verse flood you, inundate you! For the Lord's Prayer is constructed from the top downwards.

And to end, if *"Forgive us our debts as we forgive our debtors"* makes us already live the last judgement; if in the eschatological sense: *"Lead us not into temptations"* signifies: *"when the trial of fire comes, make it so that I will not be consumed"* — for God will test us by the fire of His Love. Make it so that the flame of Thy Mercy does not burn me, but warms me! For, behind the sufferings — so sublime is the mystery — is the trial of the fire of the Love of the Trinity for us. If *"But deliver us from the evil one"* makes us accept without reservation that we shall be deified by God, invaded by Him, filled with Him, shall be nothing outside of Him, this is to save us from the last malice of the demon: the last danger of being devoured, of being crushed by the divine Power and the divine Love. To understand His words, it is necessary to disappear, to desire nothing other than "God *all* in all." This is what is called the 'second death.' Then the transfigured world will burst and God will say to us: *"You are not only Me; you are My friends."*

And having prayed in this manner, let us say

Amen! Amen! Amen!

PART THREE

SOME COMMENTARIES BY THE FATHERS ON THE LORD'S PRAYER

CHAPTER EIGHTEEN

COMMENTARIES BY ORIGEN

After the brief commentary above, we shall now offer a few passages from the writings of the Church Fathers about the Lord's Prayer. We will first quote Origen (third century), then Saint Cyprien of Carthage (third century), and finally, Saint Cyril of Jerusalem (fourth century,) author of the famous *"Mystagogical catechism"*.

Origen writes: [152]

"Our Father who art in heaven"

"We must investigate carefully whether there is a single prayer in the Old Testament which calls God 'Father'. Until now, despite our efforts, we have not found one. We do not mean that God is not called Father, nor that true believers are not called the children of God, but nowhere, in a single prayer, is God named Father as did the Saviour in his most intimate address which He has transmitted to us.

"We often find that God is called Father and those who have responded to the call of God are called sons, for example in Deuteronomy: '*You have abandoned the God who begot you, you have forgotten the Lord who created you.*'[153] And again: '*Is it not Him who is your Father, who has held you as his own heritage, who has made and created you*'[154] And further on he says: '*My sons have lost faith.*'[155] In Isaiah we find: '*I have engendered children, I have raised sons and they have abandoned me.*'[156] And in Malachi: '*The son honours his father and the servant reveres his master, If I am thus your father, where in you is the fear and respect that I am entitled to?*'[157]

"Therefore, if we call God Father, and call those His sons who are born of Him because they came to hear his word, even then we will not be able to find anywhere in the ancients any exact and clear affirmation of this sonship. The passages we quoted show that those described as sons should be better regarded as subjects. We can see this from the Apostle's statement that: '*As long as the heir is underage, although he is autonomous in everything, he is in no way different from the slave; he is put under the authority of tutors and guardians until the date determined by his father.*'[158]

The Spirit of Adoption

"The fullness of time is with us with the Incarnation of our Lord Jesus Christ when those of goodwill become adopted according to the teaching of Saint Paul: '*Let it be known that you have not received the spirit of servitude to relapse into fear: you have received the spirit of adoption which enables us to cry: Abba, Father!*'[159] And from the Gospel of St. John: '*But to all who have received Him, who believed in his name, he gave power to become sons of God.*'[160]

"Because of this spirit of adoption, the Roman Catholic epistle of Saint John says of the children of God that: '*Whoever is born of God does not sin, because he bears the divine spark within him, He cannot sin, because he is born of God.*'[161]

Let us behave as true sons

"Now if we reflect seriously on the meaning of these words of Saint Luke: '*When you pray, say Father,*'[162] let us be very careful about calling Him by this name if we are not true sons. Otherwise we surely run the risk of adding to all our sins that of impiety. Let me express my thought more clearly: in his first epistle to the Corinthians Saint Paul says: '*Therefore I want you to understand that nobody speaking by the Spirit of God ever says "Let Jesus be cursed!" And nobody can say "Jesus is Lord" except by the Holy Spirit.*'[163] The words Holy Spirit and Spirit are synonymous. What exactly the words mean: '*...to say Lord under the influence of the Holy Spirit,*' is far from clear. Thousands of hypocrites, numerous heretics and sometimes even demons, overcome by the force of this name, have uttered this phrase. Surely, nobody would seriously claim that when all these people spoke the word 'Lord Jesus' they were filled with the Holy Spirit. But they would not be able truly to say '*Lord Jesus*' because only those who serve the word of God can truly say that Jesus is their Lord. This is true of the just. On the other hand, by their corrupt ways sinners make a blasphemy of the word of God, and their works cry out: '*anathema to Jesus.*'

"But those who are born of God do not sin but bear the divine spark in their hearts, they turn away from sin: and by their conduct they proclaim: Our

Father who art in heaven. The Holy Spirit Himself joins with their spirit in order to certify that they are sons of God; His heirs and joint heirs with Christ. They suffer with Him so that they may also be glorified with Him.[164]

"In accordance with their conduct these children of God do not say Abba, Father, half-heartedly. With all the purity of their heart, which is the source of right action, they truly believe in order to be justified, and accordingly, *'they confess with the mouth, and so they are saved.'*[165]

The Saints are the images of the Son

"Therefore all their actions, all their words, and all their thoughts that the Word of God shapes in His image are a reflection of the invisible God and creator *'who makes His sun rise on the evil and on the good, and sends rain on the righteous and on the unrighteous.'*[166] Therefore they are bearers of the celestial Word which is in itself the image of God.

"In this way, then, they are the image of the Image, the Son being the Image, and from then on they reflect His filiation not merely by external resemblance but by a deep assimilation. They are transformed by a spiritual renewal and on a very intimate plane they come to resemble He who is made manifest in the body of glory."

Sinners are the children of the Devil

"If, as we have seen, this is a description of those who truly say: *'Our Father who art in heaven,'* it should be evident that *'he who commits sins is a child of the devil,'* as Saint John says in his epistle, *'for the devil has been sinning from the beginning.'*[167] The spark of God which dwells in the renewed soul has an immunizing effect on those who reflect the image of his Son; but the seed of Satan infests those who commit sin and his presence prevents the necessary spiritual correction. Because the Son became manifest to destroy the works of the devil, the presence of the Word of God in our souls is capable of destroying in us the works of the devil, of extracting the infamous seed planted in us, and so making us children of God."

Becoming Divine

"Let us not imagine that we have only learned the formulation of a prayer to be said at fixed moments. If we truly understand what we have learned of the imperative *'we must pray without ceasing,'* our whole life will be an uninterrupted prayer that will enable us to proclaim: *'Our Father who art in heaven!'* Our city will no longer be on earth, but in heaven which is the throne of God, because the Kingdom of God will have been installed in all those who bear the image of the divine Word, and therefore they will have become divine."

NOTES

[152] Excerpts from *De Oratione*, ('On prayer', Migne, Greek Patrology, II, 485-549.) French Translation in A.G.Hammam, *Le Pater Explique par les Peres,* (Paris, Editions franciscaines, 1952,) pp 50-54.

[153] Paraphrase of Deuteronomy 32:18.

[154] Deuteronomy 32:6.

[155] Based on Deuteronomy 32:19-20.

[156] Isaiah 1:2.

[157] Malachi 1:6.

[158] Galatians 4:1-2.

[159] Romans 8:15.

[160] John 1:12

[161] An unusual translation of 1 John 3:9.

[162] Luke 11:1.

[163] I Corinthians 12:3.

[164] See Romans 8:16-17.

[165] Romans 10:10.

[166] Matthew 5:45.

[167] 1 John 3:8.

CHAPTER NINETEEN

The passage from Origen that we quoted in the previous chapter led us into the depth of the Lord's prayer.

In his turn, Saint Cyprien also analyzed each section of the Lord's prayer. Here we will quote some essential parts of his brief commentary.

It is interesting to note that right from the beginning he emphasises the communal and ecclesiastical character of this prayer. This was his main preoccupation. We must not forget that, after Saint Paul, Saint Cyprien was the fiercest advocate of the principle of the Church as community, communion with God as well as communion between men: a co-operative unity.

Saint Cyprien writes: [168]

"Let our Prayer be public and communal"

"And first, the Master of peace and unity did not want us to pray alone and individually, so that he who prays will not pray for himself alone. We do not say: 'My Father who art in heaven,' nor: 'Give me my daily bread.' And none of us prays only for himself that God cancels his debt; or that He exempts only him from temptation and He delivers him alone from Evil.

"Our prayer is public and communal, so when we pray we do not pray for one person alone but for a whole people, because with the whole people we are one. The God of peace and the master of harmony who teaches unity wanted each of us to pray for all, just as He carried all of us as one in Himself.

"The three youths in the furnace followed this law of prayer; they were united in prayer and become a single chorus. The scripture urges us to do so and teaches us how to pray; it gives us an example to imitate in order to follow its path. *'Thus these three in a single voice sang and thanked God ...'* [169]

"They spoke in a single voice although Christ had not yet taught them to pray. Their request was strong and effective because a calm, simple and spiritual prayer impresses God: *'All these, it is said, constantly devoted themselves to prayer, as did certain women, including Mary the mother of Jesus, as well as his brothers.'* [170]

They persevered in prayer as of one heart, which testifies to their great ardour and their unity. Because God, who gathers in his house the single hearted, admits in his divine and eternal quarters only those who pray in communion, each together with all the others."

We say "Father" because we have become sons

"How generous and marvelous is the richness of the Lord's prayer! This richness is gathered together into few words, but it has a boundless spiritual density, so that no part is missing from this summary of the heavenly doctrine that forms our prayer. It is said: '*Pray in this way: Our Father who art in heaven.*'

"The new man, who is born anew and returned to his God by His grace, first says: 'Father,' because he has become a 'son.' '*He came to His own, and His own people did not accept Him. But to all who received Him, who believed in His name, he gave power to become children of God.*'[171] He who believes in His name and who has become a son of God must start by giving thanks and openly declare that he is a son of God. And when he calls God in heaven his 'Father,' by this he states that he renounces his carnal and earthly father, the father of his first birth, in order to know only one father, the one who is in heaven. Indeed, it is written: '*Who said of his father and mother "I regard them not...he ignored his kin and did not acknowledge his children. For they observed your word and kept your covenant.*'[172]

"In the gospel our Lord also asks us to refrain from calling anybody on earth 'our father.' To the disciple who speaks of his deceased father He says: '*Let the dead bury the dead.*'[173] The disciple spoke of a father who was dead, while the father of those who believe is alive."

God is the Father of those who believe and have been born again by Him

"It is not enough, dear brethren, to become aware that we are calling the Father who is in heaven, so we add: 'Our Father,' that is, Father of those who believe, of those who have been sanctified by Him, and have been born anew by the spiritual grace: they have begun to be sons of God.

"These words are also a condemnation and criticism of the Jews. In their lack of faith they despised the Christ who had been announced to them by the prophets, and sent to them first of all, and more, they put him to death cruelly. They can no longer call God their Father, because the Lord said to their confusion: '*You are from your father the devil, and you choose to do your father's desires. He was a murderer from the beginning and does not stand in the truth, because there is no truth in him.*'[174]

"And through the prophet Isaiah, God shouted in indignation:
*I reared children and I have brought them up,
but they have rebelled against me.
The ox knows its owner,
and the donkey its master's crib;
but Israel does not know me,*

and my people do not understand.
Ah, sinful nation, a people laden with iniquity,
offspring who do evil,
children who deal corruptly,
who have forsaken the Lord,
who have despised the Holy One in Israel,
who are utterly estranged. " [175]

"To blame them, Christians say in prayer: *Our Father;* in truth he has become our father and has stopped being father to the Jews when they abandoned Him. The treacherous people cannot be sons; but those whose sins were forgiven merit this title and have been promised eternity according to the word of the Lord; '*Everyone who commits sin is a slave to sin.* ' [176] The slave does not remain forever in the house, but the son lives there forever."

If God is Father, we must behave like sons

"How great is the Lord's mercy, how great is his goodness and kindness that he allows us to pray in the presence of God, even to the ultimate favour of calling Him Father; and since Christ is the Son of God, so it is with us who are also called sons. Nobody among us would have dared to use this word in our prayer: it was the Lord Himself who encouraged us to do so.

"But we must remember, beloved brothers, that when we call God *our Father*, we must behave like sons of God. If we delight in having God for Father, then He must also find delight in us. We must be like temples of God, a place in which men can encounter His presence. Our conduct must not betray the Spirit; we have begun to become heavenly and spiritual, so now we must think and do only what is heavenly and spiritual. The Lord Himself said: '*For those who honour me I will honour, and those who despise me will be treated with contempt.* '[177] The apostle says in his epistle: '*You are not your own, for you were brought with a price; therefore glorify God in your body.*" [178]

Let us pray that holiness will dwell in us

"After this, we say: '*Hallowed be thy name.*' Not that we wish that God should be sanctified by our prayers, but rather we ask of Him that His name should be sanctified in us. For who could sanctify God when it is He Himself who sanctifies? But when we hear this word: '*You shall be holy to me; for I the Lord am holy,*'[179] we ask that, because we have been sanctified by baptism, we will persevere in what we have begun to be. And we must ask for this every day. It is imperative that we sanctify ourselves every day, because we sin daily;

we must cleanse ourselves of our sins by step by step sanctification without ceasing. These aspects of the sanctification that we owe to the divine compassion are best expressed by these words of the apostle: '*Fornicators, idolators, adulterers, male prostitutes, sodomites, thieves, greedy, drunkards, revilers, robbers — none of these will inherit the kingdom of God. And this is what you used to be. But you were washed, you were sanctified, you were justified in the name of the Lord Jesus Christ and in the Spirit of Our God.*'[180]

"He thus declares us sanctified in the name of our Lord Jesus Christ and in the spirit of our God. We therefore turn to prayer so that this sanctity can remain in us. Let us remember that our Lord and Judge asked the man whom He had just healed and made alive again *'to sin no more, so that nothing worse would happen to him;'*[181] this is why, for our part, we pray unceasingly, why we pray night and day in order that, with the help of God, we might be able to retain the sanctity and life which we owe to the divine grace."

We ask that the kingdom should come, as God has promised us

"'*Thy Kingdom come,*'that is how the prayer continues. We now ask that the Kingdom be made manifest to us in the same way that we wished His name to be made holy in us. Is it possible that God might not rule? When can something begin which has always existed and can never end? We pray for the coming of the Kingdom that has been promised, bought for us by the blood and the Passion of Christ. Before, we were slaves, now we ask that we might reign under the sovereignty of Christ. He Himself promised it to us, when He said: '*Come, ye blessed of my Father, inherit the kingdom prepared for you from the foundation of the world.*'[182]

"It is even possible, dear brethren, that the Kingdom of God refers to Christ in person, Him that we call on every day in our devotions and whose coming we wish to hasten by our attentions. Just as He is our resurrection — for in Him we are restored to life — he can also be the Kingdom of God, for it is also in him that we will rule.

"With good reason we ask for the Kingdom of God, that is, for the rule of heaven, which includes within it that of earth. But the one who challenged the common thinking of the world is above honours and kingdoms. That is why he who has given himself to God and to Christ does not yearn for the rule of earth, but of heaven.

"We have an unceasing need to pray, so that we will not lose the kingdom of heaven, as happened to the Jews who were promised the kingdom but lost it, according to the Lord's words: '*Many will come from the East and West, and will sit down with Abraham, and Isaac, and Jacob, in the kingdom of heaven, but the children of the Kingdom shall be cast out into outer darkness: there shall be weeping and gnashing of teeth.'*[183]   By these words He shows that the Jews were heirs of the Kingdom as long as they remained sons of God. When the paternity of God ended, the kingdom also came to an end. That is why we Christians, who call God *Our Father*, also pray that His Kingdom come within us."

We pray that Your will be done within us

"And we add: *'Thy will be done on earth as it is in heaven.'* This is not so that God may do as He wishes, but so that we may do what He wishes. For who can restrain God from doing what He wants? But we are opposed by the devil, who prevents our accepting the will of God both within ourselves and externally. This is why we ask that His will be done within us; but for this to occur we need His help. Nobody is strong enough in his own resources, but his strength resides in the goodness and mercy of God.

"The Lord himself showed the weakness He had assumed, when he said: *'My Father, if it is possible, let this cup pass from me.'*[184]   And to show His disciples that it was not His own will that prevailed, but that of God, he added: *'Yet not my will but yours be done.'*[185]   Elsewhere He is more specific: *'For I came down from heaven, not to do my own will, but the will of him that sent me.'*[186]

"If the Son Himself endorsed the necessity to do the will of God, how much more important is it that the servant do the will of the Lord, as is expressed in the *Epistle of John: 'Love not the world, neither the things that are in the world. If any man love the world, the love of the Father is not in him. For all that is in the world — the lust of the flesh, and the lust of the eyes, and the pride of life — is not of the Father, but is of the world. And the world passeth away, and the lust thereof: but he that doeth the will of God abideth forever.'*[187]   Those who wish to live forever must do the will of God, who is eternal."

Christ did and taught the will of God

"The will of God is what Christ did and taught. Humility in conduct; firmness in faith; modesty in speech; justice in judgements; kindness in almsgiving; discipline in human morality; acting without prejudice; dignity and understanding when we are its victims; keeping the peace with our brothers; loving God with all our heart; to love Him because He is Father, and to fear Him because He is God; to prefer nothing above Christ, as He has preferred us above all; to bind ourselves unconditionally to His spirit of charity, but to take up our cross with courage and confidence; when the time comes to enter the battle in His name or in His honour; to demonstrate confidence in difficulties so as to remain strong in the struggle; patience in death in order to earn our crown. All of this is a clear sign of our will to be co-heir of Christ, to act according to the law of God, to do the will of God."

We pray that the will of God be done on earth
as it is in heaven,
that is to say: in our soul and in our body

"We ask that the will of God be done in heaven and on earth, because both of these contribute to our salvation. The body is from the earth and the soul from heaven, therefore we are heaven and earth. And we pray that in both, meaning in both our body and our soul, the will of God be done. Now there is a conflict between the flesh and the soul and every day there is a continuous struggle between the two. We do not do what we want: the soul seeks what is from heaven and from God, and the flesh seeks what is from earth and from the world. Thus we ask fervently that the help of God should impose harmony between the two, that the will of God should be done in the soul and in the body, and that the soul that God has made anew should be saved.

"This is what Saint Paul tells us very clearly: *'For what the flesh desires is opposed to the spirit, and what the spirit desires is opposed to the flesh; for these are opposed to each other, to prevent you from doing what you want. But if you are led by the spirit, you are not subject to the law. Now the works of the flesh are obvious: fornication, impurity, licentiousness, idolatory, sorcery, enmities, strife, jealousy, anger, quarrels, dissensions, factions, envy, drunkenness, carous-ing, and things like these. I am warning you, as I warned you before: those who do such things will not inherit the kingdom of God. By contrast, the fruit of the spirit is love, joy, peace, patience, kindness, generosity, faithfulness, gentleness and self-control.'* [188]

"This is why each day, even at each moment, we ask in our prayers that the will of God be done in heaven as on earth, because the will of God is that the things of the earth must give precedence to the things of heaven, that the share of the spirit and of God be the winner."

Another explanation of the same request

"Dear brethren, these words can also mean something else: as you know, our Lord urges us to love our enemies and to pray for those who persecute us. Thus we must pray for those who are still of this world and not of heaven, we must pray that they also accomplish the will of God that Christ accepted so perfectly for the salvation of humanity.

"Christ calls his disciples not earth, but 'salt of the earth,' and the Apostle says that the first man was extracted from the dust of the earth, and the second from heaven; we must come to resemble our heavenly Father who makes the sun rise on the pious and the impious, who bestows rain on the just and the unjust; for this reason, Christ makes us pray for the salvation of all men. In heaven, that is, the heaven within us, through faith, the will of God imposes itself in us and we are becoming divine; in the same way on earth, that is, in non-believers, we ask that the will of God be done: we also ask that those still in their first birth and still earthly become divine by a new birth through water and the Spirit."

NOTES

[168] De oratione dominca, (On the Lord's prayer, Migne, *Latin Patrology*, 4,521-538. The subtitles are taken from that work.)

[169] Attributed to Daniel but not found.

[170] Acts 1:14.

[171] John 1:11-12.

[172] Deuteronomy 33:9.

[173] Matthew 8:22.

[174] John 8:44.

[175] Isaiah 1:2-4.

[176] John 8:34.

[177] I Samuel 2:30.

[178] I Corinthians 6:19-20.

[179] Leviticus 20:26.

[180] I Corinthians 6:9-11.

[181] John 5:14.

[182] Matthew 25:34.

[183] Matthew 8:11-12.

[184] Matthew 26:39.

[185] Luke 22:42.

[186] John 6:38.

[187] I John 2:15-17.

[188] Paraphrased from Galatians 5:17-23.

CHAPTER TWENTY

COMMENTARY OF
SAINT CYPRIEN OF CARTHAGE
(Continued)

We ask for our bread, that is Christ;
so that we take leave neither of His blessing,
nor of His body

"As we continue, we say: *'Give us our daily bread.'*[189] These words may be taken in their spiritual or their literal meaning: in their providential design both meanings are made to contribute to our salvation.

"Our bread of life is Christ, and this bread does not belong to everybody, but it belongs to us. As we say *"Our Father"* because He is the Father of those who have faith, in the same way we call Christ our bread because He is the bread of those who constitute His body. To obtain this bread we pray each day: as we are in Christ and receive the host each day as nourishment for our salvation, we assume that we would not, because of a more serious sin, be deprived of holy communion. This would deprive us of the heavenly bread, as well as severing us from the body of Christ, as he warns us.

"He says: *'He who eats this bread will live eternally,'* in order to confirm that those who extend their hand toward His Body and receive the Host in communion may live; on the other hand we must ask with fear that those who voluntarily separate themselves from the Body of Christ may not exclude themselves from salvation. Our Lord warned us: *'Verily I tell you, unless you eat the flesh of the Son of Man and drink His blood, you have no life in you.'*[190] Therefore each day we ask to receive our bread, that is, Christ; to continue to live in Christ, and we also ask not to be separated from grace and His Body."

We must ask for our food each day,
not at long intervals

"It is also possible to understand this request in the following way: we have renounced the world; with the help of faith we have rejected its opulence and its seductions; we simply ask for the food we need, for as the Lord said: *'So therefore, none of you can become my disciple if you do not give up all your possessions.'*[191] He who is beginning to be a disciple of Christ and gives up everything, according to the word of the Lord, must ask for his daily nourishment but must not be concerned for the very long term. For again the

Lord said: *'Do not worry about tomorrow, for tomorrow will bring worries of its own. Today's trouble is enough for today.'* [192] The disciple justly asks his food for today because it is forbidden for him to worry about tomorrow. Therefore, it is not logical that those who ask for the early coming of the kingdom of God should want to prolong their stay in this world. The apostle warns us of this in order to train, strengthen and affirm our faith and our hope. *'For as we brought nothing into the world, so we can take nothing out of it; but if we have food and clothing we should be content with these. But those who want to be rich fall into temptation and are trapped by many senseless and harmful desires that plunge people into ruin and destruction.'* [193]

Christ teaches us that riches are more than contemptible: they are dangerous

"Christ teaches us that riches are more than contemptible: they are dangerous, they contain the root of all evil whose seducing and misleading appearances lead the human spirit astray. To the foolishness of the rich man who indulged in the opulence of the world and boasted about his overwhelming harvest God replied: *'You fool! This very night your life is being demanded of you. And the things you have collected, whose will they be?'* [194]

"This fool boasted about his harvest when that same night he was to die. He was thinking about his unlimited supplies while life had already abandoned him. On the other hand, the Lord declares that he who is perfect sells all that he has, gives it to the poor, and builds himself treasure in heaven.

"Moreover he adds that we can follow his traces and imitate his glorious Passion if we make ourselves free and liberate ourselves from the worry of everyday affairs, if also, in ridding ourselves of our belongings, we offer them to God as a sign of our offering of ourselves."

To him who possesses God, nothing is lacking if he does not fail God

"Daily bread cannot be lacking to the just, because it is written: *'The Lord does not let the righteous go hungry.'* [195] And elsewhere: *'I was young and I grew old; I have never seen one of the just abandoned nor his descendants look for bread.'* [196] Thus the Lord promises: *'Therefore do not worry saying, What shall we eat? or What will we drink? or What will we wear? For it is the gentiles who strive for all these things; and indeed your heavenly Father knows that you need all these things. But strive first for the kingdom of God and His righteousness, and all these things will be given you as well.'* [197]

"To those who are seeking the Kingdom and the justice of God He promises to give everything else. In truth everything belongs to God; he who possesses God lacks nothing if he himself does not fail God. In this way, when Daniel was thrown in the lions' den on the king's orders he received his meal from God; and this man of God began eating among the famished wild beasts who spared him.[198] Elijah was also given food during his journey and also while he was being persecuted, when in solitary confinement, ravens and other birds came to him and brought him food.[199] Alas, what detestable cruelty we find in humans: animals show concern, birds bring food, but men erect obstacles and exercise their cruelty."

After asking for our food,
we ask that our sins be forgiven, so that nobody
is in error about his innocence

"After that we pray for our sins. *'And forgive us our trespasses as we forgive those who have trespassed against us.'* After our food we ask that our sins be forgiven. He who is fed by God must live in God and be preoccupied not only with the present temporal life but also with the eternal. It is possible for him to reach it if his sins are forgiven. The Lord calls those sins *'debts'*, according to the Gospel: *'I forgave you all that debt because thou desiredst me.'*[200]

"Indeed it was necessary, wise, and salutary for the Lord to remind us that we are sinners by asking us to pray for our sins. In this way as we resort to God's indulgence we recall the state of our conscience. In order that nobody regards himself complacently as if he were innocent, nor loses himself in this vanity, when he is asked each day to pray for his sins, he is reminded that he sins each day.

"John also warns us in his epistle: *'If we say that we have no sin, we deceive ourselves, and the truth is not in us. If we confess our sins, he who is faithful and just will forgive us our sins and cleanse us from all unrighteousness.'*[201] In his epistle he combines two things: we must pray for our sins, and in this prayer we must ask to be forgiven. He affirms that the Lord is faithful to pardon our sins according to His promise. Because He who teaches us to pray for our debts and our sins, at the same time promises a fatherly blessing and forgiveness."

By which rule are sins forgiven?

"The Lord specifies the conditions for his pardon: He forces us to remit the debts of our debtors to us in the same way that we ask that our sins be remitted. We cannot ask for the remission of our sins unless we act the same way towards our own debtors. Elsewhere He says: *'For with the judgment you make you will be judged, and the measure you give will be the measure you get.'*[202]

"The servant had been cleared of his debts by the master, but he refused to do the same towards one of his companions and he was therefore put in jail. He refused to pardon his companion, and he loses the pardon given him by the master.[203] In this instruction Christ teaches this truth in a very harsh way: *'And when ye stand praying, forgive, if you have aught against any; that your Father also which is in heaven may forgive you your trespasses.'*[204]

"You will therefore have no excuse on judgment day when you will be judged according to your own behaviour: you will go through exactly what you had others go through. God commands us to keep peace and harmony in his house and to live according to the law of the new birth; now that we have become sons of God we must be the guardians of the peace of God. To the unity of the Spirit must correspond the unity of souls and hearts. God does not accept the sacrifice of those who are causes of disunity, He sends them away from the altar so that they may make peace with their brothers: God wants to be pacified with prayers of peace. The most beautiful offering to God is our own peace, our own harmony, the unity of all the faithful in the Father, the Son and the Holy Spirit."

God accepts only the prayer of the peaceful

"During the times of the early sacrifices offered by Cain and Abel,[205] God did not consider the offering but the hearts: the gifts were acceptable if the hearts were. Abel, the just and peaceful, who offers his sacrifice with a pure soul, shows everyone how to present himself in the act of sacrifice, that is, in fear of God, with a simple heart and a sense of justice, harmony, and peace.

"In offering the sacrifice to God with such an attitude, he had the honour of himself becoming a precious offering and the first man called to the confession of martyrdom. He was foreshadowing the passion of the Lord by the glory of his blood, because in him dwelt the justice and peace of the Lord. Such beings are entitled to the crown, such beings, on Judgement day, will be judges alongside Christ.

"The dissidents, on the other hand, those who do not live in peace with their brothers, are condemned by the apostle and by the Bible; even if they were willing to be killed in the name of Christ they would remain guilty of having created disharmony among their brothers, for it is written: *'All who hate a brother or a sister are murderers, and you know that murderers do not have eternal life abiding in them.'*[206]

"He who prefers to imitate Judas rather than Christ cannot be with Christ. How terrible is this crime that even the baptism of blood cannot cleanse it! How severe is this accusation that even martyrdom cannot remove it!"

The enemy can do nothing against us
unless God has given permission

"The Lord insists on another request: '*Do not bear to see us tested by adversity.*'[207] By these words it seems the enemy can do nothing against us unless God has given permission. Therefore, our fear, our affection, and our attention must always be turned towards God, because in our numerous temptations the power of the Devil depends on the power of God. This the Scriptures prove when they say: '*Nebuchadnezzer of Babylon came up to Jerusalem and the city was besieged and the Lord delivered it into his hands.*'[208]

"According to the scriptures the devil is given this power against us because of our sins:

'Who gave up Jacob to the spoiler
and Israel to the robbers?
Was it not the Lord,
against whom they have sinned
in whose ways they would not walk
and whose law they would not obey?
So He poured upon Israel the heat of his anger.[209]

"And in connection with Solomon, who was sinning and deviating from the Lord's way, it is said: '*And the Lord raised Satan against him.*'"[210]

This power is granted either for our punishment or for our glory.
This request centres us on our weakness.

"God can give power to the devil in two ways: for our punishment when we have sinned, or for our glory if we are exposed to temptation. We saw that this was the case with Job: '*Very well, all that he has is in your power; only do not stretch out your hand against him!*'[211]

"In the Bible the Lord says: '*You would have no power over me unless it had been given you from above.*'[212] Therefore, when we pray not to be tempted we remember our weakness so that nobody thinks of himself as invulnerable, nobody thinks himself as better than he is, nobody gives himself credit for his faithfulness or his passion,[213] when the Lord Himself teaches humility as he says: '*Keep awake and pray that you may not come into the time of trial; the spirit indeed is willing, but the flesh is weak.*'[214] If we first show true humility, we will give everything we ask for back to God with fear and reverence, we can be assured then that His kindness will grant what we request."

The last request concerns everything
that the enemy is plotting against us

"After this our prayer ends with a conclusion that summarizes all the other requests. In the end we say: *'But deliver us from Evil.'* With these words we refer to what the enemy can muster against us, but we can rest assured that we have a powerful ally if God delivers us, if He helps those who implore Him. Thus when we say: *'Deliver us from Evil,'* there is nothing more to request: we have asked for the protection of God against the Devil. Having said this prayer we have become strong against all the schemes of the devil and the world. Who can fear the world if God is his protector in this world?"

NOTES

[189] As with the other Latin Fathers, Saint Cyprien speaks of 'daily bread,' while the Greek Fathers speak of 'Superessential' *(epiousion)* bread, or in an ancient Latin translation, 'supersubstantial'. But this changes nothing of the spiritual commentary. See the meticulous analysis by Origen of this term *epiousios* in his commentary on the Lord's Prayer.

[190] John 6:53.

[191] Luke 14:33.

[192] Matthew 6:34. Definitely a paraphrase to meet the needs of contemporary people.

[193] Again paraphrased from 1 Timothy 6:7-10.

[194] Luke 12:20.

[195] Proverbs 10:3.

[196] Psalms 37:25.

[197] Matthew 6:31-33.

[198] See Daniel 6:17-24.

[199] 1 Kings 17:4-6 and 19:5-8.

[200] Matthew 18:32.

[201] 1 John 1:8-9.

[202] Matthew 7:2.

[203] Matthew 18:23-25.

[204] Mark 11:25.

[205] Based on the story of Cain and Abel; See Genesis 4:1-16.

[206] 1 John 3:15.

[207] Saint Cyprian uses this phrase: *'to be led into temptation'* (see p.99.)

[208] Seems to be an unusual rendering from 2 Kings 24:10.

[209] Isaiah 42:24.

[210] Saint Cyprian interprets the phrase from the first book of Kings: '*The Lord raised up an adversary against Solomon*'[211] referring to a prince of Edom (see also 11:23) as meaning the Adversary or Satan.

[212] Paraphrased from Job 1:12.

[213] John 19:11.

[214] In the classical sense of being 'passive' to events. (Ed.)

CHAPTER TWENTY-ONE

COMMENTARY OF SAINT CYRIL OF JERUSALEM
(Extracts.)

In his fifth mystical catechism, Saint Cyril of Jerusalem also comments on the Lord's prayer: [215] *"Afterwards, we say the prayer that the Lord taught to His disciples; with a pure heart we call God our Father, and we say: 'Our Father who art in Heaven.'* God's love for men is infinite. To those who had erred from Him and had thrown themselves in the worst of calamities He gives His full pardon for their wrongdoing; this pardon is of such immense import that it allows them to say to Him: *'Father! Our Father who art in Heaven.'*

"Heaven also means all those who bear in themselves the celestial image; God resides in them because He has established His abode in them.

"'Hallowed be thy Name.' The Name of God is sanctified by nature, whether we realize it or not. But our sins have defiled it, as it is written; *'Because of you my Name is blasphemed continually each day.'*[216]

"Thus we ask that His Name be sanctified in us; not that it has to become holy as if it had not always been so, but rather because of the fact that we strive that we should become sanctified and live as saints of God.

"'Thy Kingdom come.' Only a pure heart can say with confidence *'Thy Kingdom come.'* One must have followed Paul's teachings so as to say: *'Therefore do not let sin exercise dominion in your mortal bodies...'*[217] Only he who keeps himself pure in his actions, his thoughts, and his words, can say to God: *'Thy Kingdom come.'*

"'Thy will be done in heaven as it is done on earth.' The holy angels of God do the will of God. Indeed, in Psalms David says: *'Bless the Lord, O you his angels, you mighty ones who do his bidding.'*[218] When you pray in this way, you say, essentially: *'As the angels in heaven do your will, Lord, let it be the same on earth: let Thy will be done in me.'*

"'Give us today the bread necessary for our subsistence.'[219] It is not ordinary bread that is needed for our nourishment, but holy bread: it must nourish the substance of the soul. This kind of bread does not go through digestion and decomposition, rather it expands throughout your being for the health of your soul and your body. Here 'today' means every day; this is how Paul expresses his thought when he says: *'While it is called today.'*[220]

"'Forgive us our trespasses as we forgive those who trespass against us.' We have committed numerous sins. We sin in thought, in speech, and in a great number of our actions which are truly reprehensible. *'If we say that we have no sin, we deceive ourselves.'*[221] We make a contract with God when we ask him

to forgive our sins as we forgive those who have sinned against us. Let us make sure that we really think about what it is that we receive and at what cost. Let us not wait and refuse to forgive others. Those wrongs of which we are victims are minimal, insignificant and without much consequence; those, on the contrary, that we have committed against God are important and it is only through the divine charity that we can be pardoned. So make sure that you are not refused the pardon of your very serious sins committed against God because you have refused to pardon small offenses.

"'*Lord, do not lead us into temptation.*' Must we think that the Lord expects us to pray that we should never be tried at all? It is said in the Scriptures: '*He who has never been tried has not proved himself.*'

"And elsewhere: '*Whenever you face trial of any kind, consider it nothing but joy.*'[222]

"But would not 'to be tried' in our text mean 'to be overwhelmed by trials?'

"Indeed, it may seem that this trial is a very strong current that is most difficult to cross. Those who are not overwhelmed by the trial are the only ones who can overcome it; they are, so to speak, good swimmers who are not washed away by the current. The others, as they try, drop to the bottom.

"Let us take Judas, for instance; he was tempted by greed. He could not, in a way, swim across this temptation; he was lost, body and soul. Peter, on the other hand, was tempted to give up; but in the end he avoided disaster, managed to reach the other shore and was rescued. In another text the choir of saints who had remained pure sings its gratitude:

"*For you, O God have tested us;*
you have tried us as silver is tried
You have brought us to the net;
You laid burdens over our backs;
You let people ride over our heads;
we went through fire and water;
yet You have brought us out to a spacious place."[223]

"Take good notice of the joy they experienced because they made the crossing without perishing. '*And you have brought us out*' it is said, '*to a spacious place.*' Spacious place here means: to come out of the test.

"'*But deliver us from Evil.*' If '*do not lead us into temptation.*' meant to remove all trials, Jesus would not have added '*But deliver us from Evil.*' Evil is the devil, and we ask to be delivered from him.

"And at the end of this prayer you say: '*Amen.*' This means that you confirm everything that is contained in this prayer."

122

NOTES

215 Mark 14:38.

216 Mystical Catechism (Migne, *Greek Patrology* 33, 11117-1124). French trans. in Le Pater explique par les peres (ibid. pp. 106-109).

217 Isaiah 52:5 Based on the French Bible text which is very different from the English.

218 Romans 6:12.

219 Psalms 103:20.

221 Hebrews 3:13.

222 1 John 1:8.

223 James 1:2.

CHAPTER TWENTY-TWO

Prayer at the dawn of Christianity;
the Apostolic tradition

Having considered the previous wonderful commentaries, let us now see how the faithful prayed at the dawn of Christianity. We will quote from two passages; one from the Apostolic Tradition and the other from the works of Origen.

The Apostolic Tradition[224] tells us of *"the time of prayer,"* which is very close to what we call now the large and small hours of liturgy.

Let us recall here the famous alphabetical Psalm 119 [225] in which the psalmist urges us to rise seven times a day, (that is, seven times during each 24 hours) to praise the Lord.

The Time of Prayer

"Let all the faithful, men and women, as soon as they come out of sleep in the morning, wash their hands and pray to God, and then go to their occupations.

"If, however, there is a sermon, one must give it priority, as we are convinced that God speaks through the words of the preacher. He who has thus prayed with his brothers is provided against the burden of the day. He who fears God must feel it a loss not to participate in the gathering, especially if he can read.

"When the preacher has arrived, all the faithful must hurry to the place of meeting where the homily will be given. There, the preacher will speak to each one. You will hear things about which you were not thinking, and you will profit from what the Spirit tells you from the mouth of the person who is speaking. In this way your faith will be strengthened by what you will hear. You will also be told how to live correctly in your home. Yes indeed, each one of you must remain firm in your habit of going to the gathering where the Holy Spirit brings His riches to you all. *'On days when there is no instruction let each of you bring home a holy book and read for the profit of your soul.'"*

Hours Of Prayer

"If you are at home, pray at the third hour [226] and praise God. If you are somewhere else at that time pray with all your heart, because it is at that hour that Christ was put to the cross. For this reason, the Law of the Old Testament ordered the shewbread to be offered at that hour — a sign of the Body and Blood of Christ — and to sacrifice a witless lamb which was a prefiguration of the perfect Lamb. Indeed, Christ is the shepherd, just as He is the bread that has come from heaven.

"You will pray in the same way at the sixth hour [227] while remembering Christ on the cross as the day had ended and darkness was everywhere. At that hour you will pray in a very forceful way to imitate He who prayed for the unbelieving Jews when the universe was in darkness.

"At the ninth hour,[228] extend your prayer and your praise to imitate the souls of the just who praise the God of truth, He who remembered His saints and sent the Word to bring them light. At that hour, with His chest open, shedding water and blood, he illuminated the dusk of that day until His dying. And by bringing together the return of light with His sleep, He gave an image of His resurrection.

"Pray also before you rest your body. Around the middle of the night, get up, wash your hands with water, and pray. If your wife is there, pray together. If she is not a Christian yet, go into another room and pray, then go back to sleep.

"Do not neglect this prayer. He who is married is not impure for that: '*One who has bathed does not need to wash, but is entirely clean.*'[229] While signing yourself with your humid breath, and in holding your saliva in your hand, your body is entirely clean, right down to your feet. Because the gift of the Spirit, and the rite of the lustral water which bursts out like a spring [230] and is received in a pure heart, have purified the faithful.

"We must then pray at that hour because the Ancients, from whom we take this tradition, have taught us that at that moment the whole of creation falls still to pray to the Lord. The stars, the trees and the water stop for a moment; and the whole choir of the angels unite with the souls of the just to sing the praises of God. It is thus very important that the faithful pray at that hour.

"The Lord Himself confirms this when He says: '*Here is the bridegroom! Go out to meet him.*'[231] And he concludes: '*Therefore stay awake, for you know neither the day nor the hour.*'[232]

"At cock-crow get up one more time and do the same. At the hour when the cock was crowing the sons of Israel adjured Christ whom we knew through faith; we are waiting for the day of the resurrection of the dead, in the hope of eternal light.

"Therefore, you who are faithful, if you behave that way and remember the mysteries while teaching each other and setting a good example for the catechumens, you will neither fall into temptation nor lose your souls, because you remember Christ unceasingly."

"In all circumstances make an effort to sign yourself in a noble way. This sign of the Passion is a well-tried defense against the Devil, as long as you do it in a spirit of faith and not in vain display, thus protecting yourself as with a shield. When the Enemy sees the inner force represented externally, which signifies our resemblance to the Word, he flees, not because you scare him but because of the Spirit which breathes in you. Moses sacrificed a lamb and sprinkled the threshold and the sides of the doors. In this way he signified the faith that we now have in the perfect Lamb. Let us sign our foreheads and our eyes with our hand in order to chase away the One that seeks our loss."

NOTES

[224] Attributed to Saint Hypolyte of Rome, third century, (see other translation in Sources Chretiennes, no. 11 bis). The quotations reproduce paragraphs 41 and 42.

[225] Psalm 119 in the numbering of the Hebrew psalm-book, 118 in the Latin (Vulgate) psalm-book. The present quotation refers to verse 164.

[226] That is, at approximately 9 o'clock.

[227] Noon.

[228] Three o'clock in the afternoon.

[229] John 13:10.

[230] Reference to baptism.

[231] Matthew 25:6.

[232] Matthew 25:13

CHAPTER TWENTY-THREE

Prayer at the dawn of Christianity: Origen

Origen speaks of the value of prayer; of its transformative force. He teaches us that Christ and the angels pray with us. Then he shows us how to pray unceasingly, and comments on the content of the petition, on the act of meditation, and on the place of prayer.[233]

The fruits of prayer

"I believe that one who prays correctly according to his abilities receives numerous advantages from prayer. First, it is very important to set one's mind to prayer; through this preparation the faithful brings himself into the presence of God, he prepares himself to speak to Him, as to someone he sees, someone who is present. If it is true that certain images, certain memories of the past remain present in our mind to such a degree that they confuse our thoughts, how important is it to recognize the beneficial effects of the mind of God present in us when the faithful becomes conscious of this look which penetrates the innermost secret of his heart; and how important that the soul tries to please this heavenly witness who probes all his spirit, who sounds people's hearts.

"Even if we assume that the faithful who sets his soul to prayer does not profit in any other way, we should not underestimate the spiritual benefits of such an effort. If he makes a habit of it, how well he avoids sin and how much progress he makes towards virtue. Those who truly persevere in prayer know this well through experience. If the thought and memory of a great man is already enough to bring out the best in us and inhibit our tendency towards evil, in prayer how much more does the remembrance of God, the Father of the Universe, support those who perceive that He is present, those who speak to Him, those whom God sees and hears."

To accept everything without complaint

"It is evident that he who prays thus has no sooner finished praying than he hears the answer: '*Here I am.*' This is on condition that before praying he removed any difficulty concerning Providence; this is what is meant by these words: '*If you remove the yoke from among you, the pointing of the finger, the speaking of evil.*'[234]

"He who accepts everything that comes to him is free from any enslavement, he does not raise his hands to a God who orders what he wants for our formation. He does not even whisper secret thoughts which go undetected by other men. It is the characteristic of unworthy servants to complain; they complain against what comes to them without raising their voice, but with all the force of their soul, as if they wanted to hide the object of their complaints from providence and from the Lord of the universe.

"It is this, it seems to me, that the book of Job refers to: '*In all this Job did not sin with his lips.*'[235] In relation to earlier sufferings it is written: '*In all this Job did not sin or charge God with wrong-doing.*'[236] And on this subject we find in Deuteronomy: '*Be careful that you do not entertain a mean thought, thinking, the seventh year, the year of remission, is near.*'"[237]

He who prays in this way, participates in the prayer of the Word

"He who prays in this way receives all the graces, so that he becomes more able to unite with '*the Spirit which fills all the universe.*'[238] and who lives on earth and in heaven according to the word of the prophet: '*Do I not fill heaven and earth says the Lord.*'[239]

"Furthermore, by this purification which was mentioned earlier, he will participate in the prayer of the Word of God, who stands even among those who ignore Him, and who is absent from nobody's prayer. He prays to the Father in union with the faithful of whom he is the mediator. Indeed, the Son of God is the High Priest of our offerings and our advocate with the Father;[240] He prays for those who pray, He pleads for those who must defend themselves. But he refuses his fraternal assistance to those who do not pray through Him with perseverance; He does not make His own the cause of those who ignore His command: '*You must pray always and not lose heart.*'[241]

"Indeed it is written: '*he told them a parable about their need to pray always and not to lose heart: in a certain city there was a judge, etc.*'[242] And before that: '*And he said to them, "suppose one of you has a friend, and you go to him at midnight and say to him, 'Friend, lend me three loaves of bread; for a friend of mine has arrived and I have nothing to set before him, etc.'*"[243] And further on: '*I tell you, even though he will not get up and give him anything because he is his friend, at least because of his persistence he will get up and give him whatever he needs.*'"[244]

The angels and the saints pray for us

"The High Priest is not alone in uniting with the faithful who really pray, there are still the angels, who, the Scriptures say, rejoice in heaven for a single sinner who repents more than for the other ninety-nine who do not have to repent.[245]

"It is the same with the souls of the saints who have fallen asleep."

"The highest virtue, according to the divine word, is charity towards our neighbour; we must admit that the saints who are already dead practice this virtue towards those who struggle in this life, even more so than those who still have to experience human weakness and who manage to help those weaker than them. For: '*If one member suffers, all suffer together with them; if one member is honoured, all rejoice together with them.*'[246] That is realised by those who love their brothers. But it is also possible to apply, to the love which is exercised in the life beyond the present life, the word of the apostle: '*The preoccupation of all Churches! If one is weak, let me be weak, if someone falls, let fire devour me?*'[247]

"Does not Christ himself say that He is ill in each of his saints who are ill, that He is in prison, that He is naked, that He is homeless, that He is thirsty?[248] Of those who have read the Bible, who does not know that Christ made all the suffering of believers His own?"

The gathering of the angels around Christ

"If the angels came to Jesus to serve Him[249] it must not be assumed that this ministering towards Jesus was limited to the short time of His stay on earth among men, and thus that He found Himself among the faithful, not: '*For whether is greater, he that sitteth at meat, or He that serveth?*'[250]

"We may wonder how many angels serve Jesus, who wishes to gather each and every son of Israel and those of the diaspora;[251] who saves those who fear Him and pray to Him? And in number how many more than the apostles work to extend the reach of the Church.[252] We read in the Revelation of Saint John that the angels are at the head of the Church.[253] It is thus no surprise that angels are seen ascending and descending around the Son of man, and that they become manifest to those who are illuminated by the light of knowledge."[254]

...and around those who pray

"At the time of prayer, the angels are informed by the person who prays of the needs that press on him, and they act according to their powers by the universal mandate they were entrusted with. Let me make a comparison to illustrate what I mean. Let us imagine a physician near a sick person who has prayed for her recovery.

"This physician knows how to cure a disease. We can be sure that he will give the right prescription to his patient, convinced that in this way he accomplishes the will of God, in himself answering the prayer of the patient.

"Or let us imagine a man who is blessed with a superabundance of earthly possessions; he is a charitable man who hears the petition of a destitute person who asks God for help. Here again it is certain that the rich man will help the poor person, acting as an agent of the divine will. Intentionally, God has come near, at the moment of prayer, to the one who has made the request and also to the one who is in a position to help; He has not let the latter remain insensible to the needs of the former.

"In such encounters it would surely be incorrect to assume that they came to be by chance only; the truth here is that God, who has counted all the hairs on the saints' heads,[255] has brought together the one who can help and the one who is waiting for him.

"In the same way we may think that the angels are near those who pray and help in the answer to their prayers because they are the intendants and helpers of God. Moreover, the angel assigned to each of us, even those who have a small place in the Church, unceasingly sees the Face of the Lord who is in heaven[256] and contemplates the divinity of our Creator. He prays with and sustains us according to His powers."

How to pray without ceasing

"In the same way that the work of virtue and the accomplishment of the commandments are part of prayer, he who joins prayer to necessary works and the works to prayer prays without ceasing. In this way only can we consider that the injunction to pray without ceasing is feasible. The essence of this injunction is to consider the totality of the life of the saint as a great prayer, of which what we usually call prayer is but a small portion. This latter type of prayer must be done three times a day, as in the case of Daniel, who prayed three times a day when he was threatened by danger.[257]

"Peter also went up to the roof to pray, around the sixth hour, when he saw coming down from heaven, a sort of large sheet lowered to the ground by its four corners.[258] This relates to the second of these three prayers, which David spoke of before him:

"O Lord, in the morning you hear my voice; In the morning I plead my case to you, and watch."

"The third prayer is expressed by these words; *And the lifting up of my hands as an evening sacrifice.*[259]

"We do not even go through the night without praying, as David says: *At midnight I rise to praise you because of your righteous ordinances.*[260]

"And from Paul, the Acts say: *'About midnight at Phillippi, Paul and Silas were praying and singing hymns to God, and the prisoners were listening to them.'"* [261]

What we must ask

"Now let us meditate on this word: *'Ask the important things and the small one will be given to you in addition; ask for the blessings of heaven and those of the earth will be given to you in addition.'* [262] Compared to the reality of the true and spiritual blessing, all the images and figures are weak and base. But the word of God urges us to imitate the prayer of the saints so that we can receive in reality what they received in images. It reminds us also that the celestial and important goods are signified by earthly and modest goods. As if He were saying: *'you want to be spiritual beings? In your prayers ask for the blessings of heaven, and once you have received them you will inherit the kingdom of heaven: once you have become strong you will receive even greater blessings. As for the usual earthly goods which you need for your daily sustenance, the Father also gives them to you as they become necessary.'*

Attitudes in prayer

"It seems to me that he who is about to pray must turn inwards and prepare himself somewhat in order to be more alert, more attentive to the context of the prayer. He must also disperse all anxieties and all affliction of the mind, and try to remember the immensity of God whom he approaches. He must keep in mind that it is baseness to stand before Him without concentration, without effort, and without due respect. Finally, he must remove all unnecessary thought.

"In coming to prayer one must, so to speak, present his soul before his hands, raise his spirit before his eyes, extricate his spirit from the world before rising to present it to the Lord of the universe. And finally, if he wishes God to forget the evil that he has committed against Him, against his neighbour, or against reason, he must rid himself of all resentment about offenses of which he has supposedly been victim.

"As the postures of the body are numerous, to express with our body the image of the dispositions of our soul during prayer, that position in which we extend our hands and raise our eyes towards heaven must have priority over all others. We say that we must act this way when there is no obstacle. But sometimes circumstances force us to pray in a sitting position when, for example, we have sore feet; or sometimes in bed because of a fever. For the same reason, if, for example, we are on a ship, or our occupations do not allow us to withdraw into privacy to do our prayer duty, it is permissible to do away with exterior dispositions.

"As for kneeling prayer, this is obligatory when we confess our sins before God, asking Him to heal and absolve them. This prayer is the symbol of the prostration and submission about which Paul spoke when he wrote: '*For this reason I bow my knees before the Father, from whom every family in heaven and on earth takes its name.*' [263] This kneeling is called spiritual because every creature adores God in the name of Jesus and humbles itself before Him. The apostle appears to refer to this when he says: '*So that at the name of Jesus every knee should bend, in heaven and on earth and under the earth.*'" [264]

The place of prayer

"As for the place, one must know that any place is appropriate for him who prays correctly. However, if one wants to do his prayers in greater quiet and less distraction he may choose a specific place in his home, if it is possible, a consecrated place, so to speak, and pray there.

"There is a particular grace and a certain utility in the place of prayer, by this I mean the place of gathering of the faithful. It is certain that the powers of the angels are a part of the gathering of the faithful and that the virtue of our Lord and Saviour is also present there. Also present are the spirits of the saints, and those, if I may add, of the dead who have preceded us, as well as those of the saints who are still living, although it is difficult to explain how.

"Here is what can be thought of the angels: '*The angel of the Lord encamps around those who fear Him, and delivers them.*' [265]

Jacob tells the truth not only when he speaks about himself, but also when he speaks about all those who serve God as he says '*The angel has redeemed me from all harm.*' [266] It is therefore possible to state: in the assembly of numerous brothers gathered for the glory of Christ, each one has his angel who surrounds those who fear God, and who stands near him whom he has the task of defending and protecting. In the assembly of saints, two Churches [267] are united: that of men and that of the angels.

"If indeed the angel Raphael can say of Tobit that he presented his prayer [268] to God, and later that of Sarah, who became his daughter-in-law, what then can we not say about the assembly of those who, united in one spirit, in one thought, constitute a single body in Christ?"

EPILOGUE

This book on the technique of prayer aims only at the opening of the soul, spirit, and will of man to the divine life. If one does more than read it, if he takes it to the stage of an experience, the results will be beneficial; and the reader of this instruction will personally profit and progress in the way which leads to health and sanctity of being.

For this there remains one indispensable condition:
to be faithful to the message of Christ.

NOTES

[233] In the remainder of his treatise on prayer.

[234] Isaiah 58:9.

[235] Job 2:10.

[236] Job 1:22.

[237] Deuteronomy 15:9.

[238] Wisdom 1:7.

[239] Jeremiah 23:24.

[240] See John 2:1.

[241] Luke 18:1.

[242] Based on Luke 18:1-7 quoted above.

[243] Luke 11:5-8.

[244] Luke 11:8.

[245] Luke 15:5.

[246] 1 Corinthians 12:26.

[247] This is the section of Luke which has just been quoted: 18:1 to 7.

[248] Possibly a confused reference to Revelation 22: 11.

[249] See Matthew 4:11.

[250] Luke 22:27.

[251] See Isaiah 27:12 and John 11:52.

[252] How many more than the apostles are the angels who do this work?

[253] Revelation 1:20 and chapters 2 and 3.

[254] John 1:51

[255] Matthew 10:30, Luke 12:7.

[256] Matthew 18:10.

[257] Daniel 6:10.

[258] Acts 10:9 and following

[259] Psalms 141:2.

[260] Psalms 119:62.

[261] Acts 16:25.

[262] This "word" does not correspond to any literal quotation from the Bible but summarizes the dominant theme of the parable of the "lillies of the field." (Matthew 6:25 and Luke 12:22-31).

[263] Ephesians 3:14-15.

[264] Philippians 2:10.

[265] Psalms 34:7.

[266] Genesis 48:16.

[267] Church in its etymological meaning of ECCLESIA, that is, ASSEMBLY.

[268] To clarify: Raphael presented Tobit's prayer to God. See Tobit 12:152-14.

134